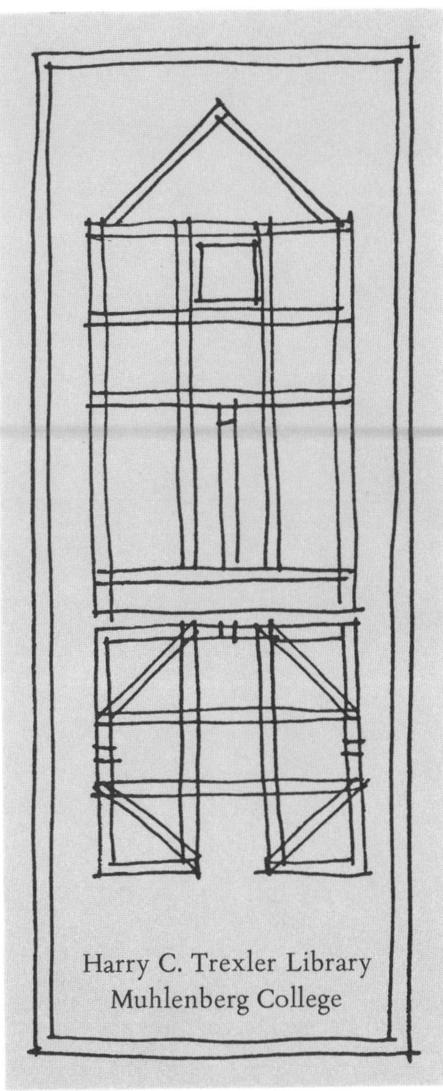
Harry C. Trexler Library
Muhlenberg College

INSIDE U.S. BUSINESS

A CONCISE ENCYCLOPEDIA OF LEADING INDUSTRIES, 1991 EDITION

INSIDE U.S. BUSINESS

A CONCISE ENCYCLOPEDIA OF LEADING INDUSTRIES, 1991 EDITION

Philip Mattera

BUSINESS ONE IRWIN
Homewood, Illinois 60430

This publication is designed to provide accurate and authoritative information in regard to the subject matter covered. It is sold with the understanding that neither the author nor the publisher is engaged in rendering legal, accounting, or other professional service. If legal advice or other expert assistance is required, the services of a competent professional person should be sought.

From a declaration of Principles jointly adopted by a Committee of the American Bar Association and a Committee of Publishers.

Acquisitions: Amy Hollands
Project editor: Susan Trentacosti
Production manager: Ann Cassady
Cover designer: Sam Concialdi
Compositor: Precision Typographers
Typeface: 11/13 Century Schoolbook
Printer: Arcata Graphics/Kingsport

Library of Congress Cataloging-in-Publication Data

Mattera, Philip.
Inside U.S. business : a concise encyclopedia of leading industries / Philip Mattera. — 1991 ed.
p. cm.
Includes bibliographical references and index.
ISBN 1-55623-377-9
1. United States—Industries—Handbooks, manuals, etc. I. Title.
II. Title: Inside US business.
HC106.8.M337 1991
338.0973—dc20 90–15020

Printed in the United States of America

1 2 3 4 5 6 7 8 9 0 AGK 8 7 6 5 4 3 2 1

ACKNOWLEDGMENTS FOR 1991 EDITION OF INSIDE U.S. BUSINESS

Given the broad range of topics covered in this book, I had to depend a great deal on other published sources of business information. I made use of innumerable articles in the business press, especially *The Wall Street Journal, Business Week*, and *Fortune*. In the case of the latter magazine, I learned an enormous amount as a member of the staff and as a reader of the publication.

Among the hundreds of other written sources I consulted—including books, reports, pamphlets, and press releases—there are several that should be mentioned, as I drew on them for nearly every chapter. *Everybody's Business: An Almanac*, edited by Milton Moskowitz, Michael Katz, and Robert Levering (Harper & Row, 1980), was of enormous assistance for historical information. That volume's success in making business narrative readable and compelling was an inspiration for *Inside U.S. Business*, which in part tries to do for industries what *Everybody's Business* did for individual corporations. In the general discussions of industries, I also made great use of the Standard & Poor's Industry Surveys and the *U.S. Industrial Outlook*, published annually by the Commerce Department. The sections on labor relations for each industry take a great deal of their historical information from *Labor Unions*, edited by Gary M. Fink (Greenwood Press, 1977). And assembling the Source Guides in each chapter was made easier by consulting Lorna Daniells' *Business Information Sources* (University of California Press, rev. ed., 1985).

As for human assistance, I would like to thank Amy Hollands at BUSINESS ONE IRWIN and my agent Edythea Ginis Selman for their faith in the project. My appreciation also goes to Ray Rogers and everyone else at CCI for their patience during the time I was producing this revised edition. My family, especially my father and young son Thomas, provided essential support. But my greatest debt is to Donna Demac, my live-in editor and endless source of encouragement, patience (during late nights at the keyboard), and inspiration.

Philip Mattera

HOW TO USE THIS BOOK

Like most people who are in the business world or who study it, you probably need to do your research in a hurry. *Inside U.S. Business* has been produced with that in mind. Its goal is to provide readers with general orientation to major industries. Rather than having to plow through countless books, articles, and other materials, you can quickly acquire the foundation for further reasearch and analysis.

Each chapter starts with a few basic facts and observations and then goes through an outline of the history of the industry, bringing the account up to the present day. The latter part of the narrative includes discussion of recent trends in competition, technology, regulatory climate, and other issues key to understanding where the industry has been and where it is going.

Other major features include:

- A ranking of the top companies in the industry.
- Brief profiles of the leading firms.
- An account of the industry's labor relations.

In addition, each chapter includes a guide to the specialized information sources you will need to pursue your research. These include:

- Leading analysts and experts.
- Trade associations and labor unions.
- Data sources and directories.
- Online databases.
- Trade publications.
- Books and reports.

Having read the text of a chapter, you will be in a position to use these information sources more intelligently. You will have a sense of what additional information to seek and what questions to ask. Overall, *Inside U.S. Business* is the most efficient means to develop a basic understanding of major industries and a research plan for broadening that knowledge.

CONTENTS

PART 4
ENERGY

PART 5
FINANCE

PART 6
HEAVY INDUSTRY AND TRANSPORTATION

INTRODUCTION

Walter Wriston, former chairman of Citicorp, once said that "information about money has become as important as money itself." America's preoccupation with business is also a preoccupation with business information. Everyone from young professionals to investors to public-interest activists wants to know what is going on in management, finance, and the like.

Yet most people have a problem knowing how to begin. Even if they have studied business, the gap between what is learned in school and the current state of things is often quite wide. *The Wall Street Journal* and the rest of the business and trade press provide up-to-date information, but the reader who is new to the subject is usually given too little background to understand fully the latest developments.

Getting oriented to a subject can require an enormous amount of background reading—a luxury that is often simply not available in the business world, where all too many research projects are assigned on an "I need the answer yesterday" basis. And even when there is the time it is often difficult to find the appropriate information.

Inside U.S. Business has been written to fill the gap. Each chapter provides a succinct but wide-ranging introduction to a major industry (or several closely related ones). The reader is given a general orientation to the field and a survey of the history of the industry, including its triumphs and failures, its achievements and scandals. Special attention is paid to the transformation of industries brought about by new technologies, mergers, foreign competition, and upstart companies like

McCaw Cellular Communications, Sun Microsystems, Next Inc., and PacifiCorp.

The narratives take the reader right up to the current competitive situation of each industry and the major technological and regulatory issues it faces. There are also short profiles of the most important companies and surveys of the industry's labor relations, especially in such cases as coal mining, where workers have played a central role in the history of the industry.

Each chapter also includes a Source Guide, which directs the reader to the best people, organizations, and publications that can provide additional information. This includes the names of leading experts and analysts, trade associations and unions, specialized data sources and directories, online databases, trade publications, and major books and reports on the industry and its players. Many of these sources are not widely known outside of the individual industries.

Because of the complexity and rapidly changing nature of American commerce, *Inside U.S. Business* cannot pretend to provide definitive accounts of the industries it covers. Nevertheless each chapter has been thoroughly researched and written to include discussion of all the major issues one needs to know about in getting oriented to an industry. The chapters are certainly not the last word on the subjects, but they do prepare the reader to engage in further research more efficiently.

Inside U.S. Business does not cover all aspects of the commercial world. The industries chosen are those that, in the opinion of the author, are of greatest importance for the American economy today and that are integrated enough—unlike, say, construction and real estate—to be discussed in fairly general terms.

Business outside the United States is for the most part beyond the scope of this book. The focus of the chapters is on commercial activities within the United States, though the overseas operations of U.S.-based companies and the foreign competition faced by American firms are also covered when they are crucial to understanding an industry.

Inside U.S. Business has been written with the widest possible audience in mind. Technical details of scientific and financial issues have been kept to the essentials, and as little business jargon as possible has been employed. The information provided was the most current available when the book went to press in early October 1990. The author hopes that people of all levels of business sophistication will find this volume a useful tool as well as interesting reading.

PART 1

COMMUNICATIONS

CHAPTER 1

BOOK PUBLISHING

Book publishing is a schizophrenic business. On the one hand it is a sizable industry with revenues of about $14 billion a year and constituting an important part of the giant media/information/entertainment sector. Yet book publishing, more than its brethren in that sector, is also an intellectual endeavor. Because it is a major disseminator of ideas, the industry has sometimes been called a "guardian of culture." The conflict between these two roles has been intensifying in recent years as one part of the industry has plunged headlong into commercialism and another has stubbornly sought to remain faithful to literary ideals.

As a business, book publishing has some peculiar economics and practices. First of all, it is a relatively small industry as big business goes. If all publishers were combined into one, the resulting firm would rank only 26th or so on the Fortune 500. While a small number of major houses account for the lion's share of publishing revenues (especially for paperbacks), there are an extraordinarily large number of producers, estimated at 20,000 in the United States alone.

Publishing is also unique in producing such an immense number of different products; some 50,000 new titles are issued each year. Unlike other consumer goods, for which consumption is somewhat predictable, the demand for any given title cannot be easily projected. Brand loyalty does not exist in this sector, and each product must be marketed and promoted individually.

Hardcover publishers lose money on most of their titles and depend greatly on a few best-sellers and the proceeds from the sale of paperback rights. In many cases books are treated like perishable goods: If titles do not sell quickly they are taken off the shelves by booksellers, who can return them to the publishers for full credit within a certain period.

Publishing is characterized by a rather old-fashioned method of distribution. Publishers' sales representatives and booksellers negotiate over each and every title. Given the continuous flood of new volumes, many books are given little opportunity to find their readership; some barely appear in shops at all. Wholesalers (among the largest are Baker & Taylor and Ingram Book Co.) deal mainly with libraries and play a limited role for bookstores.

Leonard Shatzkin, a veteran of the publishing industry, lambasted this system a few years ago in his book *In Cold Type* and proposed a merchandising system (such as that used for greeting cards) in which the publisher would determine how many copies of each title to provide to the bookseller within a specified inventory value. There has been minor movement in this direction, but distribution by negotiation is still the rule.

What has happened at the retail end is an enormous growth in influence of the chain stores. The two leading chains are the Barnes & Noble/B. Dalton group, consisting of some 1,300 stores, and Waldenbooks (owned by K mart Corp.), with about the same number of stores.

Publishers go to great lengths to please the chains. There are stories of houses changing covers and titles that didn't appeal to Dalton and Walden buyers consulted in advance of publication. The size of orders from these chains can make or break a title. Competition among the chains is intense, and Dalton and Walden have joined with others such as Crown Books in discounting best-sellers. In 1990 the large chains launched book club-type programs in which customers pay a membership fee and then receive a discount on all their purchases. These "preferred readers" will get other special services, and the chains will be able to track their purchases.

The chains were also involved in a Federal Trade Commission (FTC) complaint brought against six publishers during the final days of the Reagan administration. The FTC charged the publishers with violations of the Robinson-Patman Act by giving the chains higher discounts than those given to independent stores.

CULTURE AND COMMERCE

Before World War II, the publishing business was stodgy and in many ways not much more than a cottage industry. Some major trade publishing houses date back to the early 19th century: Harper & Row had its origins in 1817, Houghton Mifflin in 1832, and Little, Brown in 1837. They and others played an influential role in the development of American culture but remained largely untouched by the corporate modernization that began in the latter part of that century. A study of the industry by O. H. Cheney in the 1930s found many antiquated practices.

The development that began to shake up the business was the rise of the paperback. There had been brief experiments with softcover volumes in the 1830s and 1880s, but they did not endure. In 1939 Robert de Graff persuaded Simon & Schuster to invest in a venture designed to follow the lead of Penguin Books, established in England four years earlier. The resulting enterprise, called Pocket Books, brought out a series of successful paperbacks priced at 25 cents each. The acceptance of paperbacks by both regular readers and people who had not previously read books was stimulated during World War II, thanks to the distribution of large quantities of "Armed Forces Editions" to the troops.

After the war, paperback publishing took off, with new houses such as Bantam and New American Library entering the business. Established booksellers shunned this new, inexpensive product, so paperbacks were distributed in an entirely different way from hardcovers: magazine and independent distributors simply supplied an assortment of titles rather than negotiating with the retailers, which were drugstores, newsstands, cigar stores, and later supermarkets.

These titles, mainly popular fiction with lurid covers, came to be known as mass market paperbacks and in 1989 accounted for $1.2 billion in revenues, according to the Book Industry Study Group, compared with $2.6 billion for adult trade (general interest) hardcovers. The mass market business is much more heavily concentrated than hardcover publishing. The leading houses are: Avon (owned by Hearst), Ballantine (Newhouse), Bantam and Dell (the German company Bertelsmann), Berkley (MCA), Pocket Books (Paramount), and Warner Books (Time Warner).

During the early 1950s Jason Epstein convinced his superiors at Doubleday that there was also a market, especially among college students, for inexpensive paper editions of the classics and the more serious titles that had been issued by the trade publishers. Doubleday went along with the idea, and the Anchor list, first issued in 1953, was a great success. Other trade houses such as Alfred A. Knopf (Vintage Books) and Beacon Press jumped on the bandwagon that came to be called quality paperbacks. Known since the early 1970s as trade paperbacks, this segment accounted for $1.1 billion in sales in 1989.

During the late 1950s and the 1960s, publishing also prospered because of the rapid growth of the textbook business, a result of soaring educational enrollment. This business is especially attractive to publishers because it is considerably less precarious than trade books: Demand for individual titles is higher and more predictable; manufacturing and marketing costs are much lower, as are discounts to retailers; and a title can sell for many years.

The textbook business did suffer somewhat during the 1970s, as college enrollment slipped, but it has since recovered. Texts for elementary, secondary, and college students together accounted for $3.5 billion in revenues in 1989. McGraw-Hill opened a new market in 1989 when it began producing customized textbooks. The arrangement allowed teachers to pick and choose among different elements according to their syllabus, and McGraw-Hill would combine the desired materials and print only as many copies as the individual instructor needed.

CONGLOMERATION AND CONCENTRATION

The growth of publishing in the 1950s and 1960s forced many houses to abandon the genteel operating practices that had existed for more than a century. The need for capital for expansion prompted houses such as Houghton Mifflin and Random

House to go public. This put the firms under much greater public scrutiny and forced publishers to pay greater attention to financial results. Bennett Cerf, cofounder of Random House, wrote that after the company went public, "We were publishing with one eye and watching the stock with the other."

The industry also elicited a great deal of attention from the large electronics and media firms, which regarded book publishers as keys to the burgeoning educational market. The result was a frantic acquisitions binge in publishing throughout the 1960s. ITT bought Bobbs-Merrill; Litton Industries bought Van Nostrand Reinhold; RCA bought Random House; CBS bought Holt, Rinehart & Winston; Raytheon bought D. C. Heath; and Time Inc. bought Little, Brown. A latecomer to the party was Gulf + Western, which acquired Simon & Schuster in 1975.

Although some of these buyers later sold off their publishing assets when the fast bucks were not forthcoming, conglomerate ownership became a significant controversy. Groups such as the Authors Guild charged that parent companies were forcing publishers to reduce the variety of titles and to concentrate on potential best-sellers. While many parent firms have maintained a hands-off posture, there have been some egregious cases of meddling. For example, ITT told Bobbs-Merrill in 1978 to drop fiction from its list and to concentrate on cookbooks and self-help. (Even that did not help the troubled house, which was purchased by Macmillan in 1985 and dissolved.)

The fear and loathing of conglomerate ownership were intense enough among Houghton Mifflin authors to prompt a public protest when that venerable house was the target of a takeover attempt by Western Pacific Industries in 1978. Writers such as Archibald MacLeish and John Kenneth Galbraith denounced the bid, and Western eventually decided to abandon its effort.

The defenders of conglomerate ownership argued that the new parent companies injected much-needed capital into publishing operations and forced them to be more sophisticated about finance. They also pointed to the steady growth in the number of publishers as evidence that diversity was not endangered. (In fact, there has been a flowering of small presses in recent years. Notable examples include California houses such as Ten Speed Press, North Point Press, and Black Sparrow Press as well as Soho Press, Carroll & Graf, and Thunder's Mouth Press of New York.)

While conglomerate ownership does have its drawbacks, the main tendencies of publishing in the past 20 years—increasing commercialization and concentration of ownership—have proceeded even among those houses that were untouched by the conglomerate invasion.

The new merger wave that hit publishing beginning in the late 1970s has taken place mainly "within the family." Houses have been buying up each other at an accelerating pace. Harper & Row bought both Crowell and Lippincott; the Dutch publisher Elsevier purchased Dutton, which was later acquired by an investment group that turned around and sold the house to New American Library, which was later purchased by Britain's Penguin Publishing; Viking merged with Penguin; Putnam bought Grosset & Dunlap; Macmillan bought Scribner's as well as Bobbs-Merrill; Gulf + Western bought Prentice-Hall and textbook publisher Esquire Inc.; the West German Holtzbrinck Group bought Holt, Rinehart's trade division and restored its original name, Henry Holt & Co.; Time Inc. purchased leading textbook publisher Scott, Foresman (and later resold it to Harper & Row); Germany's Bertelsmann acquired Doubleday; Rupert Murdoch's News Corp. bought Harper & Row; Britain's Pearson took over Addison-Wesley; France's Hachette acquired Grolier; and Random House purchased Crown Publishers. In 1988 a bitter contest for Macmillan was set in motion after Robert Bass made a bid for the company. The company tried to bring off a leveraged buyout led by Kohlberg, Kravis, Roberts & Co., but in the end it was British media tycoon Robert Maxwell (thwarted a year earlier in a bid for Harcourt Brace Jovanovich) who won the battle at a price of $2.6 billion. Little, Brown and Warner Books became corporate cousins (and were later combined into a single operating unit) after Time Inc. and Warner Communications merged in 1989. HarperCollins (the name taken by Harper & Row's parent company) sold Lippincott to Holland's Wolters Kluwer in 1990.

The fact that many of these acquirers are foreign is an indication of the internationalization of book publishing. Ever since Alex Haley's *Roots* became a best-seller in Europe, popular American writers such as Stephen King and Danielle Steel have attracted readers among the same overseas consumers who have learned to enjoy films, television programs, and records from the United States.

THE BLOCKBUSTER COMPLEX

Publishers, merged and unmerged, have also been succumbing to what has been termed the blockbuster complex. In his 1981 book by that name, Thomas Whiteside placed the origin of modern commercialism in publishing in 1957, when Art Linkletter used his television show to plug his book *Kids Say the Darndest Things* all the way to the best-seller list.

By the 1970s the links between books and television and films had been cemented, and publishers were putting more and more emphasis on surefire categories such as pulp fiction, self-help, dieting, and celebrity biography; virtually anything else had to be by a "brand-name" writer. These popular authors were becoming celebrities, appearing regularly in the gossip columns and even more so on the TV talk shows, where they shamelessly promoted their books.

Thanks to superagents such as Scott Meredith, Irving "Swifty" Lazar, Lynn Nesbit, and Morton Janklow, film and TV deals became major elements in negotiations between authors and publishers. Richard Snyder, chairman of Simon & Schuster, has remarked, "In a sense we are the software of the television and movie media." The promise that a book would become a major multimedia property prompted publishers to offer huge amounts, especially for paperback rights.

In 1968 Fawcett paid $410,000 for the paperback rights to Mario Puzo's *The Godfather*. By 1976 Avon was willing to pay $1.9 million for Colleen McCullough's *The Thorn Birds*. The peak was reached in 1979, when Morton Janklow arranged an auction for the rights to Judith Krantz's best-seller *Princess Daisy* in which the bidding *began* at $1 million; Bantam ended up paying $3.2 million.

Although the slump that hit the industry in the early 1980s slowed down this escalation for a while, publishers soon resumed shelling out huge amounts to a favored few authors. In the mid-1980s, the rage was for political memoirs: David Stockman received an advance of $2 million from Harper & Row to tell his story, and Jeane Kirkpatrick, Geraldine Ferraro, and Tip O'Neill each got about $1 million from other houses. Random House paid $3 million for an authorized biography of Ronald Reagan.

The fact that one of these advances (to Ferraro) was paid by Bantam, a traditional paperback house, indicates the changing relationships between hardcover and softcover publishing. During the 1970s several trade houses acquired mass market paperback publishers, and now paperback houses such as Bantam and Warner Books are branching into hardcover trade publishing. In 1986 Hearst Corp., owner of trade publisher William Morrow and paperback house Avon, paid $5 million for hard- and softcover rights for James Clavell's novel *Whirlwind.*

When not encroaching on one another's turf, hardcover and paperback publishers have increasingly joined with one another in copublishing ventures. Rather than one house contracting with the author to publish the hardcover version and then selling the paperback reprint rights to another house, copublishing involves the publishers of the two versions entering into the deal from the start and sharing production and marketing expenses. Bantam has been especially active in these arrangements, joining with hardcover houses such as William Morrow and Crown Publishers.

Another novel arrangement was introduced by Whittle Communications in 1989. Whittle, known for its advertising innovations in magazine publishing, launched a series of books containing ads. Whittle's plan was to commission topical works of nonfiction from well-known writers and to give away large numbers of copies of the books to so-called opinion leaders.

In the late 1980s the blockbuster trend reached new heights as brand-name authors such as Mary Higgins Clark, Jean Auel, and Stephen King received eight-figure advances for multibook deals. In some cases even first novels were getting advances in excess of $100,000. In 1989 *Time* magazine described book publishing as "an industry on a binge, featuring publishers betting millions, authors getting rich and agents calling the shots." In part, this heady atmosphere was justified by rapidly rising sales figures for the top titles. During the 1980s, 25 hardcover titles enjoyed sales in excess of 1 million—a figure once attained only by a few mass market paperbacks.

By the end of the decade, however, the industry was taking a turn for the worse as sales and profits slumped. In 1989 Paramount Communications (the new name taken by Gulf + Western) took a $140 million write-off for Simon & Schuster. McGraw-Hill shut down its general books division. Among the other victims of the new reality were the top editors at E. P. Dutton, whose jobs were eliminated when parent company Penguin USA folded the operation into New American Library, and Random House chief executive Robert Bernstein, who was forced out by the Newhouse interests that own the company. Intent on cutting costs, Random House later cut back the list of its prestigious imprint Pantheon Books and forced the resignation of André Schiffrin, its highly respected managing director. The actions set off a storm of protests by authors, who accused the Newhouse empire of engaging in economic censorship.

LABOR RELATIONS

Publishing has traditionally been a poorly paid and nonunion industry. In the 1970s many employees, especially women in clerical jobs, began to challenge that state of affairs. Several hundred employees of Harper & Row went on strike in 1974 for 17 days and managed to win substantial pay increases. Soon afterward, District 65 of the United Automobile Workers launched an organizing drive among publishers and succeeded in signing up houses such as Harper & Row and Viking Penguin. Yet most of the 74,000 people who work in the industry are still unorganized.

Signs of activity have also begun to be seen among those who write the books. In 1990 the National Writers Union launched a campaign to get book publishers to reform various provisions in the standard contracts they sign with authors.

The 15 Largest U.S. Book Publishers (1989 Revenues in $ Millions)

1. Simon & Schuster	$1,319
2. Time Warner	1,148
3. HarperCollins	1,131
4. Reader's Digest Books	944
5. Random House	850
6. Harcourt Brace Jovanovich	825
7. Bantam Doubleday Dell	775
8. Encyclopaedia Britannica	624
9. Maxwell-Macmillan	530
10. McGraw-Hill	500
11. Times Mirror Book Group	500
12. The Thomson Corp.	496
13. Penguin USA/Addison-Wesley	477
14. Grolier	447
15. Houghton Mifflin	404

Source: *BP Report*, October 22, 1990 © 1989 Simba Information Inc.

LEADING COMPANIES

Bantam Doubleday Dell is the result of the American acquisitions of Bertelsmann Publishing of West Germany. For the 35 years following its founding in 1945, Bantam was known as

Estimated 1989 Revenues of the 10 Largest Publishers of General Books in the United States ($ Millions)

1. Random House	$850
2. Bantam Doubleday Dell	595
3. Simon & Schuster	305
4. HarperCollins	268
5. Penguin USA	230
6. Putnam Publishing	189
7. Time Warner Trade Group	160
8. Macmillan	150
9. Hearst Trade Group	135
10. St. Martin's	100

Source: *BP Report*, July 30, 1990 © 1989 Simba Information Inc.

the leader of the paperback industry. The company, which went through a series of owners before ending up with Bertelsmann, has paid record amounts for the paperback rights for best-sellers, including the all-time high of $3.2 million for Judith Krantz's *Princess Daisy* in 1979. In the 1980s Bantam entered the hardcover trade market and brought out a succession of major hits, such as the autobiographies of Lee Iacocca, test pilot Chuck Yeager, and actress Shirley MacLaine. By the mid-1980s it was challenging Simon & Schuster for the role as the "hottest" house in the industry. Doubleday was for many years the lumbering giant of the industry. Frank Doubleday, who founded the house in 1877 with S. S. McClure, developed close relationships with writers such as Rudyard Kipling and Joseph Conrad, while his son Nelson, who took charge in the late 1920s, had no literary pretensions. Nelson Doubleday, Jr., took over the company in 1978 and, overcoming his reputation as a bon vivant, confronted the growing financial crisis of the publishing operation. After some severe cost-cutting, including the shutting down of Dial Press in 1985, the business began to turn around. In 1986 the publishing operation was sold to Bertelsmann for $475 million.

Harcourt Brace Jovanovich, founded by Alfred Harcourt and Donald Brace in 1919, had its first success with a book by John Maynard Keynes and went on to publish such authors as Sinclair Lewis, Carl Sandburg, and T. S. Eliot. William Jovanovich took over the company in 1954 and remained chief executive through the end of 1988. (His son Peter later assumed the post.) An author himself, Jovanovich diversified the house into areas such as Sea World marine parks and moved its headquarters to Orlando, Florida, in 1983. In 1986 Harcourt agreed to purchase the educational and professional publishing operations of Holt, Rinehart & Winston from CBS for $500 million. The following year the company thwarted a takeover bid by British media baron Robert Maxwell by taking on more debt and paying a special dividend. The resulting financial instability forced the company to sell off its theme parks to Anheuser-Busch in 1989. John Herrington, former energy secretary, was brought in as chairman in 1990.

HarperCollins had its origins in the early 19th century when James Harper and three of his brothers set up a printing company to service booksellers. The operation soon turned into a publishing house and grew so rapidly that by 1853 Harper & Brothers was the world's largest publisher, with authors including Herman Melville and Mark Twain. In the 20th century the company, led by Cass Canfield, published popular writers such as E. B. White and James Thurber. The name Harper & Row was adopted in 1962 after a merger with textbook publisher Row, Peterson & Co. A few years later Canfield sought to protect the company against a takeover by selling a large block of stock to the Minneapolis Star & Tribune Co. Harper & Row purchased publishers Lippincott and Crowell in the late 1970s and in 1987 became a takeover target itself. The winning bidder was Rupert Murdoch's News Corp., which paid about $300 million. Half ownership of Harper & Row was later transferred to British publisher William Collins, which was itself 42 percent-owned by News Corp. and which later came under the complete control of the Murdoch holding company. The combined company was later renamed HarperCollins. In 1989 Harper purchased the Scott, Foresman textbook operation from Time Warner for $455 million. In 1990, Harper shocked the book world by purchasing the rights to three books by Jeffrey Archer for an amount reportedly in excess of $20 million.

Random House has lost its top spot among U.S. book publishers but remains one of the most prestigious, with imprints such as Alfred A. Knopf and Pantheon as well as Random House itself. The firm was founded in 1925 when Bennett Cerf bought the Modern Library series from his employer Horace Liveright and went into business with Donald Klopfer. The company made a name for itself by challenging the obscenity laws and winning the right to publish James Joyce's *Ulysses* in the 1930s. Random House was purchased by RCA during the conglomerate mania of the 1960s and was sold to the Newhouse publishing empire in 1980. Random House itself entered the merger game in the 1980s, gobbling up Schocken Books, Crown Publishers, Vanguard Press, and a group of British houses including Jonathan

Cape. When business started to slide in late 1989, S. I. Newhouse, Jr., forced out long-time Random House chief executive Robert Bernstein; a few months later André Schiffrin, the managing director of prestige imprint Pantheon Books, got the same treatment.

Simon & Schuster emerged in the 1980s as the most aggressive of the big trade publishers. Under the leadership of Richard Snyder since the house was purchased by Gulf + Western in 1975, S&S has epitomized the unabashed commercialization of book publishing. Concentrating on big-name authors and investing heavily in promotion, Snyder turned S&S into the largest and perhaps most successful trade publisher. He has been aided by S&S editor-in-chief Michael Korda, who cultivated major authors and was himself author of several books celebrating ruthlessness in business. S&S has also expanded rapidly in the fields of educational, technical, and professional publishing. With the purchase of Prentice-Hall and textbook producer Esquire Inc. in the 1980s, S&S became the largest U.S. book publishing company.

INDUSTRY DATA

Book Publishing	*1989*	*1988*	*1987*
Value of shipments	$14.0 billion	$12.7 billion	$11.6 billion
Total employment	74,000	71,500	70,300
Value of imports	$760 million	$801 million	$744 million

Source: U.S. Department of Commerce.

SOURCE GUIDE

Leading Stock Analysts and Experts

Oscar Dystel, former head of Bantam and now a consultant based in White Plains, New York, is an expert on the paperback business.

Kevin Gruneich, analyst at First Boston.

J. Kendrick Noble, Jr., analyst at Paine Webber.

Ivan Obolensky, former publisher now an analyst at Josephthal & Co.

Trade Associations and Unions

American Booksellers Association, 137 West 25th Street, New York, NY 10001. Tel.: (212) 463–8450.

Association of American Publishers, 220 East 23rd Street, New York, NY 10010. Tel.: (212) 689–8920.

Authors Guild, 234 West 44th Street, New York, NY 10036. Tel.: (212) 398–0838.

Book Industry Study Group (an industry-sponsored research body), 160 Fifth Avenue, New York, NY 10010. Tel.: (212) 929–1393.

District 65, United Automobile Workers, 13 Astor Place, New York, NY 10003. Tel.: (212) 673–5120.

National Writers Union, 13 Astor Place, New York, NY 10003. Tel.: (212) 254–0279.

Data Sources and Directories

American Book Trade Directory, an annual directory of booksellers in the United States and Canada (New York: R. R. Bowker).

Book Industry Trends, an annual statistical volume (New York: Book Industry Study Group).

The Bowker Annual Library and Book Trade Almanac, a review of the industry and compilation of statistics (New York: R. R. Bowker).

Industry Statistics, annual (New York: Association of American Publishers).

Literary Market Place, an annual directory of U.S. book publishers, agents, associations, suppliers, and other individuals and organizations in the trade (New York: R. R. Bowker). A companion volume, *International Literary Market Place*, covers 160 other countries.

Publishers Directory, annual (Detroit: Gale Research).

Publishers, Distributors & Wholesalers of the United States, an annual directory (New York: R. R. Bowker).

Publishers' Trade List Annual, a set of volumes that reproduce the catalogs of publishers (New York: R. R. Bowker).

Trade Publications

American Bookseller, monthly.

BP Report, weekly.

Publishers Weekly.

Books and Reports

Dessauer, John. *Book Publishing: What It Is, What It Does.* 2nd ed. New York: R. R. Bowker, 1981.

Cheney, O. H. *Economic Survey of the Book Industry 1930–1931.* Reprint. New York: R. R. Bowker, 1960.

Coser, Lewis; Charles Kadushin; and Walter W. Powell. *Books: The Culture and Commerce of Publishing.* New York: Basic Books, 1982.

Shatzkin, Leonard. *In Cold Type: Overcoming the Book Crisis.* Boston: Houghton Mifflin, 1982.

Tebbel, John. *A History of Book Publishing in the United States.* 4 vols. New York: R. R. Bowker, 1978–1981.

Whiteside, Thomas. *The Blockbuster Complex.* Middletown, Conn.: Wesleyan University Press, 1981.

CHAPTER 2

BROADCASTING AND CABLE

There is little doubt that electronic media have become the most important influence on the imagination of the American people. A significant portion of the population spends more time with radio and television than with any other activity, including working and sleeping. The most important influence that program purveyors hope to have on audiences is on buying habits. Although newspapers still command the largest dollar share of total advertising expenditures, the country's 1,092 commercial television stations play the leading role in the dissemination of ads for national companies. TV networks took in $9.6 billion in ad revenues in 1989, while station owners directly received another $11.8 billion. The share of radio (with 9,230 commercial stations) was $8.4 billion, and cable television got $2 billion. Taking into account cable subscription fees of $13.7 billion, the total TV and radio business had some $45 billion in revenues.

Yet the media industry is no longer a simple money machine. The emergence of a variety of competing program delivery systems—from cable to satellite to microwave—has turned the business upside down more than once. The players are changing with dizzying speed, and the previously invincible networks have been losing audience share and finding themselves up for grabs in the takeover wave. The upheaval has been encouraged by the Federal Communications Commission (especially during the Reagan administration), which has moved eagerly to undo 50 years of regulation.

A WIRELESS WORLD

The discovery of radio waves by Heinrich Hertz in the late 19th century inspired numerous experiments with wireless forms of telephone and telegraph. The first to perfect the technology for transmitting Morse code through the air was a young Italian named Guglielmo Marconi. His device took the world by storm and opened up a new industry in Europe and abroad. In 1899 the Marconi Wireless Company of America was formed to provide communications for ships at sea.

The technology was improved in the United States by Reginald Fessenden, whose work led to the first wireless voice transmission in 1906, and by Lee De Forest, who invented the audion vacuum tube that served as the basis for radio receivers. By the 1910s there was lively activity in radio by hobbyists, the military, and a few corporations (such as United Fruit, which used it to communicate with its banana boats going to and from Central America).

Radio's first great moment came in 1912, when a young operator for American Marconi picked up a distress signal from the Titanic and stayed at the receiver for 72 hours straight, relaying information. That operator, incidentally, was David Sarnoff, who went on to become one of the preeminent figures in American broadcasting as head of RCA.

During this time the advance of radio was impeded by the conflicting patent claims of American Marconi, De Forest, AT&T, and others. The problem was eased during World War I, during which time the federal government ordered companies—including light-bulb makers General Electric and Westinghouse—to produce radio components without regard to patent rights. At the end of the war, the U.S. Navy was lobbying heavily to get Congress to make radio a government monopoly under the navy's control. This particular plan was shot out of the water, but the idea of monopoly remained alive.

In 1919 the federal government was alarmed at the attempt of American Marconi, as the subsidiary of a foreign firm (British Marconi), to purchase certain essential patents owned by General Electric. As an alternative, the Wilson administration worked with GE to create a new company called Radio Corporation of America (RCA), which absorbed the assets of American Marconi. RCA, essentially a subsidiary of GE with a large minority interest owned by AT&T, was the vehicle by which a small group of companies attempted to dominate the new industry through the pooling of patents—so much so that soon after Westinghouse Electric entered the arena, it was invited to join the combine (as was United Fruit).

It was Westinghouse's establishment of the first commercial broadcasting station in Pittsburgh in 1920 that gave rise to a mass mania over radio. After KDKA went on the air, would-be listeners rushed to purchase the few receivers on the market (produced by Westinghouse) or more often badgered hobbyists they knew to put together simple crystal devices. Westinghouse expanded to Newark, New Jersey, with station WJZ, which made a splash by broadcasting the 1921 World Series.

During 1922, hundreds of new stations were licensed by the Department of Commerce, which ran out of three-letter designations and had to switch to four. The largest number of stations were run by companies (especially radio manufacturers and dealers) for publicity reasons. Many others were established by newspapers or educational institutions. All were assigned the same frequency, which meant that they had to alternate transmission times in some areas. The initial programming was sparse and unpolished, but a new age of communications had begun.

Corporate harmony was not part of the new era. The greatest tension was between AT&T and its partners in the radio combine. An agreement concluded in 1922 gave the phone company the exclusive right to produce and sell radio transmission equipment, while receiving apparatuses would be manufactured by GE and Westinghouse and marketed by RCA.

Yet AT&T sought to expand its domain through the promotion of radiotelephony (i.e., allowing people to buy time for their own broadcasts over the air). AT&T established several such toll broadcasting stations, including WEAF in New York and WCAP in Washington. It also claimed extensive rights over all broadcasting because of its patents in the field of transmission technology. The situation was clarified considerably in

1926, when AT&T agreed to quit broadcasting and sell its stations in exchange for a monopoly on wire connections between stations.

THE RED AND THE BLUE

At the same time, a new entity called National Broadcasting Company (NBC) was formed to operate AT&T's former stations and RCA's outlets. It was agreed that NBC—50 percent owned by RCA, 30 percent by GE, and 20 percent by Westinghouse—would pay AT&T generous rates for guaranteed access to landline connections.

NBC began its network broadcasting with a November 1926 gala production originating at the old Waldorf-Astoria Hotel in New York City and at other sites. By early 1927, NBC had two radio networks: NBC-Red, fed by WEAF, and NBC-Blue, which originated with WJZ.

That same year, the Columbia Phonograph Record Co. joined with a struggling operation called United Independent Broadcasters to form a serious rival to NBC. The venture nearly went under but was rescued by a group of investors that included the owners of the Congress Cigar Co. of Philadelphia. William Paley, the 26-year-old son of one of the partners in Congress Cigar, ended up as president of what had become known as the Columbia Broadcasting System (CBS).

Although CBS would later dominate the broadcast industry, in the late 1920s NBC reigned supreme. But the comfortable arrangement of the radio combine was shaken in 1930, when the Justice Department brought antitrust charges against RCA, GE, and Westinghouse. The industry was stunned but worked out a consent decree they could live with. The final deal was for GE and Westinghouse to give up their ownership interests in RCA. The latter was allowed to keep its radio manufacturing facilities, and GE and Westinghouse would be allowed to compete in that business after a 30-month interval.

After taking office the Roosevelt administration made clear its intention of creating a comprehensive regulatory framework for radio and the emerging technology of television.

FDR personally affirmed the importance of radio with the inauguration of his "Fireside Chat" broadcasts in 1933.

Federal oversight of broadcasting started back in 1912 with a law—prompted by the Titanic disaster—establishing strict requirements for ship radios. In the 1920s the Commerce Department held a series of National Radio Conferences to deal with the chaos caused by the sudden appearance of hundreds of stations on the air. Following the 1923 conference, the Commerce Department established rules for different classes of stations (depending on transmission power), placing them on different frequencies. Legislation passed in 1927 created a Federal Radio Commission, which expanded the regulatory structure; but the delicate issue of controlling advertising on the new medium was sidestepped.

In 1934 the Roosevelt administration succeeded in getting Congress to approve legislation that overhauled federal regulation of broadcasting as well as telephones (on the latter, see Chapter 5). The legislation established the Federal Communications Commission (FCC) and charged it with overseeing the airwaves with a view to promoting the public interest, which was said to include a diversity of programming at both the local and the national level. Stations were to be licensed for no more than three years, and it was made clear that broadcasters were simply being given temporary rights to use a public resource.

The FCC was not allowed to directly censor programming or advertising, but the commission soon realized that its license renewal power gave it great sway over broadcast policies. When it wanted to discourage practices such as radio lotteries or liquor advertising, the commission simply issued a statement saying such things might not be in the public interest. This so-called raised-eyebrow approach got the message across to broadcasters, who usually complied without a direct order.

By the late 1930s radio was in full flower. More than 25 million American homes were equipped with the large receiving consoles, and listening to comedians such as Jack Benny and serials such as "The Green Hornet" had become part of the ritual of daily life. The first major broadcast demagogue, Father Coughlin, was on the air, and radio was beginning to supply dramatic reports on the growing crisis in Europe. In 1938 the power of the medium was made alarmingly clear as a Halloween Eve dramatization of "The War of the Worlds," aired over CBS by Orson Welles's Mercury Theater, caused widespread panic until people realized that a martian invasion was not actually taking place.

By this time the networks were firmly in control of the business. NBC led the field with its Red and Blue networks, followed by CBS and the even smaller Mutual Broadcasting System, launched in 1934. There were also some 20 regional networks.

The growing degree of concentration of broadcasting power began to generate concern at the FCC. In 1938 the commission launched an antitrust investigation. The result was the *Report on Chain Broadcasting*, which raised questions about NBC's ownership of two national networks and about the CBS "network option" policy of being able to preempt local programming at any time. The report also suggested it was not appropriate for the networks to own artist bureaus (in effect, talent agencies), since their role as users of performers created a conflict of interest.

The networks moved quickly to divest themselves of the artist bureaus but resisted the other changes. They brought pressure to bear on FCC chairman James Fly through conservative members of Congress. Fly fought off the attacks, and the reforms were implemented and upheld by the Supreme Court. The NBC Blue Network was put up for sale and was purchased for $8 million by Edward Noble, a candy manufacturer of Lifesavers fame. Noble revamped the operation and renamed it the American Broadcasting Company.

But critics of the industry were not satisfied. There was still the issue of what many regarded as the excessive amounts of commercials and recorded music on the air; local stations were not living up to their responsibility to provide a diversity of programming. A 1946 report for the FCC by Charles Siepmann and Dallas Smythe, entitled *Public Service Responsibility of Broadcast Licensees* and more commonly known as the Blue Book, proposed stricter standards for limiting advertising and promoting discussion of public issues and local live programming. The industry attacked the report ferociously, and the commission did little to implement the Blue Book's proposals.

In fact the commission backtracked by reversing the so-called Mayflower decision, which barred broadcasters from editorializing without due regard for balance. It also rescinded the AVCO ruling, which called for competitive bids in license transfer cases. Then, in 1952, the industry got Congress to pass legislation prohibiting the FCC from considering applicants other than the proposed transferee. In the view of some analysts, these actions tended to move away from the spirit of the 1934 Communications Act and pushed broadcast channels closer to private property.

TELEVISION TAKES HOLD

As soon as World War II was over, RCA moved ahead aggressively in the development of television. Experiments in TV technology dated back to the 1920s, and RCA's Sarnoff was the most enthusiastic promoter. Commercial television had its debut in a transmission from the 1939 World's Fair in New York, but the industry developed slowly, and expansion was brought to a halt by the war.

RCA's bullishness on television was not shared by the entire broadcast industry. Some people felt that the rise of TV would spell the doom of radio. Matters were complicated further by the efforts of Edwin Armstrong to win favorable treatment for his invention of frequency modulation (FM) radio. FM broadcasting, which Armstrong pushed as a superior technology to AM, had been approved on an experimental basis but found itself in competition with television for certain parts of the frequency spectrum. In 1945 the FCC opted for the RCA position, giving a full-speed-ahead signal for television. Armstrong entered into a drawn-out lawsuit against RCA and ended up killing himself in 1953.

By 1948 the FCC had licensed about 100 television stations. It then instituted a freeze, saying that the interference problem had to be studied. At the same time, the network system took firm hold in the TV industry. NBC took the lead, while CBS held back to await the outcome of a dispute over competing methods of color broadcasting. When it did jump on the bandwagon, it had to buy most of its allotment of stations rather than establishing new outlets.

ABC struggled to keep up with its stronger rivals, and a shortage of capital forced it to merge with United Paramount Theaters. (The exhibition arm of the Paramount movie studio, it had been spun off as an independent company as a result of a federal antitrust case.) The fourth national network, Dumont, had great difficulty getting affiliates; in 1955 it disbanded the network and sold off the stations it owned to Metromedia.

During the 1950s television took hold of the American imagination to an even greater extent than radio did in the 1930s. When a TV station began operations in a city, theater and movie attendance, nightclub patronage, and even use of taxicabs declined markedly. By 1952 there were some 15 million sets in use in 64 cities, and countless people were already addicted to such programs as the "Texaco Star Theater" (with Milton Berle, known as Mr. Television), "I Love Lucy," and "Your Show of Shows."

TV was also assuming growing importance in the political process, as seen in Eisenhower's commercials during the 1952 presidential race and his running mate Richard Nixon's televised "Checkers" speech, in which he denied charges of financial impropriety. Broadcasting also played a central role in the witch hunts of the period. A group calling itself Aware Inc. published lists of purported "subversives" working in the industry. Network executives succumbed to intimidation, firing many producers and writers and instituting a blacklist.

Yet television also played a role in the downfall of McCarthyism. Edward R. Murrow and Fred Friendly of CBS took on the Wisconsin senator in a series of "See It Now" programs and did much to change public opinion. The televising of McCarthy's 1954 hearings to investigate supposed subversion in the army also swayed people by providing a close-up view of the senator's unsavory methods.

A "VAST WASTELAND"

By the late 1950s, however, TV programming had to a great extent shifted away from public affairs and serious drama. There was a great craze for quiz programs until it was revealed that many of them were fixed. Live programs became a rarity, replaced by telefilms that were produced by Hollywood studios seeking new revenue sources to substitute for the declining movie business. During the same period, much of commercial radio abandoned any semblance of diversity and adopted formula formats such as Top 40 hits.

This new direction for TV was strongly encouraged in the early 1960s by CBS, whose president James Aubrey encouraged less sophisticated programs. In a famous memo, he called for more "broads, boobs, and busts." This is precisely what CBS dished up in the form of comedy series such as "The Beverly Hillbillies," "Petticoat Junction," "Mr. Ed," and "The Munsters."

Things reached such a state that President Kennedy's FCC chairman Newton Minow decried what he called the "vast wasteland" of television programming. Minow encouraged the expansion of educational TV—promoted since the early 1950s by the Ford Foundation—and paved the way for the creation of the Corporation for Public Broadcasting in 1967 and the Public Broadcasting Service in 1969.

The 1960s also witnessed the flowering of the public-interest movement in broadcasting. Activists, seeing the growing influence of mass media in American life, began demanding that broadcasters pay more attention to minorities and issues of social change. In 1964 one of the pioneering organizations, the Office of Communication of the United Church of Christ, working with local groups, began monitoring the output of TV stations in Jackson, Mississippi.

The organization found that the white-owned stations ignored the black population, which made up 45 percent of their audience, as well as the civil rights movement sweeping the South. On that basis the group petitioned the FCC to deny license renewals to the stations. The FCC claimed that public-interest groups had no standing to intervene in such cases because they had no economic stake. A federal appeals court overruled the commission and stated that organizations such as the United Church of Christ could indeed intervene. During this period public-interest groups succeeded in getting the FCC to regulate the equal employment practices of broadcasters.

Television station owners and the networks also found themselves under increasing criticism because of the amount of advertising on the air (particularly the commercials aimed at children), the increasing amount of violence (especially in the action-adventure programs that ABC came to specialize in), and the portrayal of women and minorities. In 1969 the Supreme Court, in what is known as the Red Lion decision, affirmed the responsibility of broadcasters to air conflicting views on public issues. In 1970 the FCC continued its efforts to limit the power of the networks by restricting the role the networks could have in the production and syndication (selling old series for rebroadcast) of programming.

THE WIRED NATION

Within a few years the issue for the networks was no longer how much power they would be allowed to amass but rather how they would cope with the rise of competing TV delivery systems: cable television and various forms of pay-TV.

Cable, originally known as community antenna television, started out as a technique for delivering broadcast signals to areas that could not be reached by regular transmissions. A powerful antenna would receive the signal and relay it to households via a coaxial cable. The first community antenna was erected in 1949 to allow a group of residents in Astoria, Oregon, to pick up weak TV signals from Seattle. The first cable television company was formed the following year in Lansford, Pennsylvania.

For many years cable remained a relatively insignificant element of the television business, though broadcasters frequently complained that cable operators were making money by receiving their signals and selling them to households. The FCC approached the issue of cable regulation gingerly, given that the business did not involve broadcasting and was not conducted across state lines. In the absence of FCC rules, many local authorities asserted jurisdiction over cable, demanding that operators obtain franchises.

As cable began to grow in importance, expanding out from remote areas, the FCC began to pay more attention. In 1965 the commission finally acted, issuing rules that required cable operators to deliver signals of any broadcast stations within 60 miles (what became known as the must-carry rule) and that limited the cable transmission of programs being shown over local stations. The commission, concerned that the growth of cable would inhibit local broadcasting (especially UHF stations), issued a series of other rules that restricted the industry's development. The industry was also tainted in 1971 when Irving Kahn of Teleprompter, a leading promoter of cable, was convicted of bribing local officials in Johnstown, Pennsylvania, to obtain a franchise.

The vitality of the cable business began to improve in the late 1970s. The FCC relaxed a number of its rules, and a new kind of programming was appearing on cable systems: pay services providing uncut movies, sporting events, and other features not available on broadcast stations.

The notion of pay television—as opposed to free (i.e., advertiser-supported) TV—first arose when the medium was developing in the late 1940s. A major proponent was Zenith, which tested a "phonevision" system, in which scrambled broadcasts were unscrambled via signals transmitted over telephone lines. The idea did not catch on, but various subscription TV schemes came and went in the following years, usually eliciting an angry reaction from theater owners, who feared the medium could lead to their demise. To appease both motion picture and broadcast interests, the FCC adopted rules limiting the spread of pay-TV systems.

In the mid-1970s cable and pay-TV were joined in a novel programming service created by Time Inc. In 1972 Time had started Home Box Office (HBO) as a pay service for the company's cable system in New York. HBO was soon offered to other cable operators and began spreading at a modest rate. The turning point came in 1975, when HBO began distributing its program via satellite rather than microwave. The service was thus able to market its programs nationwide. This gave a tremendous boost both to HBO and to the cable systems it was supplying.

HBO's success inspired other programmers to turn to satellites. Broadcaster Ted Turner used the technology to turn his Atlanta TV outlet, WTBS, into the first "superstation" beamed to cable systems across the country. He later supplemented this with an all-news service called Cable News Network (CNN). Turner's services were advertiser-supported and were included in the price of a basic cable subscription, whereas HBO and competing pay services (such as Showtime) that soon emerged required an additional monthly fee. By the late 1970s the once-sleepy cable industry was one of the hottest businesses around. A sign of the times was the $650 million Westinghouse agreed to pay in 1980 to acquire Teleprompter.

As companies rushed to wire the more attractive communities (mainly wealthier urban and suburban areas), they found themselves up against local authorities eager to get the best possible terms in the franchise agreement. Cable companies often had to form alliances with local public figures and make generous service commitments. Promises of state-of-the-art systems with 100 or more channels (including noncommercial ones for public access) and with interactive capabilities led to rapidly escalating construction costs for systems, especially in areas where the cable had to be placed underground.

By about 1983 the bloom was off the cable business. Operators, in addition to being bogged down in franchise disputes and heavy capital costs, discovered that subscriptions were not growing as fast as earlier forecasts had suggested. A disturbing number of subscribers were canceling services. This process, called churning in industry jargon, became a particular problem for the pay services.

Moreover, cable was being confronted with the emergence of a variety of competing "wireless" delivery systems, including DBS (direct broadcast satellite: beaming of programs from satellites to receivers in the home), MDS (multipoint distribution systems: transmissions via microwave to special rooftop antennas), and SMATV (satellite master antenna television:

systems in which an apartment building or complex receives satellite signals through a common earth station and distributes them to individual households via wire).

As it turned out, none of those technologies ended up as a major challenger. DBS all but disappeared, and the others remained limited in scope. Consequently, by the mid-1980s the future for cable began to appear quite promising. The optimism was largely inspired by the passage of the Cable Communications Policy Act of 1984. The law gave the FCC a defined mandate for regulating cable but also decreed an end to most cable rate regulation beginning in 1987. Then in July 1985, a federal appeals court struck down the must-carry rule, freeing cable operators to convert more channels to lucrative pay services. The ruling was widely interpreted as an affirmation of the cable industry's claim, based on First Amendment arguments, that it should be immune from the regulatory strictures of the 1934 Communications Act. In 1986 the FCC adopted a more limited must-carry rule that represented a compromise between the demands of cable operators and broadcasters; but that too was struck down in the courts.

The end of rate regulation (except in those few areas where the FCC decided there was no effective competition from broadcast stations) unleashed a rapid acceleration of subscription fees. A 1989 report by the General Accounting Office found that fees were increasing by about 15 percent a year, far in excess of general inflation rates. For the cable industry this was a financial boon. Profit margins increased, and the value of cable systems—hundreds of which were being bought and sold each year—soared. Among the biggest deals in the late 1980s were the $1.6 billion acquisition of Storer Cable by a joint venture of Tele-Communications Inc. and Comcast, and the merger of United Artists Communications (no relation to the MGM/UA film studio) and United Cable Television to form United Artists Entertainment (56 percent of which is owned by Tele-Communications).

At the same time, the growing popularity of pay-per-view channels provided an additional source of revenue and allowed the pay cable services to regain some of the ground lost to videocassettes. The industry was also benefiting from the fact that the country was nearly fully wired. By the end of 1989, some 80 million homes had access to cable, and 49 million of them (61 percent) were subscribing.

While the industry was enjoying its prosperity, a backlash was in the making. The escalation of subscription rates elicited a large volume of protests, which came to the attention of politicians such as Senator Albert Gore, Jr., of Tennessee. Citing huge increases—100 percent or more—in cable rates in various communities of his state, Gore has led a campaign to reregulate what he calls the "cable Cosa Nostra." The FCC started to get the message. In 1990 the commission voted to examine whether or not stricter regulation of cable was in order. Congress also moved toward reregulation.

Cable operators have also been facing renewed challenges from competing technologies. The telephone companies have been seeking federal permission to deliver entertainment and information services to homes via fiber optics. Given the vast capacity of fiber-optic connections, consumers would have a much wider range of options—including films on demand, banking services, and electronic mail—than with cable. There has also been a renewed push in DBS. In early 1990 NBC, Rupert Murdoch's News Corp., Cablevision Systems, and the Hughes Communications subsidiary of General Motors announced a $1 billion joint venture called Sky Cable to deliver up to 108 channels of programming to subscribers, who would use small receiving dishes costing about $300 each. A similar project, called K Prime, was announced by a joint venture of General Electric and a group of cable operators.

DISHES AND PIRATES

While the cable industry and the phone companies compete to see who will deliver entertainment via wires, and the DBS providers seek a niche in providing wireless service to subscribers with special receivers, there is a growing number of viewers who pull the programming they want right out of the sky. These are the owners of private earth stations, more commonly known as satellite dishes.

Back in 1979 these dishes were still an amusement for the wealthy; the Neiman-Marcus catalog offered one for $36,500. But in the following years the price dropped sharply, and people in remote areas not served by cable began buying the devices to supplement the limited broadcast programming they were able to receive. The dishes turned famine into feast. People in the most isolated areas were able to pluck dozens of channels out of the air, including pay services and even raw feeds (unedited transmissions).

Once earth stations reached a certain presence, pay-TV providers such as HBO began to complain that dish users were in effect stealing their signals. Thus began the great debate over "signal piracy." The term often also encompassed people who tapped into cable lines without subscribing and those who used illicit converters to receive pay services via the cable. In 1983 police in Pennsylvania arrested a man calling himself "The HBO Kid," who ran a million-dollar operation selling such converters.

By the early 1980s the cable industry, estimating the losses from piracy at $500 million a year, began to fight back. HBO and other services stepped up legal actions against pirates and announced plans to begin scrambling their satellite signals at the source. At the same time, owners of earth stations banded together—led by a group called SPACE (Society for Private and Commercial Earth Stations)—to affirm their right to receive satellite signals.

The issue found its way to Congress, where Senator Barry Goldwater sponsored a bill that became part of the 1984 cable act. The provision represented a compromise between the two sides. It legalized the ownership and use of dishes for the purpose of receiving *unscrambled* signals. Programmers were supposed to develop plans for providing converters so that dish owners could view decoded scrambled signals at a reasonable fee.

The law stimulated rapid growth in earth station sales, and the number of dishes in operation by 1986 was estimated at 1.5 million. Yet after HBO finally began scrambling its signal in January 1986, the tensions between programmers and dish owners heated up again, and dish sales cooled off. Earth station users charged that cable operators and programmers were conspiring to monopolize the sale of decoding equipment. In the meantime, dish owners were slow to purchase the $400 decoders and pay the monthly fees that were also required to view scrambled programming.

One irate dish dealer in Florida made his position known by interrupting an HBO transmission with an antiscrambling message. This new form of hacking, by someone who identified himself as Captain Midnight, panicked the satellite industry. But there was a bit of relief when the culprit, who also worked as a satellite engineer, was tracked down and persuaded to plead guilty to a charge of unauthorized transmission of an interfering signal.

Most dish owners responded to scrambling in a less flamboyant manner—they simply purchased black-market devices that unscrambled signals and thus avoided the subscription fees. The satellite television industry has used both criminal prosecutions and new technologies to try to foil the pirates, but at the end of 1989 only 700,000 dish owners (out of an estimated 2.6 million) were legitimate subscribers.

DEREGULATION AND MERGER MANIA

While these new technologies were going through their growth pains, the television networks began to experience a decline in viewing levels. The network share dropped from around 90 percent of the prime-time audience in the early 1970s to less than 70 percent in the late 1980s. National advertisers started to get concerned and began to spend some of their money on cable networks. But even this did not help once videocassette recorders began invading American homes, allowing people to tape programs and then "zap" commercials (fast-forward through them) while viewing the shows later. These factors contributed to a slowdown in network revenues, which unfortunately occurred while production costs for programming were rising rapidly. The result of all this was a squeeze on ABC, NBC, and CBS. Of the three, NBC managed to make the best of a declining situa-

Leading Cable Operators (as of 12/31/89)

	Number of Subscribers (in millions)
1. Tele-Communications	4.62
2. ATC (Time Warner)	4.40
3. United Artists Entertainment	2.62
4. Continental Cablevision	2.57
5. Warner Cable	1.72
6. Comcast	1.57
7. Cox Cable	1.56
8. Storer	1.53
9. Cablevision Systems	1.47
10. Jones Spacelink	1.43

Note: Subscribers include those of systems in which the company had at least a majority interest. ATC and Warner Cable, now both owned by Time Warner, are listed separately because the merger of Time Inc. and Warner Communications was not completed until January 1990.

Source: Paul Kagan Associates, Inc., Carmel, California.

tion, holding a commanding lead in the ratings throughout the late 1980s and thus earning nearly all the profits.

There was, however, good news coming from Washington for the networks and other broadcasters. After taking office in 1981, the Reagan administration embarked on a crusade to dismantle much of the regulatory structure that had been built since 1934. While some deregulatory moves were made under

Leading Pay-TV Services (as of 12/31/89)

	Number of Subscribers (in millions)
1. HBO	17.4
2. Showtime	7.4
3. Cinemax	6.4
4. Disney Channel	4.9
5. The Movie Channel	2.7

Source: Paul Kagan Associates, Inc., Carmel, California.

Leading Advertiser-Supported Cable Services (as of 12/31/89)

Company	Homes Reached (in millions)
1. ESPN	54.8
2. Cable News Network (CNN)	53.8
3. WTBS	52.1
4. USA Network	50.8
5. Nickelodeon	49.7
6. Music Television (MTV)	49.3
7. Nashville Network	48.3
8. C-SPAN	48.0
9. The Family Channel	48.0
10. Lifetime	47.0

Source: Paul Kagan Associates, Inc., Carmel, California.

Carter, Reagan's FCC chairman Mark Fowler argued that the advent of new technologies had made the premise of regulation—the need to protect a scarce resource—obsolete.

With unbridled laissez-faire zeal, Fowler went after the commission's key regulatory principles. Starting in 1981 the FCC:

- Eliminated limits on commercial time for radio and television and ended requirements for minimum amounts of public affairs programming.
- Relaxed rules governing children's television.
- Abolished the requirement that stations keep program logs open for public inspection.
- Lifted the requirement that license holders must operate a station for at least three years before reselling it.
- Reduced detailed renewal procedures to the point that a licensee could seek a renewal simply by sending in a postcard (in addition, in 1981 Congress extended the traditional three-year license period to seven years for radio and five years for television stations).
- Attempted to abolish all ownership limits but reached a compromise with Congress under which the old 7-7-7 limit (7 TV, 7 AM radio, and 7 FM radio stations) was raised to 12-12-12, though Congress insisted that the po-

tential audience of the 12 TV stations could not exceed 25 percent of the total TV households in the United States.

- Abolished the fairness doctrine, which required broadcasters to air opposing points of view on controversial public issues. (When Congress voted in 1987 to write the fairness doctrine into law, President Reagan vetoed the bill.)

The commission also attempted to repeal the rules that limit network participation in program production and syndication; but apparently Hollywood got to President Reagan, and Fowler was told to back off. (An exception to the deregulatory trend came in the area of "indecent" programming. In 1987 the FCC began applying stricter standards to objectionable broadcasts, though it allowed greater freedom after midnight. Congress, led by Senator Jesse Helms, passed legislation in 1988 requiring the FCC to apply the indecency rules on a 24-hour-a-day basis.)

Among these changes, the expansion of the ownership limits probably had the most far-reaching effect. In fact it can be seen as a major factor in the extraordinary wave of media mergers that occurred in 1985. In that one year an estimated $30 billion worth of electronic media properties (including two of the networks) changed hands, with the blessing of the FCC. The largest transactions announced during the year were the following:

- General Electric purchased RCA for $6.3 billion.
- Capital Cities purchased ABC for $3.6 billion.
- Kohlberg, Kravis, Roberts & Co. took Storer Communications private for $2.3 billion.
- A group led by Tele-Communications and ATC agreed to purchase Group W Cable for $2.1 billion.
- Rupert Murdoch purchased seven independent TV stations from Metromedia for $2 billion, later selling off one of them for $450 million.
- The Tribune Company purchased Station KTLA in Los Angeles for $510 million, the most ever paid for a single broadcast outlet.

The acquisitions by Murdoch and the Tribune Company represent more than picking up attractive properties. Each deal was an element in the race to create a fourth commercial television network. Murdoch, working through the Twentieth Century-Fox film studio, which he also bought in 1985, began using the Metromedia stations as the basis for affiliating independent TV outlets around the country. Tribune Company, which owned six stations after buying KTLA, was after the same goal.

The quest for a viable fourth network has been around for years. Dumont attempted to play that role after the war but could not attract enough affiliates. Other companies such as Paramount and Metromedia made stabs at the goal but did not get far. Of the new efforts, Murdoch's has been the most successful. By the end of 1989 his Fox Broadcasting Company had more than 125 affiliates to which it was supplying about eight hours of programming a week. Fox was posing a serious challenge to the big three networks during at least one prime-time night a week.

During this period, radio has been going through an upheaval of its own. Most dramatic has been the rapid decline of AM radio. Whereas more than two thirds of the radio audience went to AM in 1970, FM had more than 76 percent by 1989. The brassy, jingle-laden sound of AM has lost its appeal for many people. Some AM stations have responded by seeking FCC approval to begin broadcasting in stereo, but there were no signs this would be enough to save AM. In 1990 the FCC proposed new rules aimed at improving AM reception by encouraging some stations to move to new slots in an expanded frequency band; the FCC also said it was considering allowing stereo broadcasting in that band.

Overall, the trend in broadcasting has been toward a concentration of ownership (seen perhaps most dramatically in the 1989 merger of Time Inc. and Warner Communications) and a further shift away from local programming. Even cable, which was supposed to make television available for community needs, has moved more and more toward the type of programming provided by the networks and the independents. The new technologies have provided a variety of delivery methods but relatively little in the way of diversity of programming.

LABOR RELATIONS

Workers in the radio industry responded eagerly to New Deal labor legislation by organizing to improve the poor working conditions that characterized the industry. In 1937 the American Federation of Radio Artists (AFRA) was formed, and in a few years the union was widely recognized as the bargaining agent for broadcasting talent. As for other radio workers, the Association of Technical Employees was formed in 1934 as a management-dominated union. But within a few years it began to operate independently, and in 1940 it changed its title to the National Association of Broadcast Engineers and Technicians (NABET). The union found itself in jurisdictional disputes with the International Brotherhood of Electrical Workers, but in 1951 it received a CIO charter giving it jurisdiction over the broadcasting industry. Consequently, the union substituted Employees for Engineers in its title.

In 1952 AFRA merged with the Television Authority, a federation of four performers' unions, to form the American Federation of Television and Radio Artists (AFTRA). The performers' union also had jurisdictional problems—with the Screen Actors Guild (SAG), which repeatedly rejected AFTRA's merger overtures. Finally, the two unions made a pact under which SAG would bargain for filmed television performers and AFTRA would represent performers on live or videotaped programs. During the 1950s some AFTRA officials were involved in promoting the blacklist, but the group was voted out in 1955, and AFTRA joined the forces opposing the blacklist.

AFTRA called its first national strike in 1967, forcing the networks to show reruns. The walkout was settled after 13 days, just in time for ABC to broadcast the Academy Awards ceremony. Later that same year, NABET struck ABC for two months. The union also struck NBC in 1976 and ABC again in 1977.

In 1982 AFTRA filed for Chapter 11 after a federal judge refused to stay a $10 million antitrust judgment against the union. Although unions are usually considered immune from antitrust laws, a jury found AFTRA guilty of restraint of trade for pressuring advertising agencies not to give business to a nonunion company that wrote music and jingles for commercials. The case was settled out of court.

In the 1980s the broadcast unions were under intense pressure as a result of cost-cutting measures instituted by the networks. Capital Cities, which took over ABC, and General Electric, the new parent of NBC, each had a history of taking a hard line with labor. Capital Cities, which gained a reputation as a union-buster among newspaper unions, successfully pressured NABET to allow two stations that the company had owned before acquiring ABC to remain nonunion. All three networks laid off large numbers of employees and began using more freelancers, while NBC installed robot camera operators on its evening news programs. CBS anchorman Dan Rather was prompted to write an op-ed article in *The New York Times* arguing that by making such cuts his own employer was moving "from Murrow to mediocrity." Rather also said he would take a pay cut if it would save the jobs of some of his colleagues, but CBS management declined the offer.

In 1987 management demands to have the right to dismiss workers without regard to seniority and the right to use more temporary workers prompted strikes by Writers Guild members at CBS and ABC. The walkout ended after two months, with the networks getting some of the work rule changes they had sought. A few weeks later members of NABET at NBC walked off the job. They remained out for 17 weeks but ended up giving management the right to use more temporary workers. In 1988 the Writers Guild struck television and film producers for five months over residuals, forcing a delay in the opening of the fall television season.

LEADING COMPANIES

The **American Broadcasting Company (ABC)** was created in 1945 after NBC was required by a court ruling to divest itself of one of its two radio networks. ABC struggled along, lacking the capital necessary to make a serious entry into television. To improve its resources the company merged with United Paramount Theaters in 1953. Leonard Goldenson, who headed United Paramount, ended up running the network for 30 years. Through the 1950s ABC remained a perennial also-ran in the ratings game. The network began to receive some serious audience shares in the 1960s and came close to being acquired by ITT in the latter part of the decade. In 1976 ABC suddenly leaped to first place in the prime-time ratings, thanks to the efforts of the gifted programmer Fred Silverman (known as "the man with the golden gut"). The network also became a leader in news programming. ABC had a series of disappointments in cable programming efforts but in 1984 purchased ESPN, the sports network and the largest cable service. In 1985 it was announced that ABC would be acquired in a friendly transaction by Capital Cities. The network's profits remained weak in the late 1980s, but there were signs of recovery in 1990 as ABC began cutting NBC's lead in the ratings.

CBS was formed in the late 1920s through the rescue of a small network that had been set up as a competitor to NBC. William Paley, the son of one of the owners of a cigar company that invested in the network, became head of CBS and tenaciously held on to that position for nearly 60 years. CBS was for many years the "class act" in the broadcasting business, especially with its superior news and public affairs programming. It was the invincible leader in the ratings until it was dislodged by ABC in 1976. In 1985 the network was shaken, first by an effort by a group of conservatives to change what they considered to be the liberal bias of the network. Then Ted Turner announced an audacious plan to take over CBS in a $5 billion deal that involved no cash at all. CBS defeated Turner by repurchasing 21 percent of its stock for nearly $1 billion, a tactic that ballooned the company's long-term debt. As further protection, CBS chairman Thomas Wyman asked Loews Corp. to raise its stake in the company as high as 25 percent. In September 1986 Wyman lost the support of the board, and Paley and Loews's chairman Laurence Tisch stepped in to take over management of CBS on an interim basis. They ended up staying indefinitely (though it is Tisch who effectively runs the company), moving to cut costs and to streamline operations by selling off the company's magazine division and CBS Records. This did nothing to help in the ratings, which in the late 1980s found CBS running a distant third among the networks.

Fox Broadcasting represents international media magnate Rupert Murdoch's attempt to establish a fourth commercial television network in the United States. Murdoch branched out from print to electronic media in 1985 with the purchase of seven independent TV stations from Metromedia and the Twentieth Century-Fox film company. The Metromedia deal required Murdoch to become a U.S. citizen in order to comply with FCC ownership rules. By the end of 1989, Fox had more than 125 affiliates to which it was supplying about eight hours of programming a week. The highly touted Joan Rivers talk show was a flop, but Fox prime-time shows such as "Married . . . With Children" gained a great deal of audience share beginning in the fall of 1988, when the big three networks were without new programs because of the Writers Guild strike.

The National Broadcasting Company (NBC) was the first broadcast network–in fact, it was two networks until the federal government insisted that one be divested in 1943. NBC was formed in 1926 as part of a complicated arrangement between the Radio Corporation of America (RCA) and AT&T. As part of the larger RCA organization, NBC was always financially stronger than its rivals. "General" David Sarnoff, who ran the company from its earliest days to his retirement in 1966, was the leading proponent of television in the 1930s and 1940s. He also diversified RCA into electronics and other fields. After Sarnoff's departure RCA went through a period of managerial instability that came to an end with the arrival of Thornton Bradshaw in 1981. Grant Tinker, hired by Bradshaw to head NBC, turned the languishing network around. In the 1985–86 season NBC for the first time came out on top in the ratings. The network and the rest of RCA was acquired by General Electric–its original owner–for more than $6 billion in 1986. Later that year GE named one of its executives, Robert Wright, to replace Tinker. Under Wright, NBC greatly widened its lead over the other television networks, though it moved out of radio by selling its network to Westwood One. The company moved into cable programming with the 1989 introduction of the CNBC consumer-oriented business channel and into direct broadcast satellite by joining a joint venture called Sky Cable.

Tele-Communications Inc. (TCI) is the colossus of the cable industry, with nearly 5 million subscribers and equity interests in companies with millions more. Founded in Texas in 1956, TCI was built into the nation's largest cable operator by John Malone, a former management consultant known as a ruthless negotiator. Taking advantage of the company's formidable cash flow, Malone has spent heavily to acquire entire cable systems or major equity positions, a 22 percent interest in Turner Broadcasting, and shares of such cable services as Showtime, American Movie Classics, the Discovery Channel, and Black Entertainment Television. In 1990 TCI, edged out of first place among cable operators by the merger of Time Inc. and Warner Communications, was nonetheless faced with mounting concern over its dominance in the cable industry. In response TCI announced a plan to spin off its programming interests into a separate company.

Time Warner, the nation's largest media company, is the result of the 1989 merger of Time Inc. and Warner Communications. Time had dabbled in broadcasting in the 1950s and 1960s but decided it had a better future in cable television. Beginning with a fledgling cable company in Manhattan, Time ended up with the second-largest cable system in the country. Time also created Home Box Office, which revolutionized the pay cable business. In 1989 Time entered into a friendly merger with Warner Communications (which was almost derailed by a competing bid for Time by Paramount). Aside from the Warner Brothers studio, Warner owned TV and movie producer Lorimar-Telepictures and a major cable system. The combined cable holdings of Time Warner finally created a major challenger to TCI.

The rise of Ted Turner's **Turner Broadcasting System** has paralleled the growth of the cable industry. Beginning with a billboard company inherited from his father, Turner purchased an Atlanta television station in 1969 and seven years later began transmitting its signal to cable systems around the country, making WTBS the first superstation. Turner, who gained the nickname Captain Outrageous during his yachting career, shook up television news in 1980 with the creation of Cable News Network (CNN). Initially derided as the "Chicken Noodle Network," CNN went on to become the TV news outlet of record, expanding its journalistic operations around the globe at a time when the three broadcast networks were cutting back their news organizations. In 1985 Turner made an audacious takeover bid for CBS, and the following year he purchased MGM/UA. Although Turner sold most of the movie company's assets (keeping its valuable film library), he remained stuck with a huge debt load that forced him to sell 37 percent of Turner Broadcasting to a consortium of 31 cable operators led by TCI. Turner thus lost autocratic control of the company but still managed to make audacious moves, such as the 1988 introduction of the TNT cable service (which specializes in old movies from the MGM collection) in the face of widespread skepticism.

Viacom International was formed in 1971 out of the syndication business CBS had to spin off in response to an FCC ruling forcing the networks out of that activity. Under president and chief executive Terrence Elkes, Viacom emerged as one of the fastest growing companies in the television business. Aside from syndication, it got into programming (starting Showtime in 1976 as a rival to HBO), cable system operation, and broadcast station ownership. In 1985 it went on a buying spree, acquiring (as leader of an investment group) a 15 percent interest in the Orion Pictures film studio, paying Warner Amex Cable $690 million for the MTV and Nickelodeon cable services and the 50 percent of Showtime it did not already own, and acquiring CBS's St. Louis station for $122 million. An investment group led by Elkes offered to take the company private, but that deal was rejected in 1987 by the company's board in favor of a $3 billion bid by National Amusements, a movie theater chain controlled by Sumner Redstone. Viacom—which also owns The Movie Channel and (in a joint venture with Hearst and Capital Cities/ABC) Lifetime cable services—launched a comedy service called HA! in 1990 to compete with Time Warner's Comedy Channel. The company also distributes "The Cosby Show," one of the most popular broadcast programs.

Westwood One, the second largest radio network after

ABC's, was founded in the mid-1970s by Norman Pattiz, a former sales manager of a Los Angeles television station. In 1985 the company acquired the Mutual Broadcasting System, an old-time radio network that declined to shift to television and that had come to specialize in news and talk programs such as the "Larry King Show." Two years later Westwood bought NBC's radio networks and proceeded to acquire various radio stations.

SOURCE GUIDE

Leading Stock Analysts and Experts

Peter Appert, media analyst at C. J. Lawrence.

Paul Kagan Associates, leading cable and pay-TV experts, Carmel, California.

Barry Kaplan, media analyst at Goldman Sachs.

Dennis Leibowitz, media analyst at Donaldson Lufkin & Jenrette.

Trade Associations and Unions

Alliance of Motion Picture and Television Producers, 14144 Ventura Blvd., Sherman Oaks, CA 94123. Tel.: (818) 995–3600.

American Federation of Television and Radio Artists, 260 Madison Avenue, New York, NY 10016. Tel.: (212) 532–0800.

Association of Independent Television Stations, 1200 18th Street NW, Washington, DC 20036. Tel.: (202) 887–1970.

Directors Guild of America, 7920 Sunset Blvd., Hollywood, CA 90046. Tel.: (213) 289–2000.

National Association of Broadcast Employees and Technicians, 7101 Wisconsin Avenue, Bethesda, MD 20814. Tel.: (301) 657–8420.

National Association of Broadcasters, 1771 N Street NW, Washington, DC 20036. Tel.: (202) 429–5300.

National Cable Television Association, 1724 Massachusetts Avenue NW, Washington, DC 20036. Tel.: (202) 775–3550.

Screen Actors Guild, 7065 Hollywood Blvd., Hollywood, CA 90028. Tel.: (213) 465–4600.

Writers Guild of America East, 555 West 57th Street, New York, NY 10019. Tel.: (212) 245–6180.

Writers Guild of America West, 8955 Beverly Blvd., West Hollywood, CA 90048. Tel.: (213) 550–1000.

Data Sources and Directories

Broadcasting/Cable Yearbook, a wide-ranging compilation of data and listings (Washington, D.C.: Broadcasting Publications).

Cable TV Financial Databook, an annual directory and data source (Carmel, Calif.: Paul Kagan Associates).

Gale Directory of Broadcast Media and Personnel, annual (Detroit: Gale Research).

International Television & Video Almanac, an annual compilation of data on networks, producers, group stations owners, etc. (New York: Quigley Publishing).

Television and Cable Factbook, an annual directory of broadcast stations, cable operators, and programmers (Washington, D.C.: Warren Publishing).

Online Database

BASELINE, current information on television production, distribution, and personnel (New York: Baseline Inc.).

Trade Publications

Broadcasting, weekly.

Cablevision, fortnightly.

Channels, semimonthly.

Electronic Media, weekly.

Multichannel News, weekly.

Television Business International (London), monthly.

Television Digest, weekly.

Books and Reports

Barnouw, Erik. *A History of Broadcasting in the United States*. 3 vols. New York: Oxford University Press, 1966, 1968, 1970.

Bergreen, Laurence. *Look Now, Pay Later: The Rise of Network Broadcasting*. Garden City, N.Y.: Doubleday Publishing, 1980.

Block, Alex Ben. *Outfoxed: Marvin Davis, Barry Diller, Rupert Murdoch and the Inside Story of America's Fourth Television Network*. New York: St. Martin's Press, 1990.

MacDonald, J. Fred. *One Nation Under Television: The Rise and Decline of Network TV*. New York: Pantheon Books, 1990.

Paper, Lewis J. *Empire: William S. Paley and the Making of CBS*. New York: St. Martin's Press, 1987.

Sterling, Christopher, and John Kittross. *Stay Tuned: A Concise History of American Broadcasting*. Belmont, Calif.: Wadsworth, 1978.

U.S. General Accounting Office. *Follow-Up National Survey of Cable Television Rates and Services*. Washington, D.C., 1990.

U.S. General Accounting Office. *National Survey of Cable Television Rates and Services*. Washington, D.C., 1989.

Vogel, Harold. *Entertainment Industry Economics: A Guide for Financial Analysis*. 2nd ed. New York: Cambridge University Press, 1990.

Whittemore, Hank. *CNN: The Inside Story*. Boston: Little, Brown, 1990.

Williams, Huntington. *Beyond Control: ABC and the Fate of the Networks*. New York: Atheneum, 1989.

CHAPTER 3

FILM AND VIDEO

For more than three quarters of a century motion pictures have been central to popular culture in America. They have created enduring images of life in the United States and have both reflected and shaped the changing social and political values of the country. While films in the postwar period have faced stiff competition from television, they remain a primary expression of American reality and fantasy.

Movies are also a big business. From the earliest days of Hollywood, film has been an unabashedly commercial endeavor. It is a rather unstable industry, however. The major movie-producing studios swing from boom to bust and back at an unsettling pace. The reason is a preoccupation with producing blockbuster films, which by their nature lead to either feast or famine. The huge windfalls created by successes such as *The Sound of Music* in the 1960s and *Star Wars* and *E.T.* in more recent years keep the studios chasing after the next rainbow.

This perennial problem has been made more complicated in the 1980s by dramatic changes in the patterns of film viewing. Box office receipts—about half of which go to the owners of the country's 23,000 movie screens—slumped in the middle of the decade but then recovered to reach a record $5 billion in 1989. Annual ticket purchases continued to hover around the 1 billion mark, where they have remained for more than 20 years. The reason for the lack of more dramatic growth is the challenge from videocassettes and pay-TV. By 1989 more than two thirds of U.S. households were equipped with videocassette recorders, and some 38 percent were pay-cable subscribers. While pay-TV growth has leveled off, use of videocassettes has been booming. An estimated 200 million prerecorded cassettes were sold in 1989, many of them to video shops that rent the tapes over and over again.

These new outlets, once minor considerations for the studios, have become major rivals for audiences. But they are also increasingly important sources of revenue for the movie makers. Unsure whether the rise of video spells salvation or doom, Hollywood is scrambling to find its place in this new entertainment scheme, just it it did 35 years ago when television first started substituting the living room for the neighborhood movie palace.

FROM THE KINETOSCOPE TO THE SILVER SCREEN

Toward the end of the 19th century, inventors in the United States and Europe started working on devices to produce and project moving pictures. The process was made practical by the work of Thomas Edison and his assistant William Dickson in the late 1880s, following George Eastman's creation of the first celluloid roll film.

Although Edison took out a patent for his devices, he seemed to regard moving pictures as little more than a novelty. His backers, on the contrary, saw great commercial potential, and the wizard of Menlo Park was persuaded to produce short films. This was no easy task. Edison's camera, called a kinetograph, was a large, immobile device that had to be operated indoors in a specially constructed structure (nicknamed "Black Maria" because it looked something like the police wagons that went by that name). Edison's operation first focused on animal acts and then moved on to human subjects such as boxer Jim Corbett and Japanese dancers.

The first public establishment featuring Edison's viewing device, called Kinetoscope, opened in New York in 1894. The machine was a large box inside which light was projected through a reel of film. Viewers, one at a time, looked through a peephole to see action. Before long, people were calling it a "peep show."

Other innovations came quickly. The Lumière brothers in France perfected a portable camera, and Thomas Armant in the United States developed methods for projecting films to an entire audience at once. Edison's Kinetoscope Company bought the rights to Armant's work and kept him in the background. In 1896 Koster and Bials' Music Hall in New York presented the first public performance of a motion picture, using what was called Edison's Vitascope.

American Mutoscope and Biograph Company emerged as the first serious rival to Edison, both in peep shows and in theatrical movies. The company claimed that its devices were different enough from Edison's to avoid patent infringement. Edison disagreed and launched what became a perennial campaign to protect what he saw as his exclusive rights to motion picture technology.

By the turn of the century, peep shows had gained enormous popularity; they were the leading form of entertainment for immigrants and others of the working class. Theatrical films took off when a strike of vaudeville actors in 1900 prompted theater owners to find an alternative to live shows. The process was also assisted by the efforts of Edwin Porter to transform motion pictures from short amusements into longer, more serious works of art. Inspired by the French cinema pioneer George Méliès, Porter produced the first U.S. feature film, *Life of an American Fireman*, in 1903.

As motion picture theaters, generally known as nickelodeons, spread across the country, the film industry became big business. In order to supply the exhibitors, a middleman system arose in which distributors formed companies called film exchanges that purchased or leased films from producers and rented them to theater owners.

By this time a slew of companies were defying Edison's patent claims relating to both the production and the exhibition of movies. In 1908 Edison and his leading rivals decided it was better to cooperate rather than to attack one another in the courts. They boldly established what they intended to be a production monopoly, the Motion Picture Patents Company, which claimed the right to license film exchanges and extract $2-a-week royalty payments from all exhibitors. Two years later Edison and his partners established the General Film Company, which set out to take over the distribution business.

These would-be monopolies enjoyed as little success as Edison previously did in trying to keep competitors out of the business. Independent producers remained in business and challenged the trust, as did a number of major film exchanges that resisted being bought out. By the beginning of World War I, the monopolies had crumbled, and the independents were growing in number and power in the industry.

Among the leaders of this new wave was Carl Laemmle, whose Independent Moving Picture Company established the "star system." Edison and his associates deliberately did not publicize the names of their players, in order to deny the actors too much bargaining power. Laemmle correctly assumed that audiences would be drawn in when they knew their favorite player would appear in a film. Laemmle was also one of the first to set up shop in Hollywood, the Los Angeles suburb where many producers went to be far away from the East Coast-based trust.

Another independent, Adolph Zukor, who like many producers came from an immigrant background, created a middle-class audience for movies after he imported the French production *Queen Elizabeth,* which starred prominent stage actress Sarah Bernhardt.

The rising costs of film production—a result in part of escalating salaries of star players such as Mary Pickford and star directors such as D. W. Griffith—led to the independents' consolidation into the studios that would dominate the industry for decades.

In 1920 Marcus Loew, a leading exhibitor, entered production with the purchase of ailing Metro Pictures. After a big success in 1921 with *The Four Horsemen of the Apocalypse* (starring Rudolph Valentino), Loew purchased Goldwyn Pictures, founded in 1916 by Samuel Goldfish (who later changed his name to Goldwyn). Loew then acquired the operations of a rising young producer named Louis Mayer, and the result is what became known as Metro-Goldwyn-Mayer (MGM). The other majors emerged in more or less the same manner.

Even before the start of the 1920s, leading players and directors were growing frustrated with the power of the studio moguls. In 1919 four of the biggest stars in the business decided to break away and produce films on their own. Mary Pickford, Douglas Fairbanks, Charlie Chaplin, and D. W. Griffith established United Artists (UA) as a vehicle for distributing films they intended to produce on their own. The studios were initially amused—one executive remarked that "the lunatics have taken charge of the asylum"—but UA became an important force in the industry.

THE MOVIES LEARN TO TALK

No sooner had the business achieved some structural stability than the film world was turned upside down by the arrival of a new dimension: sound. Experiments in combining images with sound had gone on since Edison invented the phonograph in 1877, but it was not until the 1920s that the technique was perfected by engineers at AT&T's Western Electric subsidiary.

The studios were initially resistant to the new technology, but the Warner Brothers studio, founded in 1923, eventually came around. After investing in Vitaphone Corp. (the company set up to market AT&T's technology), Warner brought out *Don Juan* in 1926 with an operatic sound track. But the big sensation came the following year, when the Warner production of *The Jazz Singer* with Al Jolson included the first spoken dialogue. The enthusiastic reception received by this film prompted the other studios to rush into the production of talking films. The silent era quickly came to an end.

The advent of sound certainly caused dislocation for the industry—and for those players who had poor stage voices—but it also made the medium more varied. MGM, for instance, specialized in lavish musical extravaganzas, while Warner made a name for itself with films of social realism.

The 1930s were a difficult time for the industry, which by this time was clearly dominated by a group of eight major studios. The "Big Five"—vertically integrated firms with a major presence in distribution and exhibition as well as production—were Warner Brothers, MGM, Paramount, Twentieth

Century-Fox, and RKO. The "Little Three" were Universal and Columbia (involved solely in production and distribution) and United Artists (distribution only).

The slump in the business during the height of the Great Depression forced several studios into temporary bankruptcy, and in 1938 the Justice Department began what would be a long-term effort to prosecute the major studios for antitrust violations.

Like the rest of the economy, the movie business rebounded with the mobilization for war. Hollywood eagerly produced films that fit in with the fighting spirit of the time, and in the 1940s the industry reached what was perhaps its pinnacle of influence in American culture. In 1946 weekly movie attendance reached an all-time high of 90 million, and industry profits were also soaring.

Those halcyon days did not last for long. The first blow came with the political witch hunts of the postwar period. In 1947 the House Un-American Activities Committee opened an investigation of Communist influence in the film business. Attention became focused on a group of individuals, mainly screenwriters, who were accused of leftist associations and subpoenaed to appear before the committee. The Hollywood Ten, as they came to be known, were cited for contempt after they denounced the hearings and refused to answer questions or name names. Industry leaders bowed to the committee and collectively vowed not to employ persons "believed to be Communists." Thus was the blacklist created.

The next ordeal was the culmination of the Justice Department's antitrust crusade against the industry. The government won its case, and the studios lost their appeals. By the late 1940s the five major integrated companies were forced to start divesting themselves of their theater chains. Practices such as block booking (requiring theater owners who wanted any of a studio's films to take all of them) and the fixing of minimum admission prices also went by the boards. The likes of Loew's, RKO, and Warner no longer held absolute sway over the movie business.

The third and most serious challenge to the studios was the increasing popularity of a new form of entertainment known as television. Starting in the late 1940s, TV sets were invading U.S. homes at a dizzying rate, and the small screen quickly won the cultural loyalty of America. The film producers soon felt the results in declining box office receipts. The industry fought back with gimmicks such as CinemaScope and 3-D films, but it was a futile battle. Motion pictures were no longer the country's premier leisure activity.

HOLLYWOOD IN THE AGE OF TELEVISION

Columbia was the first studio to realize that television could be turned into an opportunity. In the early 1950s the company's Screen Gems subsidiary began producing telefilms for TV. Some of these were scaled-down versions of theatrical films, while others were entirely new productions. Warner jumped on this bandwagon in 1955, and the other studios soon followed suit. By the 1960s television production was a major income-producing activity for the film companies, especially for Universal. The studios, led by RKO (which passed from Howard Hughes to General Tire and Rubber in 1955 and soon exited the production business), also generated revenue by selling the TV rights to their film libraries.

The income derived from television helped the studios survive but not necessarily prosper. Things got particularly bad in the late 1960s after a series of expensive flops. Filmmaking virtually came to a halt, and there were shake-ups in both the ownership and management of many of the leading movie companies. Transamerica bought United Artists, MCA purchased Universal, and Gulf + Western acquired Paramount. The old-line Hollywood moguls were steadily replaced by a new generation of finance-oriented executives.

By the late 1970s the industry was looking a lot more healthy, thanks largely to such blockbusters as *Jaws*, *Grease*, and *Star Wars*. Although critics often sneered at the juvenile orientation of the films of George Lucas, Steven Spielberg, and their followers, movies such as *Return of the Jedi* were box office smashes. With the number of older moviegoers apparently in decline, Hollywood went all out for the youth market.

The movie business looked attractive enough so that in 1982 Columbia, just after being purchased by The Coca-Cola Company, formed a joint venture with CBS and Time Inc.'s Home Box Office (HBO) subsidiary to create the first new major studio in decades. The venture, called Tri-Star Pictures, was the most successful of a series of projects put together by different sectors of the entertainment business. (In 1987 Tri-Star was combined with Columbia Pictures to form a new industry powerhouse called Columbia Pictures Entertainment.) The 1980s also witnessed the weakening of the grip held by the large studios on the industry. With the rise of independents such as the Cannon Group and "mini-majors" such as Orion Pictures (formed in 1978 by a group of executives, led by Arthur Krim, who left United Artists), the share of box office receipts enjoyed by the seven majors sank from close to 95 percent in 1982 to about 70 percent in 1987, when a rebound began.

This flurry of activity reflected the upheaval in the industry wrought by the rise of new entertainment media. In the early 1980s the powerhouse was pay-TV. Cable television was invading American homes at a rapid rate, and analysts were predicting the virtual demise of the theatrical film business at the hands of pay services. HBO, the leader of those services, was becoming a major force in Hollywood by financing films in exchange for pay-TV rights. Studios resented this intrusion, but many producers could not turn down the seductive deals HBO was offering. For instance, HBO was able, thanks to its position, to get early rights to the movie *On Golden Pond* for $3.5 million. Given the box office success of the film, HBO would have had to pay at least four times that amount if the deal had been struck after the theatrical run.

By the mid-1980s, however, pay-TV came back down to earth. Growth in subscriptions leveled off as many viewers found themselves dissatisfied with the few hits and lots of filler being offered by the services. People also came to realize that videocassettes offered a much wider range of choices. Videocassette recorders (VCRs), which were first offered in the mid-1970s and received a moderate response, took off in the 1980s. VCR shipments to dealers, which had been stuck below 2 million units a year, soared in 1983, and reached about 14 million in 1986. Shipments leveled off in the late 1980s, but by then the machines were in a majority of American homes.

Videocassettes suddenly became a major factor in movie studio calculations. While access to videos was certainly eating into box office receipts, owning the rights to videocassette versions of films was becoming a significant revenue source for the studios. Although many in the industry viewed the rise of video rentals—from which the industry gets no share—as a threat, it turned out that consumers would be willing to purchase prerecorded videos of hit films. This prompted some of the major studios to set up their own subsidiaries to market video versions of their films, making life harder for independents such as Vestron (which moved into production and had a hit with *Dirty Dancing*). Standard & Poor's has estimated that, on the average, new film distributors now receive only about one half of their revenues from theatrical rentals (including those abroad). Another 30–35 percent comes from home video, and 10–15 percent from television.

The success of such videos as *Raiders of the Lost Ark* proved this point and also helped to push prices for video rights up to unprecedented levels. *The Empire Strikes Back* went for an astounding $12 million. The business became all the more appealing to the studios when it turned out that a number of box office flops (*The Cotton Club*, for instance) turned into hits in cassette form.

When the market began to cool off in 1987, distributors began slashing prices to increase volume—a process aided by the addition of commercials to some videos. Paramount was able to set the price of *Top Gun* at $27 (compared to the usual price of up to $90 for popular films) by including a 30-second Diet Pepsi ad.

The market got a boost in 1988 with the video releases of *E.T.* and *Cinderella.* Although no video had ever sold more than a few million copies before, lovers of the extra terrestrial snapped up more than 12 million copies (encouraged by a $5 rebate offer from PepsiCo), and sales of *Cinderella* surpassed 7 million. The 1989 Christmas season was even bigger, with the release of *Batman* (which sold 13 million copies in the first few months), *Bambi* (10.5 million), and *Who Framed Roger Rabbit?* (8.5 million).

One significant pitfall in the videocassette business has been piracy. Hollywood had long been plagued by the sale of unauthorized prints of feature films, but the problem was generally not a major one. The advent of videocassettes made illicit duplication much simpler. Pirates simply transferred film prints onto videocassettes, which are easily reproduced. Copying of films released on videocassette could be done by anyone with a pair of VCRs.

By the early 1980s counterfeit copies of hundreds of films were being produced in massive quantities around the world. In some countries in the Middle East and Africa the pirates were said to control nearly all of the videocassette market. The situation was summed up in a 1983 headline in the trade newspaper *Variety:* "WORLD VID PIRACY AT $1-BIL MARK: MORALITY CAN'T KEEP PACE WITH TECHNOLOGY."

Hollywood has desperately sought technical solutions to combat the problem. The industry had hopes that videodiscs, which were much more difficult than cassettes to reproduce, would save the day, but the discs did not catch on with consumers. The producers of videocassettes, worried about the development of VCRs with two recording heads, began experimenting with techniques of making cassettes copyproof. In April 1985 Embassy Home Entertainment released cassettes of the *The Cotton Club* equipped with a device that prevented copying by impairing the automatic gain control of the VCR, but professional pirates were able to overcome the obstacle. The limits of technological solutions to piracy have prompted studios to explore other techniques. MCA has sought to enlist local filmmakers in South Korea to support tougher copyright enforcement by offering financial backing for the construction of new theaters in that country.

The studios' heightened concern about the losses from piracy was a reflection of the financial crunch of the industry. Yet with the average production cost of films made by the major studios continuing to rise—the figure surpassed $23 million in 1989—Hollywood had to do more than maximize its returns from the videocassette business. In the late 1980s studios began an uncharacteristic drive to reduce costs, including more frequent shooting of films in Canada and in right-to-work states, where nonunion labor can be used. Disney and Universal built studios in Florida to attract tourists for studio tours and to shift the production of some television programs out of union jurisdiction.

The studios have also been moving to gain greater control of the various outlets for their products. Taking advantage of lax antitrust enforcement by the federal government, Columbia, Paramount, Warner, and Universal's parent MCA have made investments in theater companies. Twentieth Century-Fox and MCA have purchased television stations. This has been in addition to Warner's and Disney's direct involvement in cable.

While American entertainment companies have been repositioning themselves, foreign firms have begun to invade Hollywood. Twentieth Century-Fox was taken over in the mid-1980s by Rupert Murdoch's Australia-based News Corp. In 1989 the first big Japanese assault came with Sony's $3.4 billion purchase of Columbia Pictures. A purchase of MGM/UA by Qintex of Australia collapsed in 1989 because of financial difficulties, but the replacement buyer turned out to be Pathe Communications, controlled by Italian financier Giancarlo Parretti, who had also taken over the Cannon Group. In September 1990, MCA began negotiating with Matsushita on a sale of the company to the Japanese electronics giant.

LABOR RELATIONS

The decision by the early film studios to move from the East to the West Coast was not only because of the climate. Being in Hollywood gave the industry access to the labor market of the country's largest nonunion city, Los Angeles. Organizing among studio workers began as early as 1918, when a strike of craft workers led to wage increases but no contract. After agitation resumed in the 1920s, the studios formed the Association of Motion Picture Producers mainly for the purpose of developing a united policy toward labor. Two years later they signed

Market Share of Studios Based on 1989 U.S. Film Rental Revenues*

Warner	19%
Universal	17
Disney	14
Paramount	14
Columbia	8
Tri-Star	7
Fox	6
MGM/UA	6
Orion	4

*Film rental revenues are what is left over after theater owners take their share—usually about half—of box office receipts.

Source: *Variety*, January 17, 1990.

the Studio Basic Agreement with five unions representing craft workers.

Creative personnel were slower to organize, despite the efforts of the Actors' Equity Association. In 1927 the studios tried to ward off unionization with the creation of the Academy of Motion Picture Arts and Sciences, a management-dominated entity that was supposed to represent directors, actors, writers, and technicians. After the studios tried to impose large wage cuts in 1933, the talent began seeking true union representation. The Screen Actors Guild (SAG) was formed, and the Screen Writers Guild (which was established in 1920 but which had become dormant) was revived. After a protracted battle the producers relented in 1937, and unionization for actors was established. However, management resisted recognizing the Screen Writers Guild for several more years.

In 1960 the SAG struck the industry for six weeks in order to win compensation for actors when films were sold to television. Similar walkouts occurred in 1980 and 1981 over the issue of remuneration when films were put on videocassettes or pay-TV. The Writers Guild of America (which the Screen Writers Guild became part of in 1954) struck over related issues in 1981 and 1985.

Within SAG there was controversy in the early 1980s over

the political views of its president, Ed Asner, an outspoken critic of Reagan administration policies in Central America. (Reagan, incidentally, was president of the guild for six terms beginning in 1947.) Conservative union members led by Charlton Heston waged a campaign against Asner, and though they failed to unseat him, in 1984 they did defeat an Asner-supported measure to merge SAG with the Screen Extras Guild (which later affiliated with the Teamsters).

A strike by the Directors Guild was barely averted in 1987 when the studios backed away from a demand that directors give up royalties on pay-per-view television showings of films. Yet the following year the Writers Guild staged a 22-week walkout that also centered on residuals.

LEADING COMPANIES

Columbia Pictures was started in the 1920s as a small independent producer by Harry Cohn, his brother Jack, and Joe Brandt. The company, which pioneered the practice of shooting scenes out of sequence in order to keep down production costs, specialized in low-budget features but also prospered from the social-minded films of Frank Capra. Columbia—run by Harry Cohn, the quintessential ruthless studio boss, until his death in 1958—was the first studio to move into television production. In the late 1970s Columbia was embarrassed when it was revealed that its hotshot film head David Begelman had forged more than $60,000 of company checks for personal use. The investment house of Allen & Company, which had bought a controlling interest in the studio in the early 1970s, thwarted a takeover by financier Kirk Kerkorian in 1981 by purchasing his shares. But the Allens turned around and sold their interest at a great profit to The Coca-Cola Company in 1982. Five years later Coke spun off Columbia and combined it with Tri-Star Pictures to form Columbia Pictures Entertainment (49 percent-owned by Coke). Then, in 1989, Columbia was sold for $3.4 billion to Japan's Sony, which was pursuing a strategy (already seen in the company's 1988 purchase of CBS Records) of getting involved in the entertainment software used in the company's electronic products.

MCA, which began as a small talent agency in 1924 and grew into one of the leading entertainment companies, got into the film business in 1962 with its purchase of Decca Records, which at the time owned Universal studios. Universal, which emerged in the 1920s as one of the second-tier major studios (it did production and distribution but owned no theaters), did not have many big stars under contract before 1940 and originally made its name by creating the horror genre with films such as *Frankenstein* and *Dracula.* After being purchased by MCA, Universal took the lead among film studios in television production. By the mid-1970s it was producing more than 25 percent of the prime-time programs. In the 1980s Universal had a resurgence in films. The milestones included *E.T.*, *Back to the Future*, and later *Twins* and *Parenthood.* In 1990, MCA began talks on selling the company to Matsushita.

MGM/UA Communications is the latest incarnation of the merging and splitting of what remains of two of Hollywood's old-line studios, Metro-Goldwyn-Mayer and United Artists. MGM, the product of the merger of three early film operations, was until 1959 owned by Marcus Loew's giant theater chain. With its roaring-lion trademark and motto *Ars Gratia Artis* (Art for Art's Sake), MGM produced many of the musical extravanganzas of Hollywood's golden era—above all, *The Wizard of Oz.* The studio liked to brag that it had "more stars than there are in the heavens." But MGM went into decline after World War II and suffered numerous management shake-ups. Financier Kirk Kerkorian bought control of the studio in 1969 and began selling off assets such as the prop and costume collections. United Artists was established in 1919 by four of Hollywood's leading creative personalities in an attempt to escape the control of the big-studio moguls. The founders—Mary Pickford, Douglas Fairbanks, Charlie Chaplin, and D. W. Griffith—used UA as a distribution vehicle while producing their films independently. The company, which also worked with other independent producers, went public in 1957 and was sold to the Transamerica conglomerate in 1967. In 1980 UA had the distinction of producing *Heaven's Gate*, one of the most spectacular fiascos in the industry's history. The following year Transamerica sold UA to MGM, and five years later the combined company was bought by cable television magnate Ted Turner. But Turner had difficulty putting together the financing for his acquisition and ended up with an extraordinary debt load after the $1.6 billion deal was completed. He was forced to sell MGM's real estate and film lab to Lorimar-Telepictures and later sold the United Artists portion of MGM/UA (plus the right to make films under the MGM name) back to Kerkorian, who set up MGM/UA Communications. The company remained unprofitable, so Kerkorian gutted its operations (dozens of projects were abruptly canceled in mid-1988) and put the firm up for sale. Kerkorian passed up an offer from Rupert Murdoch and instead agreed to sell to the Qintex Group of Australia; however, the deal collapsed in 1989 when Qintex was unable to put together adequate financing. In 1990 Kerkorian announced a $1.2 billion sale to Pathe Communications, controlled by Italian financier Giancarlo Parretti. Time Warner agreed to provide a bridge loan of $650 million to Parretti in exchange for distribution rights to MGM/UA's film library.

Paramount, formed by a combine of five independent regional distributors in 1914, was run with an iron fist by Adolph Zukor for decades. The company was often shaky, and its films had less of a distinctive identity than those of MGM or Warner. In 1966 the studio was acquired by conglomerate Gulf + Western, whose boss Charles Bluhdorn fired most of the management and made himself president. In 1984 the studio lost two of its top executives—Barry Diller, who went to Fox, and Michael Eisner, who left to head Disney—leaving company veteran Frank Mancuso to pull the studio back together. In the late 1980s Paramount emerged as the leader of television production for non-network stations (first-run syndication) and rose to the top tier of the movie business thanks to such stars as Eddie Murphy. In 1989 Gulf + Western changed its name to Paramount Communications and unsuccessfully tried to derail the friendly merger of Time Inc. and Warner Communications.

The film business of **Time Warner** is based on the Warner Brothers studio, which was founded in the 1920s by four sons of a Polish immigrant couple. Warner, which produced the first talking feature film, gained a reputation for movies with social and political themes, though the studio also did its share of musicals. The studio went into decline in the 1950s and 1960s, and in 1969 it was acquired by Kinney National Service Corp., a conglomerate built by Steven Ross that had begun with funeral parlors and parking lots. Under its new parent, which renamed itself Warner Communications in 1971, the studio rebounded with hits such as *The Exorcist* and *All the President's Men.* In the mid-1980s the parent company rode an earnings roller coaster after acquiring video-game producer Atari and then fought off a takeover by Rupert Murdoch. Although Ross became embroiled in a long-running feud with his largest shareholder, Herbert Siegel, the studio emerged as one of the most stable and best run in the industry. In 1989 it acquired TV and movie producer Lorimar-Telepictures. That same year Time Inc. (owner of Home Box Office and other cable properties) merged with Warner Communications to form Time Warner. The Warner studio took first place in market share in 1989 thanks to the phenomenal success of *Batman.*

Twentieth Century-Fox dates back to Fox Film Corp., an independent producer that challenged the Edison monopoly early in the century. The studio, which merged with Twentieth Century Pictures in 1935, was ruled by Darryl Zanuck for more than a quarter of a century. For many years it churned out a succession of B movies (inexpensive formula films designed to fill out double bills). After being purchased in the early 1980s by Denver oil tycoon Marvin Davis, the studio languished. Half of the company was sold to press baron Rupert Murdoch in early 1985 and the remainder later in the year.

Walt Disney Productions has sought to carry on the work of its legendary founder, who died in 1966. Although the unquestioned leader for many years in animated features, the company never became a major studio. By the 1970s Disney lost the youth market to the likes of George Lucas and Steven Spielberg. Under the leadership of Michael Eisner, Disney has focused in recent years on reaching an older audience with films such as *Splash* and *Down and Out in Beverly Hills,* the company's first R-rated feature. In 1984 Disney fought off a takeover bid by Saul Steinberg and then thwarted Irwin Jacobs with the help of the Bass Brothers. By the end of the 1980s Disney, helped by its Touchstone Pictures unit and such movies as *Good Morning Vietnam*, was finally reaching the top ranks of the industry. In 1988 it led the studios in box office market share.

SOURCE GUIDE

Leading Stock Analysts and Experts

Alexander & Associates, a New York market research company specializing in video.

Entertainment Data Inc. of Beverly Hills, California, collects information on box office trends.

Fairfield Group, a video consulting company in Westport, Connecticut.

David Londoner, entertainment analyst at Wertheim & Co.

A. D. Murphy, film industry expert who teaches at the University of Southern California and writes for *Variety*.

Harold Vogel, entertainment analyst at Merrill Lynch.

Trade Associations and Unions

Alliance of Motion Picture and Television Producers, 14144 Ventura Blvd., Sherman Oaks, CA 94123. Tel.: (818) 995–3600.

Directors Guild of America, 7920 Sunset Blvd., Hollywood, CA 90046. Tel.: (213) 289–2000.

Motion Picture Association of America, 1133 Sixth Avenue, New York, NY 10036. Tel.: (212) 840–6161.

Screen Actors Guild, 7065 Hollywood Blvd., Hollywood, CA 90028. Tel.: (213) 465–4600.

Writers Guild of America West, 8955 Beverly Blvd., West Hollywood, CA 90048. Tel.: (213) 550–1000.

Data Sources and Directories

International Film Guide, published annually (London: Tantivy Press and New York: New York Zoetrope).

International Motion Picture Almanac, a compilation of data on the industry, issued annually (New York: Quigley Publishing).

The Motion Picture Guide, a 12-volume directory of films, with an annual supplement (New York: CineBooks; distributed by R. R. Bowker).

Online Database

BASELINE, current information on film production, distribution, and personnel (New York: Baseline Inc.).

Trade Publications

Boxoffice, monthly.

Hollywood Reporter, daily.

Show Biz News, semi-monthly.

Variety, published daily in Hollywood, weekly in New York.

Video Week.

Books and Reports

Bart, Peter. *Fade Out: The Scandalous Final Days of MGM*. New York: William Morrow, 1990.

Griffith, Richard, and Arthur Mayer. *The Movies*. Rev. ed. New York: Simon & Schuster, 1970.

Lardner, James. *Fast Forward: Hollywood, the Japanese, and the Onslaught of the VCR*. New York: W. W. Norton, 1987.

Litwak, Mark. *Reel Power: The Struggle for Influence and Success in the New Hollywood*. New York: William Morrow, 1986.

McClintick, David. *Indecent Exposure: A True Story of Hollywood and Wall Street*. New York: William Morrow, 1982.

Schwartz, Nancy Lynn. *The Hollywood Writers' Wars*. New York: Alfred A. Knopf, 1982.

Shipman, David. *The Story of Cinema*. New York: St. Martin's Press, 1982.

Stanley, Robert H. *The Celluloid Empire: A History of the American Movie Industry*. New York: Hastings House, 1978.

Vogel, Harold. *Entertainment Industry Economics: A Guide for Financial Analysis*. 2nd ed. New York: Cambridge University Press, 1990.

CHAPTER 4

NEWSPAPERS AND MAGAZINES

Like book publishing, the newspaper business (and to a lesser extent magazines) has a dual identity. On the one hand it is very much a commercial endeavor, often a quite profitable one. Yet the press is also a quasi-public institution. Newspapers are vital to the political, social, and economic life of communities. This role becomes most apparent when it is interrupted; newspaper strikes create great dislocations in cities.

Newspaper publishing is also like the book industry in that it has been steadily changing from a collection of small, family-run enterprises, each bearing the mark of its founder, into a branch of big business. Attracted by the benefits of owning unregulated monopolies in the hundreds of one-paper towns, large media corporations have been gobbling up newspapers at a steady rate. Faced with tough challenges from the rise of the electronic media and the growth of the direct mail business, newspapers have nonetheless prospered in recent years. America's 1,600 daily newspapers continue to receive the largest portion of advertising spending (some 26 percent) among the media, and the total advertising and circulation revenues of the industry have climbed to more than $36 billion.

Magazine publishers also have weathered the threat from television but have experienced frequent fluctuations in advertising demand. The 11,000-title industry, which had revenues of about $20 billion in 1989 (including about $13 billion for consumer publications), has also had to confront a shift in reading tastes from general to special-interest publications.

FROM THE PENNY PRESS TO THE CHAINS

Newspapers in America date back to the late 17th century, and the tradition of a free press is rooted in the success of John Peter Zenger in the 1730s in defying censorship. Newspapers became significant as a business beginning with the rise of the *New York Sun* and other penny papers in the 1830s. The industry expanded rapidly after the Civil War, thanks to inventions such as the Linotype, web-fed rotary presses, and the typewriter. The late 1800s and the early years of the 20th century were the heyday of the great press barons, particularly Joseph Pulitzer and his *St. Louis Post-Dispatch* and *New York World*, and William Randolph Hearst (the master of yellow journalism) and his *San Francisco Examiner* and *New York Journal*. The latter part of that period also saw the expansion of the wire services—the United Press and the International News Service joined the Associated Press, which had its origins in the 1840s—and the rise of the first newspaper chains, led by those of Hearst and E. W. Scripps. The creation of the *New York Daily News* in 1919 gave rise to the tabloid format.

The period between the world wars also witnessed the development of magazines into a medium of mass communications. Henry Luce perfected the form with the introduction of *Time* in 1923 and even more so with *Life* in 1936. In between he brought out *Fortune* in order to show that business was civilized.

The social changes after World War II eventually created conditions that undermined the weakest segment of the newspaper business: the afternoon dailies. The PMs, as they are called, traditionally appealed to blue-collar workers who finished their day shifts early enough to spend some time with a paper after returning home and before eating dinner. The office workers and professionals, who grew rapidly in number during the same period, were more inclined to look at a morning paper over breakfast. The PMs have also suffered from a tendency on the part of advertisers to concentrate their spending on the one paper in town with the highest circulation. Another blow, also felt by morning papers, has been the increasing importance of suburban publications.

Some PMs prospered by switching to all-day publishing schedules, but many simply gave up the fight. Among the more prominent casualties were the *Washington Star* in 1981 and the *Philadelphia Bulletin* and *Cleveland Press* the following year. The *Los Angeles Herald-Examiner* was shut down in 1989.

Between 1950 and 1989 the number of afternoon papers dropped from 1,450 to 1,125 nationwide, while the number of morning papers increased from 322 to 530. (The latter year's figures include 29 all-day papers.) The total circulation of dailies increased steadily after World War II, but it has been flat (at a daily average of 60 to 63 million copies) for the past two decades and thus has greatly lagged behind the growth in the number of households in the nation.

Over the past 50 years a number of financially weakened papers, both PM and AM, have stayed alive through arrangements known as joint operating agreements (JOAs). Devised during the Great Depression, JOAs are arrangements in which competing papers in a city consolidate their financial and production facilities to reduce costs while keeping their editorial operations separate. For the first few decades these schemes had a precarious existence, since they could easily be struck down by the federal government as violations of the antitrust laws.

A legal challenge to the JOAs in the 1960s and the prospect of a Supreme Court decision outlawing the arrangements prompted the industry and its supporters in Congress to act. Their efforts were successful, and in 1971 President Nixon signed into law the Newspaper Preservation Act. This provided a legal basis for JOAs, though only a few new arrangements have been added to the two dozen that were established before the legislation took effect. The most recent of these was a linkup of the *News* (owned by Knight-Ridder) and the *Free Press* (Gannett) in Detroit, which was announced in 1986 and finally upheld by the Supreme Court in 1989.

Although there have been periodic rumblings, Congress has taken no action in response to the steady growth of the newspaper chains. By the late 1970s about 50 independent papers a year were succumbing to the tantalizing offers being made by the media giants. The number of independent dailies declined from some 1,400 in 1945 to 393 at the end of 1989. At the latter point there were 145 chains, which owned a total of 1,233 dailies with a combined circulation of more than 50 million copies a day.

The chains are especially attracted to cities with only one newspaper, a monopoly situation that gives the publisher enormous freedom in setting ad prices. They also like to own both of the "competing" papers in town. At the end of 1989, only 96 American cities had more than one daily, and in 53 of those cases a single chain owned both publications.

Defenders of chains argue that they bring more professional management and needed capital to smaller newspapers while permitting cost reductions through practices such as large-scale newsprint purchases. Critics of concentration of ownership, such as Ben Bagdikian, express concern about the political consequences of having such a large portion of these vital institutions controlled by a few large corporations that are far removed from the concerns of local communities.

Gannett, the largest chain, has not only bought up smaller publications but has also created a national daily that is being viewed with alarm by many papers. *USA Today*, which started publication in 1982, aims to be the first truly national general-interest newspaper. (*The Wall Street Journal* is somewhat specialized, the *Christian Science Monitor* has a limited circulation, and *The New York Times* has never succeeded in achieving large-scale national distribution.) *USA Today*, with its bite-sized articles, has been derided by many journalists as a "fast-food newspaper"; but its daring use of color and charts, extensive sports coverage, and local news from around the country have prompted many papers to make similar changes to protect their circulation. Another paper that aspired to nationwide circulation, a sports daily called *The National*, made its debut in 1990.

There is considerable disagreement on the extent to which chain ownership has affected the editorial policies of newspapers. There is no question, however, that the acquisition of papers has accelerated the technological transformation of the industry. In the 1970s many newspapers made the leap from hot

The 10 Largest Newspaper Chains (as of March 31, 1990)

Company	*Daily Circulation (in millions)*	*Number of Dailies*
1. Gannett	5.94	82
2. Knight-Ridder	3.92	28
3. Newhouse	3.04	26
4. Times Mirror	2.73	8
5. Tribune Co.	2.67	9
6. Dow Jones	2.50	24
7. Thomson Newspapers	2.15	124
8. New York Times Co.	2.07	27
9. Scripps-Howard	1.62	21
10. Cox Enterprises	1.37	18

Source: Morton Research, an affiliate of Lynch, Jones & Ryan, Washington, D.C.

type, the molding of letters out of blocks of lead using clattering Linotype machines, to cold type, in which copy is generated on computer terminals and printed via photocomposition and offset presses. While traditionalists have bemoaned the passing of the old system, the new technology has permitted papers to publish cleaner-looking pages much faster than before.

Some of the national papers, especially *USA Today* and *The Wall Street Journal*, have employed satellite technology to transmit pages from a central editorial office to local printing plants around the country. Another new technique being adopted by papers involves computerized layout systems. These are terminals that permit editors to plan and modify pages—including text, photographs, and even ads—on a single screen, thus allowing much faster and more careful creation of the paper. The leading company in providing computerized layout systems to newspapers (and some magazines) is Atex, a subsidiary of Eastman Kodak.

THE STATE OF THE MAGAZINE BUSINESS

Magazines, like newspapers, have defied those doomsayers who predicted the demise of print media as a result of the rise of television. Rather than competing with other advertising media, they tend to battle with one another, especially in key arenas such as supermarket checkout racks.

The consistent leader of the business has been Time Inc., with its stable of money-makers such as *Time, People*, and *Sports Illustrated*. But other media companies have been expanding their magazine activities, leading to a fairly hot market in magazine acquisitions during the 1980s. Real-estate developer Morton Zuckerman purchased *The Atlantic* in 1980 and four years later bought out the employee-owners of *U.S. News & World Report*, vowing to make the stodgy newsmagazine an effective competitor of *Time* and *Newsweek*. In 1984 Rupert Murdoch's News America Publishing and CBS each bought half of the Ziff-Davis magazine empire of 24 publications for a combined price of more than $700 million. CBS later sold off the publications (including *Woman's Day, Car and Driver*, and *Popular Photography*) to a group of its executives, who then resold them to the French company Hachette.

There have also been a large number of start-ups. A handful of these have been general-interest publications, including the new *Vanity Fair* (launched by the Newhouse-owned Condé Nast), *Picture Week* (which Time Inc. began test marketing in 1985 but abandoned the following year), and a film magazine called *Premiere* brought out by a joint venture of Murdoch's News America and Hachette.

Yet the vast majority of new magazines have been aimed at more specialized audiences—which is now considered the most promising path to success in the business. As a result, magazines today are usually discussed by category. Among the main genres of recent years have been the following.

Computer Magazines

With the boom of personal computers (PCs) in the early 1980s, a number of publishers, both established and new, went after a market of PC users frustrated with impenetrable instruction manuals and hungry for clear explanations of how their new acquisitions worked. Some issues of publications, such as *Byte* (McGraw-Hill), were so thick and heavy with ads that mail carriers complained about delivering subscriber copies. By 1984, with the end of rapid growth in the PC market, there was also a shakeout in the computer magazine business, and many of the dozens of PC publications have disappeared.

Fitness and Health

Taking advantage of another trend, publishers have brought out dozens of new magazines devoted to exercise, sports, nutrition, and general well-being (one is called *Self*). The overcrowding suggests that a shakeout may be in the making here as well.

Affluence

A new crop of magazines celebrates wealth, conspicuous consumption, and success in business. Some publications are aimed only at wealthy readers. *Avenue* magazine in New York is delivered by limousine to its readers, all of whom must live in Manhattan's Upper East Side. New and old magazines such as *Town & Country, Architectural Forum, Gourmet*, and *GQ* are prospering by focusing on expensive homes, expensive food, and expensive clothes. Until its demise in 1990, *Manhattan, inc.* gushed over the movers and shakers of New York. New or revamped upscale travel magazines include *Condé Nast Traveler* and *European Travel & Life* (bought by Murdoch in 1986).

By the end of the 1980s, magazine companies were planning to take the specialization process even further. Publishers began to plan editions in which advertising could be customized to the individual subscriber based on the person's demographic profile and purchasing habits. At the same time, the glut of publications led to a shakeout in which such titles as *Modern Photography, High Fidelity*, and *Venture* disappeared. Time Warner (the name Time Inc. took after merging with Warner Communications in 1989) bucked the trend by introducing *Entertainment Weekly* in early 1990. But it, like many other publications, suffered from the general slump in advertising revenues.

LABOR RELATIONS

The largest union in the newspaper business, the International Typographical Union (now part of the Communications Work-

The 10 Leading Magazine Companies, by 1989 revenues ($ Millions)

1.	Time Warner	$2,500
2.	News Corp.	1,248
3.	Advance Publications	1,141
4.	Hearst Corp.	1,019
5.	New York Times Co.	670
6.	Meredith Corp.	628
7.	Hachette Publications	573
8.	Reader's Digest	507
9.	McGraw-Hill	471
10.	Reed International	429

Source: *Advertising Age*, June 18, 1990.

ers) is also one of the oldest in the U.S. labor movement, having roots in the 1830s. Efforts to organize the editorial employees of newspapers remained tentative until the industrial union drives of the 1930s. The immediate impetus for the establishment of the Newspaper Guild was a column—actually, a call to arms—published by Heywood Broun in the *New York World-Telegram* in 1933. As a result of abysmal pay levels in the industry and the encouragement of the National Recovery Administration, unionization of the country's large newspapers (along with *Newsweek* and Time Inc.'s magazines) spread rapidly.

After the war, the Guild's growth slowed down, and the union's power varied greatly around the country. The biggest showdown between publishers and the combined forces of the Guild and the craft unions came in New York in the early 1960s. In 1962 the printers at several of the city's seven dailies walked out, and publishers of the others shut down. The strike/lockout lasted for 114 days, during which time the papers suffered heavy losses; several did not survive long even after the dispute ended.

In the 1970s unions found themselves under attack from publishers seeking to modernize their operations and cut costs. The switch to cold type made possible a sharp reduction in staff levels, which the craft unions tried mightily to resist.

One of the most bitter labor situations during that decade

arose at the *Washington Post.* After several short strikes in which the Guild and the craft unions did not honor one another's picket lines, the printers walked out in October 1975 in what became a 137-day strike related to the introduction of new technology. In part because of some sabotage of presses just before the strike began, many editorial people once again refused to join the walkout.

Management, meanwhile, had in anticipation of the strike secretly sent supervisory employees to a school in Oklahoma to learn how to take over union jobs. As a result the paper missed only one issue, and publisher Katharine Graham succeeded in defeating the strike. After the walkout ended, the Guild brought charges against some of its members for crossing the picket line. A group of those people tried to decertify the Guild, and the union only barely won the representation election that was held in 1976.

That same year magazine and book employees of Time Inc. went on strike over the demand for guaranteed rather than merit raises. The strike ended in defeat in less than three weeks, after managers and strikebreakers succeeded in putting out the magazines without interruption.

Another major confrontation at the big New York papers took place in 1978, prompted mainly by disputes involving work rules. After the press operators walked off the job, the publishers locked out the other employees, and the *Times* and *News* did not publish for 88 days (Murdoch made a deal that allowed the *Post* to resume after 56 days). In 1985 newspapers in Philadelphia were shut down for 46 days, and printers at the *Chicago Tribune* walked off the job, but the paper kept publishing. In 1990 the Tribune Co. demanded major concessions from its unions at the *News*. The workers stayed on the job after their contracts expired but sought to resist management demands for concessions by launching a boycott of the paper.

Unions in the newspaper business have responded to their weakened state by joining forces. While a number of mergers have gone through smoothly, the attempt of the International Typographical Union to find a new partner was a long-running soap opera. An effort to join with the Newspaper Guild collapsed in the early 1980s, and ITU president Joe Bingel started flirting with the Teamsters. But that attempt fizzled out after Bingel lost a reelection bid. Finally, in late 1986, the ITU membership voted to merge with the Communications Workers of America.

Gannett, one of the most antiunion companies in the industry, suffered a setback in 1989 when employees at its *Burlington Free Press* in Vermont voted to join the Graphic Communications International Union.

Magazines making use of freelancers have been confronted in recent years by a new form of labor organization. Frustrated by low payment rates and poor treatment at the hands of editors, freelancers established the National Writers Union in 1983. Although its members technically are independent contractors rather than employees, the union has succeeded in winning contracts at publications such as *Ms.* magazine, *The Nation*, and *Columbia Journalism Review.*

LEADING COMPANIES

Known to most people as the company the famous stock average is named after, **Dow Jones** is one of the leading players in the business information industry. Its biggest moneymaker is *The Wall Street Journal*, the bible of business that also has the highest circulation of any daily in the country. The *Journal* has been in the enviable position at times of having so much advertising it has had to turn some away. Editions of the paper are also published in Europe and Asia. The paper's reputation was tarnished somewhat in 1984 when it was revealed that one of its stock market columnists was giving market-sensitive information to traders before it was published in the *Journal.* The company, run by former *Journal* reporter Warren Phillips, also produces the Dow Jones News Service (the "broadwire" that the financial world depends on for speedy information) and Dow Jones News/Retrieval, a business information database. Aside from the *Journal*, the company publishes *Barron's*, a weekly for investors, and about two dozen small newspapers. It also owns a large share in the *Far Eastern Economic Review*, a weekly based in Hong Kong. The *National Observer*, a general-interest weekly created by the company in 1962, folded in 1977. A decline in *Journal* ad linage in the wake of the October 1987 stock market dive depressed the company's growth in the late 1980s.

Under the flamboyant reign of Allen Neuharth, chief executive from 1973 to 1986, **Gannett** grew from a chain of small-town newspapers into one of the premier media companies in the United States. Now the largest chain in terms of total circulation, Gannett shook up the newspaper world in 1982 with the creation of *USA Today*, a national daily. In 1985 the company accelerated its buying binge, acquiring the *Des Moines Register, Family Weekly* (a Sunday supplement), and the *Detroit News*. In 1986 it acquired the *Courier-Journal* and *Times* of Louisville, Kentucky. Right after that deal was announced, Neuharth made the surprise announcement that he would relinquish the CEO's job but remain as chairman.

Founded by William Randolph Hearst, the giant of the newspaper business in the early 20th century and the leading practitioner of yellow journalism, the privately held **Hearst Corp**. emerged from decades of lethargy to become one of the more dynamic media companies of the 1980s. Under the leadership of Frank Bennack, Jr., who took over as chief executive in 1979, Hearst went on a buying spree, snapping up book publisher William Morrow, *Esquire* and *Redbook* magazines, the *Houston Chronicle*, and various television and cable properties. The new properties—along with old ones such as the *San Francisco Examiner, Good Housekeeping*, and *Cosmopolitan*—give the secretive Hearst empire annual revenues (according to a *Forbes* estimate) of some $2 billion. In 1989 the company shut the *Los Angeles Herald-Examiner* after it could not find a buyer for the ailing afternoon paper.

Knight-Ridder, the country's second largest newspaper chain, is less well-known than other media giants but owns such important papers as the *Miami Herald*, the *Philadelphia Inquirer*, and the *Detroit Free Press*. Created by the 1974 merger of the Knight and the Ridder chains, the company gained a reputation for not imposing an editorial point of view on its publications. Losses at the *Free Press* prompted Knight-Ridder to seek (and eventually win) federal approval for a joint operating agreement with its rival, the *Detroit News* (owned by Gannett). In 1988 the company purchased Dialog Information Services, the nation's largest online information company, from Lockheed.

McGraw-Hill is the publisher of *Business Week* as well as of a wide variety of trade publications. The company, founded by James McGraw and John Hill around the turn of the century, moved from books to magazines to data. Standard & Poor's, the bond-rating and information service, was acquired in 1966, and economic forecaster Data Resources Inc. was purchased in 1979. Under Joseph Dionne, who took over as chief executive in 1983, the company began using its vast database of business information to create a variety of new products, especially online services. The various reorganizations the company went through during the 1980s did not succeed in warding off a slump that led to layoffs and a $220 million charge against earnings in 1989.

The New York Times Company is mainly known, of course, as the publisher of *The New York Times*, considered by many to be the best paper in the country and certainly the most influential. Transformed from a mediocre daily into a newspaper of record by Adolph Ochs in 1896, the *Times* has been controlled ever since by Ochs and Sulzberger family members. In 1976 the company responded to sagging readership by unveiling what it dubbed the "new *New York Times.*" This involved the creation of daily sections (Home, Living, and Weekend) meant to make the paper more appealing to an upper-middle-class suburban readership while retaining a serious commitment to news. Although the "lifestyle" emphasis has often been criticized by traditional journalists, it turned out to be a great business coup. The *Times* prospered in the 1980s, and its new sections were used as models by many other papers. The company also publishes more than two dozen small papers and magazines such as *Family Circle*.

The **Newhouse** publishing group began in 1912, when Samuel Newhouse, Sr. (still in his teens), took over the *Bayonne Times* in New Jersey. He bought the *Staten Island Advance* in 1922 and proceeded to collect newspaper and magazine properties. The founder died in 1979, and control of the business (organized under the name Advance Publications) fell to his sons Si and Donald. In 1980 they bought Random House from RCA, three years later they relaunched the magazine *Vanity Fair*, and in 1985 they purchased the *New Yorker*. By the late 1980s the Newhouses had the largest privately owned media empire in the nation, including 26 dailies (among them the *Cleveland Plain Dealer*) and the Condé Nast group of magazines (*Vogue, Glamour, House & Garden*, etc.). The family's wealth has been estimated by *Forbes* magazine at more than $5 billion.

News America Publishing is the parent company of Rupert Murdoch's American operations. Murdoch was a press baron in Australia and Britain when he invaded the United States in the early 1970s. He started quietly with two papers in San Antonio, Texas, but went on to create the *Star* as a challenger to the lowbrow tabloid *National Enquirer*. He then embarked on a string of media purchases, including the *New York Post, New York* magazine, the *Village Voice*, the *Boston Herald-American*, and the *Chicago Sun-Times*. To his newly acquired daily tabloids Murdoch brought the kind of sensationalized journalism, mixed with conservative politics, that made him notorious abroad. (A classic *Post* headline: HEADLESS BODY FOUND IN TOPLESS BAR.) In 1984 Murdoch bought 12 trade publications from Ziff-Davis, and in 1985 he became a broadcasting and film mogul by purchasing seven TV stations from Metromedia for $2 billion and the Twentieth Century-Fox film company for $575 million. The *New York Post*, the *Chicago Sun-Times*, and the *Village Voice* were sold, but Murdoch joined with France's Hachette to bring out a U.S. edition of the French fashion magazine *Elle*, and the two partners also introduced a film magazine called *Premiere*. In 1988 Murdoch spent $3 billion to buy Triangle Publications, owner of *TV Guide, Seventeen*, and the *Daily Racing Form*.

Time Warner, the quintessential media octopus, was founded by Henry Luce in the 1920s. Luce, the son of a missionary, unabashedly used *Time, Life*, and *Fortune* to promote his conservative view of the world. Through these publications Luce, who proclaimed this to be the "American century," became one of the most influential men in America. After Luce died in 1967, Time Inc. became a more traditional though far from stagnant corporation. Time expanded its book publishing operation with the purchase of Little, Brown. In the 1970s, video—including a group of cable TV companies and the HBO and Cinemax pay-TV services—became the fastest growing part of the company. But the magazine business grew as well: *Money* was launched in 1972, *People* in 1974, and *Discover* in 1980. The weekly *Life*, shuttered in 1972, was revived as a monthly in 1978. While all of these new ventures (with the exception of *Discover*) were successful, the company also had a string of conspicuous failures. With much fanfare the company bought the *Washington Star* in 1978, only to close it down three years later. Time spent nearly $50 million on a listings publication called *TV-Cable Week*, which was terminated after five months. A teletext project was also dropped. In the early 1980s, as the cable business declined, Time set up a magazine development group to explore possibilities for new publications. The main result of the group's work, a new magazine called *Picture Week*, was abandoned after about a year of market testing. In 1985 Time also broke out of its tradition by buying established magazines from others. It spent $480 million to purchase Southern Progress Corp., publisher of *Southern Living* and other publications. In 1986 the company purchased and shut down *Science 86* and *Science Digest* to reduce the competition faced by *Discover* but ended up selling the magazine a year later. In 1989 the company announced a friendly merger with Warner Communications, which was almost derailed by a takeover bid for Time by Paramount Communications (formerly Gulf + Western). The combined company brought out a new magazine called *Entertainment Weekly* in 1990.

Times Mirror, the parent company of the *Los Angeles Times*, also owns a batch of newspapers, magazines, and other media properties. The *Times*, controlled by the Chandler family, was a provincial and virulently reactionary publication until Otis Chandler took over in 1960. It is now one of the country's leading papers and one of the most profitable. In 1970 the company bought *Newsday*, the Long Island daily that is considered the country's leading suburban paper, and the *Dallas Times Herald*. In 1979 the company purchased the *Hartford Courant*, in 1980 the *Denver Post*, and in 1986 the *Baltimore*

Sun. In the latter year the company agreed to sell off the Dallas paper, while *Newsday* was making an aggressive push into New York City. In 1987 Times Mirror sold the money-losing *Denver Post* and purchased four consumer magazines (*Field & Stream, Home Mechanix, Skiing*, and *Yachting*).

The best known properties of the closely held **Tribune Co.**, built by Colonel Robert Rutherford McCormick, are the *Chicago Tribune* and the *New York Daily News*. While the *Tribune* has done consistently well, the *News* has fallen on harder times, losing its first place (in circulation) among dailies to *The Wall Street Journal*. In 1980 the *News* sought to grow by putting out an evening edition called *Tonight*; but the effort, although impressive in journalistic terms, failed to find an adequate audience and was terminated after a year. Soon afterward, the Tribune Co. management, led by Stanton Cook, put the paper up for sale but ended up keeping it after obtaining union concessions. Despite the concessions, the company launched an assault against the *News's* unions in the 1990 contract negotiations. The unions responded with a campaign against the company that included a boycott.

Washington Post Co., the publisher of the country's sec-

INDUSTRY DATA

Newspapers	*1989*	*1988*	*1987*
Value of shipments	$36.2 billion	$33.9 billion	$31.8 billion
Total employment	453,000	449,000	434,000

Magazines	*1989*	*1988*	*1987*
Value of shipments	$20.7 billion	$19.1 billion	$17.6 billion
Total employment	122,000	116,000	111,000

Source: U.S. Department of Commerce.

ond most important paper, has been run by Katharine Graham since 1963, when her husband Philip died. After being given control of the paper by Katharine's father Eugene Meyer in 1946, Philip Graham helped lift the paper from its status as a poor third to the *Star* and the *Times-Herald* (which the *Post* bought in 1954). He also purchased *Newsweek* in 1961. His widow continued the improvement of the paper, though other acquisitions (such as the *Trenton Times*—bought in 1974 and sold in 1982) have been less successful. Katharine Graham's son Don took over as publisher of the *Post* in 1979, when his mother became chairman of the parent company.

SOURCE GUIDE

Leading Stock Analysts and Experts

Peter Falco, analyst at Merrill Lynch.

James B. Kobak, a leading magazine consultant, based in Darien, Connecticut.

John Morton, a leading analyst of the newspaper industry who has his own research operation (affiliated with Lynch, Jones & Ryan) in Washington, D.C.

J. Kendrick Noble, Jr., analyst at Paine Webber.

Veronis, Suhler & Associates, a New York investment banking firm that specializes in media deals.

Trade Associations and Unions

American Newspaper Publishers Association, 11600 Sunrise Valley Drive, Herndon, VA 22091. Tel.: (703) 620–9500.

Communications Workers of America/Printing, Publishing and Media Workers Sector, 1925 K Street NW, Washington, DC 20006. Tel.: (202) 728–2300.

Graphic Communications International Union, 1900 L Street NW, Washington, DC 20036. Tel.: (202) 462–1400.

Magazine Publishers Association, 575 Lexington Avenue, New York, NY 10022. Tel.: (212) 752–0055.

National Writers Union, 13 Astor Place, New York, NY 10003. Tel.: (212) 254–0279.

Newspaper Guild, 8611 2nd Avenue, Silver Spring, MD 20910. Tel.: (301) 585–2990.

Data Sources and Directories

Editor & Publisher International Yearbook, a volume published by the leading trade journal of the newspaper business, includes statistics and a directory of newspapers in the United States and abroad as well as other organizations and companies (New York: Editor & Publisher).

Facts About Newspapers, an annual compilation of statistics (Herndon, Va.: American Newspaper Publishers Association).

The Folio: 400, a special issue of *Folio* magazine that includes rankings of the top magazines overall and by category.

Gale Directory of Publications and Broadcast Media, an annual directory of newspapers and periodicals (Detroit: Gale Research).

Newspaper Advertising Bureau, New York. An association that collects information on newspaper advertising.

Publishers Information Bureau, New York. An association that collects information on magazine advertising.

Standard Periodical Directory, a biennial directory of American and Canadian publications (New York: Oxbridge Communications).

Standard Rate and Data Service, a series of monthly volumes providing information on the circulation, advertising rates, and other commercial aspects of newspapers and magazines (Wilmette, Ill.: Standard Rate and Data Service).

Ulrich's International Periodicals Directory, a comprehensive annual directory of periodicals from around the world (New York: R. R. Bowker).

Trade Publications

Editor & Publisher, weekly.

Folio: The Magazine for Magazine Management, monthly.

MagazineWeek.

Media Industry Newsletter, weekly.

News Inc., monthly.

Books and Reports

Bagdikian, Ben H. *The Media Monopoly*. 2nd edition. Boston: Beacon Press, 1983.

Byron, Christopher. *The Fanciest Dive* (on Time Inc.). New York: W. W. Norton, 1986.

Halberstam, David. *The Powers That Be.* New York: Alfred A. Knopf, 1979.

Hynds, Ernest C. *American Newspapers in the 1980s.* New York: Hastings House, 1980.

Leab, Daniel J. *A Union of Individuals: The Formation of the American Newspaper Guild, 1933–1936.* New York: Columbia University Press, 1970.

Patten, David A. *Newspapers and the New Media.* White Plains, N.Y.: Knowledge Industry Publications, 1986.

Prichard, Peter. *The Making of McPaper: The Inside Story of USA Today.* Kansas City, Mo.: Andrews, McMeel & Parker, 1987.

CHAPTER 5

TELECOMMUNICATIONS

The telecommunications industry underwent a remarkable transformation during the 1970s and 1980s. What was once an industry dominated by a giant, regulated telephone monopoly and a few other carriers has become something of a free-for-all. Extensive deregulation and the breakup of the Bell System have given rise to a new generation of companies and new lines of business for the traditional carriers. There has also been a technological upheaval as satellites, fiber optics, and other systems have battled for supremacy in the $168 billion telecommunications service industry and the $18 billion telecommunications equipment market. The array of new services available to users—including cellular and cordless phones, fax machines, answering machines, and electronic information services via modem—has steadily increased the amount of time America spends on its 240 million phones.

FROM SMOKE SIGNALS TO THE TELEPHONE

The sending of messages over great distances dates back to early civilizations. Smoke signals and semaphores remained the state of the art until the early 19th century, when the first electrical telegraphs were devised. In the United States, Samuel F. B. Morse pioneered the use of the electromagnet in telegraphy and developed a code of dots and dashes to represent the letters of the alphabet and numerals.

Morse's original device consisted of a pen that electric currents caused to make marks on a moving strip of paper. At the suggestion of his assistant Alfred Vail, Morse changed the design to one that resembled a doorbell. He patented the sounding device in 1840 but failed to attract investor interest.

Three years later Congress appropriated $30,000 to build a test line between Washington and Baltimore. Sitting in the Supreme Court chamber of the Capitol in 1844, Morse transmitted the now legendary message "What hath God wrought." After this well-publicized event, telegraphy caught on quickly, especially with newspapers. Dozens of telegraph companies were formed, and in 1856 a group of them combined to form Western Union. The rapidly growing company completed the first transcontinental telegraph line in 1861, which promptly put the Pony Express out of business. The first transatlantic cable was laid in 1866.

As telegraphy was coming into its own, various researchers began exploring the possibility of transmitting voices in the same manner that the telegraph conveyed electric currents. One of the most successful of these men was a speech therapist named Alexander Graham Bell. Backed by the wealthy fathers of two of his students and assisted by Thomas Watson (no relation to the IBM Watson), Bell hit on a promising technique in 1876 and one of his backers rushed a description of it to the U.S. Patent Office on February 14.

Coincidentally, it was later the same day that rival inventor Elisha Gray of Chicago filed a "caveat" with the Patent Office, warning that he was working on a speaking telephone. Those few hours of difference would be decisive for Bell. The timing ended up being more important than the fact that Bell's application did not even mention telephones. It spoke of improvements in telegraphy; the crucial element, a variable-resistance transmitter, was inserted in the margin as an afterthought.

Despite the conflicting patent claims, no one had actually succeeded in transmitting a human voice. That came on March 10, when Bell, having adopted the variable-resistance idea, succeeded in sending the message "Mr. Watson, come here; I want you" after he spilled some acid on himself.

Bell's telephone gained fame later that year with a demonstration at the Centennial Exposition in Philadelphia. Even then there was skepticism about the practical applications of the device—so much so that when one of Bell's backers offered all rights to the telephone to the president of Western Union for $100,000 he was turned down.

Attitudes changed after commercial service was initiated by the Bell Telephone Company in 1877. Western Union, realizing that it had missed a big opportunity, made a deal with Elisha Gray and formed the American Speaking Telephone Company. The firm commissioned a promising young inventor named Thomas Edison, who built an improved transmitting device. Western Union decided that with its extensive wire network it was the ideal company to develop the telephone business.

Bell and his colleagues were not about to knuckle under, even in the face of a challenge from behemoth Western Union (the first truly national corporation). Led by Theodore Vail, a former telegraph operator, the Bell company launched a legal assault against Western Union. The telegraph company, inhibited by the fact that it found itself the object of a takeover campaign by financier Jay Gould, consented to a settlement in 1879. Western Union agreed to abandon the telephone business in exchange for 20 percent of the Bell company's phone rental receipts over the 17 years of Bell's patents.

The Bell company fought hundreds of other patent suits; and while it always prevailed, one case went to the Supreme Court and was decided in favor of Bell by a margin of only one vote. Although its legal rights were firmly established, Bell had difficulty financing the expansion of the system. The firm resorted to licensing others to build telephone operations in various places, and the main company went through a series of financial and management reorganizations. In 1899 the headquarters of the company were moved from Boston to New York, and the name American Telephone & Telegraph (AT&T) was adopted.

The Bell monopoly moved to dominate long-distance service and equipment manufacturing as well. Intercity service was initiated in 1881 with the connection of Boston and Providence, and Bell set up a long-lines subsidiary in 1885. To expand its output of equipment, Bell in 1881 purchased a controlling interest (later expanded to full ownership) in the Western Electric Co.—founded by Bell rival Elisha Gray—and made it the system's sole supplier.

But it was not long before the Bell monolith began to totter. Public discontent over Bell's rates (15 cents a call) escalated, and in 1885 there was the first attempt at government regulation of the business. The Indiana legislature passed legislation limiting basic phone charges to $3 a month. (The law was repealed three years later.) In the 1890s, as Bell's original patents began to expire, hundreds of independent phone companies were established.

Not long after becoming AT&T, the Bell company was the object of a takeover battle that ended in 1907 with victory for a group of bankers led by J. P. Morgan. Theodore Vail, who had left the company in 1887, was called back to rebuild the sagging monopoly. Vail promoted the idea of public service and welcomed government regulation. What he abhorred was competition. He refused to connect Bell long-distance facilities to other phone companies, and with the financial backing of Morgan he succeeded in taking over many of the independents. In 1909 AT&T even managed to win control over Western Union. Vail regarded telecommunications as a natural monopoly and intended to have AT&T run the business.

THE KINGSBURY COMMITMENT

The rest of the industry had a different view, of course, and persuaded the Justice Department to begin investigating whether AT&T was violating the antitrust laws. AT&T decided to compromise rather than fight and in 1913 reached a settlement. Making what became known as the Kingsbury commitment (named after an AT&T executive), the Bell system agreed to divest itself of its Western Union holdings, purchase no more independents without the consent of the Interstate Commerce Commission (ICC), and connect with other phone networks.

Although Vail's dream of a comprehensive national monopoly was dashed, AT&T still enjoyed many local monopolies as well as control over the long-distance business. By the 1910s state regulation of the local monopolies was spreading rapidly, and on a national level the Mann-Elkins Act of 1910 extended the jurisdiction of the ICC to telephone, though the commission ended up doing little in that direction.

In the period leading up to World War I, calls for government involvement went even further. In 1913 the Wilson administration's postmaster general began advocating nationalization (the actual term was postalization) of the phone system, as had occurred in all other major nations. Congress finally heeded this cry in 1918, and the president was empowered to take control of the country's telephone and telegraph systems. This was a strange kind of nationalization in that industry executives remained in place and shareholders continued to receive dividends.

Although federal control helped the Army Signal Corps during the war, the government had to raise phone rates and ended up with a substantial deficit. The experiment in nationalized telecommunications was terminated after a year, and the companies were returned to private hands. Private ownership under monopoly conditions was affirmed again in 1921 with the Graham Act, which exempted telephone mergers from the antitrust laws, thus allowing AT&T to consolidate local companies.

During the 1920s AT&T felt confident enough to dabble in new areas such as radio broadcasting (which it abandoned in 1926; see Chapter 2) and the development of sound systems for motion pictures (see Chapter 3). Bell Laboratories also did some early research on television.

By this time telephones were firmly established as part of everyday life for most Americans. AT&T did experience some falling off in business in the early years of the Great Depression, but it did not last long. At the end of 1937 the Bell system stood at a record 15.3 million phones.

THE UNIVERSAL SERVICE PRINCIPLE

The 1930s did, however, present a challenge to the phone industry in the form of more extensive federal regulation. The

Communications Act of 1934 established the Federal Communications Commission and gave it jurisdiction over both broadcasting and common carriers. The latter consist of services such as telephone and telegraph that are obliged to provide access to anyone on a first-come, first-served basis. With regard to telephone, the nation's policy was to be that of providing the widest possible service at the lowest possible price.

There were many in Congress who wanted not simply to regulate the telephone giant but to reduce its size as well. The greatest criticism was leveled at AT&T's ownership of Western Electric, since it was alleged that the prices charged the parent company by Western served to inflate phone service rates. In 1935 Congress ordered the FCC to explore these charges, and a massive investigation of AT&T was launched. The resulting Walker Report advocated direct regulation of Western Electric's prices, but the full commission took a softer line.

The Bell System remained intact and retained its dominance. In 1939 it controlled some 83 percent of all telephones, 98 percent of long-distance wires, and 100 percent of transoceanic radio telephony. The 16.5 million Bell phones generated 90 percent of all U.S. phone industry revenues. The largest of the independents was General Telephone, founded in 1926 and now known as GTE.

After World War II, telephone usage grew at unprecedented rates, helped by the fact that most of the Bell system had been converted to direct dialing, and the use of operators in long distance started to be phased out as well. AT&T also took up the old problem of developing transatlantic cable service, since radio telephony across the ocean (inaugurated in 1927) remained interference prone and unreliable. The task, which required sophisticated repeater devices to amplify voices through the line, was accomplished; cable service was launched in 1956.

The glory of this period for AT&T management was marred by a revival of federal legal action against the company. In 1949 the Justice Department filed an antitrust suit against the Bell System, seeking divestiture of Western Electric. After years of legal maneuvering AT&T signed a consent decree in 1956 that allowed it to hold onto Western but confined the subsidiary to manufacturing equipment for the Bell System (except for military work) and prohibited the parent company from entering any business other than common-carrier communications.

Although there was criticism to the effect that the Eisenhower administration let "Ma Bell" off too easily, the consent decree restriction on entering new businesses turned out to be a major impediment for AT&T in the emerging new telecommunications industry.

HUSH-A-PHONE VERSUS THE "BLACK BEAUTY"

AT&T's battle with the forces of competition began with the issue of customer equipment. In the 1950s a device called Hush-a-Phone, which allowed someone speaking into a phone to avoid being overheard by others in a room, was approved by the FCC and put on the market. Ma Bell, which had built an equipment as well as a service monopoly, was horrified. It was taken as a matter of faith that only Bell-produced equipment should be used in the Bell System. The idea of standardization extended to matters of style. Like Henry Ford, AT&T allowed its customers to have any kind of phone they wanted—as long as it was the standard one known ironically as the "black beauty."

Although AT&T got a federal appeals court to overrule the FCC on Hush-a-Phone, various retailers, led by Ben Jamil of New York, began selling antique and foreign phones to customers tired of the standard model. Ma Bell fought hard against these incursions, both in court and by finally introducing a slightly larger variety of models from Western Electric. But it was too late. More companies entered what became known as the interconnect industry and clamored for legitimacy. The matter was resolved in 1968, when the FCC issued its ruling in the Carterfone case.

Thomas Carter of Texas had invented a device, which he called Carterfone, that could couple a telephone handset to a mobile radio transmitter. AT&T threatened to disconnect any customers who used the device, and Carter sued. The case was referred to the FCC, which decided not only to permit the Carterfone but also to abolish all rules prohibiting the attachment of nonsystem, customer-owned equipment.

At first, however, AT&T was allowed to insist on installing (for a fee) a protective device on all such equipment, supposedly to prevent damage to the system. The FCC soon decided that these devices were superfluous and that any equipment produced by a certified manufacturer could be directly installed. The interconnect industry was off and running.

The 1960s also saw the beginning of a challenge to Ma Bell's dominance in the long-distance business. A venture called Microwave Communications Inc. (MCI) applied to the FCC in 1963 for permission to furnish private-line service via microwave between Chicago and St. Louis. While this application was being fought by AT&T, another proposal was submitted by Texas entrepreneur Sam Wyly, who wanted to offer a digital data transmission service through a company called Datran. In 1970 the FCC decided to authorize such specialized carrier operations. AT&T responded by developing its own digital service, but the FCC's green light to the specialized carriers meant that Ma Bell was not going to have a clear field in the emerging technologies.

Moreover, the Justice Department once again took aim at AT&T, filing an antitrust suit in 1974 that sought to break up the Bell System. The suit was based on charges that since the 1956 consent decree, Ma Bell had deliberately blocked the interconnection of competing equipment and had sought to prevent the establishment of specialized carriers.

The level of frustration among AT&T executives during this period reached new heights. Assailed by antitrust charges in its core business and restricted by the 1956 decree from entering new ones, Ma Bell had the worst of both worlds: being regulated as a monopoly yet losing the immunity that legitimate monopolies expected from antitrust prosecution and competition. Meanwhile upstart companies such as MCI were going after the most profitable part of the business, with none of the Bell System's responsibility for maintaining a comprehensive network for providing universal service.

The new and lucrative markets emerged as a by-product of

the computer age. By the 1960s U.S. business was heavily computerized, and the transmission of digitized data was becoming as important as voice connections in the communications activity of corporations.

In 1961 Bell began leasing the DataPhone, which was supposed to address the computer industry's transmission needs. But the data processing people were not pleased with the product, and others began pressing for the right to provide alternatives. The dispute forced the FCC to take up the thorny problem of deciding where data processing left off and communications began. In its various computer inquiries, which stretched for years, the commission never fully answered the question, but it was firm in its restrictions on AT&T. The fear was that Ma Bell could use revenues from monopoly businesses to subsidize unregulated ones and thereby gain an unfair advantage over its rivals.

BABY BELL AND THE ROAD TO BREAKUP

Pressure from AT&T finally caused the FCC to abandon this position in 1980. The commission decided that, starting in 1983, Ma Bell could enter some unregulated businesses as long as it did so through an "arm's-length," unsubsidized subsidiary—which the business press immediately dubbed Baby Bell.

Neither the Justice Department nor AT&T's competitors were happy with this arrangement and sought to block it in court. Charles L. Brown, chairman of AT&T, decided that the mess could not be straightened out until the cloud of the antitrust suit was lifted. He and the rest of Bell management began to accept the idea that the only way to do this would be to agree to the severing of the 22 Bell operating companies that provided local service around the country. Once the Reagan administration took office in 1981 the chances of such a settlement—which would avoid a complete dismembering of the Bell System—were greatly improved. By the end of the year an agreement was reached, and on January 8, 1982, the Justice Department announced that the suit would be dropped. On the same day, the government abandoned its antitrust case against IBM.

Whereas IBM got off scot-free, AT&T had to divest itself of the operating companies by January 1, 1984. Under the terms of the divestiture, drawn up and implemented under the supervision of federal judge Harold Greene, AT&T was allowed to hold onto Western Electric, the long-distance business, and Bell Laboratories and was given the right to enter unregulated businesses via Baby Bell. That subsidiary was originally called American Bell and then renamed AT&T Information Systems.

The operating companies were reorganized into seven regional holding companies (RHCs) that remained as regulated monopolies and were supposed to focus on providing local service. Judge Greene allowed them to retain the profitable Yellow Pages business and the exclusive use of the Bell name and logo in the United States. He also barred AT&T from entering electronic publishing.

The Bell divestiture—by far the largest corporate breakup in U.S. history—involved such daunting tasks as dividing up some $150 billion in assets and nearly 1 million employees among AT&T and the seven RHCs. While from a managerial standpoint this went rather smoothly, it caused unprecedented disruptions for customers. Complaints about deterioration of service skyrocketed, and delays in the installation of equipment reached unprecedented levels.

There was also an upheaval in phone rates, stemming from the fact that divestiture meant the end of the traditional Bell practice of keeping long-distance rates artificially high to subsidize local service. Under the new arrangement the charge for each call was to be determined by the cost of providing it. Thus local rates shot up while AT&T's long-distance fees began declining. The United States was divided into about 160 local access and transport areas (LATAs), with AT&T and its competitors in long distance handling calls from one LATA to another while the RHCs handled local calls.

LONG-DISTANCE SERVICE

The success of MCI and Datran in getting the FCC to authorize specialized carrier service opened up the long-distance business

The 10 Largest Telephone Utilities in 1989 (by Number of Access Lines, in Millions)

1. Bell Atlantic	17.06
2. BellSouth	16.72
3. Ameritech	15.90
4. NYNEX	14.96
5. Pacific Telesis Group	14.20
6. US West	12.31
7. GTE (U.S. only)	12.30
8. Southwestern Bell	11.44
9. United Telecommunications	3.81
10. Contel	2.59

Source: United States Telephone Association.

to widespread competition in the 1970s. Companies such as MCI built their own transmission facilities, while others leased lines from AT&T and retailed the capacity. Not having the fixed costs and the regulatory restraints of Ma Bell, these competitors were able to provide long-distance service at substantially reduced rates. The growth of these competitors was limited by customer complaints about poor connections and the fact that users had to dial a string of extra digits. By 1983 the competing long-distance companies—of which there were dozens, led by MCI and Sprint—still had well under 10 percent of the market.

After the divestiture plan was put into motion, AT&T began fighting hard to see that its long-distance business, now the main revenue producer of the streamlined corporation, remained dominant. AT&T was particularly worried what would happen after the introduction in September 1986 of "equal access," the elimination of the extra digits that users of competing long-distance providers had to dial. To pay for the conversion to equal access and the loss of the old Bell subsidy from long distance, the RHCs were allowed to begin collecting local access charges of several dollars per month from each subscriber.

This was in addition to the fees already paid by the long-distance carriers themselves to the RHCs for each connection. One reason why MCI and the other upstart carriers were able to underprice AT&T was the fact that the FCC allowed them to pay much lower fees of this sort. Since these fees were the biggest element of cost, the raising of the fees for the upstarts in the period leading up to equal access forced them to raise their rates.

As various local phone companies began converting to equal access, customers were asked to choose among the competing long-distance carriers. The companies sought to influence these choices with an extraordinary marketing blitz. Phone subscribers were bombarded with endless TV commercials, newspaper and magazine advertisements, direct mail solicitations, and phone pitches. Some $500 million was spent on these activities in 1985 alone.

It soon became clear that AT&T would remain dominant, if only because many users were too bewildered to choose, and many local companies assigned such people to AT&T by default. Many of the smaller carriers had to drop out of the business or merge. Although AT&T's lead remains huge, the company's share has been declining—from about 85 percent in 1986 to 69 percent in 1989. Since the RHCs have been kept out of the long-distance market by Judge Greene, the leading challengers in the $50 billion business remain MCI, which had 11 percent in 1989, and U.S. Sprint (a subsidiary of United Telecommunications) with 8 percent. Fourth-ranking Telecom USA agreed in 1990 to be acquired by MCI.

Long-distance prices declined steadily during the late 1980s as AT&T sought to retain its dominance in the market and as the upstarts acted to sustain their price advantage (which has become narrower). AT&T's profitability was bolstered in 1989 when the FCC shifted from a system of regulating the company's profit margin to one that controlled rates. This allowed AT&T to increase earnings, rather than to simply lower rates, as a result of operating efficiencies. The image of efficiency and technical superiority cultivated by AT&T was marred on January 15, 1990, when a malfunction shut down the company's long-distance system for nine hours.

THE EQUIPMENT BUSINESS

The failure of AT&T to block the use of non-Bell equipment allowed the interconnect industry to flourish, both in the residential phone market and the business equipment segment. In the 1970s, once subscribers were able to purchase their own phones, an astounding range of products flooded the market. Many of these were electronic "smart phones," which could store frequently called numbers, dial them automatically, and perform other feats. While many of these devices were sold, it turned out that most subscribers were satisfied buying the phone they had been leasing from AT&T.

Businesses meanwhile were growing more and more enamored of sophisticated private branch exchanges (PBXs—i.e., switchboards) that allowed internal phone systems to perform equally amazing tricks. AT&T had been facing competition in this market since 1977, when Canada's Northern Telecom introduced the first electronic digital PBX. Ma Bell responded with its Dimension switchboard, but many customers found it lacking and turned to the competition. By the early 1980s AT&T had lost a majority of the PBX market, allowing Northern Telecom to rise to first place in market share. Yet in the middle of the decade technical problems and a rebound by Ma Bell pushed the Canadian company back to second place. According to the Eastern Research Corporation, in 1989 the market share leaders in the PBX business were AT&T with 25.7 percent, Northern Telecom with 21.8 percent, Siemens/Rolm with 12.8 percent, Mitel with 8.5 percent, and Japan's NEC with 7.8 percent.

The rise of foreign competition in the business equipment as well as residential phone market caused the U.S. balance of trade in telecommunications gear to plunge into the red in 1983. The U.S. position was further eroded in 1986 when ITT abandoned its effort to develop a digital switching system for the American market and agreed to sell its European telecommunications business to France's state-owned Compagnie Générale d'Electricité. By 1989 the U.S. trade deficit in telephone equipment was more than $1.8 billion.

NEW TECHNOLOGIES: SATELLITES

The traditional method by which the Bell System provided service was through an immense network of copper wires strung between telephone poles or buried under streets and roads. Later, coaxial cables were added to the grid. The last 20 years have also witnessed the rise of technologies that have served both as new links in the established phone system and as techniques for bypassing it. One of these is the use of orbiting microwave relay stations, otherwise known as satellites.

The idea of using artificial satellites as a means of facilitating telecommunications dates back to an article published by Arthur C. Clarke in 1945. Long before it was technically feasible, Clarke envisioned extraterrestrial relays placed in a geostationary orbit (the orbit, 22,300 miles above the equator, that would keep a satellite in a fixed position relative to a part of the globe) that could serve as receivers and retransmitters of radio signals beamed up from earth.

In 1946 the U.S. Army succeeded in bouncing a radar signal off the moon, and in later years the Navy used the moon as a passive relay for signals sent from Washington to Hawaii. American space activity accelerated after the Soviet Union's dramatic Sputnik launching. By the beginning of the Kennedy administration, the use of satellites was a hot issue, and the debate centered on the control of this new resource. AT&T considered the technology a mere extension of the phone system and sought exclusive rights from NASA to develop satellites for communications. Ma Bell's request was turned down, partly because some members of Congress felt that satellites should remain under government control.

AT&T nonetheless moved ahead with its plan to launch about 50 satellites in low-altitude (i.e., nongeostationary) orbit. The low-altitude approach was less efficient for communications, since the satellites did not remain in fixed positions relative to the earth and thus had to hand off signals to one another as they orbited.

The advantage, however, was that the shorter distance the signals traveled created less of an echo on the line. Some critics of AT&T suggested that it pushed the low-altitude approach only because its leading satellite competitor, Hughes Aircraft, was far ahead in the development of geostationary techniques.

While the debate in Congress on satellites was still in progress, AT&T got the FCC to grant permission in 1961 for the launching of Telstar I, the first privately owned "bird." AT&T timed the launching carefully and worked its publicity machine overtime. The festivities included the first satellite telephone conversation; the participants were AT&T president Fred Kappel and U.S. vice president Lyndon Johnson.

Congress ended up legislating a compromise. The Communications Satellite Act of 1962 created a national monopoly in the form of the Communications Satellite Corporation (COMSAT), which was to be sponsored by the U.S. government and owned half by communications carriers and half by private investors. COMSAT also became the U.S. representative to and a primary shareholder in INTELSAT, an international satellite consortium formed in 1964.

It was not long before COMSAT's monopoly was questioned. In 1965 ABC applied to the FCC for the right to establish a private satellite network. The commission returned the application, saying it had to take some time to study the matter, given the novel legal and policy questions that were raised. Finally in 1970 the agency put aside the objections of COMSAT and ruled that any qualified applicant could enter the domestic satellite business. This so-called Open Skies policy prompted a major expansion of private satellite services, led by Western Union, RCA, and Hughes. The move was also aided by a subsequent FCC decision to deregulate the use of receive-only satellite earth stations.

IBM jumped on the satellite bandwagon in 1975 by creating a joint venture with COMSAT and Aetna Life & Casualty called Satellite Business Systems (SBS). SBS was intended to provide sophisticated, high-volume digital transmission services covering voice and data. The operation launched its satellite in 1980 and signed up its first customer the following year. Unfortunately for the partners, which ended up sinking hundreds of millions of dollars into the venture, other customers did not follow in great numbers. In the early 1980s SBS switched its emphasis to the consumer, entering the long-distance sweepstakes. It failed at this too, and in 1985 the operation was handed over to MCI as part of a major investment by IBM in the leading upstart carrier.

The satellite business turned out to be somewhat more lucrative for the companies that focused on customers such as cable television networks. Turner Broadcasting and Home Box Office led a move to satellites that included many TV programmers and other media operations such as *The Wall Street Journal*, which used the technology to transmit pages to printing plants around the country.

To get around FCC rate regulations on common carriers, Hughes Aircraft started a trend toward selling the transponders (the relay devices on the satellites) rather than leasing them. But by the early 1980s there were signs of a transponder glut, and some carriers had difficulty selling their satellite condominiums.

The tendency toward a surfeit of transponders continued through the end of the decade. In 1989 the satellite services business—with 1,400 civilian transponders available worldwide, about a quarter of which were unused—still had revenues of only $750 million. There was some excitement over the use of the super-high-frequency Ku band, which generates more powerful transmissions, allowing the signals to be received by smaller, less expensive antennas. There was also a new push in direct broadcast satellites for entertainment as a result of the $1 billion Sky Cable plan announced by a consortium of NBC, Hughes Aircraft, Rupert Murdoch's News Corp., and Cablevision Systems. Yet the future of satellites was clouded by the development of a rival technology called fiber optics.

FIBER OPTICS

The development of modern telecommunications and calculating equipment has been based on the manipulation of electrons. Yet as early as the 1870s Alexander Graham Bell explored the use of light as an alternative to electricity, though the approach remained impractical. The development of the laser in the early 1960s revived the quest.

Companies such as Corning Glass, ITT, and AT&T began experimenting with the use of glass fibers through which voice and data are transmitted in the form of bursts of light. One of the advantages of glass fibers is that they save an enormous amount of space. Copper wires permit about 48 conversations at a time—with electromagnetic interference and "leakage" as frequent problems—while the fibers can handle hundreds of times as many. Fibers also make possible vastly greater transmission speeds than copper wires. The glass fibers also avoid the problem of corrosion and do not require the repeater devices needed every mile or so on copper wire lines. The drawback of what came to be called fiber optics is that photons cannot be easily switched. They work well in transmitting from Point A to Point B but not if other connections have to be made.

As fiber optics techniques were refined in the early 1980s, various companies rushed into the market. AT&T announced plans to install a cable along the East Coast between Boston and Richmond, Virginia. Various railroad and pipeline companies joined the party by offering their rights of way for the laying of the fiber cables. By 1984 the business press was full of predictions that fiber optics would make satellites obsolete by reducing the cost of land-based communication to a pittance.

However, it was not long before the signs of excess capacity appeared here as well. By the late 1980s the long-distance companies had virtually completed their shift to fiber optics, and the RHCs were moving slowly in making the conversion in the local loop. There was a bright spot in the laying of new submarine systems (such as the TAT-8 cable from the United States to Europe, which began operation in 1988), but overall the outlook for fiber optics has become more sober.

BYPASSING THE GRID

The traditional phone companies have employed satellites and fiber optics, but those technologies are also being used by rival telecommunications providers and their customers to avoid all or part of the phone system and thereby obtain higher quality and/or lower cost services. This practice, known as bypass, was pioneered by MCI's microwave proposal of the early 1960s. After being authorized by the FCC, MCI and other specialized carriers began offering a variety of new services.

For residential customers, this mainly meant bypassing AT&T's long-distance network by using the independent facilities of MCI, U.S. Sprint, and others. For business users the choices, more sophisticated and varied, included:

- Private lines that enabled companies to bypass the local telephone company in gaining access to long-distance carriers.
- Private lines—involving coaxial cables, microwave relays, and satellites—that permit companies to bypass both the local phone companies and the long-distance carriers.
- So-called value-added networks, such as Tymnet and Telenet, that not only permit high-quality data transmission but also include services such as error checking and data storage, and procedures such as packet switching that permit lower-cost transmissions.

Some bypass is taking place through facilities called teleports, which give companies access to satellite, microwave, and fiber optics facilities outside the control of the phone companies. One of the largest is Teleport Communications Group (majority-owned by Merrill Lynch), in New York City.

The rise of bypass has represented a particular threat for local phone companies, which are estimated to lose several billion dollars a year in revenues from the practice. Even AT&T has promoted local bypass and in 1985 got FCC permission to follow the procedure in connecting business customers to WATS and 800 services. All of this has fueled the desire of the regional holding companies to go beyond the limits placed on them in the course of the AT&T breakup.

THE GROWING ASPIRATIONS OF THE RHCs

Not long after they were set off on their own, the regional holding companies spun off from AT&T decided they were not satisfied with an existence largely limited to the relatively unexciting business of providing local telephone service. The very names that some of the RHCs adopted were meant to convey a dynamic high-tech or at least nontelephone image: NYNEX

(New York and New England), Ameritech (the Midwest), Pacific Telesis (California and Nevada), and US West (Rocky Mountain and northwestern states). The other three—Bell Atlantic (mid-Atlantic), BellSouth, and Southwestern Bell (Texas, Oklahoma, Kansas, Missouri, and Arkansas)—kept the Bell name but were equally aggressive in wanting to branch out.

The RHCs (or Baby Bells, as they came to be called) entered fields such as computer retailing, software, real estate, and financial services. By the end of 1986 the RHCs had spent an estimated $3.5 billion to purchase new businesses and a large but undetermined amount to start new ventures from scratch.

Judge Greene, who retained authority over the RHCs in the aftermath of divestiture, frowned on these outside activities. He ruled that the RHCs could engage in some of the proposed businesses only if they got permission for each venture and did not allow the outside activities to account for more than 10 percent of revenues. The RHCs submitted to these restrictions reluctantly and kept the pressure on Judge Greene. In 1986 some of the RHCs began pushing to enter the long-distance business, and Ameritech won permission to produce telecommunications equipment overseas. Later that year a federal appeals court reversed one of Judge Greene's decisions and allowed the RHCs to market specialized services outside their geographical areas.

Throughout the rest of the 1980s the RHCs kept up their crusade to win greater freedom to enter new lines of business. Judge Greene remained adamant in his refusal to let the Baby Bells enter the long-distance market or the equipment manufacturing business (a position that was upheld by a federal appeals court). The RHCs were permitted to enter the data transmission business, particularly the providing of gateways to electronic database services. Judge Greene has been unwilling to allow the RHCs to generate computer-based information services, but in 1990 an appeals court told him to reconsider the matter.

Frustrated with Judge Greene's limitations on their operations, the RHCs have conducted an intensive "Free the Bells" movement to get Congress to shift oversight of the industry from Judge Greene to the FCC—a proposal that was more realistic once the commission came under the leadership of Alfred

Sikes in 1989. Sikes was more acceptable to congressional Democrats than his Reagan-era predecessors, free-market hardliners Mark Fowler and Dennis Patrick.

At the same time, the Baby Bells satisfied their urge for diversification by going abroad and making deals with foreign governments and companies. US West, for example, got a cable television franchise in Hong Kong and set up a cellular telephone business in Hungary. Pacific Telesis developed the first private cellular operation in West Germany and invested in three cable television companies in Britain. NYNEX bought 50 percent of the telephone company in Gibraltar. Ameritech and Bell Atlantic purchased the privatized state-owned telephone company in New Zealand.

CELLULAR TELEPHONES

One business that the RHCs were allowed to enter from the start was a new form of mobile telephone service. The combination of telephones and automobiles dates back to 1946, when the first mobile radiotelephone service was inaugurated in St. Louis. More widespread service was established in the 1960s. The problem with the traditional kind of mobile phone service was the limitation on the number of channels—23 per city. This meant that users often had difficulty obtaining a dial tone, and even when calls were completed the service was often poor.

Back in the late 1940s telephone researchers figured out that capacity could be greatly expanded if the same frequencies could be used simultaneously in different areas. This required a shift from a single-transmitter/receiver system to an arrangement of multiple antennas, each operating at lower power and covering a limited range. As an automobile moved from one area, or cell, to another the call would be "handed off" from one system to the next.

It was not until the 1970s that advances in electronic switching equipment made this technique possible. AT&T set up the first trial system in Chicago in 1978, and it proved a great success. In 1982 the FCC began accepting applications for cellular telephone licenses in the 30 largest cities. The plan was to allow two competing systems in each market, one of which would be awarded to a phone company.

Dozens of companies joined the cellular gold rush; when the FCC opened up the next 60 largest markets, some 150 firms filed about 1,000 applications. The commission decided to adopt a lottery system rather than to use comparative assessments in granting the licenses, and in 1984 the FCC allowed the applicants for the second 60 markets to form a giant consortium to divide up the business among them.

After Judge Greene allowed the RHCs to enter the cellular business outside their primary service areas, there was a takeover frenzy. Among the biggest deals were Southwestern Bell's 1986 purchase of most of the cellular operations of Metromedia for $1.4 billion, and BellSouth's 1989 acquisition of the cellular and paging properties of Mobile Communications Corp. of America for $710 million in stock. Yet it was a non-Baby Bell by the name of McCaw Cellular Communications that emerged as the industry leader through aggressive acquisitions and liberal use of debt. In 1990 McCaw acquired a controlling interest in LIN Broadcasting, its largest non-Bell rival, for $3.4 billion.

By the end of 1989, with cellular phones being used by everyone from farmers to drug dealers, there were 3.3 million of them in operation in the United States. Standard & Poor's estimates that the number will reach 35 million by the year 2000. Cellular companies are enjoying the boom, along with a trend toward deregulation of rates, but state regulators have begun to question the duopolistic arrangement in each market. In 1990 an upstart company called Federal Digital Cellular began to lobby the Bush administration to support an expansion from two to three systems, but the frequencies that would be used were ones currently being employed by GTE for air-to-ground pay phones on commercial airlines.

THE FUTURE

The trend among all telecommunications suppliers is toward the complete digitization of transmissions; the catchphrase is integrated services digital network (ISDN). This notion, pushed

The 10 Largest Cellular Telephone Service Providers (as of December 31, 1989)

	Number of Subscribers
1. BellSouth	419,260
2. McCaw Cellular Communications	386,000
3. Southwestern Bell	382,000
4. Pacific Telesis	381,000
5. Ameritech	242,000
6. GTE	232,300
7. NYNEX	213,000
8. Bell Atlantic	188,500
9. Cantel	177,400
10. LIN Broadcasting	169,740

Source: Paul Kagan Associates, Inc., Carmel, California.

particularly by AT&T, involves a single system for transmitting (via fiber optics phone lines) voice, data, video, and anything else that could be put in digital form. The transmission speeds possible with ISDN are astonishing—128,000 or more bits of information a second. By 1989 there were several dozen ISDN trials underway for large corporate and institutional customers; residential and small business use is still some years away.

ISDN represents an attempt by phone companies to reestablish their grid as an all-purpose transmission medium. Its success will require the adoption of technical standards that rival the networks being developed by the computer companies, led by IBM. Whatever approach prevails, there is no question that the development of methods of sending more and more information of different sorts at faster and faster speeds will continue to dominate telecommunications.

LABOR RELATIONS

Communications workers have the distinction of being in one of the few relatively high-tech industries that are extensively unionized. As a result they, among all union workers, have probably had the most experience in dealing with technological change and automation. The leading company in the industry, AT&T, was until its breakup the largest private employer in the United States.

From the earliest years, telephone workers have tended to fall into two categories: electrical craftsmen and less skilled phone operators. At first, teenage boys were employed as operators, but they proved too unruly. They were replaced by adult women, and the job remained a pink-collar ghetto until the 1970s.

Labor organizing in the phone industry started slowly but accelerated after the founding of the International Brotherhood of Electrical Workers (IBEW) in 1891. A male-dominated craft union, the IBEW ignored the operators until a wave of militancy began in Boston around 1912. The union reluctantly offered some assistance to the operators and ended up taking them into the organization, but only in a separate, second-class department.

The IBEW had some success after World War I, but telephone management moved to create company unions, which remained in place until the early 1930s. Even the fact that AT&T cut many jobs during the early years of the Great Depression while keeping the dividend intact did not lead to serious unrest. It was the passage of the Wagner Act that revived independent unionism in the industry, and in 1939 the National Federation of Telephone Workers (NFTW) was formed.

The organization remained highly decentralized and rather weak. As a result, pay for telephone workers fell behind that for workers in other industries. Amid the postwar labor militancy in 1946, the NFTW threatened a strike and got AT&T and the operating companies to bargain on a national level for the first time.

The following year the federation sought another big raise, but management declined to resume national bargaining. This time the strike was carried out. More than 300,000 workers around the country walked out in what was the most widespread strike in U.S. history. The NFTW had not prepared adequately for the action, and after several weeks the strike began to crumble. Local unions began settling with individual operating companies for small wage increases. Later that same year the NFTW decided to reorganize itself into a more centralized body and to change its name to the Communications Workers of America (CWA).

The CWA conducted a number of regional strikes in the 1950s, including a 72-day walkout at Southern Bell in 1955. In the 1960s the union had to fight off raids from the Teamsters and contend with the spreading automation of the system.

In the 1970s the threats to the CWA were from an organizing offensive by the IBEW, especially in the interconnect industry, and the uncertainty of what would happen if and when the Bell System was broken up. The union won a substantial wage increase after a weeklong national strike in 1971, and three years later AT&T agreed to national bargaining. The CWA sided with Ma Bell in its battle against competition, but after divestiture was announced the union set out to minimize the impact on AT&T's workers. There were signs that the RHCs would resist national bargaining and that a less regulated AT&T would be harder to deal with.

The latter proved true in 1983, when AT&T sought to hold the line and the CWA ended up calling a national strike. The walkout lasted about three weeks and ended with an 8.5 percent wage increase over three years.

The CWA has worked hard to adapt to the new environment created by deregulation and the breakup of the Bell System. In 1981 the union created its Committee on the Future, which examined changes in the industry and recommended bargaining strategies such as an emphasis on retraining. Recognizing that its domain had to extend to the entire information industry, the union vowed in 1985 to organize IBM. In the great long-distance wars of the 1980s, the CWA spent several million dollars promoting AT&T because it continued to use operators while the upstart carriers were completely automated.

This cooperative approach did not stop AT&T from announcing in August 1985 that it planned to eliminate 24,000 jobs in its Information Systems unit. A strike over the action was narrowly averted when the CWA and AT&T reached an agreement limiting the layoffs and restricting the use of subcontracting. The union also had to confront the fact that several of the RHCs were setting up nonunion subsidiaries and were indicating they would take tough stances when CWA's contracts expired in 1986.

Things turned out to be no easier with AT&T after the union and the company agreed to complete their negotiations before talks began with the RHCs. The CWA rejected the company's offer of an 8 percent wage increase over three years and initiated a national strike. AT&T stood fast and made its pitch directly to workers through newspaper advertisements. The two sides reached a settlement that included the same wage package but also had special provisions for job retraining, and the strike ended after 26 days. A few weeks later CWA talks with some of the RHCs broke down, and some 70,000 workers went on strike for about a week until settlements were reached.

In the 1989 round, a strike was averted at AT&T when the company agreed to a settlement package that included innovative improvements in family benefits (though the cost-of-living adjustment was eliminated). Things did not go so smoothly at the RHCs. Workers at four of the seven companies walked out, in most cases to resist management demands for reductions in health benefits. At the peak some 200,000 people were on strike. While three of the companies settled within a few weeks—with the health-care issue being resolved by agreements to establish preferred provider systems to keep down costs—the strike at NYNEX in the Northeast grew more bitter. It was only after 16 weeks that the deadlock was broken. NYNEX agreed to drop its effort to shift health-care costs to workers, and the unions agreed to a smaller wage package.

LEADING COMPANIES

American Telephone & Telegraph (AT&T) was until the mid-1980s virtually synonymous with the telephone business. Challenges to Ma Bell's monopoly began in the 1950s and culminated in the 1984 breakup of the company. AT&T held on to its manufacturing operation of Western Electric and its long-distance business, and Bell Labs was allowed to enter unregulated businesses through a subsidiary. Local telephone service became the province of seven independent regional holding companies. AT&T faced increasing competition in the equipment and long-distance markets but fought back aggressively. The company made repeated efforts to cut costs, but the biggest boost to the bottom line was the 1989 decision by the FCC to end its control over AT&T's profit rate.

Of the seven regional holding companies created by the breakup of AT&T, **BellSouth** in many ways has emerged as the leader of the pack. The largest of the group (in terms of revenues and assets), BellSouth is also the most technologically advanced. It has been especially aggressive in the cellular business, moving to first place by the end of 1989, ahead of McCaw Cellular Communications (in terms of number of subscribers). Like other Baby Bells, BellSouth has gone abroad for opportunities, setting up deals in such countries as France, Argentina, and Australia.

GTE has long been the largest among the independent telephone companies that control the small sector of the industry that was never absorbed into the Bell System. Founded as General Telephone in 1926, GTE later got into the telecommunications equipment and electronics businesses, the latter through the purchase of Sylvania in 1958. The company acquired the Telenet data communications network in 1979 and the U.S. Sprint long-distance service in 1983. U.S. Sprint, which had a hard time competing with AT&T and MCI, was spun off into a joint venture with United Telecommunications in 1986. During the same year, GTE took on Siemens as a partner for its switching-equipment operation. In 1988 the company reduced its stake in U.S. Sprint to 20 percent and in 1990 sold that remaining share to United Telecommunications. In the latter year GTE moved to strengthen its cellular business by agreeing to buy the Providence Journal Co.'s cellular properties in the Southeast. Later in 1990, GTE moved to expand both its cellular and local telephone business by agreeing to acquire Contel.

IBM saw the increasing fusion of data processing and communications as an opportunity to invade some of AT&T's traditional markets. IBM led a joint venture called Satellite Business Systems (SBS), which failed to attract enough high-volume users of data transmission systems. SBS was also a disappointment in the long-distance business, and the operation was handed over to MCI in 1985 when IBM took an equity position in that company. IBM also had difficulty achieving results after its 1984 purchase of Rolm, a leading telecommunications equipment producer. In 1988 IBM sold Rolm to West Germany's Siemens for $844 million.

McCaw Cellular Communications emerged out of the tumult of the cellular telephone business in the 1980s to become the largest firm in the industry. Craig McCaw, who had been expanding a cable television business started by his father, jumped into the cellular business when the FCC opened bidding on licenses in 1982. Taking on a mountain of debt and selling 22 percent of the company to British Telecom, McCaw began feverishly buying up licenses around the country. Following a nasty battle with BellSouth, McCaw in 1990 acquired a controlling interest in LIN Broadcasting and its lucrative cellular businesses in such cities as Los Angeles, Houston, and New York. For his efforts Craig McCaw received an astounding $54 million in salary, bonuses, and stock options in 1989.

MCI (or Microwave Communications Inc., as it was originally called) has played a major role in introducing a greater degree of competition to the telecommunications business. The company was founded by John Goeken, owner of a mobile-radio business, who applied to the FCC in 1963 for permission to construct a microwave radio system between Chicago and St. Louis. AT&T fought the idea, but the company persevered, especially after William McGowan took over in 1968. The FCC finally allowed MCI and others to provide private-line service as well as discount long-distance calling in competition with AT&T. MCI, which became the leading rival to AT&T in the long-distance business, was bolstered in 1985 when IBM purchased an 18 percent stake in the company (and turned over its Satellite Business Systems long-distance operation). MCI suffered some rough years in the mid-1980s because of falling prices and more serious competition from U.S. Sprint, but by the end of the decade MCI was enjoying a rebound and was taking market share away from AT&T. In 1990 MCI moved to fortify its position by agreeing to acquire Telecom USA, the fourth-largest long-distance carrier, for about $1.2 billion.

Northern Telecom Inc., the U.S. subsidiary of Northern Telecom Ltd. (which in turn is 52 percent-owned by Bell Canada), has emerged as a leader in the telecommunications equipment business. It introduced the first digital switchboard in the United States and temporarily took first place in the PBX market. Northern stumbled in the mid-1980s in that market and fell to the second position following a rebound by AT&T.

U.S. Sprint, the third-place contender in the long-distance market, was purchased by GTE from Southern Pacific in 1983 and spun off into a joint venture with United Telecommunications in 1986. (GTE reduced its interest from 50 to 20 percent in 1988 and in 1990 sold that remaining share to United Telecommunications). U.S. Sprint lost several billion dollars in the

INDUSTRY DATA

Telecommunications Services	*1989*	*1988*	*1987*
Operating revenues	$167.9 billion	$161.2 billion	$153.6 billion
Total employment	874,000	907,000	914,000

Telecommunications Equipment	*1989*	*1988*	*1987*
Value of shipments	$18.0 billion	$17.3 billion	$17.5 billion
Total employment	100,000	106,000	111,000
Import penetration	17.1%	15.9%	14.1%

Source: U.S. Department of Commerce.

course of constructing a 23,000-mile fiber optics network, but the company developed into a credible and aggressive challenger to MCI. In early 1990 the FBI began an inquiry into charges that U.S. Sprint illegally obtained confidential bid information about its competitors in the course of the company's successful effort to win a huge telephone contract from the federal government.

SOURCE GUIDE

Leading Stock Analysts and Experts

John Bain, analyst at Raymond, James & Associates, St. Petersburg, Florida.

Eastern Management Group, Parsippany, New Jersey.

Edward Greenberg, analyst at Morgan Stanley.

Jack Grubman, analyst at Paine Webber.

Robert Morris, analyst at Goldman Sachs.

Northern Business Information, New York.

Yankee Group, Boston.

Trade Associations and Unions

Communications Workers of America, 1925 K Street NW, Washington, DC 20006. Tel.: (202) 728–2300.

North American Telecommunications Association (interconnect industry), 2000 M Street NW, Washington, DC 20036. Tel.: (202) 296–9800.

United States Telephone Association, 900 19th Street NW, Washington, DC 20006. Tel.: (202) 835–3100.

Data Sources and Directories

Moody's Public Utility Manual, an annual collection of financial information on publicly held carriers (New York: Moody's Investors Services).

Phone Facts and *Statistics of the Local Exchange Carriers*, both annual (Washington, D.C.: U.S. Telephone Association).

Statistics of Communications Common Carriers, annual (Washington, D.C.: Federal Communications Commission).

Telephone Industry Directory, an annual guide to carriers and equipment suppliers (Potomac, Md.: Phillips Publishing).

The World's Telephones, an annual compilation of statistics (Morris Plains, N.J.: AT&T).

Trade Publications

Communications Daily.

Data Communications, monthly.

Satellite Communications, monthly.

Telecommunications, monthly.

Telecommunications Reports, weekly.

Telephony, weekly.

Books and Reports

Bolter, Walter G.; James W. McConnaughey; and Fred J. Kelsey. *Telecommunications Policy for the 1990s and Beyond*. Armonk, N.Y.: M. E. Sharpe, 1990.

Brock, Gerald W. *The Telecommunications Industry*. Cambridge, Mass.: Harvard University Press, 1981.

Brooks, John. *Telephone: The First Hundred Years*. New York: Harper & Row, 1976.

Brooks, Thomas R. *The Communications Workers of America*. New York: Mason/Charter, 1977.

Coll, Steve. *The Deal of the Century: The Breakup of AT&T*. New York: Atheneum, 1987.

Crandall, Robert W. *U.S. Telecommunications in a More Competitive Era*. Washington, D.C.: Brookings Books, 1990.

Demac, Donna A., ed. *Tracing New Orbits: Cooperation and Competition in Global Satellite Development*. New York: Columbia University Press, 1986.

Goulden, Joseph C. *Monopoly*. New York: G. P. Putnam's Sons, 1968.

Green, James Harry. *The Dow Jones-Irwin Handbook of Telecommunications*. Homewood, Ill.: Dow Jones-Irwin, 1986.

Hudson, Heather E. *The Communication Satellites: Their History and Future*. New York: Free Press, 1989.

Kahaner, Larry. *On the Line: The Men of MCI*. New York: Warner Books, 1986.

Kleinfield, Sonny. *The Biggest Company on Earth: A Profile of AT&T*. New York: Holt, Rinehart & Winston, 1981.

Organisation for Economic Co-operation and Development. *The Telecommunications Industry: The Challenges of Structural Change.* Paris, 1988.

Schacht, John N. *The Making of Telephone Unionism, 1920–1947.* New Brunswick, N.J.: Rutgers University Press, 1985.

Tedeschi, Anthony Michael. *Live via Satellite: The Story of COMSAT and the Technology that Changed World Communication.* Washington, D.C.: Acropolis Books, 1989.

Tunstall, W. Brooke. *Disconnecting Parties: Managing the Bell System Breakup—An Inside View.* New York: McGraw-Hill, 1985.

U.S. Congress, House Committee on Energy and Commerce. *Telecommunications in Transition: The Status of Competition in the Telecommunications Industry.* Washington, D.C., 1981.

U.S. General Accounting Office. *Telephone Communications: Bypass of the Local Telephone Companies.* Washington, D.C., 1986.

U.S. International Trade Administration. *A Competitive Assessment of the U.S. Cellular Radiotelephone Industry.* Washington, D.C., 1988.

U.S. International Trade Administration. *A Competitive Assessment of the U.S. Fiber Optics Industry.* Washington, D.C., 1984.

_______. *International Competitiveness Study: Fiber Optics Industry.* Washington, D.C., 1988.

U.S. National Telecommunications and Information Administration. *Issues in Domestic Telecommunications: Directions for National Policy.* Washington, D.C., 1985.

PART 2

CONSUMER GOODS AND SERVICES

CHAPTER 6

BEVERAGES

Americans are a thirsty people: The year-round demand for ice-cold beverages that are either sweet or alcoholic or both seems insatiable. Drinks are often used like medicines: People consume them to perk up or calm down, when they are busy or when they are relaxing. The satisfying of this need was once taken care of through home brews or the concoctions at the local druggist or soda fountain.

Today the packaged beverage industry—including $25 billion in soft drinks and $21 billion in alcoholic beverages—is very big business, and American products such as Coca-Cola have changed the drinking habits of people around the world. The authors of a book called *The Cola Wars*, noting the extraordinary spread of soft drinks to all kinds of societies, have declared: "Aside from physiological and biological similarities, the human race may not have a more common denominator than these drinks."

"THE PAUSE THAT REFRESHES": SOFT DRINKS

The soft drink business in the United States emerged out of the tonics and elixirs that druggists used to prepare for customers in order to cure a variety of ailments. One popular formula combining coca leaves and the kola nut was invented in 1886 by Atlanta druggist John Styth Pemberton. The rights to the product, Coca-Cola, were acquired by Asa Griggs Candler, who proceeded to market it in syrup form to soda fountains around the country.

Candler was not interested in the idea of bottling the product for direct sale to consumers, and in 1899 he sold the rights to do so to a group of Tennessee businessmen for $1. Candler ultimately turned out to be more concerned with politics than commerce, and control of The Coca-Cola Company was acquired by Georgia financier Ernest Woodruff in 1919. Woodruff's son Robert, who took over in 1923, remained chief executive until 1955 and continued to exercise great influence over the company until his death in 1985.

Thanks to aggressive marketing, Coca-Cola came to assume a prominent place in American life. As it was introduced around the world, Coke became a leading symbol of the United States, and the company went to great lengths to cultivate this status. Incidentally, the company resisted the nickname Coke for many years because of the association with cocaine. The small trace of the drug in the original Coca-Cola formula was eliminated in 1903.

Right after Pearl Harbor, Woodruff vowed to make Coca-Cola available to everyone in the military. Thanks to Eisenhower's fondness for the drink, dozens of bottling plants were set up around the world, often right behind the frontline troops.

While Coke, in its familiar green bottle, dominated the soft drink market up to and through the 1940s, a serious competitor was slowly gaining ground. Pepsi-Cola was invented by North Carolina pharmacist Cabel Bradham in the 1890s. The Pepsi-Cola company grew rapidly around the turn of the century but later ran into serious financial difficulties, falling into bankruptcy several times and passing through a variety of owners. The company got a boost during the Great Depression, when it started selling Pepsi in 12-ounce bottles for the same nickel price as Coke's 6-ounce serving.

Still, Pepsi remained a distant second until the 1950s, when the company turned to what would later be called lifestyle advertising, associating the drink with young "sociables." The company scored a major coup in 1959 when Khrushchev was photographed drinking Pepsi at an exposition of American products in Moscow. After that point Pepsi was a true contender; and Donald Kendall, the executive who arranged to have Khrushchev drink the product, was promoted to chief executive of the company. Kendall's friendship with Richard Nixon helped Pepsi get the first foothold in the Soviet market in the early 1970s. (The company now supplies Pepsi in exchange for the right to sell Stolichnaya vodka in the United States.) Coke later used its contacts with Jimmy Carter (through Atlanta lawyer Charles Kirbo) to get the first shot at the Chinese market.

Beginning in the 1960s Coke and Pepsi escalated their rivalry with a succession of advertising campaigns aimed at tapping into the changes in the American psyche and getting people to associate one or the other cola with one's personal identity. In the place of traditional slogans such as Coke's "The pause that refreshes" and "Pepsi-Cola hits the spot," the companies spent millions on promoting notions such as "You've got a lot to live, and Pepsi's got a lot to give" and "Coke is the real thing."

Until the early 1960s the two leading companies had only one soft drink brand apiece. A much smaller competitor, Royal Crown, then paved the way to a giant new market by bringing out the first major sugar-free soft drink. The Coca-Cola Company brought out Tab in 1963, and Pepsi-Cola soon followed with its own low-calorie brands. The two big companies also launched assaults on the market of their much smaller competitor, the Seven-Up Co., by pushing their own lemon-lime drinks: Coke's Sprite and Pepsi's Mountain Dew.

BRAND PROLIFERATION

The introduction of new brands continued into the 1970s but really took off in the early 1980s. The impetus was a challenge by the Seven-Up Co. on the issue of caffeine. Unlike colas, 7UP contains no caffeine, but for many years this distinction seemed to make little difference to consumers. Seizing on the health consciousness of the 1980s, the Seven-Up Company began emphasizing the caffeine issue in order to bolster its flagship brand and to generate interest in a new caffeine-free cola called Like that the company was introducing.

At first the majors dismissed the caffeine controversy, but

Pepsi soon got scared and decided to introduce its own Pepsi Free. (This was in addition to Pepsi Light, a lower-calorie, lemon-flavored version brought out in 1977.) Soon The Coca-Cola Company, which had just introduced the sugar-free Diet Coke, went with the tide and brought out caffeine-free versions of Coke, Diet Coke, and Tab. These six cola varieties were joined by Cherry Coke in 1985.

In the intensified battle for supermarket shelf space (the industry term is *facings*), Pepsi began to give Coke the most serious competition ever. In the 1970s Pepsi had begun challenging Coke on taste rather than on the traditional price basis, using a series of taste-test ads. By the 1980s this "Pepsi Challenge" was paying off as Coke's market share slipped. The corporate share for The Coca-Cola Company was bolstered by the tremendous success of Diet Coke, but when regular Coke's share plunged several percentage points from 1983 to 1984, the company began to run scared.

The people in Atlanta were prompted to make the most radical decision in the history of the company. In April 1985 chief executive Roberto Goizueta announced that the company would make the first major change in the formula of Coke in the 99-year history of the product. The new Coke was to have a smoother, sweeter taste that some people decided was much closer to that of Pepsi.

The company had spent more than four years evaluating a change in formula and was convinced the new Coke would be a hit. It soon became clear, however, that consumer loyalty to the old taste was much stronger than the company had anticipated. The majority of consumers not only expressed their dislike of the new Coke but also began organizing to get the company to return to the traditional taste. Organizations such as Old Coke Drinkers of America were formed and began talking of filing lawsuits against the switch.

In July, only three months after the fanfare of the introduction of the new Coke, Goizueta in effect admitted defeat. He announced that the company would resume selling the old Coke, to be dubbed Coca-Cola Classic, alongside the new Coke. This brought the company's cola line up to eight permutations and created a marketing nightmare. The new Coke was to remain the company's flagship brand, yet results began to come in showing that the Classic version was selling better in many parts of the country. As McDonald's and other leading restaurant chains abandoned the new Coke, the company struggled to keep the brand alive.

As the Coke and Pepsi lines slugged it out for market dominance, their smaller competitors such as Royal Crown and Dr Pepper often suffered as a result of the ensuing price war. The two majors also stepped up the pressures on their bottlers—which, aside from those few that are corporate-owned, are independent companies—to carry more of their products. 7UP was a particular victim of this process. The bottlers were barred from distributing directly competing products, but many handled 7UP, for instance, rather than Sprite or Teem, another lemon-lime brand brought out by Pepsi-Cola.

The heightened competition hurt the smaller cola producers, as well as Dr Pepper (which is technically not a cola). In addition, a good deal of the action in soft drinks began shifting to new markets. One of the fastest growing areas was that of soft drinks containing fruit juice. The Pepsi-Cola company took the lead here with its Slice brand, which even seized market share from 7UP.

Some other large companies have attempted to claim a portion of the lucrative soft drink market. In 1980 Procter & Gamble acquired Orange Crush and Hires root beer. Four years later R. J. Reynolds, the tobacco giant, purchased Canada Dry (the leading producer of mixers such as ginger ale) as well as Sunkist (the leader in the orange drink market). In 1986, after a disappointing experience in the business, Reynolds announced the sale of its soft drink operation to Britain's Cadbury Schweppes.

The power of the industry's Big Two would have gotten much greater if the companies had been allowed to proceed with deals announced in 1986. PepsiCo planned to purchase Seven-Up for $380 million, and Coca-Cola was ready to pay $470 million for Dr Pepper. Both mergers were blocked by the federal government for antitrust reasons. The domestic business of Seven-Up was instead purchased in a leveraged buyout by Hicks & Haas of Dallas, which had earlier acquired Dr Pepper in the same manner.

Coca-Cola did, however, go ahead with the acquisition of two of its largest independent bottlers for a combined price of more than $2 billion. The company then sold 51 percent of the bottling operation to the public through a stock offering. PepsiCo has also moved to increase its control of bottling. In 1989 the company spent $1.7 billion to acquire the bottling business of General Cinema.

In the late 1980s the cola war reached new levels of intensity. Coca-Cola and PepsiCo engaged in frequent price cutting and aggressive ad campaigns in the quest for market share. The results were ambiguous: Coca-Cola's share of the overall soft drink market expanded, yet PepsiCo's share of retail store sales continued to climb. In 1990 PepsiCo suffered a blow when Burger King announced it was switching to Coke products in its restaurants.

According to figures from analyst John C. Maxwell of Wheat First Securities, the market shares of the leading brands in 1989 were as follows:

1. Coke Classic	19.7%
2. Pepsi	17.8
3. Diet Coke	8.7
4. Diet Pepsi	5.7
5. Dr Pepper	4.4
6. Mountain Dew	3.6
7. Sprite	3.6
8. 7UP	3.0
9. Caffeine-free Diet Coke	2.4
10. Royal Crown Cola	1.6

The corporate totals were Coca-Cola 40.2 percent, PepsiCo 31.5 percent, Dr Pepper/Seven-Up 9.5 percent, Cadbury Schweppes 6.1 percent, and Royal Crown 2.8 percent.

ALCOHOLIC BEVERAGES

The production of intoxicating beverages has been an important U.S. industry since the earliest days of the country. Alcoholic beverage consumption reached a peak in the early 19th century, when the hard-edged pioneers of the West guzzled large quantities of whiskey.

German immigrants arriving in the middle of the century brought with them the brewing skills of Europe; before long, beer became the most popular drink among Americans. Consumption of hard liquor along with beer remained high enough to inspire a dogged temperance movement, which succeeded by 1919 in having the production of all forms of alcoholic beverages banned. If anything, Prohibition probably increased the demand for liquor, and after its repeal in 1933 the business boomed. Seagram was the first company to establish national liquor brands and thus secured a position at the top of the industry.

The first major shift in drinking habits came after World War II as many consumers switched from "brown goods" of the whiskey family to "white" drinks such as vodka and gin. Another upheaval began in the 1970s. Alcohol consumption stopped growing at its usual healthy rate, and large numbers of people switched from liquor to wine. The beer business remained healthy, but only because companies such as Miller introduced lower-calorie "light" brands. By the 1980s the talk was of the "new abstinence," and the most dramatic beverage growth was seen in sparkling water, of all things.

The industry was put on the defensive by a new temperance movement that succeeded in getting the drinking age increased to 21 in many parts of the country and that began seeking federal legislation to ban beer and wine ads from radio and television (the networks voluntarily prohibit commercials for liquor). Congress passed legislation requiring that health warnings be placed on all alcoholic beverages beginning in November 1990. While resisting restrictive laws, the industry has also jumped on the sobriety bandwagon by pushing less intoxicating sweet drinks such as wine coolers and even nonalcoholic beer and wine.

THE BEER BRAWL

Back in the 19th century most beer was consumed in taverns or by sending a youngster to the bar to fill a tin pail and bring it home. The beer was produced on the tavern's premises or in a nearby brewery. Producers gradually grew larger, but many brewers were wiped out by Prohibition. After its repeal the beer industry was dominated by small, regional, often family-owned brewing companies. A few companies such as Anheuser-Busch and Schlitz sold on a national basis, but the business remained a distinctly sleepy one.

The event that shook things up was the purchase of Miller Brewing by the tobacco giant Philip Morris in 1970. The aggressive marketers of Philip Morris instilled new life in what had been the seventh-ranked brewer by improving the quality of the product and launching the now famous "Miller Time" ad campaign. Picking up early on the increased calorie-consciousness of the population, the company led the way in the light segment with the introduction of Miller Lite.

Miller's aggressiveness propelled the company into second place behind Anheuser-Busch, which was forced to adopt similar marketing tactics. Anheuser-Busch brought out a light version of Budweiser, the number-one brand, along with a variety of other products across the price spectrum. By 1980 the two companies had established a solid hold over the industry, sharing 50 percent of the market between them. During the early 1980s Anheuser-Busch continued its climb toward its stated goal of a 40 percent share, while Miller faltered. The latter's flagship brand, Miller High Life, began sinking and was surpassed by the company's own Lite brand.

In the meantime there was an intensifying battle among the second tier of producers. Regional brewers, such as Heileman in the Midwest, began buying up their weaker brethren as consolidation appeared as the only alternative in a business beset by declining levels of demand. The Stroh Brewery Co. bought F. & M. Schaefer and Joseph Schlitz. Pabst acquired Olympia and was then itself the subject of a drawn out and complicated takeover battle. Heileman was purchased by Australia's Bond Corp. In late 1989 Coors offered to purchase Stroh's but later backed away from the deal because of Stroh's weak market position.

Industry leader Anheuser-Busch kept the heat on by competing in terms of price as well as quality and by moving quickly into the low-alcohol segment, bringing out a brand called LA (for low alcohol) in 1984. LA's appeal turned out to be fleeting, while Miller made a splash with its Genuine Draft. In the late 1980s Anheuser-Busch led the way as U.S. brewers rushed to exploit the new appeal of dry beer. Developed in Japan, dry beer has a lower sugar content and less aftertaste.

Competition has also been heightened by the increasing popularity of foreign brands such as Heineken, Molson, and Beck's. Imports rose from 1.1 percent of the U.S. market in 1975 to 5 percent in 1988 but then slipped to about 4.5 percent in 1989—the first decline after decades of growth. One of the great imported beer fads, Mexico's Corona, suffered an especially large drop in sales.

According to the trade newsletter *Beer Marketer's Insights*, the shares of the domestic beer market of the top U.S. producers in 1989 were as follows:

1. Anheuser-Busch	42.1%
2. Miller Brewing	21.8
3. Stroh Brewery Co.	9.6
4. Coors	9.2
5. Heileman	6.8

THE SOBERING PICTURE FOR LIQUOR

For much of its history, America was a hard-drinking country. Even Prohibition and the poor quality of much of the bootleg products did little to depress consumption levels. Tastes changed after World War II, thanks to Heublein's aggressive promotion of drinks such as Bloody Marys and screwdrivers that just happened to require the company's leading product, vodka.

Yet it took the health obsession of the 1970s to put a serious dent in liquor consumption. White wine or nonalcoholic beverages replaced scotch on the rocks and martinis as the status drinks. Brown goods of the whiskey family are on their way to becoming extinct as younger people's tastes change.

The industry's leaders have responded in several ways. First, they put more emphasis on premixed sweet and flavored drinks, such as Seagram's Captain Morgan Spiced Rum, which have been growing in popularity. They also moved further into the faster-growing wine business. Seagram, which already produced Paul Masson wines, purchased Coca-Cola's Wine Spectrum division in 1983 (later sold off), and in 1985 Brown-Forman Distillers acquired the leading company in the wine cooler business.

Aggressive advertising is also part of the plan. Britain's Guinness, best known for its stout and now a major force in the liquor industry through acquisitions of distillers in its home country and Schenley Industries in the United States, has employed bold "image" ads to promote Scotch as part of a young, hip lifestyle. Seagram has also sought to improve the image of liquor with an ad campaign arguing that the alcohol content of liquors is not disproportionately high in relation to beer and wine. Other producers such as Jack Daniel's (owned by Brown-Forman) went after new markets such as women who might be induced to switch over to harder drinks. To go along with the new image, Seagram in 1990 began national test marketing of a "light" whiskey product with one third less alcohol and one third fewer calories than traditional brown goods.

According to *Business Week* (June 25, 1990), the leading brands in 1989 were:

Brand	*Cases Sold (in millions)*
1. Bacardi rum	8.00
2. Smirnoff vodka	6.91
3. Seagram's 7 Crown	4.15
4. Popov vodka	3.83
5. Seagram's gin	3.75
6. Jim Beam bourbon	3.72
7. Canadian Mist	3.65
8. Jack Daniel's bourbon	3.55
9. Seagram's V.O.	2.56
10. DeKuyper cordials	2.42

The corporate market shares in 1989, according to the Impact Databank compiled by Shanken Communications, were:

Grand Metropolitan	17.2%
Seagram	13.6
Jim Beam	9.7
Brown-Forman	7.5
Hiram Walker	6.9

SOURING GRAPES FOR THE WINE BUSINESS

Until the 1930s wine production was an underdeveloped industry in the United States. In the years following the repeal of Prohibition the business began to grow, especially in California, where the industry was aided by the expert research conducted at the University of California at Davis. The liquor company Schenley (now owned by Britain's Guinness) bought two wineries in the state in 1939, and Seagram purchased Paul Masson in 1946.

But the real powerhouse in the industry was the operation established in 1933 by two brothers, Ernest and Julio Gallo. Through tireless marketing and bold modernization after the war, Gallo went on to become the giant of the industry and helped to create a significant national market for wine.

The industry took off like a rocket in the 1970s as people began switching from liquor, and even the likes of The Coca-Cola Company jumped in. By the early 1980s the bloom was off, due partly to a shift in tastes away from alcoholic beverages entirely and partly to rising import penetration. By 1982 shipments of U.S. wineries were flat after a decade of 10 percent average annual growth.

Just as the industry was worrying that it would end up in the same boat with the liquor business, salvation came in the form of a simple idea: wine mixed with citrus juices. These drinks, dubbed coolers, were invented in the 1970s by Californian Michael Crete to enliven beach parties. Crete eventually turned his idea into a business called California Cooler, which he sold to Brown-Forman for about $150 million. Other beverage companies such as Stroh, Seagram, and Gallo also jumped into wine coolers, and the business zoomed to more than $1 billion by the mid-1980s. Then, almost as quickly as it grew, the industry began to decline as many consumers lost their taste for the sweet and highly caloric product. A major victim was Matilda Bay, a cooler introduced by Philip Morris just as the market was beginning to slide.

Amid the changes in the wine market there have also been dramatic changes in the structure of the industry. In early 1987 Heublein (owned by RJR Nabisco) agreed to purchase Almaden Vineyards from National Distillers and shortly thereafter was itself sold to Britain's Grand Metropolitan. That same year Seagram sold most of its wine business—including Paul Masson and Taylor—to a new company called Vintners International.

By the late 1980s the entire $3 billion wine business was in the dumps. For the first time since the repeal of Prohibition there was a significant decline in sales, and profit margins were squeezed by rising grape prices and increased competition from low-cost imports. Vintners International, facing mounting losses, announced in 1990 that it planned to sell its Taylor unit. At the same time, a number of foreign winemakers began setting up operations in California, and domestic companies such as Gallo began to look for growth in higher-priced varietal rather than jug wines.

According to the Impact Databank compiled by Shanken Communications, the leading wine producers in 1989 were:

Gallo	27.4%
Grand Metropolitan	10.0
Vintners International	7.7
Canandaigua	5.9
Wine Group	5.5

LABOR RELATIONS

The most controversial labor issue in the soft drink industry was an international one. After workers at the Coca-Cola bottling operation in Guatemala organized a union in the 1970s, the organization suffered attacks from right-wing death squads, which resulted in the deaths of more than a dozen people. An international campaign led by the International Union of Food & Allied Workers Associations prompted The Coca-Cola Company to put pressure on its Guatemalan franchisee to see to it that the union's rights were recognized. There was some improvement in the situation, but the plant was closed in early 1984. The workers occupied the facility for more than a year, and then Coca-Cola arranged to keep the operation going under the control of a new set of investors.

Coca-Cola has frequently been charged in the United States with allowing migrant workers employed by its Minute Maid orange juice subsidiary to live in miserable conditions. In 1985 the company caused a controversy with American unions when it introduced a line of Coca-Cola clothes that were produced overseas. Following protests, the company agreed to switch to U.S. production for all clothes sold in the United States.

The main labor controversy in the beer industry has concerned Coors. Unions and civil rights groups have accused the company of discriminatory hiring practices and of intimidating employees with lie detector tests. The Brewery Workers Union went on strike at Coors in 1977 over these issues, and the AFL-CIO organized a boycott of the company's products. After the strike stretched out for more than 18 months, Coors workers voted to decertify the union. The AFL-CIO finally called off its boycott in 1987 in exchange for a promise by Coors not to interfere with union organizing drives.

Other brewing production employees, such as those at Anheuser-Busch, are members of the Teamsters union. Anheuser-Busch suffered a three-month strike in 1976.

The United Farm Workers (UFW) scored a major victory in 1967 when it signed a contract with Gallo. But in 1973 the giant winemaker made what the UFW charged was a sweetheart deal with the Teamsters union. The UFW, after challenging an election that certified the Teamsters as the representative for Gallo workers, launched a national boycott of the company's products that lasted until 1978. In 1980 other workers at Gallo and at United Vintners represented by the Distillery, Wine and Allied Workers union staged a 17-day strike, the first in the union's 35-year history. In 1986 the union agreed to wage concessions but went on strike against a dozen wineries to resist industry efforts to reduce benefits and change work rules. The walkout ended abruptly after eight weeks when the wineries threatened to bring in permanent replacement workers.

LEADING COMPANIES

Anheuser-Busch, whose Budweiser brand has long been the country's leading beer, is by far the leading brewing company in America. Built by Adolphus Busch in the late 19th century and run ever since by members of the Busch family, Anheuser-Busch weathered a strong challenge from Miller Brewing in the 1970s and emerged all the stronger for it. Under the leadership of August Busch III, the company modernized its marketing and management techniques and made some diversification moves. Thanks to a strong line of beers across the price spectrum, Busch steadily gained market share, reaching and surpassing its stated goal of 40 percent. In 1987 the company was shaken by a scandal involving several executives who allegedly received kickbacks.

The Coca-Cola Company was the pioneer in the soft drink market and for many years had a commanding lead over the business. The company jealously guards the secret formula for Coke's flavoring ingredients, code-named Merchandise 7X, going so far as to abandon its operation in India when a court in that country ordered the company to hand over the secret to the local bottlers. The company branched out into other parts of the beverage business in 1960 when it acquired Minute Maid, the pioneer in the frozen orange juice field. The company bought Taylor Wines in 1977 and developed a sizable presence in the wine business. But the operation did not meet the company's profitability standards, and the business was sold to Seagram in 1983. Coca-Cola got into the entertainment field through the purchase of Columbia Pictures in 1982. But the soft drink maker was not happy in the movie business either, so Columbia was sold to Sony in 1989. The company scored a big success with Diet Coke in 1982 but was forced into an embarrassing position in 1985 when a change in the formula of Coke proved a flop.

Coors is the most controversial of the major beer companies. Founded by Adolph Coors in the 1870s, the ultraconservative members of the Coors family running the company came into conflict with unions and civil rights groups in the 1970s. The company's product, produced in a single brewery in Golden, Colorado, for years held a kind of cult status in many parts of the country. This was in part because the beer was not sold east of the Mississippi, a marketing policy necessitated by the fact that Coors, being unpasteurized and containing no preservatives, had a limited shelf life. The management of the company, which introduced Coors Light in 1978 and began national distribution, passed in 1985 to a new generation of Coors family members. In late 1989 Coors agreed to buy the beer assets of Stroh, but the Colorado brewer later put the deal on hold as Stroh's market position declined.

Dr Pepper/Seven-Up Companies was the result of a 1988 marriage of two veteran but struggling beverage firms that had both been taken over by leveraged buyout firm Hicks & Haas in separate deals in 1986. Dr Pepper has long been a favorite in the south and has a respectable following elsewhere in the country. In 1980 it overtook 7UP as the third-ranked soft drink but was later surpassed by Diet Coke. The Dr Pepper Company purchased mixer maker Canada Dry in 1982 but sold the business to R. J. Reynolds in 1984. The firm was taken private in a $512 million leveraged buyout in 1983. Family-owned until 1967, Seven-Up Co. doggedly promoted its lemon-lime product as an alternative to the colas. Other companies brought out their own lemon-lime products in the 1960s, but it was not until the 1980s—after Seven-Up was purchased by tobacco company Philip Morris—that a counterattack was launched in the form of a campaign highlighting the absence of caffeine in 7UP. An attempt by PepsiCo to purchase Seven-Up was thwarted by federal regulators in 1986.

Gallo is the behemoth of the wine industry. Founded by brothers Ernest and Julio Gallo in the 1930s, the secretive privately held firm has led the way in the modernization of wine production in the United States. The Gallos have always had a good sense of changing tastes. They developed Thunderbird for the ghetto market, Boone's Farm for the late 1960s "pop wine" boom, and in the 1970s started placing greater emphasis on higher-quality table wines. In 1985 they brought out Bartles & Jaymes, which became the leading wine cooler. During the late 1980s Gallo fought the slump in the industry by putting more emphasis on upscale varietal wines, and in 1989 the company announced it was getting out of the skid-row wine market.

The **G. Heileman Brewing Co.** of La Crosse, Wisconsin, ranked 31st among U.S. brewers in 1960, went on to acquire a series of weaker competitors and claw its way up to fourth place by the mid-1980s. Chairman Russell Cleary fought Anheuser-Busch and Miller in its midwestern stronghold while expanding nationally. The company engaged in a long battle for Pabst Brewing, from which it ended up with some of that company's assets. In the mid-1980s it bucked the tide of overcapacity in the industry by announcing plans to build a new brewery in Milwaukee. Heileman itself succumbed to a takeover move in 1987 when it was acquired by Bond Corp. of Australia.

The roots of **Heublein** date back to the 1870s in Connecticut. The company bottled the first prepared cocktails in the 1890s and survived Prohibition by pushing A-1 Steak Sauce. Heublein bought the rights to Smirnoff vodka in 1939 at a time when the drink was largely unknown in the United States. Heublein skillfully created a market for the stuff after the war with promotion of new mixed drinks containing vodka and an ad campaign stating that vodka left the drinker "breathless." The company got into the wine business with the purchase of United Vintners in 1969 and then took a plunge in fast food with the acquisition of Kentucky Fried Chicken in 1971. In 1982 Heublein was acquired by cigarette maker R. J. Reynolds. Five years later RJR sold the company to Britain's Grand Metropolitan for $1.2 billion.

PepsiCo, the parent company of Pepsi-Cola, has evolved from a perennial also-ran into a serious challenger to industry leader Coca-Cola. Through savvy advertising and risks such as entering the caffeine-free market, the company has risen to within a few points of Coca-Cola's market share. Chief executive Donald Kendall began diversifying the company in the 1960s, buying Frito-Lay foods as well as businesses outside the food and beverage field. During the mid-1980s Kendall began shedding acquisitions of the latter sort, including North American Van Lines and Wilson Sporting Goods.

Philip Morris, the leading cigarette producer, entered the beverage field in 1970 with the purchase of ailing Miller Brewing Co. The master marketers at Philip Morris shook up the 115-year-old beermaker and brought out the hugely successful Lite beer, thus making Miller one of the great Cinderella stories of the 1970s. The company lost its luster during the 1980s, largely as a result of a drop in popularity in the flagship brand Miller High Life. Philip Morris tried to work the same earlier magic with Seven-Up after the company was acquired in 1978, but it was not to be. The lemon-lime drink continued to lose market share, and a caffeine-free cola called Like, which Seven-Up introduced in 1982, never received wide acceptance. In 1986, after an attempt to sell Seven-Up to PepsiCo was blocked by federal antitrust regulators, the domestic operations of Seven-Up were sold to Hicks & Haas. Matilda Bay, Philip Morris' late entry into the wine cooler business, was a flop.

Royal Crown has been the leading innovator in the soft drink field but has not had the resources to market in a manner comparable to Coca-Cola and Pepsi. In the early 1960s the company brought out Diet Rite, the first national diet soft drink, and in 1980 it introduced the first caffeine-free cola, RC 100. In 1984 the company was taken private by financier Victor Posner.

Seagram, the largest producer of liquor in the world, is based in Montreal but does a majority of its business in the United States. Seagram's distilling business was built by brothers Sam and Allan Bronfman beginning in the 1920s. Much of their Canadian-produced liquor ended up in the

United States during Prohibition, and after repeal the company kept on selling in grand proportions. The company developed the first national liquor brands with the introduction of Seagram's 5 Crown and 7 Crown, blended whiskies that were lighter and smoother than the rye and bourbon Americans previously drank. Under the autocratic control of "Mr. Sam" Bronfman, the company kept its control of the brown goods market but was slow to follow the move to white goods such as vodka and gin. Sam's son Edgar, who took over in 1971, expanded Seagram's presence in the wine business by buying Coca-Cola's Wine Spectrum subsidiary in 1983 and ventured into the soft drink business with the introduction of a line of mixers in 1983. Seagram enjoys substantial revenue from its 22 percent ownership of Du Pont, which it ended up with as a result of an unsuccessful battle with the chemical giant for the Conoco petroleum company in 1981. Day-to-day control of the company has been passed to Edgar Bronfman, Jr., who has

INDUSTRY DATA

Alcoholic Beverages	*1989*	*1988*	*1987*
Value of shipments	$21.5 billion	$20.8 billion	$20.2 billion
Total employment	51,300	52,600	53,900
Import penetration	12.1%	13.0%	13.4%

Soft Drinks	*1989*	*1988*	*1987*
Value of shipments	$25.2 billion	$23.7 billion	$22.0 billion
Total employment	91,100	93,300	95,300
Import penetration	0.9%	0.8%	0.7%

Source: U.S. Department of Commerce.

sought to bolster the company by emphasizing overseas sales, especially in the Far East, and nonalcoholic beverages. In 1988 Seagram moved into the orange juice business with the $1.2 billion purchase of Tropicana Products from Beatrice. Much of the company's wine business was sold off in a 1987 leveraged buyout that resulted in a new firm called Vintners International.

Stroh Brewery Co., a family-owned and -operated business since its founding in the 1850s, emerged in the 1970s as one of the nation's fastest-growing beer producers. Under the leadership of Peter Stroh, the company acquired F. & M. Schaefer in 1981 and Joseph Schlitz Brewing Co.—once the country's largest beermaker—in 1982. Known for its "fire brewing" process, the company has expanded its national advertising and distribution and entered new product markets such as low-alcohol beer and wine coolers. In late 1989 Stroh agreed to sell its beer assets to Coors, but the Colorado brewer later put the deal on hold as Stroh's condition in the market deteriorated.

SOURCE GUIDE

Leading Stock Analysts and Experts

Michael Bellas, president of Beverage Marketing Corp., New York City.

Emanuel Goldman, analyst at Paine Webber.

Gomberg, Fredrikson & Associates, San Francisco-based consultants to the wine industry.

John C. Maxwell, Jr., veteran analyst now at Wheat First Securities, Richmond, Virginia.

Jesse Meyers, publisher of the newsletter *Beverage Digest*, Old Greenwich, Connecticut.

Marvin Shanken, editor and publisher of *Impact* and *Market Watch*, leading newsletters for the alcoholic beverage industry, New York City.

R. S. Weinberg & Associates, a consultant to the beer industry, based in St. Louis.

Trade Associations and Unions

Beer Institute, 1225 I Street NW, Washington, DC 20005. Tel.: (202) 737–2337.

Distilled Spirits Council of the U.S., 1250 I Street NW, Washington, DC 20005. Tel.: (202) 628–3544.

Distillery, Wine and Allied Workers International Union, 66 Grand Avenue, Englewood, NJ 07631. Tel.: (201) 569–9212.

National Soft Drink Association, 1101 16th Street NW, Washington, DC 20036. Tel.: (202) 463–6732.

Wine Institute, 165 Post Street, San Francisco, CA 94108. Tel.: (415) 986–0878.

Data Sources and Directories

Beverage Industry Annual Manual, directory and data (Cleveland: Edgell Communications).

Brewers Almanac, an annual statistical volume (Washington, D.C.: Beer Institute).

Brewer's Digest publishes an annual directory issue (Chicago: Siebel Publishing).

Business Week publishes an annual survey of liquor brands selling 500,000 cases or more, in June.

Hereld's 5,000—The Directory of Leading U.S. Food, Confectionary and Beverage Manufacturers, published quarterly (Hamden, Conn.: Hereld Organization).

Impact Yearbook, annual directory and statistical compilation (New York: M. Shanken Communications).

Jobson's Wine Marketing Handbook and *Jobson's Liquor Handbook*, annual volumes of data (New York: Jobson Publishing).

Modern Brewery Age Blue Book, an annual directory and compilation of statistics (Norwalk, Conn.: Business Journals Inc.).

National Beverage Marketing Directory, annual (New York: Beverage Marketing Corp.).

Sales Survey of the Soft Drink Industry, published annually (Washington, D.C.: National Soft Drink Association).

Who Owns Whom in the U.S. Food, Confectionery & Beverage Manufacturing Industry, quarterly (Hartford, Conn.: SIC Publishing).

Trade Publications

Beer Marketer's Insight, semimonthly.

Beverage Digest, semimonthly.

Beverage Industry, monthly.

Beverage World, monthly.

Brewer's Digest, monthly.

Impact, semimonthly.

Market Watch, quarterly.

Modern Brewery Age, weekly.

Wines & Vines, monthly.

Books and Reports

Cahalan, Don; Ira H. Cisin; and Helen M. Crossley. *American Drinking Practices*. New Brunswick, N.J.: Rutgers University Center of Alcohol Studies, 1969.

Cavanagh, John, and Frederick Clairmonte. *Alcoholic Beverages: Dimensions of Corporate Power*. New York: St. Martin's Press, 1985.

Clairmonte, Frederick, and John Cavanagh. *Merchants of Drink: Transnational Control of World Beverages*. Penang, Malaysia: Third World Network, 1988.

Dietz, Lawrence. *Soda Pop: The History, Advertising, Art and Memorabilia of Soft Drinks in America*. New York: Simon & Schuster, 1973.

Enrico, Roger, and Jesse Kornbluth. *The Other Guy Blinked: How Pepsi Won the Cola Wars*. New York: Bantam Books, 1986.

Jacobson, Michael; Robert Atkins; and George Hacker. *The Booze Merchants*. Washington, D.C.: Center for Science in the Public Interest, 1983.

Kahn, E. J., Jr. *The Big Drink: The Story of Coca-Cola*. New York: Random House, 1960.

Louis, J. C., and Harvey Z. Yazijian. *The Cola Wars*. New York: Everest House, 1980.

Newman, Peter. *King of the Castle* (on the Bronfmans and Seagram). New York: Atheneum, 1979.

Oliver, Thomas. *The Real Coke, The Real Story*. New York: Random House, 1986.

CHAPTER 7

CIGARETTES

The cigarette industry is one of the most controversial and most profitable areas of commerce. For decades its products have been denounced as health risks, yet Americans still consume more than 500 billion cigarettes a year. The business is dominated by six companies, which have been trying since the early 1970s to stimulate growth by introducing a dazzling array of new brands, ranging from "designer" cigarettes to noname generics. Despite repeated predictions of doom the cigarette industry remains very much alive. Yet the Big Six have hedged their bets, investing large sums in nontobacco enterprises.

TOBACCO'S ROAD

The tobacco industry in America began with the leaves that some of the natives of the New World presented to Columbus (who initially thought them worthless). The production of the plant that the Indians loved to smoke became an important enterprise in the colonies and remained so after independence. George Washington and Thomas Jefferson were among the prominent tobacco growers of their day.

For a long time the main form of tobacco consumption in America was chewing, with cigars and pipes being common only among the more "respectable" strata of society. The smoking of hand-rolled cigarettes gained some popularity in the first half of the 19th century, but that habit remained socially suspect.

The rise of the cigarette as the dominant tobacco product was ushered in by the development of large-scale rolling machines in the 1880s. One man who recognized the potential of mechanization and mass production was James Buchanan ("Buck") Duke, the young proprietor of a tobacco enterprise in North Carolina. Duke signed James Bonsack, the inventor of one of the more promising rolling machines, to an airtight contract. Duke used his control over Bonsack's machines to take over most of the tobacco industry and in the process turn the United States into a country of cigarette smokers.

A ruthless competitor, Duke either drove his rivals out of business by undercutting their prices or else seized control of their companies through purchase of majority interests in their stock. By the end of the century Duke had turned his American Tobacco Company into what outsiders called the Tobacco Trust, which controlled some 90 percent of the cigarette production—and much of the rest of the tobacco industry—in the entire country.

Duke soon turned his sights abroad, plotting an invasion of the British market. Knowing the trust's power, the independent producers in Britain banded together in defense, creating the Imperial Tobacco Co. They then fought Duke by threatening to invade his comfortable domain in the United States. The enemies decided cooperation was more prudent than all-out competition. They agreed not to poach on one another's markets and set up the British-American Tobacco Co. to sell jointly to the rest of the world.

Buck Duke was on his way to achieving quite literally a monopoly of the U.S. tobacco industry, but the sentiments of the Progressive Era eventually undermined his empire. In 1911 the Supreme Court ordered the dismemberment of the Tobacco Trust into a number of independent firms, including American Tobacco, R. J. Reynolds, Liggett & Myers, and Lorillard (the latter three being companies that the Trust had earlier gobbled up).

As separate companies these four continued to dominate the industry. The popularity of cigarette smoking increased rapidly during and after World War I, and the big producers sought to create national brands. The first product to fit this description was Reynolds' Camels, introduced in 1913. American's Lucky Strikes followed suit beginning in 1916. Liggett's Chesterfields completed what stood as the Big Three of the business for more than 30 years.

SELLING THE IMAGE

The success of the leading brands was in large part a result of the heavy advertising of the tobacco companies. Slogans such as "I'd walk a mile for a Camel" and "Reach for a Lucky instead of a sweet" were constantly drummed into the national consciousness and resulted in increased sales. Even today, despite the ban on radio and television commercials, cigarettes are the country's most heavily advertised product. More than $2 billion a year is spent on appealing to smokers and potential smokers.

The reasons for the heavy promotion are, first, the fact that there is basically very little product differentiation among the various little white tubes filled with leaves; winning over a customer in most cases means selling the image that the producer chooses to associate with a particular brand. The other reason is that cigarette companies are peddling a product that is not terribly healthy, and there is always the danger that people may start taking the health warnings too seriously if their habits are not constantly reinforced by ads.

Concocting illusory product differentiation and responding to the health alarms have been the twin preoccupations of the cigarette industry in the postwar period, especially since the 1952 publication of an article in *Reader's Digest* that alerted people to the dangers of smoking. Although there had been some earlier reports of the problem, it was that article and follow-ups in the magazine that received enormous media attention and generated public concern. Cigarette sales began to drop for the first time, and the industry began to worry.

But it also found an appropriate—and lucrative—way to respond. The manufacturers started promoting filter-tip cigarettes as a safer version of what were already known as "coffin nails." Existing but obscure filter brands were given new life, along with newly developed filter products such as Winston, which went on to become one of the perennially best-selling brands in the United States.

The greatest marketing coup of the era was undoubtedly the relaunching of a minor brand called Marlboro by Philip Morris, a cigarette maker founded in Britain in the 1840s (and Americanized in 1919) that grew into one of the leading firms. Working with advertising wizard Leo Burnett, Philip Morris turned what was previously a "woman's brand" into a macho product by associating it with that quintessential image of American virility—the cowboy. The evocation of "Marlboro Country" (the rugged West) created a giant success for the brand and eventually helped Philip Morris attain the largest market share of the cigarette producers.

ON THE DEFENSIVE

Having survived the *Reader's Digest* assault of the 1950s, the tobacco industry was able to breathe easily until the early 1960s, when the health controversy broke out once again. In 1962 the British Royal College of Physicians published a study arguing that smoking was unequivocally linked to lung cancer and other diseases. The U.S. Surgeon General followed suit in 1964 with a report that scared large numbers of smokers into giving up the habit, at least temporarily, and prompted Congress to pass legislation requiring warning labels to be printed on every package of cigarettes.

The Surgeon General's report also brought about a public policy debate on smoking that continues to the present. Anti-smoking forces gained strength after 1964 and succeeded in getting Congress to ban cigarette advertising on radio and television beginning in 1971. In the 1970s federal transportation agencies established rules requiring separate smoking sections in airplanes and intercity buses.

President Carter's secretary of health, education and welfare, Joseph Califano, launched a major federal assault on smoking in 1978. But intense pressure from tobacco-state politicians such as Jesse Helms of North Carolina swayed Carter and contributed to Califano's removal in 1979. During the Reagan administration Surgeon General Dr. C. Everett Koop spoke out strongly on the hazards of cigarettes and argued that smoking, rather than occupational health hazards, was the main cause of cancer among American workers. He also issued a report labeling smoking an addiction and equating nicotine with heroin. A federal ban on smoking on commercial airliners during flights of two hours or less took effect in 1988. The following year Congress passed a smoking ban on all domestic flights (except those beginning or ending in Hawaii or Alaska that lasted more than six hours). At other levels of government, hundreds of municipalities have passed laws limiting smoking in public places or workplaces. Increasing numbers of companies have prohibited or restricted smoking in their offices.

In addition, the controversy over cigarette advertising continues. In 1985 the American Medical Association's policymaking body voted to support a ban on the advertising of tobacco products in any medium. Efforts continue to be made in Congress toward this same end. In 1990 Massachusetts senator Edward Kennedy introduced a bill to create an agency with the power to regulate tobacco along the lines of the Food and Drug Administration.

The industry has fought back with advertising campaigns noting the economic power of smokers and promotional efforts in which restaurants, hotels, and other establishments are enlisted to make smokers feel welcome. Yet the momentum seems to be on the other side. In 1990 Reynolds was forced to cancel a brand aimed at black smokers amid a wave of protest led by Health and Human Services secretary Louis Sullivan. Reynolds and other companies have also come under attack for marketing efforts that critics say are meant to appeal to children. The state of California has launched an aggressive antismoking campaign financed by cigarette taxes, and a group called the Tobacco Divestment Project began a drive to get institutions to rid their portfolios of tobacco company securities.

On another front, during the early 1980s the cigarette industry had to confront a rapid rise in the number of product liability suits brought against it. Despite the tilt toward plaintiffs in that general area of law, the industry has used armies of lawyers and unabashedly aggressive legal tactics to wear down many of its adversaries even before cases come to trial. The tobacco companies have been no less successful in those cases that do end up before a jury. In 1986 a federal appeals court ruled that the warning labels on cigarette packages protected the industry from claims that consumers were not adequately alerted to the dangers of smoking.

Yet in the late 1980s the industry's unbroken winning streak came to an end. In 1988 a federal judge declared that the evidence brought out in a trial showed that the industry had engaged in a "conspiracy vast in its scope, devious in its purpose and devastating in its results" to mislead the country about the dangers of smoking. The jury in the case did not, however, find the defendants—Liggett, Lorillard, and Philip Morris—guilty of conspiracy but did find Liggett liable in the death of Rose Cipollone from lung cancer. The jury found that the company had failed to alert smokers to the health risks of cigarettes in the period before the federal warning label started to be used. The verdict, which involved a modest award of $400,000 to Cipollone's husband, failed to act as an inducement to more lawsuits. In early 1990 a federal appeals court overturned the verdict and ordered a new trial because of improper jury instructions by the judge. At the same time the appeals court opened the door to suits covering the period after warning labels began to be used.

SELLING THROUGH THE STORM

The tobacco industry has stood firm in the face of the criticism. On the health issue the industry has tirelessly argued that there is no absolutely certain causal link between smoking and lung cancer and other diseases. The cigarette companies no longer imply, as they did back in the 1920s and 1930s, that smoking is healthy; they simply shield themselves behind the agnostic statement that no one knows for sure whether cigarettes are dangerous. Until it is proved to their satisfaction that there is a cancer link, they are perfectly willing to go on selling their product.

And a profitable product it is. Cigarettes provide one of the highest returns on sales of any industry, and most of the six major U.S. producers continue to generate healthy earnings despite the stagnant level of demand.

One of the sources of prosperity for some time was the low-tar-and-nicotine segment of the market—what the industry refers to as high-filtration or "hi-fi" brands. In the 1970s this market did for the industry what filters accomplished in the 1950s. In the intense battle for market share, the industry began producing dozens of new hi-fi as well as full-flavor (i.e., high-tar-and-nicotine) brands as segmentation became the rule of the day.

A bolder step was taken by Reynolds in 1987 when it introduced a new brand called Premier, which was dubbed the first smokeless cigarette. The product passed warm air through tobacco rather than burning it, thus producing only small amounts of smoke and ash. In theory Premier solved the problem of passive smoking (the exposure to harmful substances that occurs when one breathes the smoke produced by someone else's cigarette), but it did not go over very well with smokers themselves. Many people likened smoking Premier to inhaling fumes from burning plastic. Test marketing of the product was suspended after several months. Despite Reynolds' flop, reports began to emerge in 1989 that rival Philip Morris was developing a very-low-nicotine brand.

During the past 15 years the industry has tried almost every imaginable variation and gimmick to stimulate sales. These ranged from "prestige" brands such as Philip Morris' Players and Reynolds' "designer" brand Ritz (emblazoned with the Yves St. Laurent name) down to the generic products that were pushed heavily by Liggett beginning in 1980. To respond to the popularity of generics, other producers began offering packages containing 25 or 30 rather than 20 cigarettes for the same price; they also created discount brands priced to be competitive with the generics. By 1989 discount cigarettes accounted for about 15 percent of the market. Some of the other responses to Liggett's initiative were not so benign. In 1990 the company won a $149 million judgment against Brown & Williamson for engaging in anticompetitive pricing aimed at discouraging Liggett from continuing with its sale of generics. However, that award was later thrown out by a federal judge.

The biggest challenge for the industry in recent years was to recover from the drop in demand brought about by the doubling (to 16 cents a pack) of federal excise taxes that took effect in 1983. This first rise in levies since 1951 raised the price of a pack to more than $1 in major cities. Many state excise taxes have also been rising.

Cigarette consumption has been declining, but higher prices—along with export growth, especially to the Third World and the Soviet Union—have allowed the industry to continue increasing its aggregate revenues. The battle for position among the six major producers has remained intense. The biggest success has been Philip Morris, which passed longtime leader Reynolds in 1983. In 1989, according to the annual *Business Week* survey (February 19, 1990), the rankings by market share were as follows:

1. Philip Morris	41.9%
2. R. J. Reynolds	28.5
3. Brown & Williamson	11.4
4. Lorillard	8.0
5. American Brands	7.0
6. Liggett	3.2

Although the cigarette business remains attractive for the moment, the leading producers are hedging their bets. Actually, the diversification began after the Surgeon General's 1964 bombshell. American Tobacco got into biscuits and bourbon, and in 1970 changed its name to American Brands. Reynolds bought businesses involved in food, shipping, and packaging; in 1970 it, too, took "Tobacco" out of its name and replaced it with "Industries." Philip Morris bought Miller Brewing and Seven-Up.

More recently the two industry leaders have taken additional giant steps into the food business: Reynolds bought Nabisco Brands for $4.9 billion and took the name RJR Nabisco. Philip Morris purchased General Foods for $5.7 billion and Kraft for $13 billion. Nonetheless, cigarettes continue to be their biggest moneymakers.

In 1988 the top management of RJR Nabisco, particularly chief executive F. Ross Johnson, decided that those profits could be used to meet the interest costs in a leveraged buyout of the firm. Johnson's $18 billion bid, made in partnership with Shearson Lehman Hutton, was topped by the investment firm of Kohlberg, Kravis, Roberts, & Co. which ended up paying $25 billion—the largest deal ever—to take the company private.

LABOR RELATIONS

Beginning with the Tobacco Trust, the cigarette industry was not a great friend of organized labor. The Tobacco Workers International Union (TWIU), formed at the turn of the century, had its main organizing successes with smaller producers. It was not until after the Supreme Court ruled favorably on the constitutionality of the National Labor Relations Act in 1937 that several of the major companies signed with the TWIU. R. J. Reynolds held out and remains nonunion to this day. The tobacco company dismissed 12 percent of its workers in 1989, several months after parent company RJR Nabisco was taken private in a leveraged buyout.

A more radical alternative to the TWIU was chartered by the Committee for Industrial Organization (CIO) in 1937. The union, which eventually took the name of the Food, Tobacco, Agricultural and Allied Workers Union (FTA), concentrated on organizing agricultural workers. The FTA faced strong opposition to its attempt to bring black and white workers together in one organizational structure, as opposed to the segregated locals formed by unions such as the TWIU. The FTA was expelled from the CIO in 1949 because of Communist party influence in the union, which ended up merging with the Distributive, Processing and Office Workers of America.

The ranks of cigarette production workers have declined steadily in recent years as a result of mechanization and plant closings by the weaker producers. The number of hourly employees in the industry in 1989 was about 22,000.

LEADING COMPANIES

American Brands is the descendant of the company that Buck Duke used to corner the tobacco business in the late 19th century. Divested (by a 1911 Supreme Court ruling) of the other cigarette companies it had acquired, American went on to produce Lucky Strikes, one of the top national brands for many years. American was slow to jump on the filter bandwagon in the 1950s and ended up losing a major chunk of its market share. Yet it remained profitable in its less dominant role in the industry. The company made major moves into non-tobacco businesses in the 1960s and 1970s, acquiring companies such as Jim Beam Distilling, Swingline staplers, and Franklin Life Insurance. In 1988 the company successfully defeated a takeover attempt by E-II Holdings through the use of the Pac-Man defense (i.e., acquiring the predator).

Brown & Williamson (B&W) has been a subsidiary of British-American Tobacco (now BAT Industries) since 1927. B&W had a big success with Kool menthols but remains one of the least exciting companies in the industry. The parent company is the world's largest cigarette maker, with revenues of $14 billion and sales operations around the world. It began diversifying in the 1960s, buying cosmetics companies, department stores such as Saks Fifth Avenue, and other businesses.

Liggett Group (formerly Liggett & Myers) began as a snuff manufacturer in the 1820s. In 1899 it was swallowed up by the Tobacco Trust and reemerged in 1911. Its major brand for many years was Chesterfield, one of the three leaders along with Camels and Lucky Strikes. After World War II the company began a steady slide to last place among the major producers. Liggett showed some renewed life in the 1980s, when it led the push into generics. The company was acquired by Grand Metropolitan of Britain in 1980 and then sold to New York investor Bennett LeBow in 1986. Liggett's parent company changed its name to Brooke Group in 1990.

Lorillard is the country's oldest tobacco company, with its origins back in 1760. The company was part of the Tobacco Trust from 1899 to 1911. It enjoyed some success in the 1950s, thanks to Kent, one of the first filter cigarettes, and in the 1970s, thanks to several low-tar brands. The company was acquired by Loews Corp. in 1968.

Philip Morris, one of the leading U.S. marketers, has its roots in a London cigar and cigarette maker established in the 1840s. The company entered the U.S. market in 1902 and was taken over by American shareholders in 1919. Thanks to the phenomenally successful relaunching of Marlboro in the mid-1950s, the company rose to the top ranks of the tobacco industry and took the number-one spot in market share in 1983. A favorite of Wall Street, Philip Morris also turned Miller Brewing, which it bought in 1970, into the country's second-largest brewer. In 1981 the company outmaneuvered R. J. Reynolds to purchase a 22 percent share of Rothmans International, the tobacco arm of the South African-based Rembrandt Group. In 1985 Philip Morris purchased General Foods for nearly $6 billion; three years later it spent $13 billion to acquire Kraft. The company has worked hard to overcome the image problems associated with tobacco by spending large sums for cultural and artistic donations.

R. J. Reynolds, the king of the North Carolina tobacco business, emerged from the Tobacco Trust in 1911 and turned Camel into the country's first national brand. The company led the way to the filter era with the introduction of Winston, still the number-two seller, in 1954. Reynolds began diversifying in the 1960s, buying companies such as Chun King foods, Del Monte, and Sea-Land shipping. In 1982 it bought Heublein and in 1985 Nabisco Brands. Confident in the future of the cigarette industry, Reynolds spent $1 billion in the early 1980s constructing the world's largest and most modern cigarette factory—with an annual capacity of 5 billion packs—near Winston-Salem, North Carolina. In 1987 the company, renamed RJR Nabisco, agreed to sell Heublein to Grand Metropolitan for $1.2 billion. The following year chief executive F. Ross Johnson attempted a leveraged buyout of the company but was outbid by Kohlberg, Kravis, Roberts, & Co. which paid

$25 billion to take the company private. In 1989 the company withdrew its highly touted "smokeless" Premier brand from the market in the face of unfavorable consumer response, and in early 1990 it was forced to cancel a brand aimed at black smokers amid a wave of protest led by Health and Human Services secretary Louis Sullivan.

INDUSTRY DATA

Cigarettes	*1989*	*1988*	*1987*
Value of shipments	$20.4 billion	$19.2 billion	$17.4 billion
Total employment	30,000	31,200	32,000
Import penetration	0.1%	0.1%	0.1%

Source: U.S. Department of Commerce.

SOURCE GUIDE

Leading Stock Analysts and Experts

Marc Cohen, analyst at Sanford C. Bernstein.

Emanuel Goldman, analyst at Paine Webber.

John C. Maxwell, Jr., veteran analyst now at Wheat First Securities in Richmond, Virginia.

Trade Associations and Unions

Bakery, Confectionery and Tobacco Workers International Union, 1041 Connecticut Avenue, Kensington, MD 20895. Tel.: (301) 933–8600.

Tobacco Institute, 1875 I Street NW, Washington, DC 20006. Tel.: (202) 457–4800.

Data Sources and Directories

Business Week publishes an annual survey of cigarette industry market shares by brand and by company, in January or February.

Tobacco Industry Profile, an annual statistical publication (Washington, D.C.: Tobacco Institute).

World Tobacco Directory, an annual volume listing manufacturers, dealers, associations, and others in the industry (Redhill, Surrey, England: International Trade Publications).

Online Database

SMOKING AND HEALTH (Rockville, Md.: U.S. National Institute of Health; available via DIALOG).

Trade Publications

Tobacco Industry Litigation Reporter, semimonthly.

Tobacco International, fortnightly.

Tobacco Reporter, monthly.

Books and Reports

Finger, William R., ed. *The Tobacco Industry in Transition*. Lexington, Mass.: Lexington Books, 1981.

Sobel, Robert. *They Satisfy: The Cigarette in American Life*. Garden City, N.Y.: Anchor Press, 1978.

Taylor, Peter. *The Smoke Ring: Tobacco, Money and Multinational Politics*. New York: Pantheon Books, 1984.

White, Larry C. *Merchants of Death: The American Tobacco Industry*. New York: William Morrow, 1988.

CHAPTER 8

DRUGS AND HEALTH CARE

Over the past few decades, health care has emerged as one of the largest spheres of activity in the United States. By the end of the 1980s more than 11 percent of GNP was devoted to the treatment of illness. Of the estimated $600 billion spent in 1989, the largest share (some $230 billion) went to hospital care.

From a strictly commercial point of view, the main business involved in health care has traditionally been the production of drugs, which by 1989 was a thriving $47 billion industry, yet one tarnished by a long list of products that turned out to be harmful. In recent years private enterprise has also been expanding its presence in health care by taking over hospitals and other institutions from the public and nonprofit sectors. What has emerged is a "medical-industrial complex" that is exercising ever more influence over the practice of medicine.

FROM SNAKE OIL TO ANTIBIOTICS

The use of botanical substances in the treatment of illness dates back to early civilizations. Apothecary shops have been in existence in Europe for at least 900 years. While some traditional herbal remedies were effective, treatment was often a hit-or-miss proposition.

Modern pharmacology might be said to begin with the English physician Edward Jenner, who in 1796 discovered a way to vaccinate people against smallpox. In the early 19th century researchers learned how to isolate drugs such as morphine and quinine from plants. But it was many decades before drug production started to become scientific.

In the interim, traditional pharmacy was becoming more commercial. The first U.S. drug manufacturing operation was established in Carlisle, Pennsylvania, in 1778 to supply medicines to George Washington's troops. The industry that developed in the 19th century was often less than respectable. For decades it was dominated by so-called patent medicine producers, who sold a variety of extracts, tinctures, syrups, and other concoctions. (Actually very few of these products were patented, since that would have required disclosure of their contents. They are more properly designated as proprietary drugs.)

The patent medicine men made elaborate claims for their products, often listing on the label dozens of ailments that would supposedly be cured quickly and cheaply. Some of the nostrums were merely ineffective solutions made up mainly of water. Yet others contained quantities of addictive substances, such as opium, or were poisonous.

By making their pitch directly to users, patent medicine companies came into conflict with the medical profession. The American Medical Association warned the public about the dangers of self-medication and in the process also came to the aid of its physician-members who prepared their own medicines. Yet some doctors saw that there was money to be made in large-scale production of legitimate pharmaceuticals. Companies such as Abbott Laboratories, Miles Laboratories, and Upjohn were established by physicians in the 1880s. During the same period, a variety of pharmacists, chemists, and entrepreneurs also began creating "ethical" drug houses such as Eli Lilly, A. H. Robins, and G. D. Searle. At the time, "ethical" referred to producers who revealed the contents of their products and who sold to doctors rather than consumers. Today ethical drugs are those sold by prescription, while proprietary ones are those sold over the counter.

Despite advances such as the introduction of aspirin by the German company Frederich Bayer in 1899 and the development of a typhoid vaccine at about the same time, drug production was not put on a scientific basis until the work of the German biochemist Paul Ehrlich. He pioneered the idea that different bodily tissues have a selective affinity for specific chemical substances. He also built on the earlier work of Louis Pasteur that established the role of living organisms called bacteria in illness and other biological processes. Ehrlich paved the way for the development of sulfa drugs and antibiotics that fought against particular forms of bacteria, and he himself produced the first chemotherapeutic drug, which was used to treat syphilis.

In the following years advances in the discovery and production of drugs came much more frequently. Research in endocrinology led to the identification of insulin, and in 1928 the British physician Alexander Fleming discovered penicillin, the first of the great antibiotics but one that was effective for a limited range of diseases.

THE AGE OF WONDER DRUGS

In the late 1940s the creation of a series of antibiotics capable of fighting a broad spectrum of diseases ushered in what became known as the era of "wonder drugs." Newly prominent drug companies were frantically searching for new substances to turn into disease fighters while also devising methods for producing them in large quantities.

The pace quickened even more in the 1950s. The next wave of products consisted of tranquilizers such as Librium and amphetamines such as Dexedrine that were hailed as major advances in the treatment of mental illness. In 1954 Jonas Salk produced a vaccine for poliomyelitis. This period also saw important developments in research on hormonal chemistry. A small company in Mexico called Syntex found a way to produce large quantities of the female sex hormone progesterone from yams and synthesized a substance called norethiserone that controlled ovulation. Researchers for G. D. Searle separately produced a similar substance. While Searle and Parke-Davis (working with Syntex) put these discoveries on the market in 1957 as drugs to treat menstrual disorders, they realized they had the basis of an oral contraceptive. Parke-Davis was reluctant to market what was then a controversial product, but Searle brought out Enovid—the first version of what became known as "the pill"—in 1960. Within several years there was evidence linking Enovid with problems such as thrombophlebitis (inflammation of a clotted vein), but Searle managed to convince the Food and Drug Administration (FDA) that the pill was safe enough to remain on the market.

Although drug companies had become the darlings of Wall Street, they were considerably less popular in other quarters. No sooner had the pharmaceutical industry risen to fame with its miracle drugs than it was the subject of increasing criticism regarding both the safety and the pricing of its products.

The safety issue actually stemmed back to the late 19th century, when Dr. Harvey W. Wiley led a 25-year battle against the harmful quack medicines of the era. His efforts helped bring about the Pure Food and Drug Act of 1906 and the creation of the FDA. Unfortunately the Supreme Court interpreted the law as prohibiting only mislabeling. The Sherley Amendment of 1912 forbade false and fraudulent therapeutic claims. But the courts decided that fraudulent intent had to be proven—a difficult matter—so there was still no effective legislation against harmful medicines.

The turning point came in the 1930s. The Roosevelt administration was pushing for stricter regulation, which the industry as usual was fighting. Then came the case of the S. E. Massengill Company of Bristol, Tennessee. The firm was producing Elixir of Sulfanilamide, the first liquid version of an effective antibiotic. The product was not tested, and it turned out that the substance in which the active ingredient was dissolved had a devastating effect on the kidney. More than 100 users suffered a slow, agonizing death before the cause was discovered. The outcry over the Elixir case helped bring about passage of the Food, Drug and Cosmetic Act of 1938, which established much stricter safety standards and rules for testing.

Although the industry grumbled about the cost of the testing procedures and the delays in FDA approval, it was widely thought that the days of harmful medicines were over. That notion began to dissolve with the case of Chloromycetin, an antibiotic that was introduced by Parke-Davis in 1949 and was believed to have fewer side effects than other drugs of the sort. Although the drug was originally supposed to be used for typhoid fever, Parke-Davis promoted it heavily, and by the early 1950s it was being prescribed for a wide variety of less serious ailments. Soon the drug was being linked to severe and irreversible anemia. Parke-Davis defended its product, and after an investigation the FDA allowed it to remain on the market with a warning label.

The industry also came under fire for the high costs of its products, which stemmed in part from changes in the marketing practices of the industry. Traditionally, drug companies dealt mainly with pharmacies, and doctors made out their prescriptions according to generic names. With the rise of the wonder drugs, physicians began specifying brand names. The industry started spending huge sums encouraging this practice. Armies of "detail men" (sales representatives) were sent out by the drug houses to visit doctors to familiarize them with the latest products and make pitches for their own brands. The companies also spent large sums advertising in medical journals and mailing out free samples and lavishly printed brochures to doctors.

The industry also encouraged brand-name consciousness by labeling new products with catchy, easy-to-remember brand names and cumbersome, hard-to-remember generic designations. For example, the Swiss company Hoffman-La Roche's popular tranquilizer Librium was generically called chlordiazepoxide hydrochloride. This practice meant that once a drug's 17-year patent protection expired, doctors would be likely to go on prescribing the brand name even if cheaper generic equivalents had come on the market.

All of these practices inflated the expenses of the big drug houses, which, along with high research costs, were reflected in their prices. Some felt the process had gotten out of hand, and in 1959 Senator Estes Kefauver of Tennessee opened hearings on the subject. The senator kicked up a storm and in 1961 issued a report concluding that prescription drug prices were unreasonable in relation to production costs.

Kefauver's proposed legislation to remedy this and other

problems relating to the industry was going nowhere when another drug tragedy occurred. This time it was the linking of the sedative Thalidomide to serious birth defects in the children of women who took the drug while pregnant. Approval to sell Thalidomide in the United States had been refused by the FDA, but after reports on its hazards appeared abroad, there was concern about the thousands of U.S. patients who had been given the drug on an experimental basis.

Amid the scare, Congress revived and passed Kefauver's bill but without the pricing provisions. The 1962 legislation set stricter standards for manufacturing and rules for reporting to the FDA, made it easier for the government to stop the sale of drugs found to be harmful after approval, required certification of each batch of antibiotics, and required that drugs be effective as well as safe. The pricing issue was brought up again by Senator Gaylord Nelson of Wisconsin in 1967 hearings and at other times but it never resulted in restrictive legislation. Allegations of improper testing and lax FDA enforcement were also persistent, particularly later during the Reagan administration.

THE SEARCH FOR "MAGIC BULLETS"

By the early 1970s the drug business was under a cloud. The number of new drugs had been steadily declining, falling from more than 300 in 1959 to fewer than 100 in 1973. Companies that had grown fat on various wonder drugs of the early postwar period were facing patent expirations. Federal government impatience with the rising cost of medicine had prompted plans to require medicaid and medicare patients to use the cheapest available form of drugs—low-priced generics rather than the brand-name products that brought healthier profits to producers. The FDA and the Federal Trade Commission were also getting tougher on the advertising claims made for over-the-counter products. A number of drug companies turned to other businesses—including cosmetics and medical equipment—to sustain their profits.

It was not long, however, before some rays of sunshine began to appear for the industry. Advances in molecular biology and biochemistry were promising a new generation of highly effective drugs for specific ailments. Researchers, who were systematically studying thousands of possible chemical structures in the search for "magic bullets," began to achieve impressive results.

The most successful of the new wave of drugs to reach the market was Tagamet, a major breakthrough in the treatment of peptic ulcers. Developed and sold by Smith, Kline and French (now SmithKline Beecham), Tagamet's virtue was that it did not merely help the body deal with the effects of an ulcer but actually stopped the production of acid. The drug became one of the most widely prescribed pharmaceuticals in the world and propelled the formerly sleepy SmithKline to the upper ranks of the industry.

Tagamet also prompted an industry scramble—dubbed "Tagamania"—to find similar superdrugs. Companies started escalating their research budgets, which in the aggregate increased from about $1 billion in 1976 to $4 billion in 1985. The buzzword was "custom-designed drugs," meaning those that interacted with specific cellular processes in the body. Taking advantage of new knowledge concerning "receptors" (complex proteins on cell surfaces, where reactions with drug molecules take place), researchers started with the chemistry of the tissue and then tried to devise an appropriate drug. There was also a move toward drugs that did not simply treat the symptoms of disease but actually attacked the cause of the problem at the cellular level. The areas of greatest activity included cardiovascular drugs ("beta blockers" and calcium antagonists to prevent angina and hypertension), drugs to treat arthritis, and anti-inflammatory drugs.

BLEMISHES ON THE INDUSTRY'S RECORD

While some observers were comparing these breakthroughs to the wonder-drug era of the 1940s, the reputation of the industry was being marred by a series of controversies over the safety of its products. Among these were the following.

Accutane

This potent prescription drug for the treatment of acne resulted in hundreds of birth defects in the 1980s in children delivered by women who took the drug during pregnancy despite clear warnings that Accutane could do great harm to a fetus. Given the dangers, the FDA in 1988 ordered Accutane manufacturer Hoffman-La Roche to take extraordinary measures to reduce the use of the drug by pregnant women.

Copper-7

Copper-7 was an intrauterine contraceptive device (IUD) introduced by G. D. Searle in 1974. Hundreds of lawsuits linking use of the device to problems such as pelvic infections and infertility prompted Searle to take Copper-7 and its other IUD product off the market in 1986. Two years later a federal jury found the company negligent in the testing and marketing of the device.

Dalkon Shield

The Dalkon Shield was a contraceptive device sold by A. H. Robins from 1971 to 1974. Many users ended up having problems with infertility and sometimes fatal infections. By the mid-1980s the company had been hit with more than 10,000 lawsuits. Deciding that it did not have the resources to handle all the settlements, the company filed for Chapter 11 protection in 1985 and was acquired several years later by American Home Products, which agreed to pay out more than $2 billion to Dalkon Shield victims.

Darvon

Darvon is a painkiller introduced by Eli Lilly in 1957 as a nonnarcotic alternative to morphine and codeine. The drug had a huge success, but it was later accused of being less effective than aspirin yet quite addictive. Despite many calls to ban the drug, the FDA simply criticized Lilly for inadequate warning labels and allowed it to keep Darvon on the market.

DES

Diethylstilbestrol (DES) was a drug originally synthesized in 1938 and used by women to prevent miscarriages. Despite evidence that it caused cancer in animals, the product was marketed by several companies. By the 1970s daughters of women who had used DES were reporting complications including vaginal and cervical cancers.

Depo-Provera

Depo-Provera is a long-lasting contraceptive injected into a woman. The product was never approved in the United States despite years of effort by its producer, Upjohn. Yet it has been marketed aggressively abroad (especially in the Third World), where it has been linked to serious side effects and birth defects.

Oraflex

Oraflex was an antiarthritis drug introduced with great fanfare by Eli Lilly in 1982. There were soon reports linking the drug to internal bleeding and kidney and liver problems. In 1985 Lilly pleaded guilty to charges that it had failed to inform the FDA about four deaths and other illnesses linked to the drug.

Despite these setbacks, the drug business at the beginning of the 1990s was riding high. Impressive new drugs continued to come out of the research pipeline, and demographic trends—namely the increasing elderly proportion of the population—suggested a growing demand for the industry's wares. The side effects of life in modern industrial society continued to create market opportunities. Along with ulcer treatment (pioneered by SmithKline's Tagamet, which was later surpassed by Zantac, sold by Britain's Glaxo Holdings), the big drug growth areas have involved hypertension, cholesterol, and heart attacks. Drugs to treat high blood pressure, such as Squibb's Capoten and Merck's Vasotec, have competed intensely for a multibillion-dollar market. Warner-Lambert's Lopid and Merck's Mevacor are among the cholesterol-lowering drugs vying for a share of a growing business. Genentech introduced TPA and SmithKline brought out Eminase to compete with streptokinase, sold by Hoechst of West Germany to dissolve blood clots associated with heart attacks.

New diseases such as AIDS, while a tragedy for thousands of

victims, represented lucrative potential markets for the industry. The first company to succeed in this area was Burroughs Wellcome (the U.S. subsidiary of Britain's Wellcome), which developed a drug called azidothymidine, or AZT, which did not destroy the AIDS virus but in many cases stopped it from reproducing. The excitement over AZT was dampened by the high price of the drug—about $10,000 for a year's dosage—as marketed by Burroughs Wellcome with the brand name Retrovir. Responding to protests by AIDS activists, the company reduced the price by 20 percent in 1987, but that was not enough to prevent Burroughs Wellcome from being regularly denounced as an AIDS profiteer. A wave of protests in 1989 prompted another 20 percent price cut, yet AZT has remained one of the most expensive drugs ever sold. Several weeks later Lyphomed announced it would give away a drug that prevents pneumonia in people infected with the AIDS virus. The FDA, under pressure to release new AIDS drugs more quickly, announced in 1989 that it would allow wide distribution of an experimental drug called dideoxyinosine, or DDI, while it was still being tested.

The drug industry was also enjoying a boom in more prosaic products. Aspirin makers were prospering thanks to studies suggesting that the everyday drug actually serves to reduce the risk of heart attacks and has other surprising properties. New markets were also opening up in "cosmeceuticals"—more sophisticated versions of health and beauty aids that promised to reverse (at least in some people) what were previously thought to be irreversible bodily processes. Retin-A, a prescription acne medicine produced by Johnson & Johnson's Ortho Pharmaceutical, was found to eliminate wrinkles in sun-aged skin. In 1988 Upjohn got FDA approval for Rogaine, the first recognized treatment for male-pattern baldness.

Some companies even made the best of the rise of generics, which reached about one third of the drug market in the late 1980s, by selling so-called branded generics: versions of drugs priced midway between brand-name products and those from generic producers. Yet other companies tried to argue the superiority of original brand-name products and were accused of using scare tactics when they insisted on the remote possibility that generics might be harmful.

In the middle of 1989 it began to appear that those warnings were not so far-fetched. A scandal arose amid reports that several producers of generics had falsified test results submitted to the FDA and that several agency officials had taken bribes. The FDA, which had simplified its approval process for generics as a result of the 1984 Waxman-Hatch Act and had relaxed its overall enforcement as part of the deregulatory trend of the Reagan era, was forced to investigate a large part of the generic industry. Manufacturing and record-keeping irregularities were found at 10 of 12 firms examined. There were no documented cases of deaths or injuries from the improper practices of the generic producers, but the scandal did give new ammunition to the crusade of the brand-name manufacturers.

The industry has also had success on Capitol Hill. In 1982 Congress passed legislation that provided increased tax incentives for companies to devote research efforts to so-called orphan diseases, those for which the potential number of users is too small to make it commercially attractive to develop drugs. The law also gave companies that produce orphan drugs (defined as those needed by fewer than 200,000 patients) exclusive marketing licenses for seven years when the substances do not qualify for patent protection. The Waxman-Hatch Act expedited the approval process for generics but gave branded drugs patent extensions of up to two years to make up for time taken up in the approval process. In 1986 Congress passed a bill permitting the export of drugs not approved for sale in the United States. The law also set up a federal program to compensate children injured by vaccines.

During most of the 1980s there was a high degree of stability among the leading drug companies; the pharmaceutical industry seemed to be immune to the takeover epidemic that had overcome much of American business. By the end of the decade that tranquility was ending. Several companies engaged in an intense bidding war for A. H. Robins, which had filed for Chapter 11; American Home Products came out on top. Also in early 1988, the Swiss company Hoffman-La Roche made a hostile bid for Sterling Drug, best known as the producer of Bayer aspirin. Eastman Kodak arrived on the scene as a white knight, purchasing Sterling for $5.1 billion. The emerging pattern was one in which companies with strong marketing operations sought to join forces with firms strong in research and development. In 1989 SmithKline Beckman, in a weakened condition because of declining Tagamet sales, agreed to merge with Britain's Beecham Group. Several months later Squibb agreed to a $12.6 billion friendly merger with Bristol-Myers. The same year, Dow Chemical acquired Marion Laboratories and merged it with its Merrell Dow subsidiary.

On the horizon is increased competition from the Japanese. Until the late 1980s the Japanese drug companies were a minor factor in a world pharmaceutical industry dominated by American and a few European producers. Yet after gaining proficiency in making antibiotics, Japanese companies such as Takeda Chemical, Fujisawa, and Tanabe Seiyaku began moving into more advanced products. They have also been moving directly into foreign markets by buying companies and forming joint ventures, such as the one Takeda created with Abbott Laboratories.

THE BIOTECHNOLOGY REVOLUTION

Another force transforming the drug industry has been the rise over the past two decades of an advanced form of biochemistry. Called genetic engineering or biotechnology, this new field involves the manipulation of DNA molecules to produce miraculous new drugs.

The story of biotechnology is basically that of the combination of scientific and entrepreneurial instincts. As biochemical researchers grew more sophisticated in their ability to rearrange genetic material, some of them quickly appreciated the commercial implications and acted on them. Cetus Corp., the oldest biotechnology firm, was established in California in 1971 by microbiologist Ronald Cape. Biotechnology pioneer Herbert Boyer of the University of California at San Francisco joined with venture capitalist Robert Swanson in 1976 to form Genentech, which went on to become the industry leader. Biogen was established in 1978 by an international group of scientists.

In the early years these companies did little more than research, so it was a sensation when Biogen announced in 1980 that it had succeeded in genetically restructuring bacteria to produce interferon, a highly effective disease-fighting agent found naturally in the body but only in very small amounts. Interferon was widely considered a potential cure for some forms of cancer as well as a variety of viral diseases.

A Supreme Court decision in 1980 was the Magna Charta for the industry. The Court ruled that new forms of life are eligible for protection under the patent laws. The new status of the industry made it more attractive to established companies. The limited investment in biotechnology by large corporations developed into a new gold rush. Some bought into the existing ventures, while others—among them numerous drug companies—set up their own biotechnology operations.

By the mid-1980s the biotechnology industry had come of age. In the United States several hundred companies were making use of about $2.5 billion of invested capital. The industry had succeeded in synthesizing human insulin and was awaiting FDA approval for interferon. Research was also proceeding on a new generation of safer and more effective vaccines as well as a substance called tissue plasminogen activator (TPA), which dissolves clots that block arteries during heart attacks. Most exciting was the report from the National Cancer Institute in 1985 that a substance called Interleukin-2, synthesized by Cetus, was showing impressive results in treating cancer patients.

In 1986 the FDA approved the first genetically altered vaccine for human use. Designed to protect against hepatitis B, the vaccine was developed by Chiron Corp. and was to be marketed by Merck. The next big breakthrough came in 1987, when the FDA ignored the advice of its advisory committee and approved the sale of Genentech's TPA product (given the brand name Activase). In 1990 the company won a patent dispute regarding TPA, but it had to contend with the introduction of a competing drug called Eminase produced by SmithKline Beecham as well as the release of a study that found TPA to be no more effective than streptokinase, an older and much less expensive heart attack drug.

Biotechnology shipments did surpass the billion-dollar figure in 1989, but there was a shadow over the industry. Observers, particularly those in the investment world, were dissatisfied with the rising costs of research and the slow pace at which products made it to market. At the end of the decade there was the beginning of a shakeout among the 500 or so firms in the industry, with several dozen liquidating, filing for Chapter 11, or selling out. Some of those sales were to foreign firms. Japan, in particular, made a major push during the 1980s to build a biotechnology industry of its own, using both U.S. acquisitions and domestic investment. Yet the most significant foreign incursion into the U.S. industry was the 1990 sale of 60 percent of Genentech to Roche Holdings (parent of Hoffman-La Roche) of Switzerland.

From its earliest days biotechnology has been the subject of major controversy over safety. Critics have charged that the industry's practice of gene-splicing—the separation of DNA molecules and recombination of genetic material from different sources—could create dangerous organisms that, if accidentally released, could have disastrous health consequences.

Congressional efforts to establish new safety laws were inconclusive, and in 1978 the Department of Health, Education and Welfare asked the FDA and the Environmental Protection Agency to regulate the field through existing laws and National Institute of Health guidelines. A 1987 report by a panel of the National Academy of Sciences concluded that genetic engineering did not present any unique ecological hazards.

The safety crusade on biotechnology has to a great degree been the work of one man, Jeremy Rifkin, working out of a small organization in Washington called the Foundation on Economic Trends. Since the mid-1970s Rifkin has been warning of the hazards of genetic engineering and has effectively used the political and legal systems to carry on his crusade. In 1986 he forced the Agriculture Department to suspend the license of a small firm, Biologics Corp., whose genetically engineered vaccine for pigs was just beginning to be used by farmers. The license was restored, but Rifkin had made front-page news. Rifkin has also been the leading critic of a set of guidelines issued by the Reagan administration in 1986 for the supervision of biotechnology by five government agencies.

Another setback for the industry came in 1990 when an FDA advisory committee refused to approve Interleukin-2, saying that its manufacturer, Cetus Corp., had not demonstrated that the drug was sufficiently effective in the treatment of cancer.

Despite these various obstacles, industry leaders remain optimistic about the future of biotechnology. At the beginning of the 1990s, the new areas include treatment of anemia with erythropoetin (EPO), medications for autoimmune diseases such as diabetes and multiple sclerosis, so-called antisense drugs that could prevent genes from producing disease-causing proteins, and the possibility of a vaccine for AIDS. The latter possibility came closer to reality in June 1990, when researchers announced that a vaccine made by Genentech appeared to protect chimpanzees against infection from the AIDS virus.

THE RISE OF THE HOSPITAL

While drug production in the United States has always been a commercial endeavor, the institutional treatment of the ill has taken several different forms. Starting in the late 1960s the nearly extinct for-profit hospital began to make a dramatic comeback. While the growth in the new "hospital industry" started to slow down in the mid-1980s, corporations have staked out a major role in the practice of health care.

The role of hospitals of any kind in systematic health care is less than a century old. Before the late 19th century, hospitals were indistinguishable from almshouses, serving mainly as repositories for the ailing poor—what Paul Starr has called "places of dreaded impurity and exiled human wreckage."

Health care was largely performed by individual physicians in their offices or in the home of the patient. Since surgery was limited and health technology was primitive, there was little need for large institutions aside from those that sheltered victims of chronic diseases.

This situation began to change after the Civil War, the result to a great extent of the professionalization of nursing, the widening use of anesthesia, and the adoption of Joseph Lister's antiseptic techniques. The latter encouraged a greater range of surgical procedures by reducing the chances that the patient would die of infection.

Many of the early hospitals were established as profit-making endeavors by physicians with the backing of wealthy sponsors. Larger hospitals were set up as "voluntary" institutions, meaning they were supported by religious or philanthropic groups rather than by the government. As hospitals came to assume a more and more dominant role in the health care system in the 20th century, it was these nonprofit institutions that prevailed. Of the 4,306 U.S. hospitals in 1928, 1,889 were voluntary, 1,877 profit-making, and the remainder public. By 1960 there were only 856 for-profits while the voluntaries had grown to 3,291. The growth of the nonprofits was aided by the Hill-Burton Act of 1946, which provided federal subsidies for their construction.

At the same time, the entire health system grew more and more complex. The voluntary hospitals established Blue Cross private health insurance plans beginning in the 1930s. These were joined by Blue Shield plans, set up by medical societies to cover doctors' fees for hospital treatment. Various attempts to create a national insurance system were unsuccessful, though in the 1960s the federal government created health programs for the elderly (medicare) and the poor (medicaid).

In fact, it was these programs—which brought enormous amounts of federal funds into health care—that stimulated the revival of profit-making hospital companies. Starting in the late 1960s companies such as Hospital Corporation of America (HCA) and Humana Inc. began purchasing nonprofit hospitals or else taking over their management. Many hospital administrators welcomed this trend. In a period of rapidly rising costs and complicated government regulations, they found they could no longer manage effectively. Many joined nonprofit chains to take advantage of lower-cost purchasing and other economies of scale. Yet particularly in the West and Southeast, administrators turned to the private sector.

Calling themselves proprietary or investor-owned, chains such as HCA introduced businesslike practices in the institutions they took over—so much so that critics charged that they were eroding the quality of health care. The pattern of the private chains, it was charged, was to "skim off" the most profitable patients, those fully insured people who needed short-term treatment not involving expensive procedures. Those without coverage or those requiring long-term care tended to be shunted off to public or nonprofit hospitals. The private chains have also been accused of reducing staffing to inadequate levels and charging higher prices than nonprofit institutions.

Despite the controversy HCA and the others grew at rapid rates for two decades. By 1984 about 1,700 of the nation's 6,800 hospitals were investor-owned. The industry talked boldly about seeking to introduce brand-name consciousness into health care by setting up their own insurance plans or health maintenance organizations, so that a company would be associated with all aspects of care.

What brought the halcyon days to an end was the decision by the federal government finally to do something to control the problem of galloping hospital costs. In 1983 Congress established a prospective payment system for medicare. This involved the creation of some 470 diagnostic related groups (DRGs) and the setting of fixed reimbursement levels (adjusted for different regions of the country) for them. A medicare patient who entered the hospital had to be categorized according to a DRG, and the hospital would be reimbursed no more than the amount fixed for the DRG. If the institution could provide the care for less than the fixed amount, it could keep the difference; if not, it had to absorb the loss.

At the same time, the attempts by corporations to cut down on employee health costs by raising deductibles and otherwise restricting medical insurance plans tended to reduce the amount of care people were seeking. Simultaneously there was an accelerating trend toward outpatient treatment for ailments that were previously handled in hospitals. Private companies began building freestanding clinics and emergency rooms (so-called Docs-in-the-box) to handle these procedures. The spread of health maintenance organizations (HMOs)—both nonprofit ones and for-profit chains such as Maxicare

Health Plans—also reduced hospital visits by concentrating on preventive medicine. Consequently hospital utilization rates began to fall, reaching 62 percent in 1985 compared with 75 percent at the beginning of the decade.

All of this spelled financial trouble for hospitals. The nonprofits responded by seeking new forms of revenue. Many of them diversified into profit-making areas like home health care or even such non-health-related businesses as catering, data processing, janitorial services, and health clubs. Given their lack of entrepreneurial experience, many hospitals ended up failing at these new initiatives.

The for-profit companies have also been hurting. In October 1985 HCA announced that its earnings would probably be flat in 1986. The next day American Medical International, another leading chain, reported a fourth-quarter earnings drop of 38 percent. Wall Street, used to much more favorable news from the industry, panicked and began dumping hospital stocks. The companies as a group lost some $1.5 billion in market value in a single day.

Aside from the loss of investor confidence, the for-profits experienced disappointing results in their attempts, led by Humana, to set up their own insurance programs. In 1987 HCA attempted to stabilize its operations by selling off more than 100 of its less-profitable facilities to a new company owned by employees through an employee stock ownership plan. The remainder of the company underwent a leveraged buyout in 1989; American Medical International also went private that year. Humana, meanwhile, remained public and stuck with its strategy of creating a network of insurance plans and participating doctors to feed patients into the company's hospitals; by the end of the 1980s the plan finally appeared to be paying off.

Although troubled, the private hospital industry will surely survive. So will nonprofits, but many of them have, aside from diversifying, been forced to adopt private-sector techniques such as advertising and product differentiation (luxury suites and other amenities) to attract patients. Health maintenance organizations also have their problems. Although total HMO enrollment doubled during the second half of the 1980s, reaching 36 million in 1989, there have been signs

The 20 Largest Medical and Health-Care Companies, by 1989 Medical and Health-Care Revenues ($ Millions)

	Company	Revenues
1.	Aetna Life & Casualty	$19,671
2.	Bristol-Myers Squibb	9,189
3.	Lincoln National	8,081
4.	SmithKline Beecham	8,006
5.	Baxter International	7,399
6.	Kaiser Permanente	6,800
7.	Merck	6,551
8.	John Hancock Mutual Life	6,368
9.	McKesson	5,853
10.	Johnson & Johnson	5,842
11.	Prudential Insurance	5,700
12.	Abbott Laboratories	5,379
13.	American Home Products	5,263
14.	CIGNA	4,998
15.	American General	4,227
16.	Eli Lilly	4,176
17.	Pfizer	4,118
18.	Humana	4,068
19.	Eastman Kodak	4,009
20.	Bergen Brunswig	3,923

Source: *The Medical & Healthcare Marketplace Guide*, MLR Publishing Company, Philadelphia, Pennsylvania.

that the growth is levelling off. Part of the reason is increasing employer disenchantment with the plans. Whereas participants have long complained about the quality of care in many HMOs, bosses are now frustrated with HMO premiums, which have been rising almost as fast as those of conventional insurance plans.

The seemingly unstoppable health-care inflation has forced business to rethink its attitude toward health policy. Leading executives such as Chrysler's Lee Iacocca, arguing that the private sector simply cannot solve the problem, have begun to push for what the corporate world traditionally regarded as anathema: a government-sponsored national health-care plan. The prospects for such a reform have been improving, but what remains unclear are the issues of how extensive the coverage would be and what role would be played in it by the for-profit health industry.

LABOR RELATIONS

The growth of hospitals has been accompanied by the creation of a large nonprofessional labor force characterized by low status and low pay. Some union organizing began in San Francisco-area hospitals after World War I, but it was not until the late 1950s that the movement began to grow. One major obstacle to overcome was the fact that in 1947 nonprofit hospitals had succeeded in getting Congress to exempt them from the provisions of federal labor law.

The new wave of hospital organizing was closely linked to the civil rights movement, in that minority workers were heavily represented in the industry. The spearhead of the drive was New York's Local 1199 of the National Union of Hospital and Health Care Employees, a small union representing mainly drugstore workers. The union staged a 46-day strike against seven hospitals in 1959, winning improvements in wages and working conditions but not recognition. The union struck again in 1962, and the impasse was resolved only when Governor Nelson Rockefeller agreed that if the walkout was ended, he would press the state legislature to provide labor law protection for employees of nonprofit hospitals.

The law was passed, and Local 1199 was firmly established as the collective bargaining representative in the voluntary institutions. Meanwhile, District Council 37 of the American Federation of State, County and Municipal Employees organized workers at the city's municipal hospitals, and Local 144 of the Service Employees International Union signed up employees at many of New York's proprietary institutions.

The organizing successes in New York spurred campaigns in other parts of the country. By 1967 some 8 percent of the country's hospitals had unions for all or some of their workers, compared with less than 3 percent in 1961. Outside of large northern cities, successes did not come so easily. In Charleston, South Carolina, it took a 110-day walkout, including massive demonstrations and a threat by longshoremen to shut down the port, to win recognition.

Organizing was helped by the decision of Congress in 1974 to extend national labor law protection to workers at voluntary hospitals. Yet management in many parts of the country—including the Sunbelt regions, where the new private chains concentrated their activity—fought hard against unionization. Hospitals were among the most aggressive users of antiunion management consultants. By the mid-1980s the industry was still only about 20 percent organized. But the labor movement was hopeful that organizing gains would come faster following the 1989 announcement by the National Labor Relations Board (NLRB) of new rules regarding appropriate bargaining units for health-care workers.

In 1984 the National Union of Hospital and Health Care Employees separated from its parent (the Retail, Wholesale and Department Store Union), with which it had been on unfriendly terms for some time. However, Local 1199 in New York, which accounted for about one half of the hospital union's 150,000 members, remained with the parent union. Local 1199, which had struck New York's voluntary hospitals in 1976, staged another militant strike of 47 days in the city in 1984. Local 1199 went through several years of intense internal disputes, but in 1989 the union skillfully used short strikes and a pressure campaign to get a generous settlement from the voluntary hospitals.

After a contentious affiliation debate, the National Union of Hospital and Health Care Employees was dissolved in 1989, with about two thirds of its 75,000 members joining the Service Employees International Union and the remainder going with the American Federation of State, County and Municipal Employees.

Unionized workers in the pharmaceutical industry are represented mainly by the Oil, Chemical and Atomic Workers Union and the International Chemical Workers Union. The most notable confrontation of recent years occurred at industry leader Merck, which in 1984 locked out 730 workers in New Jersey, precipitating a strike at several Merck plants and a corporate campaign against the company. The strike was settled after three months.

LEADING COMPANIES

Abbott Laboratories was founded in 1888 by Dr. Wallace Abbott, who pioneered the use of pills consisting of only active ingredients rather than fluid extracts of entire plants. Abbott, an aggressive promoter, ran into trouble with the American Medical Association over his sale of shares in the company to doctors. In the following years the company devised products such as sodium pentothal (the so-called truth serum) but in the 1970s had repeated difficulties in its production of intravenous solutions and was the subject of the FDA's largest product recall. Abbott decided to put more emphasis on the medical diagnostics business, and by the late 1980s it was the leader in the field.

Bristol-Myers Squibb is the result of a friendly $12.6 billion merger of two drug giants in 1989. Bristol-Myers, founded in the late 19th century, was known mainly for its health and beauty aids, including Clairol hair coloring, Ban deodorant, and Bufferin and Excedrin headache remedies. The company launched a campaign in the early 1980s to build its ethical drug business but had not achieved any dramatic results. Squibb was formed in 1858 by a former Navy doctor and over the next 100 years grew into one of the country's leading drug companies. In 1951 Squibb merged with Mathieson Chemical, and the combined company merged with Olin Industries several years later. The Squibb operation languished until it was spun off as an independent company once again in 1968. For several years Squibb tried diversifying its operations—buying Beech-Nut, Life Savers, and other nondrug properties—but during the 1970s it focused itself on pharmaceuticals. Squibb remained generally lackluster but did well in the 1980s with its Capoten cardiovascular drug, though that success was later diminished by the rise of a competing drug called Vasotec sold by Merck.

Genentech became the leader of the biotechnology industry that emerged in the 1970s. Founded by a leading biochemist and a venture capitalist, the company came to epitomize the excitement of genetic engineering in the minds of many people. When Genentech went public in 1980 there was a scramble to buy shares, which on the first day more than doubled from the initial price of $35. The company succeeded in synthesizing human insulin and a growth hormone called Protropin and became a leader in the development of interferon. In 1987 the company got FDA approval for TPA, a blood clot dissolver for heart attack victims. Genentech fought off a patent challenge on TPA and captured two thirds of the market for heart attack drugs but found itself with more competition when SmithKline Beecham introduced its Eminase product in 1990. Shaken by its faltering stock price, the company agreed in 1990 to sell a 60 percent interest to Swiss drug giant Roche Holdings for $2.1 billion.

Hospital Corporation of America (HCA) is the McDonald's of the private hospital business. It was established in 1968 by Dr. Thomas Frist of Nashville, his son Dr. Thomas Frist, Jr., and Jack Massey, one of the founders of Kentucky Fried Chicken. HCA became the largest of the commercial chains, and in 1986 it owned 258 institutions and managed 219 others. A 1983 attempt to acquire American Hospital Supply—a controversial deal because of that company's dominant role in its field—was defeated by a rival bid from Baxter Travenol Laboratories (now Baxter International). Faced with declining profitability because of low occupancy rates and inadequate medicare reimbursement, HCA moved to stabilize itself in 1987 by selling off 104 of its facilities to an employee-owned entity. Two years later the remainder of the company was taken private in a leveraged buyout.

Humana, which along with HCA led the growth of the for-profit hospital industry, was founded in the 1960s in Louisville, Kentucky, by a pair of lawyers. Humana has been more aggressive than HCA in marketing, using among other things the enormous publicity from the artificial heart transplants performed at the company's hospitals. When the industry began to suffer from declining occupancy rates and reduced medicare reimbursements in the 1980s, Humana began to develop its own health insurance plans and a network of participating doctors to steer patients into the company's facilities. It took a number of years, but by the end of the decade the strategy was beginning to pay off.

Eli Lilly, one of the grand old names in the drug business, has been plagued in recent years with safety problems. Its Darvon analgesic was accused of being less effective than aspirin yet highly addictive. It was one of the producers of the estrogen

DES, which has been linked to cancer in the daughters of women who used it. In 1985 Lilly admitted that it failed to inform the FDA about several deaths and other illnesses linked to its antiarthritis drug, Oraflex. Lilly was founded in 1876 in Indianapolis by Eli Lilly, inventor of a process for coating pills with gelatin to make them easier to swallow. In the 1920s the company made its mark through the sale of insulin (extracted from animals) and was later a major producer of penicillin and the Salk vaccine. From 1930 to 1960 it was usually the leader in the prescription drug business. The company received another black eye in 1989, when the FDA criticized quality-control procedures at Lilly's factory in Indianapolis and found that false or incomplete data had been submitted to the agency by employees at the plant. In 1990, the company was faced with accusations that its antidepressant drug Prozac caused suicidal tendencies in users.

Merck, the leader of the ethical drug industry in the United States, is a descendant of a German pharmaceutical house dating back to the 17th century. U.S. operations began around the turn of the century and became independent of the German Merck during World War I. Merck, one of the most highly regarded drug companies, was a leader in the development of vitamins and antibiotics and since the mid-1970s has brought out a variety of new drugs. In 1983 the company bought a majority interest in Banyu Pharmaceutical of Tokyo. In the late 1980s Merck began selling the first genetically engineered human vaccine (for hepatitis B) and the first cholesterol-lowering drug, called Mevacor. It also brought out a successful blood-pressure drug called Vasotec to compete with Squibb's Capoten. While other drug firms got caught up in mergers, Merck instead formed a series of joint ventures with such companies as Johnson & Johnson and Du Pont.

Pfizer started out as a chemical company in the 19th century and achieved recognition as a drug house in the 1940s, thanks to its successes in improving the production of penicillin. Pfizer was the first drug company to use aggressive marketing techniques, which shook up the genteel traditions of the industry but ended up being adopted. Pfizer developed a good reputation, but in the mid-1980s there were reports linking its antiarthritis drug Feldene to sometimes fatal internal bleeding. In 1986 Pfizer was pressured to remove from the market a heart valve made by a subsidiary. The valves were reported to have resulted in several hundred deaths. In 1990 Pfizer came under fire as a result of a congressional investigation that concluded that the company knew about the problems with the valves but failed to notify the FDA or the medical community in a timely fashion.

G. D. Searle, purchased by Monsanto for $2.7 billion in 1985, was founded in the Midwest in the 1880s. Searle became a full-line manufacturer and starting in 1949 enjoyed a great success with Dramamine, a drug for treating motion sickness that was turned into an over-the-counter product in 1954. In 1960 the company introduced the first oral contraceptive, Enovid. Management of the firm was taken over by former Defense Secretary Donald Rumsfeld in 1977, and the Searle family sold off its interest in 1984. By the 1980s the company was facing hundreds of lawsuits based on harmful effects suffered by users of its Copper-7 intrauterine contraceptive device. After a federal jury in one case found the company negligent, Searle began settling the other suits out of court.

SmithKline Beecham (or Smith, Kline and French, as it used to be known) is one of the oldest U.S. drug houses. Founded in Philadelphia in the 1830s, the company produced a wide range of products and was the first regularly to send free samples to doctors. After World War II SmithKline was a leader in the development of tranquilizers and amphetamines. After a slump in the 1960s the company achieved a phenomenal success with Tagamet, an antiulcer medicine that was one of the most prominent of the custom-designed drugs that started to appear in the 1970s. In 1982 SmithKline spent $1 billion to purchase Beckman Instruments. During the late 1980s the company's performance slumped as Tagamet and its other leading product—the blood-pressure drug Dyazide—faced increasing competition. SmithKline saved itself from a possible hostile takeover in 1989 by agreeing to a friendly $8.3 billion merger with Britain's Beecham Group.

INDUSTRY DATA

Drugs	*1989*	*1988*	*1987*
Value of shipments	$46.8 billion	$43.1 billion	$39.1 billion
Total employment	176,000	172,200	170,000
Import penetration	9.7%	8.3%	7.4%

Source: U.S. Department of Commerce.

SOURCE GUIDE

Leading Stock Analysts and Experts

John Hindelong, hospital analyst at Donaldson, Lufkin & Jenrette.

Viren Mehta, analyst at Mehta & Isaly, a New York stock research company specializing in pharmaceuticals.

Linda Miller, biotechnology analyst at Paine Webber.

Raymond Moran, drug analyst at Cowen & Co.

Ronald Nordmann, drug analyst at Paine Webber.

Ronald Stern, drug analyst at Tucker, Anthony.

Trade Associations and Unions

American Federation of State, County and Municipal Employees, 1625 L Street NW, Washington, DC 20036. Tel.: (202) 429-1000.

American Hospital Association, 840 N. Lake Shore Drive, Chicago, IL 60611. Tel.: (312) 280–6000.

Association of Biotechnology Companies, 1120 Vermont Avenue NW, Washington, DC 20005. Tel.: (202) 842–2229.

Federation of American Health Systems (for-profit hospitals), 1405 N. Pierce, Little Rock, AR 72207. Tel.: (501) 661–9555.

Industrial Biotechnology Association, 1625 K Street NW, Washington, DC 20006. Tel.: (202) 857–0244.

Local 1199 of the Retail, Wholesale and Department Store Union, 310 West 43rd Street, New York, NY 10036. Tel.: (212) 582–1890.

Pharmaceutical Manufacturers Association, 1100 15th Street NW, Washington, DC 20005. Tel.: (202) 835–3400.

Service Employees International Union, 1313 L Street NW, Washington, DC 20005. Tel.: (202) 898-3200.

Data Sources and Directories

American Drug Index, an annual listing (St. Louis: J. B. Lippincott).

Biotechnology Directory, an annual guide to products, companies, research, and organizations (New York: Stockton Press).

Directory of Investor-Owned Hospitals, Hospital Management Companies and Health Care Systems, annual (Little Rock, Ark.: Federation of American Health Systems).

Drug and Cosmetic Catalog, an annual directory (Cleveland: Edgell Communications).

Dun's Guide to Healthcare Companies, an annual directory (New York: Dun's Marketing Services).

Genetic Engineering and Biotechnology Firms Worldwide Directory, annual (Kingston, N.J.: Sittig & Noyes).

International Biotechnology Industrial Directory, annual (Maplewood, N.J.: CTB International Publishing).

Medical and Healthcare Marketplace Guide, an annual directory and ranking of companies throughout the health industry (Philadelphia: International Bio-Medical Information Service).

Pharmaceutical Manufacturers of the United States, a triennial directory (Park Ridge, N.J.: Noyes Data).

Pharmaceutical Marketers Directory, annual (Boca Raton, Fla.: CPS Communications).

Physicians' Desk Reference, an annual guide to prescription drugs (Oradell, N.J.: Medical Economics).

Prescription Drug Industry Factbook, triennial (Washington, D.C.: Pharmaceutical Manufacturers Association).

Online Databases

BIOBUSINESS (Philadelphia: Biosis; available via BRS and DIALOG).

BIOCOMMERCE ABSTRACTS (Slough, United Kingdom: Biocommerce Data; available via DIALOG).

BIOTECHNOLOGY ABSTRACTS (London: Derwent Publications; available via DIALOG and ORBIT).

CURRENT BIOTECHNOLOGY ABSTRACTS (Nottingham, United Kingdom: Royal Society of Chemistry; available via DIALOG).

DIOGENES, covering drug regulation (Rockville, Md.: Diogenes; available via BRS and DIALOG).

HEALTH PLANNING AND ADMINISTRATION (Bethesda, Md.: U.S. National Library of Medicine; available via BRS and DIALOG).

INTERNATIONAL PHARMACEUTICAL ABSTRACTS (Bethesda, Md.: American Society of Hospital Pharmacists; available via BRS and DIALOG).

PHARMACEUTICAL NEWS INDEX (Louisville, Ky.: UMI/Data Courier; available via BRS and DIALOG).

Trade Publications

Biomedical Business International, monthly.

BioTechnology, monthly.

Drug and Cosmetic Industry, monthly.

Drug Topics, semimonthly.

F-D-C Reports, weekly.

Genetic Engineering News, 10 times a year.

Health Business, weekly.

Health Care Financing Review, quarterly.

Hospitals, fortnightly.

IMS Market Letter, weekly.

McGraw-Hill's Biotechnology Newswatch, fortnightly.

Modern Healthcare, weekly.

Scrip: World Pharmaceutical News (Richmond, Surrey, United Kingdom), semiweekly.

Books and Reports

Braithwaite, John. *Corporate Crime in the Pharmaceutical Industry*. Boston: Routledge & Kegan Paul, 1984.

Egan, John W.; Harlow N. Higinbotham; and J. Fred Weston. *Economics of the Pharmaceutical Industry*. New York: Praeger Publishers, 1982.

Fink, Leon, and Brian Greenberg. *Upheaval in the Quiet Zone: A History of Hospital Workers' Union Local 1199*. Champaign, Ill.: University of Illinois Press, 1989.

Kotelchuck, David, ed. *Prognosis Negative: Crisis in the Health Care System.* New York: Vintage Books, 1976.

Mahoney, Tom. *The Merchants of Life: An Account of the American Pharmaceutical Industry.* New York: Harper & Brothers, 1959.

Mintz, Morton. *By Prescription Only.* Boston: Beacon Press, 1967.

———. *At Any Cost: Corporate Greed and the Dalkon Shield.* New York: Pantheon Books, 1985.

National Academy of Sciences. *Agricultural Biotechnology: Strategies for National Competitiveness.* Washington, D.C.: National Academy Press, 1987.

———. *Biotechnology: An Industry Comes of Age.* Washington, D.C.: National Academy Press, 1986.

———. *The Competitive Status of the U.S. Pharmaceutical Industry.* Washington, D.C.: National Academy Press, 1983.

National Institute of Medicine. *The New Health Care for Profit.* Washington, D.C.: National Academy Press, 1983.

———. *For-Profit Enterprise in Health Care.* Washington, D.C.: National Academy Press, 1986.

Organisation for Economic Co-operation and Development. *Biotechnology: Economic and Wider Impacts.* Paris, 1989.

Rosenberg, Charles E. *The Care of Strangers: The Rise of America's Hospital System.* New York: Basic Books, 1987.

Starr, Paul. *The Social Transformation of American Medicine.* New York: Basic Books, 1982.

Teitelman, Robert. *Gene Dreams: Wall Street, Academia, and the Rise of Biotechnology.* New York: Basic Books, 1989.

U.S. Congress, Office of Technology Assessment. *Commercial Biotechnology: An International Analysis.* Washington, D.C., January 1984.

———. *U.S. Investment in Biotechnology.* Washington, D.C., July 1988.

Wohl, Stanley. *The Medical Industrial Complex.* New York: Harmony Books, 1984.

Yoxen, Edward. *The Gene Business.* New York: Harper & Row, 1983.

CHAPTER 9

FOOD AND AGRICULTURE

Agriculture was the root of all commerce, and despite the Industrial Revolution, food production remains one of the largest spheres of business activity. Yet this production is no longer limited to what is grown or raised on the farm and brought directly to market. To a great extent, supplying the means of sustenance has become simply a branch of manufacturing. Large, corporate-type farms have taken over the land, and foodstuffs go through extensive processing and packaging before they reach the consumer. Modern farming, food processing, and the industries that provide the inputs they require—tractors, seeds, fertilizers, additives, and the like—together constitute a megasector of the economy known as agribusiness. In 1989 Americans spent some $300 billion on food.

FROM CANNING TO FREEZING

While societies have for at least a millennium preserved food through techniques such as drying, salting, and smoking, the origins of large-scale food processing are to be found in the 19th century. The development that began to free people from the constraints of time and distance regarding food consumption was the invention of vacuum packing. A Frenchman named Nicholas Appert is credited with having devised the process in 1809, but for what would today be called national security reasons it was kept secret. Similar techniques using tin cans rather than jars emerged in the United States in the 1820s.

Canning started developing into an important industry with the invention in the 1850s of equipment to produce the cans automatically. The use of canned foods by both armies during the Civil War gave a further boost to the industry as large numbers of Americans grew used to tins and came to enjoy the consumption of exotic foods as well as familiar ones out of season.

It was during this period of the late 19th century that other food production techniques were devised. Gail Borden invented a meat biscuit for people on expeditions (unfortunately it had no taste) and went on to create a more successful product in condensed milk, which he patented in 1856. Wheat farming spread throughout the prairies and plains, and the great milling empires of the Washburn and Pillsbury families were established in Minneapolis. John Dorrance perfected condensed soup, and his employer Campbell Soup began marketing the product aggressively. Henry Heinz began establishing the first national brands for prosaic products such as pickles and catsup.

The meat industry also arose during this time. Cattle raising spread through the West, and once rail lines were completed Chicago became the center of the slaughtering trade. In the 1870s Gustavus Swift and Philip Armour established companies that went on to become the giants of meatpacking. Using assembly-line techniques and newly devised refrigerator cars, Swift and Armour extended the markets for their meat products across the country. But their operations did not always adhere to the most sanitary practices. The uproar caused by the publication in 1906 of *The Jungle*, Upton Sinclair's exposé of unhealthy conditions in meatpacking, prompted Congress to enact the first Pure Food and Drug Law.

The rise of factory food elicited a backlash in the form of evangelical-type nutrition movements. One of the crusaders was Mother Ellen White of the Adventist Church, who established a sanitarium in Battle Creek, Michigan, in 1866. Under the leadership of Dr. John Kellogg, the establishment became famous for having its patients eat dry, brittle food. The cereal concoctions served at Battle Creek were soon being marketed to a receptive public by, among others, William Kellogg (brother of the head of Battle Creek and founder of the Kellogg

Company) and Charles Post (a former patient at the sanitarium who called his version Grape-Nuts).

THE RISE OF THE FOOD ENGINEERS

Like the Civil War, World War II served to advance the food processing industry. Special packaging techniques used to feed the troops were later adapted to civilian use. The reluctance of women, who had gotten a taste of work outside the home during the war, to return to drudgery in the kitchen encouraged the invention of all sorts of prepared products, many of them in frozen form (the freezing of food was perfected by Clarence Birdseye, a sometime explorer, after World War I).

The creation of "instant" versions of food required a great leap forward in chemistry. Manufacturers had long grappled with the problem of making processed food more appetizing. In earlier periods this was done by adding sugar, salt, and vegetable colors. By the 1950s hundreds of chemical additives with unpronounceable names were devised and used to advance what came to be called food engineering. These included stabilizers and emulsifiers to maintain consistency, preservatives to prevent spoilage, and artificial flavors and colors to enhance taste and appearance.

Perhaps the leading paradigm of the rise of food engineering was the quest for a substance that would substitute for the cream used in coffee. In the early 1950s chemists devised an instant powdered version, dubbed Pream, that had the desired characteristics: It did not need to be refrigerated, and it was immune to spoilage. The problem was that it had the wrong taste. The Carnation Company improved on it with the introduction of Coffee-Mate in 1961. This product more convincingly imitated cream, and it stimulated an entire array of nondairy coffee "lighteners."

The notion of completely synthetic foods as the solution to world hunger enjoyed a vogue in the 1960s, along with great hopes for soybeans and fish protein concentrates. While completely lab-produced food did not advance very far, food engineering marched on. Convenience foods overwhelmed the nation's supermarkets, and it required an increasingly sophisticated knowledge of chemistry to understand the labels on foodstuffs. By the late 1970s genetic engineering was added to the industry's bag of tricks. For instance, companies such as Campbell Soup and Heinz have sponsored research aimed at developing "super tomatoes" with tough skins that allow them to be picked mechanically and shipped to soup and catsup factories with less damage. Some experiments have tried to create square tomatoes that would be even more efficient to process. Taste, of course, ends up being something less than super.

ROLLER COASTER PRICES

Whereas technology was the preoccupation of the food industry in the 1950s and 1960s, the following decade saw the laws of economics return to center stage. In the early 1970s food prices changed their traditional behavior and shot ahead of other elements of the cost of living. The sharp price increases, especially for meat, in the early 1970s turned out to be linked to a huge sale of grain to the Soviet Union. Public resentment was increased as people began to realize the extent to which food production and distribution had been taken over by the behemoth known as agribusiness. As a result of the Soviet deal, some public exposure was for the first time given to the giant grain-trading companies such as Cargill and Continental Grain.

While farmers were certainly enjoying higher income in these years, the accusatory finger came to be pointed at the food processors and distributors, which were estimated to keep 60 cents of every dollar Americans spent on food. The processing of food became one of the most profitable of industries, yet the prosperity on the farm was short-lived.

By 1976 farm prices were sinking, and farmers with medium and small operations grew restless. The insurgent American Agricultural Movement, founded in 1977, called for a farmer's strike (which did not succeed) and organized a tractor blockade of Washington in 1978. The movement's demand was for an improvement in the federal government's price-support program.

That program dates back to the Agricultural Adjustment Act of 1933, which sought to remedy the perennial problem of American farmers: overproduction and the consequent downward tendency of the prices they receive for their output. The 1933 law put the government in the business of providing subsidies and controlling acreage devoted to six basic crops. While the Agriculture Department paid out substantial sums each year to farmers—often on the condition that they not farm—the program did not protect them from severe economic crunches. In the late 1970s, the farmers' rallying cry was for complete parity—an esoteric concept that meant a guarantee of supports that would keep farm prices in the same relationship to production costs as existed in the golden era of 1910–1914.

The farm movement never succeeded in winning its full agenda in Congress, but it did manage to keep the price-support program alive even while the Reagan administration was slashing subsidies of all sorts. In part this was the result of the severe crisis of the farm sector in the first half of the 1980s, stemming from factors such as President Carter's embargo on grain sales to the Soviet Union, high interest rates, and sinking commodity prices.

The troubles in the farm sector tended to accelerate the concentration of ownership; bigger operations were better able to weather the crisis. Of the 2.3 million farms still in existence in 1985, those with more than $100,000 in sales generated almost 70 percent of farm income and received 66 percent of government subsidies. Smaller, family farmers had by 1985 fallen into desperate enough straits to warrant a charitable media event—Farm Aid—along the lines of the concerts organized for the starving people of Africa. The plight of the farmer was also worsened by the growing level of food imports. By 1986 the United States had its first trade deficit in food since 1959.

The suffering of the farm sector also brought grief to the industries that supply it, especially the farm equipment producers. Industry leader International Harvester—which suffered a six-month strike in 1979–80—experienced heavy losses and came close to bankruptcy. In 1985, after a succession of management shake-ups, Harvester dropped out of the business. It sold its agricultural equipment line to Tenneco subsidiary J. I. Case and devoted itself to producing trucks under the new corporate name of Navistar International. Deere & Co. responded to the slump by embarking on an extensive cost-cutting drive. When the market started to recover in the late 1980s, industry leader Deere found itself losing ground to Case and to Ford Motor, which became a major player in the market through the acquisition of New Holland and Canada's Versatile Corp.

Around 1987 the farm sector began to show signs of recovery. Export income was boosted by a weak dollar and a 4-million-ton wheat sale to the Soviet Union. Yet the following year saw the arrival of a different kind of crisis: the worst drought since the 1930s. Many crops were devastated, and although food prices shot up, many farmers had less to sell. The rains eventually did return, and it turned out that the drought contributed to greater prosperity for farmers in the final years of the decade because the reduction of surpluses helped keep up farm prices. Consumers, on the other hand, were unhappy to find more of their income going to pay for food.

UNCERTAINTY AND CONSOLIDATION AMONG THE PROCESSORS

Low farm prices spell prosperity rather than despair for the big food processors; for them it means reduced raw materials costs. The food industry has, however, faced a challenge in keeping up with the changing demographics and tastes of the great consuming masses.

The push toward convenience that occurred right after World War II returned with much greater force in the 1970s. The entry of millions of women into the waged labor market brought about a demand for foods that could be prepared in even less time and with appliances such as microwave ovens. But the new consumer requirements had other dimensions. There was much greater concern about nutrition and weight watching, while at the same time people were growing more sophisticated and adventuresome in their tastes.

These trends have prompted food companies to move in

two major directions. On the one side they have been furiously developing products with reduced levels of sugar, salt, cholesterol, fat, and artificial ingredients. After studies found some correlation between the consumption of oat bran and reduction in cholesterol levels, there was a mad rush to put oat bran in everything from candy bars to beer. Cereal companies such as General Mills and Kellogg pushed the fiber craze even further with the introduction of products containing the grain psyllium, though General Mills withdrew its product in early 1990 amid pressure from the FDA to substantiate health claims.

Adopting terms such as "natural" and "lite" that are not subject to federal rules, the processors have given consumers the appearance if not always the reality of healthier foods. By the late 1980s companies were growing even bolder in their health claims. As food processors began touting their products as cures for a variety of ailments, it seemed as if the supermarket was becoming a modern medicine show. The easing of federal regulation during the Reagan administration encouraged this trend, though many state governments stepped in to restrain the snake-oil claims. In early 1990 the Bush administration followed the lead of the states and announced stricter regulations on health claims. The administration also announced plans for mandatory nutritional labeling on virtually all packaged foods.

The other move has been toward upscale products that may be more pleasing to the palate but work against the health trend. For instance, super-premium ice creams, which have greatly elevated levels of butterfat, were one of the success stories of the past dozen years. Once-specialized items such as croissants are being produced and consumed on a mass level.

The industry is hoping to resolve the conflict between health and indulgence through the development of fat substitutes that would allow people to consume rich foods without worrying about their cholesterol levels. In the late 1960s scientists at Procter & Gamble discovered a substance called sucrose polyester, which has the same texture as natural fats but is indigestible by the body, meaning that it does not end up in the bloodstream. By the end of the 1980s P&G was still awaiting regulatory approval for the synthetic substance, named olestra, while NutraSweet Corp. raced ahead with its fat substitute called Simplesse. NutraSweet—a subsidiary of Monsanto, which developed the artificial sweetener aspartame—initially thought that Simplesse did not require federal approval, since it was made from natural ingredients. The Food and Drug Administration demurred, but the agency did move faster on NutraSweet's application than it did on the P&G application. In early 1990 the FDA approved the use of Simplesse for frozen dessert products. Since Simplesse cannot be used in cooking, P&G still has hopes for olestra.

Americans want their food to be not only healthy and tasty but convenient as well. By the beginning of the 1990s some 70 percent of U.S. households owned microwave ovens, and various surveys showed that 15 minutes was the maximum time most Americans were willing to spend preparing an ordinary meal. Using new forms of packaging and new food formulations, the major processors have been spending huge sums to develop new microwave products ranging from pizza to cakes to hot-fudge sundaes.

While hustling to keep up with the often contradictory desires of consumers, the food industry has also had to cope with the fact that the business has simply not been expanding at a torrid rate. Demographics have kept growth in demand rather modest.

Companies have responded in several ways. One has been an intensification of the battle for market share. When a hot new area comes along (such as granola bars a few years ago) the big firms all jump in and heavily promote their versions. The pace of new-product introductions has accelerated, reaching more than 12,000 in 1989, though it must be noted that many of these are simply modifications of existing offerings. Another element of the market-share battle has been the introduction of national brands to products (such as pasta) that were previously sold regionally or ones (such as fruits and vegetables) that were not sold by brand at all. In the late 1980s Campbell led the way in tailoring national brands to varying local tastes and otherwise customizing the marketing process.

MERGING IN THE KITCHEN

The other approach has been to grow by buying someone else's business. The once-sleepy food industry has become a hotbed of merger activity. Acquisitions have come in three phases. Starting in the 1960s many companies responded to the first signs of slower growth by diversifying into other businesses. One popular area was toys: General Mills bought Parker Brothers, and Quaker Oats acquired Fisher-Price. Meatpacker Esmark generated lots of bad jokes when it acquired Playtex, a leading producer of women's undergarments, in 1975.

Many of the food companies were not successful as conglomerates, so the second wave of acquisitions was focused on the food industry itself. Following the early lead of Beatrice, which had been snapping up hundreds of small food producers since the 1950s, other processors began hunting for firms that would fit in with their existing operations. Campbell Soup entered the dog food and pickle businesses; General Foods bought Entenmann's bakers; Heinz swept into the low-calorie market with the purchase of Weight Watchers International; Hershey acquired several pasta makers; and Pillsbury adopted Green Giant.

The third and most recent wave has been the most dramatic. Rather than simply acquiring relatively small producers, the food giants have become engrossed in a spectacular series of billion-dollar mergers—the largest outside of the oil industry. This phase may be said to have begun with the merger of Nabisco and Standard Brands in 1981. While that was billed as a consolidation of equals (the combined company was named Nabisco Brands), the following deals were more in the line of takeovers.

In 1984 Swiss food giant Nestlé offered to buy Carnation for $3 billion. The following year the big cigarette makers, seeking to diversify further out of tobacco, got into the act. R. J. Reynolds (which had already bought Del Monte in 1979) arranged to acquire Nabisco Brands for $4.9 billion. A few months later Philip Morris made a deal to take over giant General Foods for $5.6 billion.

More remarkable was the series of deals that began with a

1983 attempt by David Mahoney, chief executive of Norton Simon, to take his food-based conglomerate private through a leveraged buyout. Mahoney was thwarted when the company was instead acquired for $977 million by Esmark (the name adopted by meatpacker Swift & Company in 1973). A year later Kohlberg, Kravis, Roberts & Co. tried to take Esmark private through a leveraged buyout, only to be outbid by Beatrice, which paid $2.7 billion. In 1985 the Kohlberg firm turned around and proposed a leveraged buyout of industry octopus Beatrice. This time the buyout went through—for a final price of $6.2 billion.

The food industry takeover wave escalated once again in late 1988. In the course of only a few weeks, Britain's Grand Metropolitan made a bid for Pillsbury, Philip Morris announced its intention to acquire Kraft, and the top management of RJR Nabisco launched an effort to take the company private through a leveraged buyout. Pillsbury succumbed to Grand Met in a deal worth $5.8 billion after its poison-pill defense was struck down in court. Philip Morris won Kraft for $12.9 billion and, by combining it with General Foods, emerged with the world's second largest food company (behind Switzerland's Nestlé). A bidding war emerged for RJR Nabisco among the management-led group, Kohlberg, Kravis, Roberts & Co., and First Boston (which withdrew before the bitter end). The Kohlberg firm was victorious and ended up paying a staggering $25 billion for the food and tobacco company—by far the largest deal in history. In 1990 ConAgra agreed to pay Kohlberg, Kravis, Roberts & Co. $1.3 billion for Beatrice.

THE CRISIS OF THE MEATPACKING INDUSTRY

While many food processors look attractive to tobacco companies, one segment of the business has been mired in crisis for some time. The once powerful meatpacking industry has been crippled by changing patterns of consumption and high costs.

Actually there are two segments to the industry. The old-line producers have had the most difficulties. Some of their

The 20 Largest Food Companies by 1988 Food Sales ($ Billions)

1. Philip Morris Companies	$25.8
2. RJR Nabisco	9.9
3. Anheuser-Busch	9.4
4. ConAgra	8.6
5. IBP	8.5
6. PepsiCo	8.2
7. Coca-Cola	8.0
8. Archer Daniels Midland	7.2
9. Nestlé Holdings	6.0
10. Campbell Soup	5.7
11. H. J. Heinz	5.5
12. Borden	5.4
13. Sara Lee	5.3
14. Quaker Oats	4.9
15. CPC International	4.7
16. Ralston Purina	4.6
17. Kellogg	4.3
18. Beatrice	4.1
19. General Mills	4.0
20. Pillsbury	3.6

Source: *Food Processing*, December 1989.

tribulations were caused by the rise in the 1960s of a new generation of meatpackers—especially Iowa Beef Processors, later bought by Occidental Petroleum and called IBP—that set up their slaughterhouses right in the cattle-raising areas, thus enjoying much lower costs than the companies that were stuck with facilities in Chicago and other cities.

Most of the older packers ended up being acquired or going though other transformations: Greyhound bought Armour (and later sold it to ConAgra); General Foods bought Oscar Mayer; Swift became Esmark, and its meatpacking business was later spun off as Swift Independent Co.; and Wilson Foods, purchased by LTV in 1967, was spun off in 1981, went into Chapter 11 in 1983, and was bought by Doskocil Companies in 1988 (which in turn entered Chapter 11 in 1990).

The industry has consolidated, and the survivors are concentrating on the more profitable processed products rather than simple slaughtered meat. This meant that by the end of the decade, IBP—49 percent of which was spun off by Occidental to the public in 1987—was losing ground to companies like Geo. A. Hormel & Co., which introduced a line of shelf-stable items that required no refrigeration. At the same time, the poultry segment of the industry has gained ground as per capita chicken consumption moved ahead of beef consumption in the late 1980s.

STEPS TOWARD DEREGULATION

The initial Pure Food and Drug Law inspired by Upton Sinclair's revelations about meatpacking was followed in 1938 by the Food, Drug and Cosmetic Act. While this law provided for additional regulation of food production, it put the burden on the Food and Drug Administration to prove that any substance used in processing was unsafe.

The cancer scares of the 1950s helped bring about a series of amendments in 1958 that shifted the burden of proof to manufacturers to show that substances were safe. The 1958 legislation also included a provision, known as the Delaney Clause, that put an absolute ban on the use of any additive found in laboratory tests to cause cancer in animals or humans. The law did, however, allow manufacturers to continue employing additives already in use and generally regarded as safe. Some of these, including the artificial sweetener cyclamate, were later found to be carcinogenic, and the FDA began the long process of testing them all.

There has for many years been heated debate on the use of food additives. The industry has defended the substances as safe and essential to providing the variety of foods American consumers want. Critics have warned of possible health risks. The FDA has wavered between strong action and indulgence of the industry, delaying for many years the implementation of a ban on a group of artificial colors. The public has been perplexed.

In 1985 FDA Commissioner Frank Young began taking steps to loosen regulation. Young explicitly said that the agency would adopt an unorthodox view of the Delaney Clause: that substances posing only a *small* risk of cancer could be authorized. Young put this into action in late 1985, when the agency permitted the use of the carcinogen methylene chloride in decaffeinating coffee.

The FDA has also moved to drop the barriers to the controversial practice of food irradiation. The process, developed in the 1950s, is said to be a superior form of preservation because less heat is used than in other techniques. Irradiation is permitted in a number of other countries, but opponents in the United States argue that the long-term health effects of the practice are not known. Irradiation was given a boost in 1984 after the Environmental Protection Agency halted the use of the pesticide ethylene dibromide on stored grain. In 1985 the FDA gave approval for Radiation Technology of Rockaway, New Jersey—a leader in the business—to begin irradiating pork and later authorized wider use of the process.

The Environmental Protection Agency, which has jurisdiction over the use of pesticides, announced in 1988 that it would follow the FDA in applying a looser interpretation of the Delaney Clause, yet the agency claimed it was actually strengthening regulation since it planned to begin applying the standard to pesticides that were in use before the 1972 federal law on pesticides took effect.

While federal regulation remained ambivalent, public anxiety about food safety soared in the late 1980s. The worries seemed to reach a fever pitch in 1989 after there were reports that fruit from Chile was tainted with cyanide, that the ripening agent Alar used in growing red apples was a dangerous carcinogen, and that milk—the symbol of food purity—could contain dioxin leached from paperboard containers as well as traces of antibiotics and sulfa drugs given to cows.

Perhaps more than anything else, these scares have given a new legitimacy to what is known as alternative agriculture—the avoidance of pesticides, chemical fertilizers, and the like. Organic farming, once the province of hippie communes, is now being tried by large agribusiness enterprises.

LABOR RELATIONS

The creation of large-scale agricultural operations in California in the late 19th century brought with it the first farm labor organizing. The miserable conditions under which the mostly

Chinese and Japanese immigrant labor force toiled made the big farms a focus of agitation by the Industrial Workers of the World (IWW) in the early years of the 20th century. But the group's Agricultural Workers Organization fell prey, along with the rest of the IWW, to the repression of radicals during and after World War I.

Militancy in the fields arose again in the 1930s, especially among Mexican workers, who had become the largest immigrant group in the California farm labor force. The Communist party set up the Cannery and Agricultural Workers Industrial Union, which won some strikes in the early 1930s but found organizing difficult after California became flooded with desperate Dust Bowl refugees. Tensions between rival AFL and CIO organizers also limited the organizing progress of the period.

Greater success was achieved in Hawaii. Harry Bridges' International Longshoremen's and Warehousemen's Union (ILWU) made an impressive effort in the 1940s to organize the multiethnic labor force of the sugar and pineapple plantations of the islands. The ILWU won passage of legislation that sanctioned organizing among Hawaiian plantation workers—a right denied their brethren on the mainland. After a series of major strikes, the ILWU was firmly entrenched, and the Hawaiian farm workers got some of the best wages and conditions of agricultural laborers anywhere.

Back on the mainland there was a resumption of farm organizing after the war, but it was complicated by the establishment of the *bracero* program, under which growers were allowed to bring in low-wage workers from Mexico to toil in the fields. Established unions were once again unable to overcome their rivalries, and the major advance in farm-worker organizing did not come until the 1960s, when a Chicano organizer named Cesar Chavez put together an association closely tied to the Catholic Church.

Chavez's National Farm Workers' Association joined with Filipino workers in a mid-1960s strike against grape growers in Delano, California. Taking advantage of the fact that farm workers were exempt from federal labor law and thus were not constrained by the ban on secondary actions, Chavez expanded the strike to a consumer boycott, particularly against the products of Schenley Industries. Chavez gained the support of political figures such as Senator Robert Kennedy, and after a 230-mile *peregrinaciones* (pilgrimage) to Sacramento to request action on farm labor by the governor, the union was recognized by Schenley. Chavez's organization, which became the United Farm Workers (UFW), continued its campaign against other producers of table grapes and won contracts with the major growers in 1970.

The UFW then moved on to the California lettuce and strawberry fields, but the union ran into increasing competition from the Teamsters, who increased their foothold in agriculture by offering sweetheart deals to the growers. The two unions signed an agreement in 1977 that defined separate jurisdictions, but rivalry continued, and in 1984 the Teamsters declined to renew the pact.

Chavez scored a major victory in 1975 when he got the California legislature to enact a collective bargaining law for farm workers. The UFW made good use of the law, especially in a drawn-out but largely successful strike against lettuce growers in 1979. But the future of the UFW remained threatened by two forces: an internal rebellion in the union against the autocratic leadership of Chavez and the march of mechanization in the fields. The union also faced a less sympathetic figure in the California statehouse after George Deukmejian succeeded Jerry Brown as governor in 1983.

Through the rest of the 1980s the UFW pursued a new national boycott of table grapes, focusing on the pesticide hazards for consumers as well as workers. While the boycott attracted a fair amount of support, the union itself remained in crisis because of declining membership levels and adverse court judgments in suits brought by growers in connection with violence during previous strikes.

Since the UFW failed to expand its organizing efforts much beyond California, it was another group, calling itself the Farm Labor Organizing Committee (FLOC), that took up the plight of the migrant laborers who picked tomatoes and cucumbers in Ohio and Michigan. The committee organized a strike against the growers (who mainly supplied Campbell Soup) in

1978 and a boycott of Campbell products in 1979. Finally in 1986 the workers triumphed, getting both the growers and Campbell to sign an unusual three-party contract. In 1987 FLOC won representation rights for workers at farms in Ohio and Michigan that grow cucumbers for Heinz. In 1990 FLOC signed a new contract with Heinz and its cucumber growers that eliminated the sharecropper status of the farm workers and gave them regular employee status.

Another labor triumph occurred in 1987 at Watsonville Canning and Frozen Food in California. Some 1,100 workers (most of them Latino women) represented by the Teamsters carried out a dogged 18-month strike to resist concessions and succeeded in pressuring the company's main creditor, Wells Fargo Bank, to take over the business because of unpaid loans. The bank leased the facility to NorCal Frozen Foods, which reached the settlement with the union.

The other major area of labor confrontation in the food industry has been meatpacking. Unionism among butchers began after the Civil War as the big meatpacking operations were formed. The Amalgamated Meat Cutters union was chartered by the AFL in 1897. The union suffered major strike defeats in 1904 and 1922, and in the 1930s it saw the rise of a rival CIO union, the United Packinghouse Workers of America. The two bodies finally merged in 1968.

In the early 1980s the major meatpackers launched an all-out assault on labor costs. Companies successfully pressured the United Food and Commercial Workers (UFCW)—formed by the 1979 merger of the Meat Cutters and the Retail Clerks International Association—to grant wage concessions. In some cases plants were closed down and then reopened under new management that renounced previous labor agreements, as happened after Armour shut down its operations and sold them to ConAgra (ConAgra later agreed to pay $6.6 million to settle charges brought by the UFCW). An even more drastic approach was taken by Wilson Foods. In 1983 the company, claiming that its labor costs were unbearable, entered Chapter 11 for the purpose of abrogating its union contracts. After doing so, Wilson slashed wages by as much as 50 percent and kept operating.

Wage cuts and bankruptcy were also the fate of Rath Packing, whose owners decided to sell the business to the employees in 1980. The crisis of the industry made it difficult for this experiment in worker ownership to succeed. In late 1983 the management of Rath followed Wilson's lead by filing for Chapter 11 and getting a bankruptcy judge to set aside the labor contract. Despite the bitterness this caused, Rath's workers made further concessions; but it was not enough, and the company headed for liquidation.

The national leadership of the food workers union has tolerated concessions as an alternative to additional plant closings, but some locals have adopted a more militant posture. The leading example was Local P-9, which called a strike against Hormel (a leading pork processor and one of the last independent firms in the industry) after the company unilaterally cut wages by more than 20 percent in 1984. The local hired labor consultants Ray Rogers and Ed Allen, who initiated a corporate campaign against Hormel and urged the strikers to pursue their battle, even after the union's national leaders denounced the walkout as "suicidal" and ordered it to end. When Local P-9 kept up its defiance, the UFCW took over the local and negotiated a new contract with Hormel.

Labor relations have also been bitter at IBP, which successfully fought unionization at most of its facilities and took a hard line at those plants that were organized. Contract negotiations at its Dakota City, Nebraska, flagship plant have almost never proceeded smoothly, and violence has characterized many of the disputes. In December 1986 the company locked out 2,500 workers at the plant when they refused to accept a wage freeze. The UFCW launched a public relations campaign focusing on the dismal safety record at the plant and allegations that IBP understated the number of injuries in reports to the federal government. The campaign helped to focus public attention on the abysmal safety record of the industry and led to a record $2.6 million fine against IBP by the federal Occupational Safety and Health Administration in 1987. The dispute in Dakota City, which changed from a lockout to a strike, was settled after seven months when the union agreed to a two-tier wage system.

LEADING COMPANIES

Campbell Soup was built on the invention of condensed soup in the 1890s by chemist John Dorrance, who worked for his uncle's canning company. The firm had a big success with the product, making Campbell one of the first national food brands and still one of the most highly regarded. The firm bought Pepperidge Farm, a producer of premium baked goods, in 1961 and in the 1970s diversified into businesses such as pickles, chocolate, dog food, and restaurants. Campbell continued to pursue growth through acquisition in the 1980s with purchases such as Mrs. Paul's Kitchens, a leading frozen-fish producer, as well as through the introduction of new products such as Le Menu frozen dinners. In the latter part of the decade the company found its dominant position in the soup market eroded by a variety of challengers.

Cargill is the largest of the highly secretive half-dozen companies that dominate the world grain trade. Privately held Cargill was founded in the 1860s by Will Cargill, who along with Frank Peavey soon dominated the U.S. grain business. Under the leadership of the Cargill and MacMillan families, the company gained a reputation as a "faceless giant." It along with the other big trading companies got some unwelcome attention in the 1970s because of their role in arranging the controversial Soviet grain sales. In recent decades Cargill has branched out into a variety of other businesses, including salt mining, barge construction, and sugar. In 1978 it acquired meatpacker MBPXL, later renamed Excel. The company's staggering size was revealed in late 1985, when it made one of its infrequent disclosures of financial results: For the year ending May 1985, revenues were more than $32 billion, making Cargill the country's largest private company. In 1989 Forbes estimated that the figure had risen to $43 billion.

During the 1980s **ConAgra** was transformed from a sleepy producer of feed, flour, and poultry into a diversified and aggressive food producer. The firm became a major force in meatpacking through the purchase of Armour, Monfort of Colorado, and half of Swift Independent. By 1989 ConAgra was a leader in beef, poultry, and seafood and had turned itself into the country's fourth-largest food processing company. That position was bolstered in 1990, when ConAgra agreed to purchase Beatrice for $1.3 billion. Founded in Nebraska in 1894 as a middleman for dairy and poultry products, Beatrice grew into a large dairy producer in the first half of the 20th century. Starting in the early 1950s Beatrice went on a dazzling buying spree, acquiring several hundred food companies. Beatrice itself kept a low profile and allowed its many businesses to operate quite independently. The obsession with growth came under some criticism in the 1970s, and after James Dutt won a boardroom battle for control of the company in 1979, he set out to sell a number of money-losing and even some successful businesses. He later reorganized the company and launched a campaign to make the Beatrice name known to consumers. Dutt ran afoul of the company's board and was ousted in 1985. A few months later, Kohlberg, Kravis, Roberts & Co. arranged to take the company private for more than $6 billion. The position of chief executive was given to Donald Kelly, former head of Esmark (bought by Beatrice in 1984). Kelly then embarked on a process of selling off chunks of the company.

General Mills was put together in 1928 by Minneapolis miller James Bell and half a dozen other big millers from across the country. The company became a major figure in the cereal (Wheaties, Cheerios) and flour businesses. In the 1960s it diversified into such areas as toys and clothing, but the nonfood businesses were spun off in 1985. The company benefited greatly during the oat bran craze of the late 1980s, though it withdrew a product containing the grain psyllium after questions about its safety.

H. J. Heinz has been a leader in the production of pickles, relishes, sauces, and condiments for more than a century. It is perhaps best known for its catsup and its 57 Varieties slogan (an arbitrary number from the start). Heinz bought the Ore-Ida frozen potato business in 1965 and Weight Watchers foods in 1978. Under chief executive Anthony O'Reilly the company has emphasized cost controls and has sought to expand its already extensive foreign operations.

Kellogg, the leader in the breakfast cereal market, has resisted diversification. Founded by William Kellogg to sell what was then a health food—wheat flakes—the company survived a long Federal Trade Commission antitrust action against the leaders of the cereal industry in the 1970s. After becoming chief executive in 1979, William LaMothe launched a campaign to increase market share and discouraged a takeover by buying back 20 percent of the company's stock. Kellogg capitalized on the health concerns of the 1980s by running aggressive marketing campaigns for its cereals, including an effort to push its high-fiber All-Bran product as a cancer preventive and the marketing of a product called Heartwise that contained the grain psyllium, which was said to be even more effective than oat bran in reducing cholesterol. Nevertheless, the company lost ground in the late 1980s to General Mills amid the oat bran mania.

As part of its diversification effort, tobacco giant **Philip Morris** has made huge acquisitions in the food industry and turned itself into the largest food company in the United States. General Foods, acquired in 1985 for more than $5 billion, was for many years the major innovator in the food industry. General Foods dates back to the cereal business started by Charles Post after his time at the Battle Creek Sanitarium. Postum Cereal later merged with the Jell-O Company and Clarence Birdseye's frozen food operations. Long a leader in coffee roasting and frozen vegetables, General Foods in the early 1980s sought to reduce its dependence on mature products by acquiring companies such as Entenmann's bakers, the Ronzoni pasta company, and meatpacker Oscar Mayer. General Foods also scored with new products such as Crystal Light powdered beverage and Jell-O Pudding Pops. By the late 1980s many of the company's products were out of sync with changing tastes, causing the firm to lose ground in markets such as breakfast cereal. Kraft had its origins in the cheese business that James Kraft started in Chicago in 1903 and in a group of dairy companies. Functioning as a subsidiary of National Dairy Products, Kraft produced processed favorites such as Velveeta cheese spread and Miracle Whip salad dressing. In 1980 the company merged with Dart Industries, maker of Tupperware products, Duracell batteries, and other items. Six years later Dart and Kraft decided to go their separate ways, with Kraft keeping the food businesses and Duracell, and Dart holding onto everything else. Philip Morris paid $12.9 billion to acquire Kraft in 1988.

Pillsbury was founded in 1869 by Charles Pillsbury, who went on to become one of the pillars of the Minneapolis milling business. Known mainly as a producer of flour and other baked products (its Doughboy is one of the more famous advertising characters), the company got into the restaurant business in the 1960s with the purchase of Burger King. William Spoor, who ran Pillsbury from 1973 to 1985, arranged the acquisition of Green Giant (the largest packer of peas and corn), Häagen-Dazs ice cream, and Van de Kamp's (a specialty food producer). After the company faltered under the leadership of Spoor's successor, John Stafford, Spoor was temporarily brought out of retirement to resume his old job. The weakened company was taken over by Britain's Grand Metropolitan for $5.8 billion in 1989. Grand Met sold off Van de Kamp's and the Bumble Bee tuna business while converting Burger King and Häagen-Dazs from Pillsbury units into free-standing operations.

Quaker Oats was formed in the late 19th century by a group of oatmeal millers; the Quaker name was adopted in 1901. The company became the leader in hot cereals and was also one of the early producers of pet food. Starting in 1969 the company branched out into other food areas, such as Celeste frozen pizza and Stokely Van Camp, maker of pork and beans and Gatorade drink. It also diversified into a number of nonfood businesses, but by the late 1980s the company was narrowing its scope once again. In 1986 Quaker purchased Anderson, Clayton & Co., best known as the producer of Gaines Burger and Gravy Train dog foods.

RJR Nabisco was the result, first, of the 1981 merger of Nabisco and Standard Brands and then the 1985 purchase of the combined company by R. J. Reynolds. Nabisco itself was born of the merger of two rival baking groups in 1898. The company developed the first brand-name cracker (Uneeda) and went on to dominate the cookie and cracker market with brands such as Ritz, Oreo, and Fig Newton. Standard Brands was built on Fleischmann yeast and gin, Royal baking powder, and Chase & Sanborn coffee. Reynolds entered the food business with the 1966 purchase of Chun King Chinese foods. A 1988 proposal by top management to take the company private through a leveraged buyout prompted a bidding war in which Kohlberg, Kravis, Roberts & Co. ended up acquiring the firm for $25 billion—the largest takeover ever.

SOURCE GUIDE

Leading Stock Analysts and Experts

George Abraham, a leading meatpacking consultant, of Abraham & Associates, Sarasota, Florida.

William Leach, food industry analyst at Donaldson, Lufkin & Jenrette.

William Maguire, food industry analyst at Merrill Lynch.

John McMillin, food industry analyst at Prudential-Bache.

Trade Associations and Unions

American Frozen Food Institute, 1764 Old Meadow Lane, McLean, VA 22102. Tel.: (703) 821–0770.

American Meat Institute, 1700 N. Moore Street, Arlington, VA 22209. Tel.: (703) 841–2400.

Bakery, Confectionery and Tobacco Workers International Union, 1041 Connecticut Avenue, Kensington, MD 20895. Tel.: (301) 933–8600.

Grocery Manufacturers of America, 1010 Wisconsin Avenue NW, Washington, DC 20007. Tel.: (202) 337–9400.

National Food Processors Association, 1401 New York Avenue NW, Washington, DC 20005. Tel.: (202) 639–5900.

United Farm Workers of America, P.O. Box 62, Keene, CA 93531. Tel.: (805) 822–5571.

United Food and Commercial Workers International Union, 1775 K Street NW, Washington, DC 20006. Tel.: (202) 223–3111.

Data Sources and Directories

Agricultural Statistics, annual (Washington, D.C.: U.S. Department of Agriculture).

Food Engineering's Directory of U.S. Food Plants, biennial (Radnor, Penn.: Chilton Company).

Hereld's 5,000—The Directory of Leading U.S. Food, Confectionary and Beverage Manufacturers, quarterly (Hamden, Conn.: Hereld Organization).

Meat Packers, an annual directory (Omaha, Neb.: American Business Directories).

Who Owns Whom in the U.S. Food, Confectionery and Beverage Manufacturing Industry, quarterly (Hartford, Conn.: SIC Publishing).

Online Databases

AGRIBUSINESS U.S.A. (Johnston, Iowa: Pioneer Hi-Bred International; available via Dialog).

FOODS ADLIBRA (Minneapolis: General Mills; available via Dialog).

Trade Publications

Agricultural Outlook (U.S. Department of Agriculture), monthly.

Food Engineering, monthly.

Food Processing, monthly.

Food Technology, monthly.

Frozen Food Age, monthly.

Meat & Poultry, monthly.

Milling and Baking News, weekly.

National Food Review (U.S. Department of Agriculture), quarterly.

National Provisioner, weekly.

Books and Reports

George, Susan. *Feeding the Few: Corporate Control of Food.* Washington, D.C.: Institute for Policy Studies, no date.

Marsh, Barbara. *A Corporate Tragedy: The Agony of International Harvester Co.* Garden City, N.Y.: Doubleday Publishing, 1985.

Meister, Dick, and Anne Loftis. *A Long Time Coming: The Struggle to Unionize America's Farm Workers.* New York: Macmillan, 1977.

Morgan, Dan. *Merchants of Grain.* New York: Penguin Books, 1980.

Root, Waverly, and Richard de Rochemont. *Eating in America: A History.* New York: William Morrow, 1976.

U.S. Congress, Office of Technology Assessment. *Technology, Public Policy and the Changing Structure of American Agriculture.* Washington, D.C., 1986.

CHAPTER 10

RESTAURANTS, HOTELS, AND CASINOS

Restaurants and hotels have traditionally been among the most entrepreneurial of businesses in the sense that the barriers to entry are relatively minor. Inns, taverns, and other public places have been around for centuries and have represented the easiest route for enterprising souls who want to escape from the laboring classes. Proprietors of restaurants and small hotels work long, hard hours and put their personal mark on the establishment. This form of commerce is the quintessential small business.

Yet in early 20th century America a new approach to the business of feeding and lodging was beginning to take shape. In 1919 a man named Conrad Hilton bought and renovated a small hotel in Cisco, Texas. In 1925 Howard Johnson took over a money-losing drugstore in Quincy, Massachusetts, and made a hit selling homemade ice cream. In 1927 John Willard Marriott opened a root beer stand in Washington, D.C., and then branched into spicy Mexican food during the winter months.

From such unlikely beginnings these three men built empires that have changed the landscape of the country. Joined by McDonald's hamburger stands and Holiday Inns in the mid-1950s, these franchised and corporate-owned hotels and restaurants have replaced smaller, locally owned establishments and turned food and lodging into major industries.

THE FAST-FOOD REVOLUTION

The man who deserves the most credit or blame for transforming the eating habits of America is Ray Kroc. A sometime piano player and paper cup salesman, Kroc was 52 and the distributor of Multimixer milkshake machines when he had what amounted to a religious experience in 1954. It occurred while he was visiting a major customer, the McDonald Brothers, who operated a roadside hamburger stand in San Bernardino, California.

Kroc was overwhelmed by the volume of business the McDonalds were enjoying by serving up bags of burgers, french fries, and milkshakes with factorylike efficiency. While the brothers were satisfied with their modest gold mine, Kroc immediately envisioned a string of such establishments across the country. He made a deal with the McDonalds under which Kroc got the right to use their name and methods in franchising the concept and the brothers would get a bit more than a quarter of the 1.9 percent of the franchisees' gross to be collected by Kroc.

The McDonald's concept spread like a brush fire. The number of stores jumped from dozens to hundreds, and the number of hamburgers sold—displayed on a sign below the golden arches—soared into the billions. Kroc established rigid standards by which the stands had to be operated; in fact, he turned the management of a McDonald's into a sort of science, the precepts of which are taught to aspiring store managers at an institution called Hamburger University.

Kroc's system essentially involved the industrialization of food service: the use of equipment and procedures that were so defined that a totally inexperienced teenager—the preferred employee—could be inserted into the system and function with no difficulty. The result was a perfectly tuned machine turning out utterly predictable food in a wholesome and unthreatening environment. Kroc summarized his approach as Quality, Service, Cleanliness, and Value.

The remarkable rise of McDonald's served as the catalyst for the emergence of a national fast-food industry. The diners and greasy spoons that lined the country's roads were steadily replaced by the familiar outlets of a small number of major chains. The pattern of the hamburger business was repeated in other sectors such as fried chicken (Kentucky Fried Chicken), pizza (Pizza Hut), fish (Arthur Treacher's), and even restaurants with more extensive menus (Denny's).

The go-go atmosphere of fast food in the 1960s brought the business to the attention of large corporations. Pillsbury acquired Burger King in 1967, General Foods bought the Burger Chef chain in 1968, and Heublein purchased Kentucky Fried Chicken in 1971. Later, PepsiCo acquired Pizza Hut and Taco Bell, and Hershey Foods bought Friendly Ice Cream Corp.

The industry continued to grow in the 1970s, helped by demographic changes such as the movement of women into the waged labor market and by economic changes such as the sharp rise in the cost of food used to prepare meals at home. Aided by extensive marketing and advertising expenditures, the chains turned fast-food "dining" into a socially acceptable way for a family to feed itself. Using devices such as the Ronald McDonald character, McDonald's in particular won the loyalty of children, who became increasingly important in determining where a family was going to eat out. In 1972 McDonald's reached $1 billion in total store sales and surpassed the U.S. Army as the nation's biggest dispenser of meals.

The supremacy of McDonald's in the hamburger business began to be challenged in the 1970s. After initially holding back the necessary investment in Burger King, Pillsbury gave its subsidiary the resources to compete more effectively with the industry leader. Meanwhile, an executive of Arthur Treacher's Fish & Chips decided to establish a chain that would serve higher-quality and more substantial burgers than the ones purveyed by McDonald's. R. David Thomas named the firm after his daughter, and Wendy's eventually became one of the largest chains in the country.

By the 1980s both Wendy's and Burger King were prepared to challenge the predominance of the McDonald's empire. Burger King introduced successful nonhamburger menu items and in 1982 initiated the aggressive advertising campaign that came to be known as the Battle of the Burgers. Later Wendy's joined the fray with its now-famous "Where's the beef?" commercials, which exploited the fact that McDonald's had traditionally been stingy with the portion of meat in its hamburgers. McDonald's was temporarily shaken by these assaults but continued to grow at a handsome rate, thanks in part to popular new offerings such as Egg McMuffins (which opened the breakfast market to the chains), Chicken McNuggets, and later the McD.L.T., a burger with lettuce and tomato served in such a way that the meat remained hot and the vegetables cool until the thing was ready to be consumed. The chain, which reached the milestone of 10,000 outlets in 1988, has also added prepackaged salads to the menu and began experimenting with pizza.

While McDonald's was gaining ground, Burger King was falling behind in what the industry calls "share of stomach." A series of ad campaign flops and an inability to maintain consistently high standards among its outlets kept Burger King's average sales per store flat during the second half of the 1980s. Britain's Grand Metropolitan, which purchased Burger King's parent Pillsbury in 1988, put in a new management team and began a restructuring program, but the chain continued to decline.

Today the hamburger business remains the dominant force in the chain restaurant industry, which had sales of some $65 billion in 1989. This in turns represents more than one third of the $167 billion market in commercial feeding.

Yet there have been a number of reports suggesting that the burger business may not be able to keep up its customary rate of growth. There are signs that the chains have simply saturated the market and that customers are getting tired of the same old fare. The increased concern about nutrition and the revival of sophisticated dining among yuppies and other groups have cast a fair amount of disrepute on fast food.

The chains are dealing with the saturation problem by seeking new markets, including the placement of stores in institutional settings such as military bases, museums, and schools. Burger King went so far as to create a fleet of mobile restaurants in 1985 to capture potential customers such as workers at remote construction sites who could not get to a regular store.

As for the change in tastes, the chains seem to be banking mainly on the appeal of convenience and relatively low cost, though they have made some adjustments to their menus. Nonetheless, by the end of the 1980s there were signs that the great restaurant boom was coming to an end. The entire indus-

The 10 Largest Restaurant Chains by 1989 U.S. Systemwide Food Service Sales ($ Millions)

1. McDonald's	$12,012
2. Burger King	5,700
3. Pizza Hut	3,240
4. Kentucky Fried Chicken	3,000
5. Hardee's	2,980
6. Wendy's	2,827
7. Domino's Pizza	2,500
8. Marriott	2,120
9. Taco Bell	2,000
10. Dairy Queen	1,938

Source: *Nation's Restaurant News*, August 6, 1990.

try, from the "white tablecloth" establishments down to the fast-food chains, began to experience slower growth, leading to bitter price wars among the chains. The new conventional wisdom was that American families were frequently finding that eating at home—thanks to microwave ovens, a wider range of processed foods and take-out fare—was more convenient, after all.

THE RISE OF THE LODGING INDUSTRY

Small, locally owned hotels and motels went the same way as the mom-and-pop restaurant; large numbers of them were replaced by chains. Conrad Hilton branched out from Texas to sites across the country (and eventually abroad, until the international business was sold off). At the lower end of the business, Memphis real estate developer Kemmons Wilson set out in the 1950s to transform the motel from a disreputable rendezvous for lovers to a family institution. The company created by Wilson—Holiday Inns (renamed Holiday Corp. in 1985)—went on to become the largest lodging company in the world.

The industry enjoyed steady growth until the early 1980s, when it was especially hard hit by the recession and high interest rates. Nevertheless, the building boom continued, and many cities ended up with gluts of hotel rooms. By the mid-

1980s new rooms were being constructed at a rate of more than 15,000 a year, and occupancy rates slipped to about 64 percent, down from about 73 percent in the late 1970s.

Many of the lodging companies found they could no longer remain in their traditional market niches. They had to pay much greater attention to marketing and to developing new services.

The pressures on the $42 billion lodging industry led to an increasing segmentation of the business. Hoteliers moved up and down the scale in the search for new business. Companies such as Marriott went after the luxury market with the establishment of special concierge floors or all-suite hotels. In order to attract guests, hotels began offering services such as computers in rooms and teleconference facilities; there was even a willingness to cut prices, especially for conventions and other group functions.

At the same time there was a move toward less-expensive accommodations. Budget facilities such as Motel 6 prospered, and Holiday and Marriott built facilities that were attractive but inexpensive. By the end of the 1980s there were signs of a glut of low-cost rooms, and intensified price competition was shrinking profit margins.

In the hotel industry's more fragile state, a number of chains have been taken over by foreign interests. Britain's Ladbroke acquired Hilton International from UAL, Hong Kong developer New World Development bought Ramada's lodging unit, British brewer Bass became the owner of Holiday Inns, and France's Accor purchased the Motel 6 chain.

GAMBLING ON GAMING

Several of the large hotel chains have also diversified into casinos. The lucrative though not risk-free casino business began back in 1931 when the state of Nevada legalized gambling. Because state rules required each owner of a company to be licensed, public companies were effectively excluded. Instead the industry came to be infiltrated by a fair amount of organized crime money. It was mobster Bugsy Siegel, in fact, who

The 10 Largest U.S.-Based Hotel Chains in 1989

	Rooms	*Hotels*
1. Holiday	370,081	1,900
2. Marriott	135,901	542
3. ITT Sheraton	134,400	454
4. Days Inn of America	120,725	951
5. Quality International	120,352	1,082
6. New World/Ramada	108,134	591
7. Hilton Hotels	94,752	271
8. Howard Johnson/Rodeway	73,850	610
9. Hyatt Hotels	71,047	150
10. Motel 6	60,000	522

Source: *Hotels*, July 1990.

constructed the Flamingo, the first plush casino in the state, soon after the end of World War II. The 1969 Corporate Gaming Act allowed public companies to enter the business, and the image of the industry gradually improved. Yet there continued to be reports of mafia associations of some casino executives, and there have been a number of cases of skimming of profits.

Nevada retained its geographic monopoly on casino gambling until 1976, when the voters of New Jersey approved a referendum permitting the establishment of casinos in Atlantic City. Resorts International took a chance and purchased the biggest hotel in town before the vote took place. Its gamble enabled it to open its casino before anyone else, in May 1978, and to have the market to itself for a year.

Then the influx began. By the end of 1981 there were eight other casinos in town, built by Caesars World, Bally Manufacturing, Holiday, Ramada, and others. For a while it seemed that there was business enough for everyone. The gross win in Atlantic City—house wins minus house losses at the tables and the slots—grew at a phenomenal average rate of 68 percent a year.

This did not necessarily mean nirvana for the casino owners. They were saddled with heavy debt from the expensive construction of their properties, and they had to offer inducements (free bus service, free chips, etc.) to bring in the masses. By

1985 the 10 casinos in Atlantic City had gross winnings of some $2 billion, greater than that of the more than 50 casinos in Las Vegas. Yet the growth rate in Atlantic City had started to slow down significantly.

Analysts attributed the phenomenon to the limited hotel space and poor transportation system of the city, which meant that most visitors were day-trippers who tended to wager less than the Las Vegas conventioneers and vacationers, who drop greater sums during their visits, which averaged four to five days.

As these realities became clear, several companies abandoned partly constructed casinos in Atlantic City, while some of those in operation experienced losses. Elsinore Shore Associates, owner of the Atlantis Casino Hotel, filed for bankruptcy in 1985. Yet others were expecting a rosier future for the city. Showboat Inc., a Las Vegas veteran, entered the Atlantic City market, and New York real estate developer Donald Trump, already a partner in one casino, opened a second property in 1985 and bought a controlling interest in Resorts in part to rescue the company's faltering plan to construct an expensive new hotel-casino called the Taj Mahal. After television producer Merv Griffin made a takeover bid for Resorts in 1988, he and Trump reached an agreement under which Griffin took the firm private while Trump got the Taj Mahal. Faced with a heavy debt load and declining market share, Griffin filed for Chapter 11 bankruptcy in late 1989. At the same time Trump was experiencing financial difficulties and delays in the completion of the Taj Mahal. The Taj, as it became known, did open amid much hype in 1990, but only a few months later Trump was scrambling to meet payments on his junk bond debt.

Meanwhile things began looking up in Las Vegas. The "city that never sleeps" started increasing its gross winnings by worrying less about the high rollers and placing greater emphasis on the "grinds," the less affluent visitors who lose less per capita but who exist in much greater numbers.

Encouraged by the boom in business that began after the recession of the early 1980s, Las Vegas casinos embarked on a building spree intended to increase the number of hotel rooms by one third. Among the highest rollers were Circus Circus (known as "the K mart of casinos"), which built the 4,000-room Excalibur for some $300 million, and Golden Nugget, which earmarked twice that amount for a more lavish 3,000-room structure called the Mirage, complete with a man-made volcano.

Overseas money also began flowing into Las Vegas after a ban on foreign ownership of casinos was lifted in the mid-1980s. Tokyo-based Korean investor Ginji Yasuda paid $54 million for the bankrupt Aladdin. Japanese slot machine magnate Katsuki Manabe took over a closed downtown Holiday Inn, renovated the facility, and reopened it as the Park Hotel & Casino. Another Japanese businessman, Masao Nangaku, entered a high bid of $158 million for the bankrupt Dunes.

LABOR RELATIONS

The predominant sector of the restaurant industry, fast food, has remained almost entirely nonunion. Companies such as McDonald's and Burger King have gone to great lengths to maintain total control of their underpaid work force. McDonald's has employed what it calls rap sessions, discussions that serve both to allow workers to air their gripes and to allow supervisors to get a reading of the attitude of the troops.

There have been some serious organizing drives among fast-food workers, though few have been successful. When McDonald's sought to open its first stores in San Francisco in the early 1970s, the company found itself confronted by unions and local politicians who were opposing city approval because of the labor policies of the company. It took a long court battle before McDonald's prevailed. In the late 1970s the fast-food chains faced an intensive campaign in Detroit by an independent group called the Fastfood Workers' Union.

Aside from fighting unions, McDonald's has long lobbied for a lower minimum wage for teenagers, who make up the large majority of the company's labor force. The "teenwage" concept was finally adopted by Congress when the minimum wage was revised in 1989. However, by the late-1980s, with demographic trends reducing the size of the teenage labor force,

McDonald's and other chains began hiring older workers and the disabled. In 1990 a coalition of church, labor, and community groups in Philadelphia launched a boycott of McDonald's to protest the fact that workers at its inner-city restaurants were being paid $1 an hour less than those employed in suburban facilities.

Other parts of the feeding and lodging industry are more heavily unionized, the largest union being the Hotel Employees and Restaurant Employees International Union. This organization has been suspected of having mob connections; in 1984 a Senate subcommittee charged that the union was under the substantial influence of organized crime interests. Nevertheless, some the union's locals—especially Local 26 in Boston, which negotiated an innovative housing program for its members—have a more progressive reputation.

The union has been challenged both by employers (demands for concessions led to a bitter 75-day strike at Las Vegas hotels and casinos in 1984) and by a much smaller rival union, the United Industry Workers, which has convinced a number of groups of workers to switch their affiliation. The larger union staged a 27-day strike in New York City in 1985 that resulted in a 25 percent wage increase over five years. Hotel workers at eight of Atlantic City's casinos staged a one-day walkout in 1986. Casino workers in the city are not unionized. In 1990 musicians at five major casino-hotels in Las Vegas ended a 249-day strike after failing to force the facilities to end the use of taped music.

LEADING COMPANIES

Bally Manufacturing prospered for decades as the country's leading producer of slot machines and pinball machines and later arcade games such as Space Invaders and Pac-Man. The company's bid to expand into casino ownership in Atlantic City resulted in a ruling by New Jersey's tough-minded Casino Control Commission that founder William O'Donnell had to resign because of suspected associations with organized crime. Bally, under the leadership of chairman Richard Mullane, prospered by going after the low rollers. In late 1985 the company announced it would purchase MGM Grand Hotels, the owner of two casinos in Nevada. In 1987 Bally paid greenmail to thwart a takeover bid by Donald Trump and then proceeded to purchase Golden Nugget's Atlantic City casino.

Burger King, which became a subsidiary of Pillsbury in 1967, has engaged in a perennial battle with industry leader McDonald's. The company suffered frequent management changes in the late 1970s and early 1980s, but it emerged as an aggressive challenger to McDonald's, especially in the advertising arena. By the latter part of the 1980s Burger King was suffering from a string of unsuccessful ad campaigns and began falling further behind McDonald's. Grand Metropolitan, which acquired Pillsbury in 1988, set out to revitalize the chain (by, among other things, removing it from Pillsbury's control) but found it a formidable task.

Golden Nugget's young chief executive, Stephen Wynn, caused a stir in 1985 when he made a bid for Hilton Hotels Corp. Although the bid was unsuccessful it added to the reputation of Wynn, who was already respected for having made Golden Nugget one of the most successful of the Atlantic City casino owners. In 1987, however, Golden Nugget bailed out of that market by selling its Atlantic City casino to Bally. At the same time, the company invested more than half a billion dollars on a extravagant new hotel-casino on the Strip in Las Vegas.

Hilton Hotels Corp. originated with the $5,000 purchase of a hotel in Cisco, Texas, by Conrad Hilton in 1919. Hilton went on to acquire the Statler chain and prestigious individual hotels such as the Waldorf-Astoria in New York City and the Palmer House in Chicago. The foreign properties of the company expanded rapidly in the 1950s and 1960s, but the Hilton International operation was sold to Transworld Corp. in 1964 at the urging of Conrad's son Barron, who later became chief executive. (In 1986 Transworld sold the hotels to UAL, which then resold the business to Ladbroke of Britain shortly thereafter.) In the 1980s Hilton got into the casino business but suffered a major disappointment in 1985 when the New Jersey Casino Control Commission denied a license to the company to operate the $320 million casino it was building in Atlantic City. The casino was sold to Donald Trump. In 1985 the company fought off a takeover attempt by Golden Nugget. The company officially put itself up for sale in August 1989, but seven months later the company took itself off the market, saying that it was unable to attract adequate offers.

The **Holiday Inns** lodging empire was founded by Memphis real estate developer Kemmons Wilson in the early 1950s. Franchises and company-owned properties spread rapidly across the United States and abroad. In 1980 the company bought Harrah's casinos and by the middle of the decade was receiving 37 percent of its revenues from gambling. Chief executive Michael Rose pushed the company upscale through the creation of Crowne Plaza and Embassy Suite Hotels while also courting the budget market through the Hampton Inns chain. Restructuring moves carried out to thwart a takeover bid created financial instability in the company, prompting Rose to sell 153 hotels, including all of those abroad, to the British brewing company Bass in 1987. Two years later Holiday Corp. decided to sell the rest of its hotels to Bass and spin off its gambling business. Bass later created Promus Companies as a holding company for its Holiday operation.

Kentucky Fried Chicken originated in the supposedly unique recipe for fried chicken developed by Colonel Harlan Sanders in the late 1930s. The company started franchising in the mid-1950s; it was bought in 1964 for a mere $2 million by Kentucky businessman (and future governor) John Y. Brown, Jr. Brown built the business into a $250 million chicken empire, which he sold to Heublein Corp. in 1971. The business faltered and ended up being a drain on Heublein's profits from vodka and other products. In 1986 PepsiCo agreed to purchase the company from Heublein's parent, RJR Nabisco, for $850 million.

Marriott Corp. had its origins in a root beer stand established by John Willard Marriott in Washington, D.C. in 1927. Marriott built a string of Hot Shoppes in Washington and went on to amass a food-service empire that included the Roy Rogers and Bob's Big Boy chains as well as a large airline catering business. In 1957 the company opened the first of a chain of hotels concentrated in suburbs and airports. Since the mid-1970s, the company, under the leadership of J. W. "Bill" Marriott, Jr. (his father died in 1985), has financed much of its growth by selling off ownership of hotels to investor groups and collecting hefty management fees for running the properties. The company spent $400 million on the massive New York Marriott Marquis in Times Square and in late 1985 purchased the Howard Johnson Company for $300 million. The slowdown in fast food in the late 1980s prompted the company to put its restaurant operations up for sale. In 1990 Hardee's agreed to purchase the Roy Rogers unit.

McDonald's, the pioneer of the business, is still leader of the fast-food industry. Under the leadership of Fred Turner, chief executive from 1977 to 1987, the company continued to break all records in the food-service business. Its rate of expansion—500 or more restaurants a year through the 1980s—has been astounding. In 1988 the company reached the landmark of 10,000 stores. Having conquered the suburbs and small towns, McDonald's began focusing on cities and foreign sites. At the end of 1989 more than one fourth of its 11,000 stores were abroad, accounting for 30 percent of its $17.3 billion in systemwide sales. McDonald's continued to spend massive amounts on advertising—some $728 million in 1988, making it the eighth biggest advertiser in the United States. The company has reached a new level of status in sociological and business terms. In 1985 the original McDonald's set up by Kroc in Des Plaines, Illinois, was turned into a museum, and the shares of McDonald's Corp. were added to the elite group that make up the Dow Jones Industrial Average. While McDonald's shook off a challenge by Burger King and Wendy's in the early 1980s, by the end of the decade there were signs that the company's phenomenal growth was beginning to level off.

Resorts International, originally a paint manufacturer, has been one of the most controversial of the casino companies. Founder James Crosby used his relationship with an official of the Bahamian government to get permission to build a casino on Paradise Island in 1967. Resorts opened the first casino in Atlantic City in 1978, but in 1985 it barely convinced the Casino Control Commission to renew its license. The chairman of the commission and the state attorney general argued that Resorts was not fit to retain the license because of some company funds that ended up in the pocket of the prime minister of the Bahamas. The company denied any wrongdoing. Following Crosby's death in 1986 Donald Trump acquired a controlling interest in the firm but in 1988 found himself in a bidding war with entertainer and television producer Merv Griffin when Trump tried to take the firm private. The two adversaries ended up reaching a pact under which Griffin took the company private and Trump got the huge Taj Mahal casino-hotel that Resorts was constructing in Atlantic City. Yet the financial problems of Resorts did not disappear. Facing a heavy debt load and dwindling market share, Griffin put Resorts into Chapter 11 bankruptcy in late 1989.

Wendy's International was founded by R. David Thomas, a fast-food executive, in 1969. Its stores used a turn-of-the-century motif and higher-quality food to appeal to a more mature clientele. Wendy's gained enormous attention in the mid-1980s—and boosted its position in the adult hamburger market—with its "Where's the beef?" commercial. Yet the

INDUSTRY DATA

Hotels and Motels	*1989*	*1988*	*1987*
Receipts	$57.1 billion	$52.4 billion	$48.2 billion
Total employment	1,675,100	1,503,600	1,427,600

Eating and Drinking Places	*1989*	*1988*	*1987*
Retail sales	$167 billion	$157 billion	$147 billion
Total employment	6.4 million	6.3 million	6.1 million

Source: U.S. Department of Commerce.

chain was unable to come up with an encore, and growth in the late 1980s faltered.

SOURCE GUIDE

Leading Stock Analysts and Experts

Stephen W. Brener Associates, a hotel consultant in New York City.

Joseph Doyle, a lodging and restaurant analyst at Smith Barney.

Al Glasgow, editor of *Atlantic City Action*, a casino newsletter published in Atlantic City, New Jersey.

Lee Isgur, a casino analyst at Paine Webber.

Technomic Inc., a restaurant consulting firm in Chicago.

Harold Vogel, a casino and hotel analyst at Merrill Lynch.

Trade Associations and Unions

American Hotel and Motel Association, 1201 New York Avenue NW, Washington, DC 20005. Tel.: (202) 289–3100.

Hotel Employees and Restaurant Employees International Union, 1219 28th Street NW, Washington, DC 20007. Tel.: (202) 393–4373.

National Restaurant Association, 1200 17th Street NW, Washington, DC 20036. Tel.: (202) 331–5900.

Data Sources and Directories

Directory of Chain Restaurant Operators, an annual listing (New York: Business Guides Inc.).

Hotel and Travel Index, a quarterly directory of hotels and motels around the world (Secaucus, N.J.: Reed Travel Group).

Laventhol and Horwath, an accounting and consulting firm in Philadelphia, publishes several annual statistical volumes, including *U.S. Lodging Industry* and *U.S. Gaming Industry*. It also publishes with the National Restaurant Association the annual *Restaurant Industry Operations Report*.

Lodging Industry Profile, an annual statistical compilation (Washington, D.C.: American Hotel and Motel Association).

Lodging Outlook, a monthly compilation of statistics on hotel chains and independent hotels (Hendersonville, Tenn.: Smith Travel Research).

OAG Travel Planner/Hotel and Motel Red Book, a quarterly directory of hotels and motels in North America (Oak Brook, Ill.: Official Airlines Guide).

Trends in the Hotel Industry, published annually by a Texas accounting and consulting firm (Houston: Pannell Kerr Forster).

Trade Publications

Atlantic City Action, monthly.

Gaming & Wagering Business, monthly.

Hotel and Motel Management, monthly.

Hotels, monthly.

Lodging Hospitality, monthly.

Nation's Restaurant News, weekly.

Restaurant Business, monthly.

Restaurant Hospitality, monthly.

Restaurants and Institutions, fortnightly.

Books and Reports

Boas, Max, and Steve Chain. *Big Mac: The Unauthorized Story of McDonald's*. New York: Mentor Books, 1976.

Emerson, Robert L. *Fast Food: The Endless Shakeout*. New York: Lebhar-Friedman, 1979.

Kroc, Ray. *Grinding It Out*. The autobiography of the founder of the McDonald's empire. Chicago: Contemporary Books, 1977.

Love, John F. *McDonald's: Behind the Arches*. New York: Bantam Books, 1986.

Luxenberg, Stan. *Roadside Empires: How the Chains Franchised America*. New York: Viking Press, 1985.

CHAPTER 11

RETAILING

The buying and selling of goods has played a major role in most societies. The coming together of merchants and customers in marketplaces such as the ancient Greek agora and the Middle Eastern bazaar has allowed for the intermingling of peoples and to some extent the growth of civilization.

In more modern times the central place of commerce is seen most clearly in the United States. The growth of the great department stores starting in the mid-19th century ushered in the era of mass consumption. And the sprouting of shopping centers and malls after World War II redefined the social landscape of much of the country. Today retailing, with its annual sales of $1.7 trillion, is the largest business sector in the United States.

FROM YANKEE PEDDLERS TO MERCHANT PRINCES

The growth of retailing in the United States followed the overall development of the country. As significant numbers of settlers moved inland starting in the early 1800s, they were followed by traveling merchants. These entrepreneurs sold pioneer families items such as housewares and notions that they could not obtain from the land.

The Yankee peddlers, as they came to be known, satisfied vital needs of the frontier people, and many were willing to exchange goods for pelts, honey, or other homemade items. Yet the peddlers also had a reputation for dishonesty—for passing off inferior or counterfeit products onto unsophisticated country folk. Phrases such as "Don't take any wooden nickels" emerged from these practices. Many peddlers retained their less-than-scrupulous ways when they settled down in one place and opened a general store. The growth of the mail-order business later in the century was stimulated by the dissatisfaction of rural people with their local merchants.

Back in urban areas, retailing was also undergoing a transformation. As cities began growing rapidly in the early 19th century, some merchants began expanding traditional specialty shops into grander emporia with greater selections of dry goods. Eventually all sorts of other products were added, and by the late 19th century huge establishments known as department stores sought to satisfy every conceivable material need. There is considerable dispute about who began the first true department store in the United States—the term was not used until the 1880s—but the leading pioneers undoubtedly were A. T. Stewart, Rowland Macy, and John Wanamaker.

Stewart, an Irish immigrant who arrived in the United States in the 1820s with a stock of linens and laces, soon opened the country's largest store in lower Manhattan. The Marble Dry Goods Palace was also unusual in that it was the first store to establish fixed prices, thus ending the traditional practice of haggling between salesclerk and customer. Macy, a veteran of several unsuccessful stores in Massachusetts, adopted a similar fixed-price policy and also sold exclusively on a cash basis when he opened a large store in New York City in 1858. Wanamaker, who began operation in Philadelphia in the 1860s, sought to upgrade the quality of ready-made clothing and also pioneered the money-back guarantee. In 1896 Wanamaker branched out to New York, taking over the business of Stewart, who had died in 1876.

By the end of the 19th century these establishments and others, such as Marshall Field's of Chicago, had dramatically altered the way urban Americans shopped. Department stores in the major cities elevated the mundane activity of buying goods into something exalted; lavish emporia were the temples of consumption. Goods were displayed in ways that stimulated demand rather than simply responding to it. Leading stores had amenities such as stools for customers to sit on while considering their purchases and "silence rooms" to allow overwrought shoppers to regain their composure and go on buying.

Department stores were all the more marvelous to customers because they were the first establishments to install newly invented devices such as elevators, electric lighting, telephones, and cash registers. The stores also pleased customers with free home delivery via great fleets of horse-drawn (and later motorized) carriages.

The late 19th century saw other retailing developments that involved the shifting of business away from small, local merchants to larger enterprises. The most significant of these for what was still a largely rural population was the growth of the mail-order business. Although some limited purchasing by mail existed earlier, the father of this business was a former country storekeeper and traveling salesman by the name of Aaron Montgomery Ward. Knowing the dissatisfaction of farmers with their local country stores, Ward began selling goods by mail in 1872. The response to Ward's catalogs, which came to be known as "wish books," was strong, and the company grew rapidly.

Another pioneer of mail order, Richard Sears, got into the business accidentally in the 1880s. While working as a railroad station agent in Minnesota, Sears ended up with a COD shipment of watches that a local jeweler refused to accept. Sears made a deal with the supplier to sell the watches himself. This worked out so well that Sears quit the railroad, opened a mail-order watch business in Minneapolis, and later moved to Chicago. By the 1890s he and partner Alvah Roebuck were selling a wide variety of products through the mail, and before long they surpassed Ward.

Aided by the enactment of rural free delivery in 1896, both companies continued to prosper, building strong bonds with millions of families. The catalogs produced by the two companies helped to shape U.S. consumption patterns and are now considered classic Americana.

The great mail-order houses did not please everyone. Local merchants, seeing their livelihood endangered, fought back. They organized public catalog burnings and promoted smear campaigns that accused Sears and Ward—which were given unfriendly nicknames such as Rears & Soreback and Monkey Ward—of selling inferior merchandise. The companies took great pains to disprove these charges; Ward's went so far as to give a committee of farmers the run of its warehouse, allowing the group to tear open large numbers of packages and compare the contents against what was advertised in the catalog. The committee reportedly found nothing amiss.

The small-merchant lobby also struggled against another of the retailing developments of the period: the rise of the chain stores. The chains emerged in two kinds of shops: variety stores and groceries. The pioneer in chain-selling of food was George Huntington Hartford, who along with George Gilman opened an ornate store in lower Manhattan in 1859 to sell tea. Hartford, who later adopted the grandiose name Great Atlantic & Pacific Tea Company (known as A&P), added coffee and spices and later a full line of groceries to his stores. By keeping prices low A&P gained a loyal following, and by 1876 there were 67 A&P stores stretching from Boston to St. Paul; in 1915 the number had risen to 1,000.

Low prices were also the appeal of the variety stores that Frank Woolworth began opening in the 1870s. Limiting his goods to ones selling at 5 or 10 cents each, Woolworth built an empire that by the time of his death in 1919 included more than 1,000 stores with total sales of $119 million. Woolworth's major competitor was James Cash Penney, who opened his first store in Wyoming in 1902. Penney, who called his early shops Golden Rule Stores, expanded across the West and after 1913 began growing at a phenomenal rate across the country. By 1933 there were nearly 1,500 Penney stores.

The growth of the Hartford, Woolworth, and Penney empires and other chains gave rise to an intense anti-chain-store movement that culminated in the 1930s. Led by Representative Wright Patman of Texas the anti-chain-store forces tried to halt the march of the national retailers through discriminatory legislation. The battle was played out in a series of dramatic congressional hearings, and in the end the power of the chains prevailed. Not only did the national corporate merchants retain their empires, but many local department-store powerhouses ended up as parts of national retail holding companies such as Federated Department Stores and Allied Stores.

THE MALLING OF AMERICA

In the postwar period, chain stores and department stores were entrenched enough in American commerce to serve as the anchors of what became the predominant new style of retailing, the shopping center. The oldest planned shopping center is reputed to be Country Club Plaza, built near Kansas City in 1922. But it was only during the 1950s that these collections of stores began to transform the American landscape.

Drawing on precedents such as the Galleria in Milan, Italy (built in the 1860s) and the Old Arcade that was constructed in Cleveland in 1936, developers soon began enclosing the shopping centers and calling them malls. Like the early department stores, malls sought to immerse customers in an all-encompassing shopping environment. Climate was carefully regulated, and security and cleanliness were attended to obsessively; in short, nothing was allowed to stand in the way of the urge to buy.

In replacing traditional commercial districts, malls have in many places become the main arenas of social life. People come to them not only to shop but also to seek the company of others and even to engage in civic activities. Political organizations have used malls for leafleting, and when courts in some states upheld the right of mall owners to ban such activity, the rulings were denounced as major impediments to free speech.

While suburban malls have often been criticized for causing the decline of downtown areas, the transformation of historic structures into enclosed shopping centers has contributed to the revival of many urban districts. Beginning with Faneuil Hall in Boston, the Rouse Co. and other developers have carried out projects such as The Gallery in Philadelphia, the Grand Avenue Complex in Milwaukee, South Street Seaport in New York, and Union Station in St. Louis.

By the mid-1980s the spread of malls had slowed down, largely because of saturation in many parts of the country. Yet at the same time developers in Minnesota began work on the largest (10 million square feet) mall in the country, now expected to open in 1992.

The postwar period also saw a dramatic transformation of the food retailing business. Groceries were traditionally sold in small shops in which clerks waited on each customer. The rise of chain stores such as A&P affected the ownership but not the operating style of the shops. A Memphis grocer named Clarence Saunders is credited with being the first to break out of the mold. His Piggly Wiggly stores, the first of which opened in 1916, introduced self-service.

This concept caught on in places, but the major leap occurred in 1930 when a large cash-and-carry store called King Kullen's opened in the Jamaica, Queens, area of New York City. This was the birth of the supermarket, and in the years after World War II these food palaces rapidly replaced traditional grocery stores. A&P transformed its shops accordingly though not fast enough, and other chains such as Safeway and Kroger rose to the top ranks of retailers.

THE DISCOUNTERS' CHALLENGE

The comfortable prosperity that many of the country's large retailers enjoyed in the 1950s did not last for long. Although retailing was never a high-margin business, efficient stores made respectable income by selling goods at manufacturers' list prices. Discounting was limited to special sales or particular departments such as Filene's famous Automatic Bargain Basement.

During the late 1950s there appeared on the scene a group of retailers who sold all their goods all of the time at discounted prices. The first wave came with the factory outlet stores that were set up in abandoned textile mills in New England. Building on the principles of low overhead, high turnover, and customer self-service, the discounters began to spring up everywhere. They won the right to sell goods such as appliances below list price, and they defied local blue laws, which banned Sunday hours.

The man who came to epitomize the discounting revolution was Eugene Ferkauf. A onetime luggage dealer, Ferkauf built a national chain called E. J. Korvettes that caused an upheaval in the department store business. Ferkauf, known as the Duke of Discounting, enjoyed shaking up the stodgy retail trade with gestures such as the 1962 opening of a discount store in the middle of New York's snobbish Fifth Avenue shopping district.

Ferkauf left the company in 1968, and in 1979 Korvettes was purchased by the French retailer Agache-Willot. The new owners could not stem what was already a serious cost-control problem, and in 1981 the company filed for bankruptcy.

Another major player in the early discounting era has survived and is stronger than ever. Back in 1962 the S. S. Kresge Co. plunged into discounting with the establishment of a chain called K mart stores. These stores, which now number more than 2,000, have been a phenomenal success, propelling Kresge (which changed its name to K mart in 1977) from a sleepy variety store chain into the second-largest retailer in the United States.

During the 1980s discounting became more important than ever. There has also been an expansion from traditional discounting into other forms of low-price selling. Discounters buy at wholesale and cut their retail prices through low overhead and high volume. A new variation, known as off-price stores, involves purchasing goods at below wholesale prices by accepting manufacturers' overruns, end-of-season goods, and other irregular lots. The off-price retailers enjoy about $200 per square foot in annual sales (almost twice the level of traditional department stores) and turn over their stock nine times a year (compared with a normal level of three times). By the mid-1980s off-price stores numbered more than 10,000 and accounted for about 5 percent of sales in clothing, accessories, and footwear. Some traditional department stores have threatened to stop buying from manufacturers who sell to off-price retailers, who in turn have charged department stores with price-fixing. Most recently the off-price segment has been undercut by even more heavily discounted goods. More recent rages are wholesale cash-and-carry clubs, hypermarkets, and gray-market dealers (who obtain brand-name goods through unauthorized channels).

Some traditional retailers have responded to the discounters not by fighting them but by joining the game. None has been so successful as Kresge's K mart venture, but a number of chains have even experimented with off-price stores. In 1989 Sears plunged into discounting with an "everyday low price" strategy.

Yet this is only one of a number of directions the big chains have pursued in response to an increasingly precarious competitive situation. Following the early lead of Macy's, mass retailers such as J. C. Penney and Sears have been trying to improve their fashion image and attract a more upscale clientele. Other chains such as Woolworth, Federated, and Dayton Hudson have been opening smaller specialty-type stores instead of full-line department stores.

Food retailers, whose sales surpassed $350 billion in 1989, have also been responding to the simultaneous pressures to go upscale and downscale. On the one hand, they have gone along with the demand for low prices through the stocking of generic products and through "no-frills" practices such as reducing selections, selling out of shipping cartons, and charging for bags. On the other hand, many supermarkets have responded to increased food sophistication by adding salad bars, gourmet departments, and other amenities.

Whether upscale or down, supermarkets have been the arena for intense battles over shelf space. Despite the slow rate of growth in the market, food processors continue to introduce new products at a rapid rate. Recognizing their strong position, many retailers have begun demanding (and receiving) high fees, called slotting allowances, from manufacturers who want to be sure their new products will be on display. Some chains are also demanding "failure fees" for products that flop and are discontinued by the retailer.

RETAILING WITHOUT STORES

Another challenge facing the big chains is the rise of alternative forms of distribution that do not involve stores. The most important of these is also one of the oldest forms of retailing:

mail order. While purchasing goods from a catalog was long the practice of rural families, it has in recent years become more popular among all segments of the population.

One old-line catalog seller, Sears, has benefited from this surge, while the other major player, Montgomery Ward, could not stem the losses in its mail-order operation. Ward discontinued its catalog business in 1985, and three years later the retailer's parent Mobil Corp. sold the business to an investor group led by Ward's management for $1.6 billion.

The main beneficiaries of the mail-order boom have been specialized suppliers who sell everything from rare fruits to jewels. Yet as the number of catalogs proliferated (reaching into the thousands), direct mail companies began to complain that the competition was eating into their profits.

Besides the great catalog glut, mail-order houses have also come under pressure for their tax practices. Thanks to the wording of state sales tax regulations, companies selling by mail to out-of-state customers are not required to collect sales tax. The customers are theoretically required to come forward and pay on their own, but few do. Now state officials are seeking legislation that would close what they see as a legal loophole depriving their coffers of countless dollars of tax revenues.

The other main forms of retailing without stores are home shopping and electronic shopping. Home shopping is the name given to the marketing of goods through cable television networks devoted exclusively to sales pitches—to which viewers respond by calling special phone numbers to place orders. Although there have been reports that the supposedly rock-bottom prices offered on the networks are often no lower than those in stores, this form of retailing took off in the mid-1980s. Led by Home Shopping Network (the pioneer in the business), Cable Value Network, and QVC, home shopping revenues reached $1.5 billion in 1988.

The growth of electronic shopping, which involves the placing of orders via home computers and cable television devices, has been less dramatic. A series of videotex experiments carried out by companies such as Warner Amex, Times Mirror, and CBS discovered only moderate interest on the part of consumers in shopping electronically. The future of this sector of retailing now depends on the performance of the Prodigy online service developed by Sears in cooperation with IBM. The partners have sunk hundreds of millions of dollars into the project, which entices electronic shoppers with colorful graphics and simple keyboard commands.

TOO MANY STORES?

In the mid-1980s analysts of the retail industry began to question one of the basic assumptions of the business: that the construction of more stores led to an overall increase in the level of retail sales. A report published by the Marketing Science Institute presented a discouraging forecast regarding growth of retail sales during the remainder of the 1980s. The study raised doubts about the wisdom of the expansion strategy and gave ammunition to those who argue that the United States already has too many stores.

Advocates of the "overstoring" thesis noted that average annual sales per square foot of retail space have declined in real terms since the mid-1970s. Some retailers have been responding to this situation by closing or consolidating existing stores or reducing the size of the new ones that are opened. They are also fighting harder for increased market share.

RESHUFFLING THE DECK

Starting in the mid-1980s the transformation of retailing moved from the level of individual stores to the ownership status of the parent companies. Much of the change has been the result of takeover assaults by the likes of Dart Group, run by the Haft Family. Dart has gone after a long list of retailers (including May Department Stores, Safeway Stores, Supermarkets General, Dayton Hudson, Stop & Shop, Federated Department Stores, and Kroger), often prompting the target to take refuge in a leveraged buyout. Other firms, such as Macy's, undertook leveraged buyouts on their own initiative. May Department Stores jumped to the top ranks of retailers by acquiring Associated Dry Goods in 1986.

The other major force in the industry turned out to be Canadian real estate developer Robert Campeau, who entered retailing with his $3.5 billion acquisition of Allied Stores in 1986. He set his sights even higher in early 1988, when he made a bid for Federated Department Stores, parent company of such chains as Bloomingdale's, I. Magnin, and Bullock's. Campeau edged out a rival offer from Macy's and ended up paying $6.5 billion for Federated. It turned out that Campeau had taken on more than he could handle. Poor sales at various chains made it impossible for Campeau to keep up with the massive debt load he had assumed in his acquisitions.

In 1989 Campeau had to turn to Olympia & York Developments, the Canadian real-estate powerhouse, for help. The assistance came at a price: Campeau lost control of Campeau Corp. The new management team was unable to reverse the decline fast enough, so the company's U.S. retailing operations filed for Chapter 11 bankruptcy in January 1990. Similar debt problems had a few months earlier forced Australian-owned Hooker Corp. to seek Chapter 11 protection and liquidate its B. Altman chain; Ames Department Stores took the same step in April 1990, as did the Circle K convenience store chain the following month. Even those retailers who have avoided bankruptcy have been forced to pare back their operations. At the beginning of 1990 more than 100 department stores owned by various chains were up for sale.

LABOR RELATIONS

Although working in a store was for a long time considered a type of white-collar job and thus preferable to toiling in a factory, retail employees have experienced more than their share of mistreatment. In the early days the main grievance was the long hours. Workweeks of as much as 80 or 90 hours prompted retail workers to form "early-closing societies" aimed at reducing the number of hours shops remained open and thus the amount of time clerks were expected to be on the job. The soci-

The 15 Largest Retailers, by 1989 Retail Sales ($ Millions)

1. Sears Roebuck	$31,599
2. K mart	29,533
3. Wal-Mart	25,811
4. American Stores	22,004
5. Kroger	19,104
6. J. C. Penney	16,103
7. Safeway	14,325
8. Dayton Hudson	13,644
9. A&P	11,148
10. Campeau	10,440
11. May Department Stores	9,425
12. Winn-Dixie	9,151
13. Woolworth	8,820
14. Southland	8,275
15. Melville	7,554

Source: *Chain Store Age Executive*, August 1990. *Chain Store Age Executive* is published by Lebhar-Friedman, 425 Park Avenue, New York, NY 10022.

eties evolved into unions, and by 1890 the Retail Clerks National Protective Association (later shortened to the Retail Clerks International Association, RCIA) was chartered by the American Federation of Labor.

The RCIA continued its battle over the workweek and later turned to wages as well. The problem the union had in organizing was that the retail work force was characterized by seasonal employment and high turnover. Some of the large employers, such as Sears, J. C. Penney, and Filene's of Boston, discouraged unionization by adopting paternalistic policies, including profit-sharing plans and grievance procedures.

During the labor upheaval of the 1930s, militant locals in the RCIA, especially in New York, grew tired of the conservative leadership of the union and eventually broke away to form the Retail, Wholesale and Department Store Union. In 1979 the RCIA and the Amalgamated Meat Cutters merged to form the United Food and Commercial Workers (UFCW).

During World War II Montgomery Ward was involved in one of the most famous incidents in U.S. labor history. When Ward president Sewell Avery defied an order from President Roosevelt to renew a union contract, FDR ordered the company seized by the army under his wartime powers. When Avery refused to cooperate with the army, he was forcibly removed from his office.

After the war the retail work force expanded enormously, but the unions failed to keep up their organizing pace, especially at the new chains. In recent years the main labor relations battle in the retail field has involved supermarket workers.

For many years unionized workers at the big chains enjoyed relatively good pay, benefits, and working conditions. But as competition from nonunion chains intensified in the late 1970s, companies began efforts to reduce their labor costs.

Safeway went through some bitter strikes in 1978 over the company's use of computerized time and motion work rules. The Winn-Dixie chain was the target of a national AFL-CIO boycott because of its attempt to vacate labor agreements. Kroger, traditionally a paternalistic employer, began to get tough with the UFCW. In regions such as Pittsburgh, Cleveland, and southern Michigan the company warned that unless the union agreed to concessions, stores would be closed—and Kroger made good on that threat in numerous places. At the end of 1985 some 10,000 UFCW members struck seven supermarket chains in the Los Angeles area. Despite staying out for eight weeks, the workers had to take a pay cut.

A different way of dealing with labor costs was devised by the UFCW and A&P after the chain closed 70 of its stores in the Philadelphia area in 1982. The union got the company to agree to a plan under which many of the stores were reopened with lower wage rates. This was not unusual, but A&P also agreed that if labor costs in the stores were kept to 10 percent of sales, the company would contribute 1 percent of sales to a special fund, out of which bonuses would be paid to the employees. The union also helped employees of two of the other closed A&Ps reopen them under worker ownership and management.

After Safeway went private in a leveraged buyout, the new owners sold off large chunks of the firm, eliminating thousands of jobs. The UFCW filed suit and reached an agreement with the company under which severance payments would be made if a division were sold to company that did not retain the employees and negotiate a union contract.

Restructuring has also led to labor unrest at Sears. After the nonunion retailer began to reduce base pay amid its cost-cutting drive in 1989, some disgruntled workers began organizing drives, with the cooperation of the Office and Professional Employees International Union, at various stores around the country.

LEADING COMPANIES

Batus Inc. is the subsidiary set up by London-based tobacco giant BAT to serve as the holding company for a set of retail properties (including Marshall Field's and Saks Fifth Avenue) that BAT began purchasing in the United States in the early 1970s. Another of the properties, Gimbels (founded in the 1850s as a trading post in Indiana and merged with Saks in 1923), was dismantled in 1987. The Marshall Field's chain, the great Chicago retail empire, was acquired in 1982. Batus has been disappointed in Gimbels' performance in recent years, as the mass merchandiser faltered while its traditional rival Macy's moved upscale. It came as no surprise in early 1986 when Batus announced plans to sell Gimbels and some other stores while holding onto fashionable Saks, Marshall Field's, and other properties. In 1989 Saks and Marshall Field's were also put up for sale as part of BAT's defense against a takeover bid by James Goldsmith. The following year Batus announced the sale of Marshall Field's to Dayton Hudson and Saks to Investcorp, a partnership of Middle East investors that previously owned Tiffany & Co.

Carter Hawley Hale had its origins in the small dry-goods store Arthur Letts opened on Broadway in Los Angeles in the late 19th century. What was originally known as The Broadway grew steadily in the West and merged with Hale Brothers stores in 1950. The company became a leader in upscale retailing after acquiring Neiman-Marcus in 1968 and Bergdorf Goodman in 1972. Neiman-Marcus, best known for the unusual and extremely expensive items in its catalog, was founded in Dallas in 1907 and later expanded across the country. Bergdorf, the high-class women's clothing store in New

York, had its origins in a 19th-century tailor shop. In 1977 Carter Hawley Hale (it adopted the name in 1974) made an unsuccessful attempt to acquire Marshall Field's but the following year purchased the historic but ailing Wanamaker empire of Philadelphia. In 1984 the company defeated a bold takeover attempt by The Limited. Two years later, faced with another bid by The Limited and a partner, Carter Hawley Hale spun off its specialty retailing business. Neiman-Marcus and Bergdorf Goodman ended up under the control of General Cinema.

Dayton Hudson was formed in 1969 by the merger of two old-line department store companies—Hudson's of Detroit and Dayton's of Minneapolis. Dayton's, a fashion trendsetter, also founded the large B. Dalton bookstore chain in the 1960s but sold the business in 1986. Dayton Hudson has made various forays into discounting but sold its chain of Plum's off-price stores. A takeover bid by the Dart Group collapsed in the wake of the October 1987 stock market crash. In 1990 Dayton Hudson agreed to purchase Marshall Field's from Batus for $1 billion.

Federated Department Stores is an amalgam of more than a dozen retail groups, including famous names such as Bloomingdale's, Abraham & Straus, and Rich's of Atlanta. Federated was set up in 1929 as a holding company under the leadership of the Lazurus family of Columbus, Ohio, though the groups have always kept considerable autonomy. Filene's, for instance, retained its famous Automatic Bargain Basement, where generations of Boston shoppers have fought over special shipments of goods at extremely low prices. (Filene's Basement was sold to a management group in 1988, and the rest of the company was purchased by May Department Stores.) Bloomingdale's, founded in 1872, made a name for itself with dazzling and hip displays of goods, showing in the process how a department store could be a fashion leader. For many years Federated had fallen behind its competitors in innovation, but in the 1980s some new life was injected by Howard Goldfeder, who took over as CEO in 1981. The company paid greenmail to the Dart Group in 1987 but early the next year found itself the object of a takeover move by Robert Campeau, who ended up paying $6.5 billion for the firm. Campeau was unable to handle the heavy debt load from his acquisitions, so Federated ended up in Chapter 11 in early 1990.

The Great Atlantic & Pacific Tea Company (A&P) may not be so great any longer, but the company has shown unexpected resilience. The A&P empire began as a tea store opened by George Huntington Hartford in the late 1850s. Hartford branched out from tea to coffee and spices and eventually to a full line of groceries. A&P stores began sprouting up like mushrooms everywhere, each laid out identically. The company went along with the supermarket revolution starting in the late 1930s but was slow to modernize after the war. Still, at the end of the 1960s the company was the biggest retailer in the United States. In the early 1970s the company pushed a campaign called WEO (originally Warehouse Economy Outlet, later Where Economy Originates), in which goods were sold at the cheapest possible levels. This set off a price war that hurt A&P more than its competitors, and WEO was dropped in 1973. A&P lost considerable ground in the 1970s, and in 1975 new CEO Jonathan Scott began closing hundreds of stores and eliminating thousands of employees. The company was purchased by the West German Tengelmann Group in 1979, and in 1980 James Wood was brought in to attempt another rescue job. Wood had disappointing results with a group of Plus Stores (no-frills stores with limited selections), but he managed to stop the decline. By the mid-1980s the company was in stable financial health and was expanding and upgrading its stores. In 1986 A&P purchased the Shopwell and Waldbaum supermarket chains, putting it at the top of the New York City market, the country's largest.

K mart is the result of one of the most dramatic success stories in modern retailing. In the early 1960s the S. S. Kresge chain of variety stores recognized the potential of the discounting movement and began opening K mart stores. The experiment grew like mad and eventually took over the company in importance as well as name. K mart reached the number-two spot among retailers in the early 1980s and by 1985 was gaining quickly on industry leader Sears. The company, which purchased the large Waldenbooks chain from Carter Hawley Hale in 1984, also embarked on a process of upgrading its image of polyester and blue-light specials. Yet by the end of the 1980s K mart was being overtaken by the unstoppable Wal-Mart chain.

Kroger Co. surprised the retail world by shooting ahead of Safeway in 1984 to be the leading food retailer, based on U.S. sales alone. (Safeway does considerable foreign business.) Founded by Barney Kroger in the 1880s, the company has traditionally been strong in the Midwest but has expanded across the country. In recent years Kroger has been ruthless in the battle for market share, playing hardball with its unions and pulling out of markets where results were not satisfactory. Kroger does a large amount of its own manufacturing through several dozen food processing plants. In 1988 the company used a $5.3 billion recapitalization to thwart takeover bids by the Haft Family and Kohlberg, Kravis, Roberts & Co.

The Limited, a women's clothing empire founded by Leslie Wexner in the 1960s, has been the fastest-growing retailer of the past two decades. From the mid-1970s to the mid-1980s the company grew to 100 times its original size, and Wexner's large personal stake in the company rose in value to about $1 billion. The company achieved its record through both its own stores and the shops of the Lane Bryant chain (acquired in 1982) and Lerner stores (bought in 1984). That same year Wexner shocked the retail world by attempting a takeover of Carter Hawley Hale. The bid was eventually dropped, but Wexner went on in 1985 to acquire the high-class New York specialty shop Henri Bendel. The following year Wexner joined forces with a large real estate developer in another run at Carter Hawley Hale. Wexner was also unsuccessful in his attempts to buy Federated and Macy's, but The Limited continued to dominate the specialty retailing business.

R. H. Macy & Co. began as a dry-goods shop opened by Rowland Macy in Manhattan in 1858. Promoting the practices of fixed prices and payment in cash, Macy was also one of the first merchants to branch out into a wide variety of goods. After being taken over by the Straus family in the 1880s, Macy's kept to its cash-only policy, guaranteeing prices 6 percent lower than those in stores that sold on account. Macy's bought the Bamberger's chain in 1929 and began opening stores in New York's suburbs and around the country in the 1950s. In the 1970s Macy's, under the leadership of Edward Finkelstein, pioneered the upscale movement by creating boutiques and specialty departments within the larger stores. The company experienced a sharp decline in 1984, and a number of top executives departed. In 1986 a group of the remaining managers, led by Finkelstein, took the company private in a $3.6 billion leveraged buyout. Two years later Macy's was unsuccessful in a last-minute effort to take over Federated Department Stores after a bid had been made by Robert Campeau.

Montgomery Ward, one of the two great catalog companies, was founded by Aaron Montgomery Ward in 1872. Through his wish books Ward made available a wide variety of goods to farm families and allowed them to reduce their dependency on often unscrupulous local merchants. In the 1920s the company began opening stores in which catalog goods were put on display. Customers put so much pressure on Ward's to sell goods on the spot that the company began opening retail outlets. The company was slow to modernize after World War II and barely survived a takeover attempt by Louis Wolfson in the early 1950s. Ward's had a turnaround in the 1960s and in 1968 merged with Container Corp. of America to form Marcor, which was bought by Mobil Corp. in 1974. Ward's has not kept up with the times since then, experiencing slow growth and losses. The catalog business was suspended in 1985, and the company launched a plan to convert many of its stores into specialty outlets. In 1988 an investment group led by Ward senior managers took the company private for $1.6 billion.

J. C. Penney, one of the leading mass merchandisers, was founded by James Cash Penney with a tiny, cash-only dry-goods store in Wyoming in 1902. Penney bought out other chains and opened more stores at a rapid rate; he had nearly 1,400 by 1929. Penney traditionally sold mainly clothing and footwear but in the early 1960s introduced full-line stores. The company began returning to its old specialty in the mid-1970s and during the 1980s began seeking to improve its fashion image and attract a more affluent clientele. The company set aside $1 billion for a modernization drive, but its home shopping network was a failure.

Safeway Stores emerged from the West to surpass A&P in the 1970s as the nation's biggest supermarket chain. Founded as a cash-and-carry grocery in Idaho in 1915, Safeway has based much of its growth on private-label sales. Starting in the 1970s it moved decisively to reduce overhead and increase sales by emphasizing nonfood items. In 1980 the company started opening no-frills Food Barn stores. Following a hostile tender offer from the Dart Group in 1986, Safeway agreed to be taken private in a $4.2 billion leveraged buyout. Four years later 10 percent of the company was sold to the public once again.

Sears Roebuck & Co. is the world's leading retailer, though in recent years it has been stumbling. The company started out as a mail-order house for watches founded by Richard Sears, a former railroad station agent in Minnesota. Seeing the success of Montgomery Ward, Sears and his partner Alvah Roebuck branched out into a general line of merchandise. The company soon overtook Ward's in sales, thanks in part to Sears' extremely efficient method for fulfilling mail orders. The system, involving conveyor belts and pneumatic tubes, helped to inspire Henry Ford's automobile assembly line. The company began opening retail stores in the 1920s. Under the autocratic control of General Robert Wood, the U.S. Army quartermaster during World War I, the company set up the Allstate auto insurance business in 1931 and began expanding abroad. Franklin Roosevelt once said that the best way to convince the USSR of the superiority of the American way of life would be to drop Sears catalogs all over the Soviet Union. During the 1980s the company plunged into the financial services game by acquiring the Dean Witter brokerage house and the Coldwell Banker chain of real estate agencies. Sears also introduced a hybrid credit and financial services card called Discover, but the company's goal of becoming a financial supermarket was never fully realized. On the retail side, the company moved somewhat upscale in its appeal and launched a program to remodel 600 of its 800 stores and turn many of them into "stores of the future." However, in the mid-1980s, with competition from discounters escalating, the firm's retail revenues were flat. Investor pressure prompted the company to embark on a restructuring in 1988 that included selling the 100-story Sears Tower in Chicago (the world's tallest building) and buying back 10 percent of the outstanding stock. In 1989 the company responded to pressures from discounters by launching an "everyday low prices" strategy, but most customers were unimpressed, and the attorney general of New York State sued the company for false advertising.

Southland Corp., the owner of the 7-Eleven chain, is the leading convenience store retailer. The convenience store was born in the 1920s in Dallas, when Joe Thompson, the manager of an ice dock owned by Southland Ice Co., began to sell eggs, milk, and bread during his long opening hours. The availability of essential foodstuffs at hours when grocers were closed proved to be popular, and under Thompson's leadership Southland began opening stores at a rapid pace. Originally called Tote'm Stores, the chain was christened 7-Eleven in 1946 to reflect what were then the hours of business. By the beginning of 1986 the company had more than 7,500 stores, more than one third of them franchised. In 1983 Southland bought the Citgo refinery, and in 1984 the company was found guilty of setting up a slush fund to pay bribes to New York State officials to fix sales tax cases. The company has sought to upgrade its stores and got involved in developing a $1 billion office complex in Dallas. In 1987, when the company was faced with a possible takeover threat, the Thompson family spent $3.7 billion to buy out the shareholders and return Southland to family control. Three years later a controlling interest in the company was sold to a group of Japanese investors.

In the 1970s **Wal-Mart Stores** came out of nowhere (actually, Bentonville, Arkansas) to begin challenging the giants of retailing. Founder Sam Walton had quietly begun opening discount stores in the 1960s and was soon spreading across the Sunbelt. The unassuming Walton held onto more than one third of the stock after Wal-Mart went public, and by the early 1980s he had become a billionaire. In 1985 he rose to the top of the Forbes 400 as the country's wealthiest person. By the late 1980s Wal-Mart was replacing K mart as the chain most likely to seize the top retailing spot from Sears.

F. W. Woolworth Co. played a major role in retailing by

popularizing the five-and-dime variety store. Founded by Frank Woolworth in the 1870s, the company rapidly moved to the top ranks of American merchants—which Woolworth emphasized by erecting a headquarters in 1913 that was the tallest building in the world. The company was slow to modernize after World War II, and an attempt to follow Kresge into the discounting business through a chain of Woolco stores was a failure. That chain was shut down in 1982. In the mid-1980s, however, Woolworth found success in a batch of specialty shops—selling goods such as stationery or jewelry—that do not carry the Woolworth name.

INDUSTRY DATA

Retailing	*1989*	*1988*	*1987*
Retail sales	$1.54 trillion	$1.46 trillion	$1.36 trillion
Total employment	13.2 million	12.8 million	12.4 million

Sources: U.S. Department of Commerce (sales); U.S. Bureau of Labor Statistics (employment). Neither set of data includes eating and drinking places.

SOURCE GUIDE

Leading Stock Analysts and Experts

Kurt Barnard, retailing consultant with his own firm (Barnard Enterprises) in New York City.

Joseph Ellis, analyst at Goldman Sachs.

Jeffrey Feiner, analyst at Merrill Lynch.

Management Horizons, a retail consulting firm based in Columbus, Ohio.

Kurt Salmon Associates, a retail consulting firm based in Atlanta.

Trade Associations and Unions

Direct Marketing Association, 6 East 43rd Street, New York, NY 10017. Tel.: (212) 689–4977.

International Association of Chain Stores (food chains), 3800 Moore Place, Alexandria, VA 22305. Tel.: (703) 549–4525.

International Mass Retail Association, 570 Seventh Avenue, New York, NY 10018. Tel.: (212) 354–6600.

National Grocers Association (independents), 1825 Samuel Morse Drive, Reston, VA 22090. Tel.: (703) 437–5300.

National Retail Merchants Association, 100 West 31st Street, New York, NY 10001. Tel.: (212) 244–8780.

Retail, Wholesale and Department Store Union, 30 E. 29th Street, New York, NY 10016. Tel.: (212) 684–5300.

United Food and Commercial Workers International Union, 1775 K Street NW, Washington, DC 20006. Tel.: (202) 223–3111.

Data Sources and Directories

Chain Store Age publishes an annual listing of the top retail companies, in August.

Directory of Department Stores, Directory of Discount Department Stores, and *Directory of Supermarket, Grocery & Convenience Store Chains*, each published annually (New York: Business Guides Inc.).

Fairchild's Financial Manual of Retail Stores, annual (New York: Fairchild Publications).

Financial and Operating Results of Department and Specialty Stores and *Merchandising and Operating Results of Department and Specialty Stores*, both annual statistical volumes (New York: National Retail Merchants Association).

Financial Profiles of Public Companies in Textiles, Apparel, Retailing and Footwear and *Soft Goods Outlook*, both annual (Atlanta: Kurt Salmon Associates).

Fortune as part of its Service 500, publishes an annual ranking of the fifty largest retailers, in June.

Operating Results of Mass Retail Stores and the Mass Retailers Merchandising Report, published annually (New York: International Mass Retail Association).

Phelon's Discount Stores, a biennial directory of more than 2,000 discount and self-service stores and their key personnel (Fairview, N.J.: Phelon, Sheldon & Marsar).

Progressive Grocer's Marketing Guidebook, annual directory and statistical compilation (Stamford, Conn.: MacLean Hunter Media).

Sheldon's Retail Directory, an annual listing of major department stores, chains, and other retailers and their key personnel (Fairview, N.J.: Phelon, Sheldon & Marsar).

Thomas Grocery Register, an annual three-volume work listing information on some 62,000 U.S. and Canadian firms involved in food distribution (New York: Thomas Publishing).

Trade Publications

Barnard's Retail Marketing Report, monthly newsletter.

Catalog Age, monthly.

Chain Store Age, monthly (published in several editions).

Direct Marketing, monthly.

Discount Merchandiser, monthly.

Discount Store News, fortnightly.

Progressive Grocer, monthly.

Stores, monthly.

Supermarket News, weekly.

Books and Reports

Bluestone, Barry; Patricia Hanna; Sarah Kuhn; and Laura Moore. *The Retail Revolution*. Boston: Auburn House, 1981.

Hendrickson, Robert. *The Grand Emporiums*. Briarcliff Manor, N.Y.: Stein & Day, 1979.

Katz, Donald R. *The Big Store: Inside the Crisis and Revolution at Sears*. New York: Viking Press, 1987.

Kowinski, William. *The Malling of America*. New York: William Morrow, 1985.

Mahoney, Tom, and Leonard Sloane. *The Great Merchants*. Rev. ed. New York: Harper & Row, 1974.

May, Eleanor G.; C. William Ress; and Walter J. Salmon. *Future Trends in Retailing*. An influential study of the industry. Cambridge, Mass.: Marketing Science Institute, 1985.

Weil, Gordon L. *Sears, Roebuck, U.S.A.* Briarcliff Manor, N.Y.: Stein & Day, 1977.

CHAPTER 12

TEXTILES AND APPAREL

Spinning, weaving, and clothesmaking are among the oldest productive activities of the human race, and these businesses continue to be important to the economy of nearly every country on earth. They are also the center of the most bitter trade controversy between developed countries and less developed ones. The U.S. textile and clothing industries, shaken by steadily rising imports, have responded with a campaign for protectionist policies along with a wave of automation, new marketing strategies, and a slew of acquisitions and buyouts. Leaders of the two sectors, each of which had shipments worth about $70 billion in 1989, say they are fighting for survival.

THE LEGACY OF SLATER'S MILL

The growth of the textile industry was virtually synonymous with the Industrial Revolution in England and America. Eighteenth-century Britain witnessed a series of inventions—such as the flying shuttle, the spinning jenny, and the water frame—that turned spinning and weaving from domestic crafts into mass production.

The introduction of this technology into the New World was accomplished by Samuel Slater, a former mill supervisor in England, which in the late 18th century had strict prohibitions on the export of textile know-how. Receiving backing from merchants in Rhode Island, Slater constructed from memory a small mill based on the design of British inventor Richard

Arkwright. This operation, opened in 1790, can be seen as the beginning of American industry.

In the following years small spinning mills proliferated in Rhode Island and Massachusetts, but the creation of a true factory system was brought about through the efforts of Francis Cabot Lowell starting in 1813. After spending several years studying the British system, Lowell returned to New England with a plan to consolidate the various phases of textile production—spinning, weaving, dyeing, and printing—under one roof.

Lowell established the Boston Manufacturing Company and opened a mill in Waltham, Massachusetts, to realize this plan. The Waltham system caught on and helped to stimulate the growth of the textile industry throughout New England, including the town of East Chelmsford, which was renamed Lowell in honor of the textile magnate. The supply of the raw material, cotton, had by this time been greatly increased by Eli Whitney's invention of the cotton gin in 1793.

In its early decades the textile industry was supplying fabric that was sold in the dry-goods stores that were springing up throughout the cities and towns of the United States. The only ready-made clothing was that produced in "slop shops" and sold to sailors in waterfront outlets. This began to change with the introduction of the treadle-powered sewing machine by Isaac Singer in the 1850s. Westward expansion and the California gold rush created a demand for durable, ready-to-wear apparel for hardworking landlubbers. It was during this time that German immigrant Levi Strauss built a business in San Francisco selling tough trousers to forty-niners.

The clothing industry was given a further impetus by the large government contracts awarded for the production of army uniforms during the Civil War. As immigration accelerated in the latter part of the century, the menswear industry grew in stature and made use of this new labor pool. The shirt industry developed after World War I (during which men in the army were first exposed to shirts with attached and unstarched collars) when Arrow Shirts (owned by Cluett Peabody) introduced the process of Sanforizing, which prevented shrinking.

The women's apparel industry developed more slowly. It

was not until the early years of the 20th century that a significant degree of mass production replaced custom tailoring for this type of clothing. The trend began with undergarments and silk kimonos and then spread to shirtwaists and later to cotton dresses.

In the 1920s a group of real estate developers in New York erected buildings on Seventh Avenue designed to house workrooms and showrooms for apparel companies. The 16-block area became the center of the women's garment trade in the United States. After American fashion began to escape the grip of French haute couture in the 1930s, the garment district emerged as a design as well as production and marketing center.

SOUTHWARD, HO!

While the clothing industry remained concentrated in the Northeast, the dominance of the New England textile mills began to erode in the late 19th century. The traditional center of the industry reached its pinnacle of power with the large textile complexes in Fall River, Massachusetts (which called itself "Spindle City"); New Bedford, Massachusetts; and Manchester, New Hampshire. But during the Reconstruction era, mills began to pop up in the South, particularly in the Carolinas.

After World War II the South became the center of the manufacturing end of the textile business. Faced with increasing unionization and rising costs, many of the New England producers simply packed up their bags—their capital, that is—and transferred production below the Mason-Dixon line.

One of the more notorious practitioners of this policy was Royal Little, the founder of Textron, who got into the synthetic yarn business in the 1920s and made a killing from the vogue for rayon. After receiving government contracts in the 1940s for parachutes and jungle hammocks, Little began buying up New England competitors, including giant American Woolen. He shut down many of the mills, selling off their assets in order to set up operations in the South and to get into other lines of business. Similar moves were also made by J. P. Stevens, which laid off many thousands of workers in the North and then fought a bitter battle when unions tried to follow the company to the South.

Although labor costs and the general business climate in Dixie were hospitable to the textile mills and to the many clothing producers that also relocated there, the industry did not remain placid. First of all, there was a major upheaval in the making with the spread of man-made fibers. Rayon, which was invented in 1891, was synthetic in the sense that it derived from cellulose rather than cotton or wool. Yet the bigger change came from the use of inorganic materials.

This path was blazed by Wallace Carothers, a research scientist who began working for Du Pont in 1927 in an effort to create an artificial substitute for silk. It took Carothers seven years to find the right compound and Du Pont another four to figure out how to produce the substance efficiently. But when nylon was put on the market in 1940 in the form of women's hosiery, public acceptance was immediate. Du Pont sold 64 million pairs of nylons the first year alone.

After the war, synthetic fibers based on petrochemicals began to assume a major place in the textile and apparel business. By the 1960s material such as polyester was being used in the majority of clothing, and chemical companies such as Celanese, Monsanto, and of course Du Pont had become leading fiber producers.

No sooner were the textile and apparel industries adjusting to this sea change than they faced a challenge from another quarter: foreign competition. The first significant signs of this threat came in the 1950s, when Japan, having recovered from the war, began exporting heavily to the United States. The Eisenhower administration persuaded the Japanese to accept voluntary trade restraints in 1957, but by the early 1960s imports were mounting from other Asian countries.

The problem continued to grow, and by the early 1970s both the United States and other developed countries were eager to do something to protect textile and apparel producers from what was seen as predatory third-world competition. The result was the Arrangement Regarding International Trade in Textile, more commonly known as the Multifiber Agreement (MFA).

The MFA, which took effect in 1974, essentially represented a way for the developed countries to get around the free-trade provisions of the General Agreement on Tariffs and Trade in order to shield what was considered a vulnerable sector of their economies. Under the agreement, developed countries were able to negotiate specific import limits with third-world producers. Revisions to the MFA in 1977 and 1981 gave importing nations even more latitude.

Although the MFA gave some relief to U.S. producers, the textile and apparel industries faced a worsening crisis in the 1970s and early 1980s. The textile sector was plagued with serious overcapacity, cutthroat competition among domestic manufacturers, and fragmentation of production. Aside from howling for more protectionist trade policies, the industry responded to its predicament in several ways.

STRATEGIES FOR SURVIVAL

One tack was to move away from the traditional focus on commodity products and instead emphasize more profitable and distinctive items, such as designer towels and sheets. Fieldcrest Mills was a leader in this strategy, succeeding in foreign as well as domestic markets. Industry leaders Burlington and J. P. Stevens jumped on the bandwagon with upscale home furnishings. There was also a push in specialized new fibers used in products such as snakebite-proof pants and better bulletproof vests.

The other major strategy of the large textile companies was a massive investment in new plants and equipment. The aim here was not to increase overall capacity but to modernize old facilities and reach new levels of efficiency. The industry spent large sums—reaching about $2 billion per annum—on new technologies such as direct-feed carding in yarn production, open-end spinning, and various kinds of shuttleless looms for weaving. This surge of automation did significantly increase productivity, but it also accelerated the decline of employment levels in the industry.

Most of the 15,000 firms in the clothing sector were too

small to make major capital investments, though some of the larger companies did adopt laser cutting devices and other computerized equipment. A nonprofit operation called Tailored Clothing Technology Corporation (referred to as TC^2) was set up in the early 1980s by a group of clothing and textile firms to research further innovations. TC^2, formed with the cooperation of labor unions, in effect functions as a cooperative research-and-development effort for a pair of industries traditionally dominated by companies too small to engage in research and development on their own. Although the practical results of TC^2 have been limited, there has been increased emphasis on new technology among apparel manufacturers.

Nonetheless, apparel remains a highly labor-intensive industry, and wage costs continue to be decisive. The major producers, especially the big blue-jeans makers, have dealt with this imperative by seeking out cheaper labor wherever it might be found. Levi Strauss, for instance, has shifted a great deal of production abroad, taking advantage of Tariff Item 807, which allows a U.S. company to do some aspects of production overseas and then import the semifinished items back home and pay duties only on the value added abroad. Many of the foreign facilities are located in export-processing zones, in which tariffs and other government regulations are relaxed and labor is strictly controlled.

In the United States some aspects of production can be farmed out to subcontractors known as jobbers, who frequently make use of sweatshop or home labor to get the work done. Even in the unionized northeast, garment workers continue to be paid less than their counterparts in any other major industry.

By the early 1980s the clothing business was suffering both from a sharp drop in demand during the recession and from a general decline in the popularity of designer jeans and other brand-name apparel. (Jeans sales reached a record level of some 600 million pairs in 1981—a result, it is said, of the film *Urban Cowboy*—and then began declining.) Later in the decade the problem was intensified competition. The big department stores put more emphasis on house brands, which reduced the market for designer labels. At the same time, designer firms like Calvin Klein and Ralph Lauren began opening their own retail outlets to compete with the department stores.

The upheaval in the textile and clothing industries has also brought about a wave of changes in ownership of major firms. After some leading corporate raiders showed interest in these sectors, a batch of companies rushed to go private in order to remain independent. Dan River used an employee stock ownership plan (ESOP) to accomplish this in 1983, as did both Cone Mills and jeans producer Blue Bell the following year. In 1985 Levi Strauss was taken private in a leveraged buyout by the Haas family, descendants of the founder.

Becoming private was also the fate of Cannon Mills, which succumbed to a takeover by financier David Murdock in 1982. Cannon was then sold to Fieldcrest Mills in late 1985. At about the same time, Springs Industries agreed to acquire M. Lowenstein, and West Point-Pepperell said it would purchase Cluett Peabody. In 1986 VF Corp. (maker of Lee, the third-ranking brand of jeans) announced it would purchase Blue Bell (producer of second-ranking Wrangler). The following year Burlington was taken private to evade a bid by Dominion Textile of Canada and raider Asher Edelman. An attempt by managers of J. P. Stevens to take the company private in a leveraged buyout was thwarted by a successful takeover move in 1988 by West Point-Pepperell. West Point, in turn, was taken over by William Farley's holding company Farley Inc. (which also owns Fruit of the Loom underwear) in 1989, though Farley had difficulty handling the debt load he took on as a result of that deal. In mid-1990 he was battling with lenders to keep control of West Point.

All this restructuring, technological change, and marketing emphasis did not change the fact that imports were capturing a steadily increasing share of the U.S. textile and clothing markets. In 1985 textile imports approached $4 billion, triple the 1972 total; in 1989 they were $4.7 billion. Apparel imports meanwhile soared above $15 billion in 1985, more than seven times the 1972 level; in 1989 they were nearly $24 billion.

This trend fanned the fires of protectionist sentiment in Congress. There was particular concern over reports that certain exporting countries were arranging for their products to

The 10 Largest Textile Companies, by 1989 Sales ($ Millions)

1. Wickes	$4,802
2. Milliken	2,900
3. Armstrong World Industries	2,864
4. West Point-Pepperell	2,568
5. Burlington Holdings	2,198
6. Springs Industries	1,909
7. Amoskeag	1,402
8. OWG	1,185
9. Shaw Industries	1,176
10. JPS Textile Group	821

Source: *Fortune*, April 23, 1990; *Forbes*, December 11, 1989 (Milliken estimate).

pass through other nations in order to get around the MFA import limits. The result was legislation that took aim at what were regarded as the prime offenders—Hong Kong, South Korea, and Taiwan—by cutting their import allowances by about 30 percent and reducing levels for other countries by lesser amounts.

The Textile and Apparel Trade Enforcement Act passed both houses of Congress in late 1985 but was vetoed by President Reagan in December. The House narrowly upheld the veto the following summer. Meanwhile the trade debate continued, with the industry insisting on the need for better protection and its opponents (major retailers, for instance) arguing that legislation such as the 1985 bill would raise domestic clothing prices and that automation, not imports, was mainly responsible for the loss of hundreds of thousands of jobs over the past decade. Nevertheless the leading textile and apparel firms, along with their unions, established the Crafted with Pride in the USA Council, a body that worked to convince the public of the need to "buy American."

LABOR RELATIONS

Just as textiles were central to the development of American industry, so were the workers employed in the mills key figures in U.S. labor history. The Lowell "factory girls" were the first

The 10 Largest Apparel Firms, by 1989 Sales ($ Millions)

1. Levi Strauss	$3,628
2. VF	2,540
3. Liz Claiborne	1,411
4. Fruit of the Loom	1,321
5. Hartmarx	1,312
6. Crystal Brands	857
7. Leslie Fay	786
8. Kellwood	754
9. Russell	688
10. Phillips-Van Heusen	642

Source: *Fortune*, April 23, 1990.

Americans to be exposed to the rigors of mass production, and they were among the earliest workers to act collectively to further their lot. The first strike in the mills took place in 1824 in response to attempts by the owners to extend hours and reduce wages. The workers ended up returning to work on management's terms, but an era of labor militancy in the mills was opened.

By the late 19th century the labor force in textiles as well as clothing was changing rapidly, becoming the domain of new immigrants from Europe. Unions had been formed, but they were mostly limited to skilled native workers. By the early years of the 20th century the low-paid and overworked immigrant labor force began organizing to improve working conditions.

In the mills the decisive events included the Fall River strike of 1904 and the large-scale walkout in Lawrence, Massachusetts, in 1912. The latter event, which occurred after the American Woolen Company tried to cut wages, was a bitter 63-day affair that ended in victory for the workers and wage increases throughout the New England textile industry.

Around the same time there was upheaval among clothing workers, who were concentrated in New York. Major strikes of shirtwaist makers in 1909 and cloakmakers in 1910 resulted in the Protocol of Peace, an accord that abolished home work and inside subcontracting, limited the workweek to 54 hours, and created an arbitration process for grievances (in exchange for giving up the right to strike). The following year the deaths of 146 young women workers who were caught behind locked doors during a fire at the Triangle Shirtwaist Company brought public attention to sweatshop conditions and led to various reforms.

By World War I the International Ladies Garment Workers Union, formed in 1900, was one of the most influential U.S. labor organizations. In 1914 the Amalgamated Clothing Workers of America was formed in the men's clothing industry as a more aggressive alternative to the United Garment Workers, which was oriented to skilled tailors and cutters.

The movement of both textile and clothing firms to the South was in large measure aimed at escaping unions. The firms that established those industries in the South had set a paternalistic (though low-wage) and fiercely antiunion tone in the region. When organizers arrived in the new center of the industries after World War II, mill owners were willing to defy the law in the attempt to remain union-free.

After workers at Deering-Milliken's plant in Darlington, South Carolina, voted in 1956 for the Textile Workers Union of America (a CIO union formed in the 1930s), the company closed the operation and spent years fighting the unfair-labor-practice charges brought against it. It was not until 1980 that the company agreed to pay $5 million in compensation to the workers who had lost their jobs.

Another epic labor battle took place at J. P. Stevens. In 1963 the Textile Workers began an organizing drive at the company's plants throughout the South. Although the union won a number of representation elections (including one that inspired the film *Norma Rae*), Stevens refused to negotiate a contract. Eventually the Amalgamated Clothing and Textile Workers Union (formed by the 1976 merger of the Textile Workers and the Amalgamated Clothing Workers) adopted a strategy proposed by Ray Rogers that involved pressuring the company's outside directors and lenders. This "corporate campaign" helped bring about a 1980 agreement in which Stevens agreed to recognize the union at facilities where workers had voted in favor of representation.

Despite the J. P. Stevens settlement, unionization of southern textile mills has not progressed much further. A key election at Cannon Mills in 1985 resulted in a dramatic defeat for the union.

Clothing workers' unions have also been in a weakened condition because of rising imports and the decline in jobs. Production workers in apparel declined from 1.2 million in 1973 to about 920,000 at the end of the 1980s. During the same period, the number of textile production workers fell from 863,000 to 583,000. The clothing unions have tended to put their greatest energies in "buy American" campaigns and have not pushed too hard to end the low wage scales of the industry. The unions have also not had much success battling the resurgence of sweatshops and home labor.

The last major labor battle in the clothing industry took place at Farah Manufacturing in the early 1970s. The workers (mostly Chicano women) at the pants producer's El Paso and San Antonio plants walked out in 1972 to protest the company's refusal to recognize the union they had voted for in 1970. After 22 months and a lot of public support, Farah finally agreed to negotiate a contract.

In the late 1980s labor explored a different way of dealing with the industry. When the jobs of 8,000 workers were threatened by a plan of Farley Inc. to sell Cluett Peabody, the Amalgamated Clothing and Textile Workers launched a campaign to have Cluett taken over by an employee stock ownership plan. The effort, launched in conjunction with Nashville businessman Spencer Hays, was dropped in August 1989 after receiving an unsympathetic response from Farley.

LEADING COMPANIES

Burlington Holdings, once the world's largest textile company, got started as a producer of rayon in North Carolina in the 1920s. During the Great Depression the company began gobbling up other mills in the South and became the leader in the commodity end of the business. By the 1980s Burlington was shaking off its stodgy reputation by investing heavily in modern equipment and bringing out designer products. In 1987, faced with a takeover attempt by Dominion Textile of Canada and raider Asher Edelman, the firm's management joined with Morgan Stanley in a $2.5 billion leveraged buyout.

Hartmarx, formerly known as Hart, Schaffner & Marx, is one of the oldest names in the men's clothing business. It got started as a Chicago retail clothing store in 1872 and later moved into the wholesale end of the business. It ran the first national clothing advertising and became the leading producer of men's suits. In the 1980s the company remained strong while producers of less expensive clothing were buffeted by imports. Yet later in the decade the company faced losses at its retail outlets and began to suffer the consequences of the market shift to more stylish European designs.

Levi Strauss, the largest U.S. apparel company, is famous the world over for its blue jeans. The company was founded by a German immigrant who set up a dry goods business in San Francisco in the 1850s. A Nevada tailor named Jacob Davis approached the company in 1872 with his idea for using rivets to reinforce workpants. Strauss embraced the idea and brought out a product, the 501 Double X blue denim waist overall, that remained virtually unchanged for more than a century. Levi Strauss rode the wave of popularity of blue jeans in the 1960s and 70s but stumbled in its attempts to diversify into other lines of apparel.

Liz Claiborne, who founded **Liz Claiborne Inc.** with her husband Arthur Ortenberg in 1976, has transformed the women's clothing industry. She translated haute couture into stylish and not-too-expensive clothes that working women could wear to the office. The company, which went public in 1981, has grown by more than 40 percent a year and made it to the Fortune 500 only 11 years after its birth. After gaining control of about one third of the market for women's better sportswear, in the late 1980s Claiborne began to move into men's clothing. The company has avoided direct involvement in manufacturing and instead deals with contractors in more than two dozen countries.

Milliken & Company of Spartanburg, South Carolina, is the nation's largest privately held textile firm (Forbes estimated revenues as $2.9 billion in 1989) and certainly the most secretive. Formerly known as Deering-Milliken, the company pioneered the use of modern equipment and has been one of the most ardent opponents of unionization. President Roger Milliken stepped into the spotlight in 1985 by becoming the chief spokesman for the Crafted with Pride in the USA Council. Many of Milliken's products are unlabelled and are used in swimsuits, uniforms, and other garments. The company still prides itself on using the most up-to-date and efficient technology.

West Point-Pepperell pulled off a major coup in 1988 when it took over industry giant J. P. Stevens, thus thwarting a leveraged buyout plan proposed by Stevens managers. That move came two years after West Point acted as a white knight for Cluett Peabody, which was being pursued by raider Paul Bilzerian. West Point, formed by the 1963 merger of two mills that dated back to the mid-19th century, ended up with the lead in the bed linen market and a strong second place in towels. Yet

INDUSTRY DATA

Textiles	*1989*	*1988*	*1987*
Value of shipments	$69.0 billion	$65.6 billion	$62.9 billion
Total employment	687,000	679,000	675,000
Value of imports	$4.7 billion	$4.5 billion	$4.7 billion

Apparel	*1989*	*1988*	*1987*
Value of shipments	$72.2 billion	$67.7 billion	$65.1 billion
Total employment	1,090,000	1,069,000	1,080,000
Value of imports	$23.7 billion	$22.2 billion	$21.5 billion

Source: U.S. Department of Commerce.

in 1989 West Point itself succumbed to merger mania when it was taken over by William Farley, who had difficulty handling the debt he took on to complete the deal and in mid-1990 was scrambling to keep control of West Point.

SOURCE GUIDE

Leading Stock Analysts and Experts

Brenda Gall, textile and apparel analyst at Merrill Lynch.

Margaret Gilliam, textile and apparel analyst at First Boston.

Edward Johnson, textile and apparel analyst at Prescott Ball & Turben, New York.

Jay Meltzer, textile and apparel analyst at Goldman Sachs.

Kurt Salmon Associates, a textile and apparel consulting firm based in Atlanta, Georgia.

Trade Associations and Unions

Amalgamated Clothing and Textile Workers Union, 15 Union Square West, New York, NY 10003. Tel.: (212) 242–0700.

American Apparel Manufacturers Association, 2500 Wilson Blvd., Arlington, VA 22201. Tel.: (703) 524–1864.

American Textile Manufacturers Institute, 1801 K Street NW, Washington, D.C. 20006. Tel.: (202) 862–0500.

International Ladies Garment Workers Union, 1710 Broadway, New York, NY 10019. Tel.: (212) 265–7000.

Data Sources and Directories

Davison's Textile Blue Book, an annual directory (Ridgewood, N.J: Davison Publishing).

Fact File: The Textile/Apparel Industries and *Fairchild's Textile & Apparel Financial Directory*, annual compilations of statistics (New York: Fairchild Publications).

Fiber Organon, a monthly compilation of statistics on man-made fibers (Roseland, N.J.: Fiber Economics Bureau).

Financial Profiles of Public Companies in Textiles, Apparel, Retailing and Footwear and *Soft Goods Outlook*, both annual (Atlanta: Kurt Salmon Associates).

Focus: An Economic Profile of the Apparel Industry, an annual compilation of statistics (Arlington, Va.: American Apparel Manufacturers Association).

Textile Highlights, a quarterly compilation of data (Washington, D.C.: American Textile Manufacturers Institute).

Online Databases

TEXTILE TECHNOLOGY DIGEST (Charlottesville, Va.: Institute of Textile Technology; available on DIALOG).

WORLD TEXTILES (Manchester, England: Shirley Institute; available on DIALOG).

Trade Publications

America's Textiles International, monthly.

Apparel Industry, monthly.

Daily News Record.

Textile Industries, monthly.

Textile World, monthly.

Women's Wear Daily.

Books and Reports

Chapkis, Wendy, and Cynthia Enloe, eds. *Of Common Cloth: Women in the Global Textile Industry*. Amsterdam and Washington, D.C.: Transnational Institute, 1983.

Clairmonte, Frederick, and John Cavanagh. *World in their Web: Dynamics of Textile Multinationals*. London: Zed Press, 1981.

Conway, Mimi. *Rise Gonna Rise: A Portrait of Southern Textile Workers*. Garden City, N.Y.: Doubleday Publishing, 1979.

Dunwell, Steve. *The Run of the Mill.* Boston: David R. Godine, 1978.

MIT Commission on Industrial Productivity. "The U.S. Textile Industry," in *Working Papers of the MIT Commission on Industrial Productivity*. Cambridge, Mass.: MIT Press, 1989.

National Research Council. *The Competitive Status of the U.S. Fibers, Textiles and Apparel Complex*. Washington, D.C.: National Academy Press, 1983.

Organisation for Economic Co-operation and Development. *Textile and Clothing Industry: Structural Problems and Policies in OECD Countries*. Paris, 1983.

Rothstein, Richard. *Keeping Jobs in Fashion: Alternatives to the Euthanasia of the U.S. Apparel Industry*. Washington, D.C.: Economic Policy Institute, 1989.

Rowan, Richard L. *Employee Relations Trends and Practices in the Textile Industry*. Philadelphia: Wharton Industrial Research Unit, 1987.

Stein, Leon, ed. *Out of the Sweatshop*. New York: Quadrangle Books, 1977.

Toyne, Brian, ed. *The Global Textile Industry*. London: Allen & Unwin, 1984.

U.S. Congress, Office of Technology Assessment. *The U.S. Textile and Apparel Industry: A Revolution in Progress*. Washington, D.C.: Government Printing Office, 1987.

Waldinger, Roger D. *Through the Eye of the Needle: Immigrants and Enterprise in New York's Garment Trades*. New York and London: New York University Press, 1986.

PART 3

ELECTRONICS

CHAPTER 13

MAINFRAMES AND MINICOMPUTERS

In the mid-1950s, the process of handling data took a major technological leap with the spread of electronic computing devices. Computers, which were initially devised for military and scientific purposes, soon swept the business world, shaping the way in which corporations kept their records and did their planning. The computer industry grew into one of the major sectors of American business and provided its customers with ever more powerful and efficient processors. In 1989 the industry shipped hardware with a total value of some $70 billion. About 30 percent of this represented large-scale devices known as mainframe computers that usually sell for more than $1 million each; another 40 percent consisted of smaller machines called minicomputers and workstations. These segments are the subject of this chapter. Personal computers, software, and semiconductors are discussed elsewhere. Labor relations in the entire electronics industry are discussed in the chapter on semiconductors.

FROM ABACUS TO ENIAC

The urge to count is a fundamental human trait; and as soon as the numbers involved exceeded fingers and toes, people turned to mechanical computational aids. Until the 17th century, devices such as the abacus sufficed, but then men of science such as Blaise Pascal and Gottfried Wilhelm von Leibniz began devising machines that could take over the tedious chores of arithmetic. In the mid-19th century British inventor Charles Babbage advanced the concept with his project (never realized) of building an "analytical engine." Several decades later in the United States Herman Hollerith invented punch cards and mechanical tabulators suitable for serious computation.

Hollerith started out producing his machines for the Census Bureau but found there was an enormous demand for the devices in the business world. Yet Hollerith was a better inventor than he was an entrepreneur, and in 1910 his company was taken over by financier Charles Flint. A pioneer in promoting what would later be called synergistic mergers, Flint combined Hollerith's firm with several others to form the Computing-Tabulating-Recording Company, more commonly known as CTR.

In 1914 CTR hired a talented young marketing man named Thomas Watson to serve as general manager. Watson had been working for National Cash Register (NCR), where he rose to prominence as an aggressive disciple of John Patterson, the king of the cash register business. Patterson's ruthless tactics against the competition resulted in an antitrust suit naming him and Watson among the defendants. The original guilty verdict was overturned on appeal after Patterson made extensive use of company resources to help Dayton, Ohio (where NCR was based), recover from a devastating flood.

By the early 1920s Watson was running CTR and promoting aggressive salesmanship to turn the company into the leader of the tabulating industry. Through paternalism and a strong dose of what today is called corporate culture—there were among other things company songs and the ubiquitous slogan THINK—Watson built one of the best-managed organizations in American business. In 1924 he changed the name of the company to International Business Machines (IBM®).

While IBM was swallowing the punch-card business, work was going on in various research centers with the aim of developing more sophisticated counting machines. At Bell Labs in the late 1930s mathematician George Stibitz hit on the idea of using electric switches to represent the zeroes and ones of the binary number system. Howard Aiken, a graduate student at Harvard who was doing similar work, ended up getting some funding from IBM, which was more interested in the prestige of being associated with a Harvard project than in the practical results. Watson was skeptical of electronic computing devices and remained so until the early 1950s. When Aiken unveiled his machine—the automatic sequence controlled calculator, or Mark I—in 1944, he barely mentioned IBM, which outraged Watson and probably contributed to Watson's resistance to computers.

A separate research project at the Moore School of Electrical Engineering of the University of Pennsylvania resulted in the device that paved the way for the computer industry. Following an approach often credited to John Atanasoff of Iowa State College, John Mauchly and J. Presper Eckert assembled a machine based on electronic vacuum tubes. The huge contraption, dubbed the Electronic Numerical Integrator and Computer (ENIAC), was first demonstrated publicly on February 14, 1946—a date that could be called the birth of the modern computer age.

Eckert and Mauchly recognized the commercial potential of what they had created and sought to keep the patents in their own names. A dispute over this issue led to their departure from the Moore School and the establishment of a private company to produce ENIAC-like computers under the name of UNIVAC. The two men lacked business finesse as well as adequate capital, so in 1950 they agreed to sell the business to Remington Rand, a large office-supply outfit.

The new owners soon scored a coup when they made a deal with CBS to use UNIVAC to predict the outcome of the 1952 presidential election. The computer forecast a landslide victory for Eisenhower by 9:00 P.M. on election night, but officials were skeptical of the result and refused to air it until a much larger percentage of the actual voting results had come in. Nevertheless, Walter Cronkite helped to introduce millions of Americans to these electronic marvels, and the name UNIVAC became synonymous with computers.

THE RISE OF IBM

In the next few years other companies joined Remington Rand (which merged with Sperry Corp. in 1955 to form Sperry Rand) in the computer business, the most important of these new entrants being IBM. Thomas Watson, Jr., who became president of the company in 1952, had none of his aging father's hesitation about electronic computers. The younger Watson gave the go-ahead for development of a scientific computer that became known as the defense calculator, or the 701. With this product and its commercial version, the 702, IBM let loose its formidable sales machine on the computer business. In fact it was this marketing prowess that made 702 a huge success despite the fact that it was technically inferior to UNIVAC. IBM quickly moved on to the 705, which incorporated magnetic core memory. By 1956, only three years after the introduction of the 701, IBM had seized 85 percent of the computer market, leaving Sperry far behind with a 10 percent share.

IBM's lead was solid enough so that the company could take its time joining the rest of the industry in the move from vacuum tubes to transistors. Then, as integrated circuits were perfected and put into use, IBM began planning its major technical initiative. The results of this preparation were announced with much fanfare in April 1964. At simultaneous press conferences in 62 U.S. cities and 14 foreign countries, IBM unveiled its 360 Series—a range of computers that were supposed to address any kind of data processing need. The $5 billion that IBM risked on this entirely new generation (the industry's third) of machines represented one of the greatest business gambles ever.

There was some stumbling, but the 360 turned out to be a great success, establishing IBM as the unquestioned leader of the business. In fact, analysts started referring to the industry as "IBM and the Seven Dwarfs," the latter consisting of Sperry, Control Data Corp. (CDC), Honeywell, RCA, NCR, General Electric, and Burroughs. IBM's dominance allowed it to set the standards for the industry and gave the company's salespeople enormous leverage over the people in corporations responsible for computer-buying decisions, many of whom were persuaded that purchasing data processing equipment from anyone but IBM was an unacceptable risk.

IBM's hard sell—which often included promises of new, improved products that were far from completed—put its competitors at a severe disadvantage. After Control Data was burned by what it considered a very premature announcement of an IBM model, CDC's founder and chief executive William Norris began complaining to the Justice Department. Getting no action, Norris finally filed a private antitrust suit against IBM in late 1968, charging the industry leader with advertising "paper machines and phantom computers." Soon afterward, on the very last day of the Johnson administration, the Justice Department brought its own case against IBM.

IBM fought back against CDC but ended up settling out of court in a 1973 accord under which IBM sold its Service Bureau Corp. subsidiary to CDC at asset value and agreed to pay out about $100 million over several years. (IBM had been forced to create the Service Bureau as an arm's-length operation as part of the 1956 consent decree it signed to resolve antitrust charges brought by the Justice Department with regard to the tabulating business.) But perhaps the most important element of the settlement was the provision for destroying the computerized index CDC had compiled of the 75,000 pages of internal IBM documents it had obtained during the discovery phase of the case. The Justice Department had been hoping to get its hands on that index to aid its case against IBM (which stretched through the 1970s and was finally dropped by the Reagan administration in January 1982).

The dominance of the 360 Series had a negative as well as a positive effect on IBM's competitive position. Two new sets of rivals emerged. One group purchased IBM mainframes and leased them out to customers at better rates than IBM offered to rental customers. Another set of companies, such as Mohawk Data Sciences and Telex, began producing peripheral equipment that worked with IBM systems (the industry jargon is "plug compatible") but that was cheaper and more efficient than comparable devices made by IBM.

Big Blue, as IBM was nicknamed, fought back with various tactics, including the introduction of the 370 Series in 1970. It priced this new line of products to the disadvantage of the leasing companies and made some design changes that complicated life for producers of what came to be called plug-compatible peripherals.

These moves against the upstarts resulted in yet more litigation against IBM. Big Blue prevailed in a case brought by Greyhound Computer Leasing but lost the initial verdict in the suit brought by Telex. The federal appeals court overturned the verdict, and after Telex vowed to go to the Supreme Court the two parties settled. But IBM's legal woes mounted as about a dozen other small competitors sought their day in court. *Fortune* described the experience as "IBM's travails in Lilliput."

As if this were not enough, Big Blue was also confronted by a direct assault in its core business: the production of large-scale, general-purpose mainframe computers. IBM never quite had this market entirely to itself, but the group of competitors known as the Seven Dwarfs (who were renamed the BUNCH—an acronym for Burroughs, the Univac division of Sperry, NCR, Control Data, and Honeywell—after GE and RCA dropped out of the business in the early 1970s) were perennial also-rans. Then in 1970, Gene Amdahl, an IBM engineer who had designed the 360 Series, left the company with the intention of producing mainframes that were superior to IBM's but ran on the same software.

Amdahl's vow was initially laughed off by Big Blue, but the new company obtained funding from Fujitsu (which wanted access to the technology) and American venture capitalists. Overcoming the odds, Amdahl brought out its 470 V/6 in 1975 and began luring away some of IBM's major customers, who were impressed by the better price-performance ratio of Amdahl's machine. Before long there was a rush into the IBM-compatible mainframe business by companies such as Itel, Two Pi, and Magnuson Systems.

On another front IBM was threatened by the increasing popularity of smaller systems that allowed easier and more flexible data processing operations. This segment of the business was created back in 1957 by a young MIT engineer named Kenneth Olsen. Several years later the firm, called Digital Equipment Corp., brought out a system for $120,000 at a time when the cheapest mainframes were going for well over $1 million. These inexpensive systems (soon labeled minicomputers) found many willing customers, and DEC experienced a breathtaking rate of growth. But it was in the 1970s that minis, by then also being produced by companies such as Data General and Hewlett-Packard, came into full flower.

In all, the 1970s were a period of discomfort for IBM. Its overall market share dropped from about 60 percent to 40 percent over the decade, and its profit margins slid several points from the typical 1960s range of 24 to 28 percent. For the first time Big Blue seemed less than invincible.

BIG BLUE TRIES TO BOUNCE BACK

At the end of the decade IBM unleashed a plan to regain dominance. The industry had long been awaiting Big Blue's next major step. In 1975 the company abandoned work on something called Future System, which was supposed to replace the 370 Series. IBM's planners decided that an entirely new generation of machines would be too disruptive and instead opted for an evolutionary change. In fact it was this slower pace that gave breathing room to the leasing companies and IBM-compatible manufacturers.

In 1979 Big Blue changed the rules of the game. IBM announced the 4300 line—a new generation of medium-scale mainframes that were priced far below existing levels. The cost per megabyte of memory plunged from $75,000 to $15,000. This bargain elicited orders by the truckful. In only three weeks IBM had requests for 42,000 machines, more than twice what the company had planned to produce over the life of the series. Delivery schedules were stretched out over four years.

The overwhelming demand created problems for IBM. Customers were upset at the long waiting periods for delivery, and some turned to the IBM-compatibles instead. Many large-scale users, anticipating big price cuts to match the bargains on the smaller 4300 machines, canceled previous purchase orders and switched to leasing while waiting for announcements regarding high-end models. IBM got caught in a financial squeeze and suffered both earnings and stock price declines.

IBM's delays in bringing out new high-end machines created a new opening for the plug-compatible mainframe producers, who soon gained a total market share exceeding that of the BUNCH. By the early 1980s Big Blue appeared to abandon its previous attempts to eradicate this form of competition, and the likes of Amdahl (no longer run by Gene Amdahl) became a permanent, if still unstable, factor in the mainframe business.

This is not to say that the 1980s brought a repetition of the woes that the 1970s had visited on IBM. In fact Big Blue became more aggressive than ever, especially after the Justice Department dropped its long-standing antitrust suit in 1982. IBM eagerly adopted tactics, such as volume discounts, that it previously had shunned and brought charges against Hitachi and National Advanced Systems for theft of trade secrets. IBM also purchased a chunk of Intel to gain better access to advanced semiconductor technology.

In 1985 IBM finally launched the first of its new generation of high-end mainframes. Code-named Sierra during the development process, the 3090 Series represented a less than earth-shaking improvement over the 3080 Series. In fact the lack of a big leap—along with the price cuts IBM offered on the 3080 machines—prompted some users to decide they would be better-off buying used mainframes from the older series. In addition there were announcements of competing machines from Amdahl, Burroughs, Honeywell (a mainframe built by Nippon Electric and using Honeywell software), and National Advanced Systems (a distributor of plug-compatible machines made by Hitachi).

All of the industry suffered from the sharp falling off of growth in the computer business starting in the mid-1980s. The effect on behemoth IBM was most pronounced, with the company's earnings and stock price declining sharply. The stagnation continued through the rest of the 1980s, forcing Big Blue to do two things it traditionally avoided: eliminate thousands of jobs and resort to discounts to sell mainframes. Other companies also reduced their work forces and shut factories.

By the end of the decade it began to appear that the industry's problem was more than cyclical. Many analysts started saying that the industry was maturing and that growth rates would no longer be in the 20 to 30 percent range that computer makers had previously taken for granted.

In 1990, IBM announced a new generation of much faster mainframes in an attempt to maintain its hold over the shrinking mainframe market. However, Big Blue was upstaged somewhat by an announcement by Fujitsu of its own new generation of machines. Few of the Fujitsu computers would be sold in the United States, but the Japanese company had an indirect influence in the American market through its distribution relationship with Amdahl.

THE FUTURE OF MAINFRAMES

The boom in personal computers starting in the early 1980s turned the computer industry upside down. The increasing power and sophistication of desktop machines dethroned mainframes and minis as the workhorses of corporate data processing. During the 1980s, local area networks of PCs were the rage—particularly for office automation—and IBM gave this technology a boost in 1985 with the introduction of its own version of the network. It is true, however, that these networks usually need to be run by minis or mainframes, so any claims about the obsolescence of larger machines is still quite premature. In fact, the strategy launched by IBM in the late 1980s to save its larger systems was based on their role in linking minis, PCs, and databases.

Yet the momentum away from mainframes and minis has accelerated with the growth of the market for workstations—high-powered desktop systems that are designed for engineers and scientists but that are spreading to other users. Groups of workstations sharing storage systems are starting to take the place of networks of PCs tied to mainframes or minicomputers. During the 1980s the workstation market was dominated by an upstart company called Sun Microsystems along with Digital Equipment, Hewlett-Packard, and Apollo Computer (acquired by H-P in 1989).

Originally based on Motorola's 32-bit microprocessors, the workstation business was transformed when Sun developed its SPARC microprocessor using the reduced instruction set (RISC) technique. Sun pushed to make SPARC an industry standard and was supported in that effort by Unisys, Xerox, and AT&T (which purchased a 20 percent interest in Sun). Yet other leading companies went with competing microprocessors from Motorola, Intel, and other suppliers. Sun's position was also challenged by IBM's introduction in 1990 of a new line of relatively low-priced workstations that use Big Blue's own RISC processor.

While workstations are gaining ground at the low end, the market for the most powerful mainframes, known as supercomputers, remains quite strong. Supercomputers are systems capable of handling the huge number of computations involved in sophisticated scientific and engineering applications. Until the mid-1980s the supercomputer market was essentially owned by Cray Research; by the end of 1984 there were 130 supercomputers in place worldwide, and Cray had supplied 88 of these.

The Cray-2, introduced in 1985, offered performance in the mind-boggling range of 600 to 1,200 MFLOPS (millions of floating-point operations per second). Founder Seymour Cray then turned to the Cray-3, which was supposed to achieve a much more amazing performance of 16,000 MFLOPS through the use of gallium arsenide chips.

But life got more complicated for the company. A new generation of producers—including Convex Computer, Alliant Computer Systems, and Floating Point Systems—brought out machines dubbed mini-supercomputers, which were just as powerful as smaller Crays but significantly less expensive. At the same time, Japanese companies such as NEC, Hitachi, and Fujitsu became more serious competitors in full-fledged, high-end supercomputers. Control Data subsidiary ETA Systems tried to be another contender, but it did not win enough acceptance and was shut down by CDC in 1989.

Cray fought back with its X–MP machine, but Steve Chen—the designer of that supercomputer and a superstar of the field—resigned from Cray in a dispute over funding for the development of an even more advanced model. Chen, a leader in the development of parallel processing, set up a new company called Supercomputer Systems and got money and technical assistance from IBM. In 1989 Seymour Cray himself set up

The Top 20 Computer Companies Worldwide, by 1989 Information Systems Revenue ($ Billions)

1. IBM	$60.81
2. Digital Equipment	12.94
3. NEC	11.48
4. Fujitsu	11.38
5. Unisys	9.39
6. Hitachi	8.72
7. Hewlett-Packard	7.80
8. Groupe Bull	6.47
9. Siemens	6.01
10. Olivetti	5.57
11. Apple	5.37
12. NCR	5.32
13. Toshiba	4.60
14. Canon	3.78
15. Matsushita	3.66
16. Compaq	2.88
17. AT&T	2.87
18. NV Philips	2.81
19. Nixdorf	2.79
20. Xerox	2.79

Source: Reprinted from *Datamation*, June 15, 1990. © by Cahners/Ziff Publishing Associates, L. P.

a new company (which was spun off from Cray Research) to continue development of the Cray-3.

Even more ambitious than Cray's gallium arsenide gambit are the efforts being made to develop computers based on optics rather than electronics. Since light travels faster than electricity, optical computers could theoretically provide machines of vastly greater speed. While optical computing has a long way to go before entering the realm of the practical, the technology is being explored by researchers at various universities and at Bell Labs, which in 1990 unveiled the first (albeit primitive) digital optical processor.

LEADING COMPANIES (APART FROM IBM)

Control Data Corp. (CDC) was formed in 1957 when a group of engineers led by William Norris broke away from a subsidiary of Sperry Rand to produce sophisticated scientific computers on their own. Norris decided to mount a legal challenge to IBM in the late 1960s over pressure tactics used by Big Blue to discourage customers from buying a CDC system. A settlement of the case in 1973 allowed CDC to buy IBM's computer service operation at a bargain price. In the following years Norris placed more emphasis on the service business and the production of peripheral equipment while also sinking many millions of dollars in a computer-based learning system called PLATO. He also made a name for himself as a leading exponent of corporate social responsibility. At the beginning of 1986 Norris finally stepped down, and his successor Robert Price set out to clear up the company's financial problems. Price did make some progress in that regard, but CDC still suffered from a meager market share. In 1989 the company took a pretax $490 million charge to leave the supercomputer business and reduce its mainframe operations. Lawrence Perlman, who took over as chief executive at the end of 1989, continued the shrinking process.

Until the mid-1980s, **Cray Research** was the undisputed leader of the supercomputer business, the production of the fastest mainframes for advanced technical applications. The company was established in 1972 by Seymour Cray, a brilliant engineer who pioneered supercomputers while working for CDC. Cray Research continued developing more powerful machines, but in the 1980s it confronted challenges from two directions. A new generation of companies began producing what became known as mini-supercomputers—machines that were as powerful but much less expensive than Cray's smaller models. At the same time, companies such as NEC, Hitachi, and Fujitsu managed to build a Japanese supercomputer business in only a few years and began challenging Cray at the high end. In 1989 Cray Research spun off a new operation headed by Seymour Cray to develop an advanced supercomputer using experimental gallium arsenide technology.

Digital Equipment Corp. (DEC) was the originator of a segment of the mainframe business consisting of smaller, more flexible machines known as minicomputers. Founded in 1957 by young MIT engineer Kenneth Olsen, DEC experienced phenomenal growth until the early 1980s, becoming the second-largest company in the computer industry. Facing a slowing of growth in minicomputers, Olsen then moved to improve the company's marketing ability and succeeded in gaining customers for its VAX minis beyond the traditional scientific and technical niches. Yet DEC was soon confronted by a wave of powerful desktop machines—dubbed super-minicomputers—that provided the power of mainframes at a fraction of the price. In response to customer pressure for greater network capabilities, DEC formed a series of joint ventures and other alliances with a variety of companies to fill in its product line. DEC has also been struggling to gain a foothold in the market for engineering workstations, which has drawn many users away from minis. In the late 1980s, DEC weathered the downturn in the industry better than many other companies and retained the number-two position behind IBM. Yet in 1990, DEC announced its first loss as a public company and began a major reduction of its work force.

Hewlett-Packard (H-P), the premier instruments company, has been trying for years to break into the top tier of the computer business. Founded in a Palo Alto, California, garage in 1938 by William Hewlett and David Packard, the company first got into the minicomputer business in 1968 and remained one of the leading players in that segment. Under the leadership of John Young the company was faltering until a redesign of H-P's minicomputer line resulted in improved market share in the late 1980s. H-P tried to move to the fore of the market for workstations with its 1989 acquisition of Apollo Computer for $500 million. Yet the combined operation found it difficult to compete with Sun Microsystems.

Honeywell's roots go back to A. M. Butz's invention of the thermostat in 1883. The company got into the computer business in 1955 by buying an operation from Raytheon. In 1963 Honeywell pioneered the concept of IBM-compatibility with the introduction of its H–200, a product that prompted Big Blue to accelerate the announcement of its pathbreaking 360 Series. The company's presence in the industry took a leap after the purchase of General Electric's computer business in 1970, but Honeywell faltered and remained one of the least dynamic of the mainframe producers. By the mid-1980s Honeywell was pulling back from the production of general-purpose mainframes and concentrating on factory automation. In 1986 Honeywell's computer operations were turned into a joint venture with France's Groupe Bull and Japan's NEC. In 1987 the operation was renamed Honeywell Bull as Groupe Bull became the dominant party in the venture.

NCR, the modern incarnation of the old National Cash Register empire, entered the computer business in the early 1950s but was slow at integrating it into the rest of the company. NCR retained a foothold in the mainframe business by selling to its faithful customers in the retail and financial areas. Charles Exley, who took over as president in 1976, established a strategy of aiming at specialized markets, but the company remained a weak player in the industry. In 1986 NCR introduced its first new mainframes in seven years and became a leading supplier of machines using the Unix operating system.

Sun Microsystems burst onto the computer scene in the 1980s with a bold plan to encourage greater standardization and compatibility of systems. Founded in 1982 by several Stanford University graduates, Sun positioned itself in the emerging market for engineering and scientific workstations. The company's decision to use AT&T's Unix operating system resulted in an alliance with Ma Bell, which bought 20 percent of Sun. In the hardware area Sun developed (with Japan's Fujitsu) a microprocessor chip called SPARC that uses RISC (reduced instruction set computer) techniques. Since SPARCs are easier and less expensive to produce, Sun was able to market machines that provided processing power at a fraction of the cost of established mainframes and minicomputers. The excitement over this new approach helped Sun, led by boyish chief executive Scott McNealy, to become a billion-dollar company in only six years.

Unisys was the name taken by Burroughs after it acquired rival mainframe maker Sperry for $4.8 billion in 1986. Burroughs has been one of IBM's the most persistent competitors in the mainframe business since the 1950s, gaining a reputation for the simplicity and power of its programs. The company got into the computer business early in that decade, after making a name for itself in adding and accounting machines. But Burroughs did not have the marketing finesse to go along with its technical prowess. W. Michael Blumenthal, President Carter's first Treasury secretary, was brought in to run the company in 1980. He rescued Burroughs from a nose dive, bought memory-device maker Memorex in 1981, and in 1985 introduced a new series of mainframes to compete with IBM's Sierra line. Sperry's ancestor Remington Rand was the leader of the industry in its early days after it took over the company founded by computer pioneers John Mauchly and J. Presper Eckert. But soon the firm's UNIVAC machines fell victim to IBM's superior salesmanship. In 1971 Sperry bought the computer business of RCA and resisted diversifying out of mainframes. The marriage of Burroughs and Sperry was initially ridiculed because of the incompatible product lines of the two firms, but Blumenthal managed to improve the financial condition of the combined operation. Yet Unisys remained a distant second to IBM in the mainframe business.

Wang Laboratories, founded by An Wang in 1951 as a producer of custom-built electronic components, grew during the 1970s into the nation's leading producer of word-processing systems. The company's ascent faltered in the early 1980s, when the rise of personal computers reduced the

INDUSTRY DATA

Computers and Peripherals	*1989*	*1988*	*1987*
Value of shipments	$69.5 billion	$65.5 billion	$57.4 billion
Total employment	281,000	290,000	292,000
Value of imports	$20.5 billion	$18.6 billion	$15.1 billion

Source: U.S. Department of Commerce.

appeal of Wang's dedicated terminals. A spate of problems involving new products and financial controls further weakened the firm. An Wang's son Frederick was chosen by the board to take the president's job and lead an attempted revival. Fred Wang broadened the company's product line, introducing IBM compatible PCs and a more powerful minicomputer, but the decline continued. In 1989 An Wang, who was battling cancer (he died the following year), removed his son and replaced him with former General Electric executive Richard Miller.

SOURCE GUIDE

Leading Stock Analysts and Experts

Dataquest Inc., San Jose, California.

Gartner Group, Stamford, Connecticut.

International Data Corp., Framingham, Massachusetts.

Daniel Mandresh, analyst at Merrill Lynch.

Ulric Weil, veteran analyst now with his own firm in Washington, D.C.

Trade Association

Computer and Business Equipment Manufacturers Association, 311 1st Street NW, Washington, DC 20001. Tel.: (202) 737–8888.

Data Sources and Directories

Computer Industry Almanac, an annual compilation of data (Dallas: Computer Industry Almanac).

Computer and Business Equipment Industry Marketing Data Book, an annual volume of statistics (Washington, D.C.: Computer and Business Equipment Manufacturers Association).

Datamation 100, an annual ranking of the leading computer companies worldwide, in the June 15 issue of *Datamation*.

Gartner Group Top 100 DP Almanac, an annual statistical review of the leading data processing firms (Stamford, Conn.: Gartner Group).

Online Database

COMPUTER DATABASE (Foster City, Calif.: Information Access Co.; available via BRS and DIALOG).

Trade Publications

Computer Decisions, monthly.

Computers and People, bimonthly.

Computerworld, weekly.

Datamation, semimonthly.

Books and Reports

Brock, Gerald. *The U.S. Computer Industry.* Cambridge, Mass.: Ballinger, 1975.

Fishman, Katharine. *The Computer Establishment.* New York: Harper & Row, 1981.

Flamm, Kenneth. *Targeting the Computer: Government Support and International Competition.* Washington, D.C.: Brookings Institution, 1987.

McClellan, Stephen. *The Coming Computer Industry Shakeout.* New York: John Wiley & Sons, 1984.

Massachusetts Institute of Technology. "The U.S. Semiconductor, Computer, and Copier Industries," in *Working Papers of the MIT Commission on Industrial Productivity.* Cambridge, Mass.: MIT Press, 1989.

Rifkin, Glenn, and George Harrar. *The Ultimate Entrepreneur: The Story of Ken Olsen and Digital Equipment Corporation.* Chicago: Contemporary Books, 1988.

Shurkin, Joel. *Engines of the Mind: A History of the Computer.* New York: W.W. Norton, 1984.

Sobel, Robert. *IBM: Colossus in Transition.* New York: Times Books, 1981.

Watson, Thomas J., Jr., and Peter Petre. *Father, Son & Co.: My Life at IBM and Beyond.* New York: Bantam Books, 1990.

Weil, Ulric. *Information Systems in the 80s.* Englewood Cliffs, N.J.: Prentice-Hall, 1982.

CHAPTER 14

MICROCOMPUTERS AND SOFTWARE

At one time computers were large, forbidding devices locked in temperature-controlled rooms and tended to by a priesthood of specialists. For most people they were mysterious and marvelous machines that were becoming an increasing force in their lives yet were still hidden from view. Even computer students and aficionados could only gain access to the data processing power of mainframes via remote terminals and time-sharing arrangements. Until the early 1970s companies and institutions, not individuals, owned all of the computers in existence.

Starting in 1975 this state of affairs began to change at a remarkable pace. Small computer systems, or microcomputers, appeared on the scene and were eagerly purchased by people seeking direct and personal access to data processing and to what became a new form of entertainment. The industry that grew up around this phenomenon expanded at a rate rarely seen in the history of American business. Despite a slowdown in the late 1980s, the industry had by 1989 reached a revenue level of some $28 billion for hardware and $5 billion for software. What was once the exclusive domain of youthful entrepreneurs—a number of whom are now multimillionaires—is now a developed industry led by IBM, the traditional giant of the computer industry, and the two most successful upstart companies: Apple and Compaq.

HISTORY OF A YOUNG INDUSTRY

The pioneering company in the microcomputer industry was a now defunct firm called Micro Instrumentation Telemetry Systems (MITS). Formed in 1968 by a group of air force officers/electronics buffs stationed in Albuquerque, New Mexico, MITS started out producing radio transmitters for model airplanes. A few years later Ed Roberts, who had bought out his partners, got into calculators, and after the disastrous price war in that business he hit on the idea of producing kits that would allow hobbyists to make use of the recently developed microprocessors, the so-called computers on a chip.

Encouraged by Les Solomon, an editor at *Popular Electronics*, Roberts had the prototype ready in early 1975 when it was announced to the world on the cover of Solomon's magazine. The product was called Altair, a name suggested by Solomon's 12-year-old daughter because it was the destination of the Starship Enterprise in an episode of *Star Trek*. Pathbreaking though it was, the Altair was primitive by later standards. It had no keyboard or display screen, and after the circuit board was assembled programming could only be introduced through a series of switches.

But what excited the electronics hobbyist world was that it was indeed a computer, built on an Intel 8080 chip and capable of being programmed. It was that capability that interested two young men named Bill Gates and Paul Allen, who had been programmers since their early teens. Seeing the issue of *Popular Electronics* announcing the Altair, the two called MITS and offered to produce a version of the popular computer language Basic to run on the machine. Roberts was interested, and after Gates and Allen delivered the program six weeks later, they and MITS developed a close working relationship. Gates and Allen set up a company called Microsoft, which became one of the premier software houses. Another early programmer was Gary Kildall, an instructor at the U.S. Naval Postgraduate School who wrote the operating system CP/M, which became the standard for the first generation of micros.

The Altair was a great success among hobbyists, and MITS was soon joined in the micro business by a slew of other small companies, including IMSAI, Processor Technology, and North Star. All of these producers emerged out of the alternative computing scene of the San Francisco Bay area and Silicon Valley. This was the milieu of young "hackers" who were committed to making computers more accessible to noninstitutional users and were suspicious of those who attempted to make a big business out of micros. They were particularly unsympathetic to people such as Gates and Allen who were making money from software. The prevailing ethic was that software should be freely shared, and pirating of programs was commonplace.

Some micro buffs were more explicitly political and talked of "computer lib" as a means of social change. Lee Felsenstein initiated a project called Community Memory to provide free computerized information services to the public. Both the politicos and the techies came together with the budding entrepreneurs in a group called the Homebrew Computer Club.

SETTING UP THE APPLE CART

Two of the participants in Homebrew meetings were a pair of friends named Steven Jobs and Stephen Wozniak. The two Steves had been involved in electronics since their teens. In the early 1970s they were drawn into "phone phreaking," the production of devices called blue boxes that allowed one to make long-distance phone calls without paying for them.

Jobs, who dabbled in Eastern religion, ended up working for Nolan Bushnell at Atari. At the time, Bushnell was already a Silicon Valley success story, thanks to his invention of Pong (an electronic version of table tennis that was the first video arcade game). Pong started a video-game mania, and Atari (which means "check" in the Japanese game Go) grew like mad, especially after the introduction of home versions of Pong and other amusements.

Jobs was more interested in computers than in games. After Bushnell turned down his proposal for a micro, Jobs urged his friend Wozniak to build one independently. Wozniak, a brilliant engineer and an inveterate prankster, took on the challenge while remaining in his job at Hewlett-Packard. The resulting product, built first in Jobs's parents' house and then the proverbial garage, was christened Apple®.

After the 50 copies of the primitive Apple I were well received, Jobs and Wozniak managed to persuade Mike Markkula, a former marketing wizard at Intel who was comfortably retired in his mid-30s, to help the fledgling company get off the ground. Jobs also convinced leading Silicon Valley publicist Regis McKenna to take on the firm as a client. In the meantime Wozniak was designing an improved version of the system.

The Apple II, which Jobs insisted be as easy as possible to use and have an attractive and unforbidding design, was an instant hit. More than any other product, it helped to bring micros out of the hobbyist world and to a wide range of the general population. One of the elements of this success was the availability on the Apple II of the first financial analysis program for micros, VisiCalc®.

The machine also brought rapid growth to Apple Computer, whose operating revenues leaped from $8 million in 1978 to $117 million in 1980. The initial expansion was made possible by $517,000 in venture capital that Markkula arranged to obtain from Venrock Associates (the venture capital arm of the Rockefeller interests), Don Valentine, and Arthur Rock in early 1978. This investment paid off handsomely. When Apple went public in December 1980, the $517,000 was suddenly worth about $200 million, and the shares owned by Jobs, Wozniak, and Markkula made them centimillionaires. Thanks to the company's generous stock options, many other employees hit the jackpot as well.

Along with the success of the Apple II, the micro market exploded. Dozens of start-up companies were created, and analysts made bold predictions about the spread of micros into virtually every household; the sky was said to be the limit.

Several companies soon rose to the top of the heap. These represented the two leading strategies of the time. Commodore International, a former typewriter company, led the push into the home market. Led by Jack Tramiel, Commodore brought out the low-cost PET (named after the pet rock fad of the time). But after the company got a reputation for poor service, its sales effort was focused in Europe. In 1981 Tramiel, convinced of the demand for cheap computers in the United States, brought out the VIC 20 and priced it at $299. Tramiel's persistence made Commodore a success even while other home-computer makers got pummeled in the intensely competitive market.

By the early 1980s, Jobs's skepticism about the market for

home computers seemed to be justified; the greatest demand came from business and professional users. One company that established a strong foothold there early on was Tandy Corp., parent company of the Radio Shack chain of electronics stores. Tandy's TRS-80 series won a loyal following among serious but not necessarily hobbyist users, and the Model 100 (one of the first laptop devices) became the standard for journalists and others who needed to write or record data while on the road.

The most spectacular rise and fall in this segment was that of Osborne Computer. Adam Osborne got into the micro scene in the mid-1970s after he self-published *Introduction to Microcomputers* and started writing columns for publications such as *InfoWorld.* Osborne expanded his book publishing operation and was successful enough so that McGraw-Hill bought the business in 1979. He then decided to produce his own systems.

Introduced in 1981, the Osborne 1 was an impressive if unattractive machine. It was a no-frills micro that had a disk drive, monitor, and keyboard, all built into a portable package; several software programs were also thrown in for the price of $1,795. The Osborne took off, and by its second year the company was doing $70 million in sales. Yet in September 1983, Osborne Computer went into Chapter 11, the victim of poor management. Osborne himself disclaimed responsibility and placed the blame on Robert Jaunich, the former president of Consolidated Foods who had been brought in to run the company. Whoever was the culprit, it seems that Osborne Computer was a classic case of a company soaring too high too fast.

Osborne was not the only disaster in the business and professional segment. Dozens of small companies came and went, and neither Hewlett-Packard nor Xerox was able to make much of a splash. Apple hoped to have a clear field for a more sophisticated and expensive office system it was developing with the code name of Lisa®, but that was not to be.

ENTER BIG BLUE

By 1980 planners at computer behemoth IBM had become impressed with the growth of the micro market. Although Big

Blue had traditionally concentrated on selling large mainframe systems and had been slow to enter even the minicomputer market, IBM was confronting the 1980s with an aggressive posture, hoping to overcome the frustrations of the 1970s. An operation called Entry Level Systems (later Entry Systems Division) was set up in Boca Raton, Florida, to develop an IBM machine to compete with the micros produced by entrepreneurs who had not yet been born when Big Blue got into the computer business in the early 1950s.

The IBM PC, introduced in August 1981, took the world by storm. While it was no technological leap forward—the components were standard ones supplied by outside vendors—the machine did have the IBM cachet, and that made all the difference. Big Blue made some smart moves: The PC had an open software system, which encouraged the production of many compatible programs by independent firms, and the leap from an 8-bit to a 16-bit processor came at the right time for the industry.

IBM's machine was announced around the time the Apple III was suffering from engineering problems (which had led to major recalls) and poor marketing. IBM was able to charge ahead in the office and professional segment, matching Apple's market share only a year after the introduction of the IBM PC. In 1983 Big Blue gained more ground as Apple's new entry for the business market, the $10,000 Lisa, failed to win widespread acceptance because of its limited software and inability to communicate with other computers, especially IBM mainframes. By October 1983, *Business Week* was able to proclaim: "The battle for market supremacy is suddenly all over, and IBM is the winner."

Meanwhile, at the low end of the market a fierce price war was in progress. Atari was slugging it out with Coleco and Mattel in the game-player segment, while Texas Instruments and Atari were losing ground to Commodore and Coleco in the home computer area (defined as machines costing less than $1,000). Prices for basic home computers dropped to $99 (after rebates), causing a string of fatal losses for several producers. Among the victims in the shakeout of 1983 were Texas Instruments, Mattel, and Timex, which was selling the "mini microcomputer" created by British inventor Clive Sinclair.

Starting in 1984, Apple, having brought in John Sculley of PepsiCo to serve as president, launched its counterattack against IBM. The campaign included a new version of Lisa and a less expensive but impressive system called Macintosh®. Sculley and Jobs hoped to pitch the Mac—which offered a more powerful (32-bit) processor, excellent graphics, and a mouse input device—to smaller companies and university students.

Yet by 1985 Apple was abandoning its quest to rout IBM from the personal computer market, realizing it was more realistic to introduce devices that would make Macintoshes compatible with IBM office networks. (In 1986 Microsoft Corp. released a program enabling Macintoshes and IBM PCs to share some forms of data.) With Sculley completely in charge—he forced Jobs out in late 1985—Apple improved its margins but continued to slip in market share. Yet Sculley kept promoting the Macintosh.

Part of the reason for Apple's slide was a new force in the micro market that was challenging Big Blue as well: producers of IBM-compatible PCs. Just as happened in the mainframe and peripheral markets, a group of companies saw an opportunity in producing micros that worked on the same software as the venerable IBM PC but were better or cheaper than the machines put out by IBM itself.

The most outstanding of the clone producers was Compaq Computer, a company that racked up the amazing figure of $111 million in sales for its first year in operation (1983) and soared to more than $1 billion in 1987. Compaq started out producing portable models, and it trounced the IBM "luggable" introduced in 1984. (IBM also went nowhere with its PCjr™, a scaled-down version of the PC introduced in 1983 and discontinued in 1985.) Compaq then brought out desktop machines that competed with the basic PC, as well as with the higher-performance AT® and XT™ machines.

Compaq was also the first company to come out with a PC based on the advanced Intel 80386 processor. The 386 generation of machines started to revolutionize desktop computing. With their 32-bit microprocessors, PCs were often able to take the place of mainframes and minicomputers. Yet not long after the 386s were on the scene, IBM tried to rewrite the rules with the introduction of a series of PCs (called Personal System/2®) that used the new OS/2 operating system developed by Microsoft and a proprietary architecture called Micro Channel. The IBM machines actually included many proprietary designs, the patents on which Big Blue vowed to defend vigorously against clone producers. The Personal System/2 also employed a graphic interface that resembled that of Apple's Macintosh. In fact, the products of IBM and Apple began to converge in many respects as Apple revamped the Macintosh to make it more appealing to corporate customers.

Rather than slavishly following IBM to the Micro Channel data pathway, a group of the leading clone producers, led by Compaq, decided to embrace Extended Industry Standard Architecture, an extension of the existing AT standard. By the middle of 1990, the contest between the two standards seemed to be resulting in a draw.

In terms of general market share, IBM's lead continued to erode, and Big Blue had to share the top tier of the microcomputer market with Compaq and Apple. Even the low end of the market was consolidating, as some clone producers dropped out (or sold out, as Zenith did in selling its PC operations to France's Groupe Bull in 1989) and few newcomers entered an increasingly difficult business. According to International Data Corporation, the market shares in 1989 were:

IBM	19.6%
Apple	8.8
Compaq	6.6
Zenith	4.5
Tandy	4.3
Others	56.2

SOFTWARE TAKES CHARGE

The direction of the microcomputer software industry was to a great extent determined in 1980 when a group of pin-striped representatives of IBM visited young Bill Gates of Microsoft. Big Blue was looking for a programming language for its then-secret personal computer project and was impressed with Microsoft's work. IBM also ended up asking Gates to provide an operating system for the PC. The program, called MS-DOS® (Microsoft disk operating system) by Gates and PC-DOS® when sold by IBM, quickly became the dominant standard as the IBM PC and its clones seized a large chunk of the micro market.

Thanks to the PC's open architecture and IBM's encouragement of independent producers, the range of PC-compatible applications software expanded rapidly. For business users, integrated financial packages (ones that combined spreadsheets and graphics) were the rage, and Lotus Development's 1-2-3® (designed for the PC) soon dethroned VisiCalc, the pioneer in this field. As a result Lotus became for a time the largest independent software producer.

By the mid-1980s, as micro hardware reached a certain level of sophistication, industry analysts began saying that the future of personal computing depended much more than before on advances in software. The new wave of novice users needed more accessible programming, while those with more experience required software with greater versatility and sophistication.

These conflicting goals sometimes caused problems. Lotus brought out an advanced integrated program in 1984 called Symphony®, which was technically impressive but which many users found too difficult to use. The same problem plagued Ashton-Tate, another of the top software houses, with its dBase III® database management program. Increasing complexity of programming has contributed to major delays in such products as 1-2-3 Release 3 and dBase IV®, and when the latter did appear in 1988 it contained such serious flaws that Ashton-Tate lost a huge chunk of market share. Problems such as these have affected the industry's pricing: While the cost of micro hardware has steadily declined, software prices generally have not budged.

Another reason for the sticky prices is that software has become an oligopoly, with the market increasingly dominated by a small number of major producers, especially the Big Three:

Lotus, Ashton-Tate, and Microsoft. For a while it appeared that this would be an orderly arrangement, with each of the three focusing on its own market segment: Lotus in spreadsheets, Ashton-Tate in database management, and Microsoft in systems software. Some of the companies, however, were not satisfied with their own turf. Microsoft, which had already branched out to applications software with its popular Word® text editing program, introduced Excel® to compete with 1-2-3. Lotus brought out a variety of new products ranging from word processing to graphics. They generally did not catch on, and the company also suffered from its lack of a version of 1-2-3 for the Macintosh.

Microsoft did not capture a big share of the spreadsheet business with Excel, but the company did enhance its domination of the systems software market. It developed the OS/2 operating system, which was adopted by IBM in its new line of PCs that was introduced in 1987. And when OS/2 failed to live up to its promise of rapidly becoming the new standard, Microsoft introduced an advanced version of its Windows® program, which allowed PCs using DOS to enjoy many of the advantages that had been unique to the Macintosh. In 1990 Lotus sought to position itself to challenge Microsoft by acquiring Novell Inc., a leading producer of network software. But the $1.5 billion deal collapsed over a failure to agree on the composition of the post-merger board of directors. Microsoft may thus remain secure in its dominant position for some time to come.

The 10 Largest Independent Producers of Microcomputer Software in 1989 ($ Millions)

1. Microsoft	$952.8
2. Lotus Development	556.0
3. WordPerfect	281.4
4. Ashton-Tate	265.3
5. Autodesk	177.0
6. Adobe Systems	121.4
7. Logitech	112.0
8. Software Publishing	110.4
9. Borland International	104.2
10. Aldus	87.9

Source: *Softletter*, March 19, 1990.

COPY PROTECTION AND COPYRIGHT

One of the main reasons software companies have given for their high prices is that they incur heavy losses from the unauthorized copying of programs. Analysts estimated those losses at several hundred million dollars a year in the early 1980s.

The problem for the industry has been that software is extremely easy to copy; in fact, copying the contents of a floppy disk onto another (blank) disk is one of the first operations a micro user learns. Moreover, many of the young hackers who made the personal computer revolution happen regarded software programs as tools that should be freely available to anyone who wanted to use them.

As software companies grew larger and left the hacker mentality behind, they started spending a considerable amount of time and money to "copy-protect" their products. Yet clever hackers were easily able to break the protection codes and distribute copies to friends. By the early 1980s there were special programs, such as Locksmith, that automatically circumvented protection codes and allowed one to make copies of protected software. "Liberated" software often ended up on electronic bulletin boards from which PC users could download it through the phone lines onto disks.

Software makers fought back by developing new devices to prevent unauthorized copying. The first advanced protection device was Vault Corp.'s Prolok system, introduced in the early 1980s. This involved the placement of a tiny hole in the disk that must be in the proper place for the software to run. Later, software companies developed "lock and key" combinations of hardware and software devices to deter piracy.

While many individual micro users amassed collections of pirated disks, the software industry came to realize that the pirates who were costing them the most were corporations that purchased one or several copies of expensive business programs such as Lotus 1-2-3 and then made many additional unauthorized copies to distribute among the staff. The research firm Future Computing estimated in a 1985 study that there were as many pirate copies of business software programs in circulation as legitimate ones.

The software industry started getting tough with corporate pirates in 1984. Lotus Development charged Rixon Inc. with unauthorized copying of 1-2-3 and sued the company for $10 million. The parties settled out of court, with Rixon agreeing to make a substantial payment. In 1985 MicroPro International, producer of the WordStar® word-processing program, sued a subsidiary of American Brands, also winning a settlement. Later that year an FBI investigation led to a lawsuit against a Philadelphia publishing company for providing an unauthorized copy of a $4,800 database program to a New York typesetting firm.

Such actions prompted many companies to take the software copyright issue more seriously. Numerous large firms adopted strict internal policies against software copying, and some of them began arguing that the only practical solution was a system of software site licenses. Under this arrangement a vendor would sell a company a few copies of a program and the right to make a limited number of additional copies. Vendors had mixed feelings about site licenses, since they ended up receiving less in revenues for each copy of their programs in use, but the discounted proceeds were more than they received when extra copies were simply pirated.

At the same time, many corporate users began to put pressure on software producers to eliminate copy-protection features, which the users felt were making some programs less efficient. Fearing that they could lose more from reduced legitimate sales than from piracy, a number of leading software companies began to abandon copy protection in 1986.

Yet software companies continued battling on another legal front. In the same way that hardware producers began making clones of the IBM PC, smaller software firms developed their own versions of popular programs such as 1-2-3. In 1987 Lotus filed suit against two of the clones, raising the tricky legal question of how far a company could claim a proprietary right to the general look and feel (the technical term is "user interface") of a program. The issue became more urgent after Apple sued Microsoft and Hewlett-Packard, charging that they were selling programs (Windows and New Wave, respectively) that infringed on copyrights Apple had for the visual display of the Macintosh. (Ironically, Apple itself was belatedly sued in 1989 by Xerox, which claimed that Apple misappropriated some of its copyrights in developing the Macintosh.)

Lotus and Apple were given a boost in 1988, when the U.S. Copyright Office ruled that screen displays were covered by copyright laws. That decision helped pave the way for the 1990 court victory by Lotus against one of its clone rivals, Paperback Software International. This, in turn, emboldened Lotus to bring legal challenges against some of its larger competitors, especially Borland International, producer of the Quattro program.

The intellectual property situation has been further complicated by a trend toward the filing of patents to gain proprietary control of basic software techniques. The practice, which is already entangling leading software companies in infringement suits, could inhibit the future development of the industry.

LEADING COMPANIES

Apple Computer was not the first to produce a micro but was the pioneer in introducing personal computing to a mass audience. Founded by young hackers Steven Jobs and Stephen Wozniak, the company attracted venture capital and professional management and embarked on a dizzying rate of growth. The world became more complicated when computer giant IBM stormed into the market. Apple stumbled with several products and allowed IBM to win over the lucrative office segment. By the mid-1980s Apple had become a billion-dollar company, and Jobs's unorthodox management methods were steadily abandoned. In 1985 he was stripped of his operating authority and then ousted entirely. Under the leadership of former PepsiCo executive John Sculley, Apple finally cracked the office market with enhanced versions of its Macintosh computer (which was also introduced in a portable version). But by the beginning of the 1990s, Apple was experiencing both a sharp decline in growth and internal instability.

Ashton-Tate had its origins in 1975, when George Tate (who was repairing stereos at the time) was inspired by the announcement of the first micro, the Altair. Tate started programming, and in 1980 he formed Software Plus with Hal Lashlee. The company prospered by selling dBase II®, a database management program devised by Wayne Ratliff. Under the leadership of Edward Esber, Jr. (Tate died in 1984), the company emerged as one of the nation's largest independent software producers. Yet the long-awaited dBase IV, released in 1988, turned out to have serious flaws. Ashton-Tate moved to correct the problems, but the reputation of its product was seriously tarnished. Clone producers took advantage of the opening, and Ashton-Tate's market share plunged. The company's decline accelerated, and in 1990 Esber was ousted.

Atari was the first Silicon Valley success story of the micro age. The company was established by Nolan Bushnell, who created the first electronic arcade game (Pong) and gave rise to the video-game mania of the 1970s. Atari was purchased by Warner Communications in 1976 and for several years soared, thanks to booming sales for home video games. Poor product development, management disarray, and the decline of the game industry brought grief to the company, which Warner sold off at a bargain-basement price to Jack Tramiel in 1984. Working with his three sons, Tramiel revived the company with a more serious home computer called the 520 ST. He also brought back Bushnell as a consultant to develop video games, but the revival of that business in the late 1980s was dominated by Japan's Nintendo.

Commodore International grew up far from the magic of Silicon Valley. Founded in the Bronx in 1954 as a typewriter repair company by Jack Tramiel and Manny Kapp, Commodore first expanded into the general office equipment business and then the volatile calculator market of the early 1970s. Tramiel got into the computer business in 1976 after buying MOS Technology and the following year brought out one of the early micros, called PET. Commodore became a leader of the home computer market through its ruthless price cutting, but Tramiel was ousted in early 1984. The company went into a slump but rebounded on the strength of a sophisticated home computer called Amiga.

Compaq Computer emerged from nowhere in 1983 to become the leading IBM-compatible micro. Starting with a portable model (actually known as a "luggable" because of its 28-pound weight) and then branching out to desktop machines to match IBM's line, Compaq achieved a breathtaking rate of growth. It reached $500 million in revenues by its third year; $1 billion by its fifth. Launched by venture capitalist Ben Rosen and former Texas Instruments engineer Rod Canion, Compaq trounced IBM's portable model and brought out smaller and lighter luggables in 1986. Later that year Compaq introduced a new desktop machine that was the first personal computer to use Intel's powerful new 80386 microprocessor. Compaq began to transcend its identity as an IBM clone when it declined to follow Big Blue in its move to a data pathway called Micro Channel (and got eight other clone makers to join with it). Compaq was slow in entering the laptop market, but when it did so in 1988 its machine was very well-received. In 1989 the company brought out a super-powerful machine using Intel's latest processor (the i486), that was capable of supporting large networks of PCs.

IBM took the micro world by storm in 1981 when the colossus of Armonk, long wedded to the market for big mainframe machines, brought out a personal computer. The PC was no technological marvel, but the IBM name brought it a healthy market share and leadership of the industry. In the following years IBM introduced a succession of more powerful PCs—the XT in 1983, the AT in 1984, and the RT® in 1986—aimed at solidifying Big Blue's dominance in the office and professional market. IBM had less luck with its PCjr (a scaled-down version of the PC) and a portable PC, both of which went nowhere. In 1987 the company took the bold step of introducing a new line of PCs that used the OS/2 operating system developed by Microsoft. IBM tried to discourage cloning of the Personal System/2 series by asserting widespread patent protection for the machines, particularly for its Micro Channel, the pathway for moving data from the 32-bit processor to the monitor and other peripheral devices. Big Blue then surprised the industry by entering into an agreement with Steve Jobs's new company, Next Inc., to purchase the right to use Next's screen design, or user interface, in its new line of workstations.

Lotus Development Corp. was founded in 1982 by Mitchell Kapor, a onetime disc jockey and teacher of transcendental meditation. In the late 1970s he got involved in programming, and after the IBM PC appeared he got venture capital from Ben Rosen to bring out an integrated financial software package called Lotus 1-2-3, which went on to become the nation's best-selling program. Under the leadership of Jim Manzi (Kapor left in 1986 to pursue new ventures), Lotus became the leader of the software industry and tried to reduce its dependence on 1-2-3 by bringing out a variety of other programs. Diversification was not a great success, and the company suffered from a long delay in the production of a revised version of 1-2-3, but once that revision (Release 3) went on sale it was well-received. A move by Lotus in 1990 to take on Microsoft by acquiring Novell Inc., a leading maker of network software, collapsed because of a dispute over the composition of the board of directors.

Microsoft, the leader in systems software for micros, was founded in 1975 by William Gates and Paul Allen. The two young programmers produced a version of the Basic language for the first micro, the Altair, and went on to fame and fortune after being chosen by IBM to produce both the systems software and the programming language for its PC. Later, Microsoft expanded into applications software with well-received products such as the Word text-editing program and Excel, a spreadsheet program for the Macintosh. The company went public in a well-received offering in 1986. Microsoft developed the OS/2 operating system, which was embraced by IBM in its new line of PCs introduced in 1987; the new machines also made use of a version of Microsoft's Windows program, which allowed micro users to shift more easily between different programs. Version 3.0 of Windows, introduced in 1990, was hailed as the advance that finally fulfilled the promise of making the PC as user-friendly as the Macintosh.

Next Inc. was established in 1985 by Steven Jobs after his ouster from Apple. Helped by a $20 million investment from H. Ross Perot (as well as his own fortune), Jobs set out to produce an advanced academic computer powerful enough to do sophisticated work in science and engineering. The sleek machine, introduced in 1988, uses a version of the UNIX operating system and has an optical storage device, a high-grade sound synthesizer, and a monitor with photographic-quality images. Next leaped into the office PC market when the Businessland computer-store chain agreed to purchase at least $100 million worth of its machines to sell to companies. Among those impressed with the Next computer was IBM, which paid more than $10 million for the right to use the machine's symbols and commands (known as the user interface) in a new line of workstations that Big Blue was developing. A paucity of applications software has limited Next sales, but Jobs remains optimistic.

SOURCE GUIDE

Leading Stock Analysts and Experts

Stewart Alsop, editor of *PC Letter*, published in Redwood City, California.

Broadview Associates, a software consulting company based in Fort Lee, New Jersey.

Dataquest, San Jose, California.

Esther Dyson, editor of *Release 1.0*, a newsletter published in New York.

International Data Corp., Framingham, Massachusetts.

Michelle Preston, analyst at Salomon Brothers.

Richard Schaffer, publisher of *Technologic Computer Letter,* in New York.

Richard Sherlund, analyst at Goldman Sachs.

Jeffrey Tarter, publisher of *Softletter* in Watertown, Massachusetts.

Charles Wolf, analyst at First Boston.

Trade Associations

Association of Data Processing Service Organizations, 1300 N. 17th Street, Arlington, VA 22209. Tel.: (703) 522–5055.

Computer and Business Equipment Manufacturers Association, 311 1st Street NW, Washington, DC 20001. Tel.: (202) 737–8888.

Software Publishers Association, 1101 Connecticut Avenue NW, Washington, DC 20036. Tel.: (202) 452–1600.

Data Sources and Directories

Business Software Directory, annual (Berkeley, Calif.: Information Sources).

Computer Software Directory, annual (Omaha, Neb.: American Business Directories).

Hot List, a ranking of best-selling software programs compiled by a major distributor (Inglewood, Calif.: Softsel Computer Products).

Microcomputer Vendor Directory, a semiannual list of hardware and software suppliers (Pennsauken, N.J.: Faulkner Publishing).

The Software Catalogue, a semiannual listing of programs (New York: Elsevier).

Software Encyclopedia, an annual directory (New York: R. R. Bowker).

Online Databases

BUSINESS SOFTWARE DATABASE (Berkeley, Calif.: Information Sources Inc.; available via BRS and DIALOG).

BUYER'S GUIDE TO MICRO SOFTWARE (Weston, Conn.: Online Inc.; available via BRS and DIALOG).

COMPUTER DATABASE (Foster City, Calif.: Information Access Co.; available via BRS and DIALOG).

MICROCOMPUTER INDEX (Medford, N.J.: Learned Information Inc.; available via DIALOG).

MICROCOMPUTER SOFTWARE GUIDE (New York: R. R. Bowker; available via DIALOG).

SOFTWARE DIRECTORY (Pittsburgh: Black Box Corp.; available via DIALOG).

Trade Publications

Byte, monthly.

Computerworld, weekly.

InfoWorld, weekly.

PC Letter, semimonthly

Release 1.0, 15 times a year.

Softletter, semimonthly.

Software Magazine, monthly.

Technologic Computer Letter, 40 times a year.

Books and Reports

Butcher, Lee. *Accidental Millionaire: The Rise and Fall of Steve Jobs at Apple Computer*. New York: Paragon House, 1987.

Carlston, Douglas G. *Software People*. New York: Simon & Schuster, 1985.

Freiberger, Paul, and Michael Swaine. *Fire in the Valley: The Making of the Personal Computer*. New York: Osborne/McGraw-Hill, 1984.

Levering, Robert; Michael Katz; and Milton Moskowitz. *The Computer Entrepreneurs*. New York: New American Library, 1984.

Massachusetts Institute of Technology. "The U.S. Semiconductor, Computer, and Copier Industries," in *Working Papers of the MIT Commission on Industrial Productivity*. Cambridge, Mass.: MIT Press, 1989.

Moritz, Michael. *The Little Kingdom: The Private Story of Apple Computer*. New York: William Morrow, 1984.

Organisation for Economic Co-operation and Development. *Internationalization of Software and Computer Services*. Paris, 1989.

Rose, Frank. *West of Eden: The End of Innocence at Apple Computer*. New York: Viking Press, 1989.

U.S. International Trade Administration. *A Competitive Assessment of the U.S. Software Industry*. December 1984.

CHAPTER 15

SEMICONDUCTORS

It has been called the second industrial revolution, the new alchemy, a revolution in miniature, the micro millennium. It is transforming work, play, education, war, and virtually all other aspects of life. The end of its impact is far from sight. "It" is microelectronics; and even after discounting the hype, it is one of the true marvels of the modern age.

The source of this wonderment is a group of devices that combine thousands of electric circuits on pieces of silicon smaller than a fingernail. Rather than being wired together, the circuits are formed by unbelievably dense microscopic etching on the silicon, which has the useful quality of being a semiconductor of electricity. Some of the chips can store a million bits of information, while others form the core of a computer's ability to process data.

These memory chips and microprocessors constitute the building blocks of computers, telecommunications equipment, and other "smart" machines. The $28 billion semiconductor industry is one of the most technologically sophisticated segments of business, but it is also one of the most volatile. Competition is fierce; ruthless price-cutting in the battle for market share has undone numerous companies and has become a major point of contention between the United States and Japan. At the same time, a sharp boom-bust cycle in the industry has kept producers off-balance. It is a difficult business but one that will continue to grow in importance.

HARNESSING ELECTRONS

The science and practice of electronics emerged out of research performed by Thomas Edison using one of his inventions, the light bulb. The wizard of Menlo Park found that when a metal plate was placed in the bulb, a measurable electric current could be detected between the heated filament and the plate. The Englishman John Ambrose Fleming discovered that this device could be configured so as to detect high-frequency radio signals.

In 1906 American inventor Lee De Forest added another element to the bulb and found that it served not only to detect signals but to amplify them as well. This three-electrode audion, as improved by De Forest and others, opened up a new world of electrical communication, including radio, radio telephony, wireless telegraphy, and long-distance telephone service. These vacuum tubes also served as the main components of the first computers in the 1940s.

The next leap in electronics came during World War II, when research on radar began to focus on a class of elements known as semiconductors. These substances, particularly silicon and germanium, had the useful quality of conducting electricity more easily than insulators but not as freely as conductors and thus showed great promise as signal detectors.

After the war, scientists at AT&T's Bell Labs built on that research in an effort to find an alternative to vacuum tubes that would be less bulky and throw off less heat. In 1947 a team led by William Shockley (who was later to gain notoriety for his views on race and intelligence) found the answer in a tiny circuit made out of germanium and incredibly thin wires. Dubbed the transistor—short for transfer resistance—this "solid-state" device (i.e., one without moving parts) set off a process of miniaturization in electronics and brought a Nobel Prize to Shockley and the leading figures in his team, John Bardeen and Walter Brattain.

AT&T made the secret of the transistor widely available (for a price) but did not itself get into the business of making the devices, probably because of antitrust pressures from the federal government. Instead a slew of other firms obtained licenses from Ma Bell and took the leap into microelectronics. The Pentagon quickly recognized the value of the new forms of circuitry, and military research money began to flow into the industry.

Raytheon, one of the major vacuum-tube makers, pioneered the commercial consumer market with hearing aids and what were then called transistorized radios. Other entrants included older electronics companies such as Philco and Motorola, as well as a young firm called Texas Instruments (TI), which produced geophysical equipment for the oil industry. TI, having lured away a Bell Labs scientist, developed the first silicon version of the transistor and began its ascent to the leadership of the semiconductor industry.

In the early 1950s, Shockley got the entrepreneurial bug and decided to leave Bell Labs to produce transistors on his own. He returned to his boyhood home of Palo Alto, California, and set up Shockley Semiconductor Laboratories in 1955. This was just at the time that Palo Alto and the surrounding area south of San Francisco Bay was emerging as a hotbed of new-technology companies.

The catalyst for this was Stanford University. Early in the century Frederick Terman, a professor of electrical engineering and later provost of the university, encouraged his students to remain in the area after graduation and start new ventures rather than go to work for large corporations in the East. Two of his disciples were William Hewlett and David Packard, who in 1939 founded a company to sell audio oscillators and ended up creating one of the premier U.S. electronics firms.

By the early 1950s Stanford was leasing parts of its extensive property to technology companies such as Varian Associates and Hewlett-Packard. A critical mass of engineering talent began to appear in the area as such companies as Sylvania, Philco, and General Electric set up operations. Lockheed bought 700 acres in nearby Sunnyvale for its newly established Missile and Space Division. Gradually the orchards of the Santa Clara Valley began to be replaced by modern, low-rise industrial structures.

Shockley certainly picked the right place and the right time to set up shop, but it soon appeared he was not the right man to head such a venture. Although Shockley's reputation allowed him to attract some of the most talented young scientists and engineers in the country, the staff was soon put off by the boss's tyrannical ways.

Before long a group of seven key employees decided to leave and establish their own firm. In casting about for financial backing, the group took the fortuitous step of contacting the investment bank of Hayden Stone. It turned out that the Wall Street firm had a client, Fairchild Camera and Instrument, that was interested in entering the semiconductor business. The group persuaded Robert Noyce, a key figure at Shockley, to join them as head of the venture, and a deal was struck with Fairchild.

The "traitorous eight," as Shockley took to calling them, set out with the goal of trying to put together large numbers of transistors and other circuit elements into one tiny, solid-state unit. It turned out that a similar aim was being pursued by Jack Kilby at TI. In 1959 Kilby hit on a way of batch processing what amounted to miniature integrated circuits.

The news of Kilby's breakthrough mobilized Fairchild, and before long Noyce was able to announce a much better process for interconnecting circuit components. Fairchild applied for a patent for this planar process only five months after TI had filed. These events of 1959 set off both a legal battle (TI sued Fairchild) and a controversy over which company deserved credit for inventing the integrated circuit.

The courts and the historians resolved the issued in Solomonic fashion. It was decided that since TI was first but Fairchild had made refinements essential to commercial production, the two companies should share equal credit for integrated circuits. Thus Kilby and Noyce are generally regarded as co-inventors, and companies that wanted to produce the devices had to obtain licenses from both TI and Fairchild.

The semiconductor industry grew steadily in the 1960s, aided by the adoption of integrated circuits by the computer industry and by the Pentagon's insatiable appetite for ever smaller and ever more sophisticated electronic components. Vacuum tubes steadily disappeared from the scene as did the old-line companies that produced them. Leadership of the business was assumed by TI, Fairchild, and Motorola.

Within Fairchild, however, there was growing instability. Many of its top people were frustrated at the relationship with the parent company; and as the firm grew larger many executives grew restless, longing to return to a more entrepreneurial atmosphere. As early as 1959 several Fairchilders acted on these feelings and left to form a company called Rheem Semiconductor. In the 1960s this pattern grew more pronounced, and soon the Santa Clara Valley was dotted with start-up companies established by Fairchild defectors.

A COMPUTER ON A CHIP

Many of these new ventures went nowhere, but several emerged as leading players in the semiconductor business. Fairchild manufacturing wizard Charles Sporck went to National Semiconductor; marketing man Jerry Sanders helped found Advanced Micro Devices; and, most important, Noyce departed with research-and-development boss Gordon Moore and process-development expert Andrew Grove. Obtaining financing from venture capitalist Arthur Rock, the three set up a company called Intel.

By 1970 Intel (short for integrated electronics) had brought out several types of memory chips, which at the time had a capacity of 1K (meaning one kilobit, or more precisely 1,024 bits of information). The company also had a contract from a group of Japanese calculator producers to develop some custom chips. Faced with the difficult task of trying to cram too many chips into the allotted space, Intel engineer Ted Hoff came up with the idea of putting all of the functions on a single chip.

Working with circuit designer Federico Faggin, Hoff succeeded in this effort and thereby created the first microprocessor, sometimes called a "computer on a chip." The Japanese clients were initially skeptical about the device and gave Intel the right to sell what became the 4004. The rest of the world, still caught up with the handheld calculator, also took a while to appreciate the significance of the microprocessor.

But by the middle of the 1970s the device was being heralded as the cornerstone of the microelectronics revolution. Intel's 8080, introduced in 1974 and used to create the first microcomputer, became the industry standard. In a September 1977 article in *Scientific American,* Noyce noted that a microprocessor costing about $300 had more computing power than the original ENIAC mainframe, was 20 times faster, cost only one 10,000th as much, and took up only one-30,000th as much space.

What Intel had done with the microprocessor and its early memory chips amounted to a breakthrough in large-scale integration (LSI)—an industry phrase that referred to the cramming of thousands of circuits onto a single piece of silicon. Throughout the 1970s semiconductor makers achieved higher and higher levels of integration, quadrupling the capacity of memory chips every few years.

The leap from one generation to another did not always proceed smoothly. The 4K memory chip posed a number of manufacturing difficulties—a problem exacerbated by the slump that befell the industry in 1975. As semiconductor fabrication became more complex, the costs of development rose rapidly. Many companies simply did not have sufficient resources to keep up.

The upshot of this was a buying spree of semiconductor companies, mainly by foreign firms seeking a foothold in a business that was still dominated by the United States. The Dutch electronics giant Philips bought Signetics, a Fairchild spin-off, in 1975. Siemens of West Germany purchased Litronix and 20 percent of Advanced Micro Devices in 1977. Northern Telecom took a minority interest in Intersil (later sold to GE), and Nippon Electric acquired a company called Electronic Arrays.

U.S. companies also got into the act: Honeywell bought Synertek (later sold to AT&T), and United Technologies purchased Mostek, a prominent spin-off from TI. In 1979 the venerable Fairchild Semiconductor, by then in decline, was taken over by the French oil services company Schlumberger, which had little luck trying to revitalize the firm that had given birth to so much of what became known as Silicon Valley.

This takeover wave generated a debate within the industry on whether semiconductor companies could survive inside large corporations. It was common wisdom that electronics giants such as RCA could not make it in the chip business because of a resistance to innovation and an inability to respond to the frequent changes of the fast-paced semiconductor market.

There was some truth to the proposition, and it is significant that the top four firms in the industry—TI, Motorola, National Semiconductor, and Intel—were independent. At the same time, there was no evidence that IBM's purchase of 20 percent of Intel diminished the latter's vitality. And it should be noted that large companies such as IBM produce substantial numbers of semiconductor devices for use in their own products.

More than big-business domination, the main problem for the U.S. semiconductor industry turned out to be an aggressive competitive thrust from Japan. Until the late 1970s the Americans had nothing to worry about, controlling as they did some two thirds of the world market. But the Japanese were not about to ignore this lucrative business. In the mid-1970s agencies of the Japanese government joined with five leading electronics firms—Hitachi, Fujitsu, Mitsubishi, NEC, and Toshiba—in a research-and-development initiative called the VLSI Project.

This effort to gain a foothold in very large scale integration paid off when the industry was moving from 4K to 16K memory chips. The demand for the denser chips was much greater than expected, and U.S. companies simply could not produce the 16Ks fast enough. This created an opening for the Japanese firms, which appeared on the scene with devices that many users found to be superior to those produced by American companies.

Led by NEC and Hitachi, the Japanese gained 40 percent of the 16K market by 1980 and were well situated to take the lion's share of the next generation of memory chip, the 64K. By this time Japanese semiconductor exports to the United States had surpassed American exports to Japan. The U.S. producers, starting to panic, formed the Semiconductor Industry Association to bring their plight to the attention of the government. An industry that had always prided itself on being aloof from Washington found itself in the position of needing federal help to overcome what it characterized as unfair obstacles that American producers faced in trying to sell to Japan.

The American protestations initially had little effect. The Japanese took such a strong lead in 64K DRAM (dynamic random-access memory) chips that most American producers either dropped out of the market or never bothered to enter it. By the early 1980s the Japanese were positioned to dominate the emerging 256K generation as well.

All was not dismal with the U.S. semiconductor industry, however. The Americans, particularly Intel and Motorola, remained far ahead in the microprocessor market. In 1982 Intel announced what it called a micromainframe, a set of three chips that had the capabilities, including multiprocessing, of a large computer. By the mid-1980s microprocessors reached the 32-bit level (meaning they could process that many pieces of information at a time).

U.S. companies also prospered in the growing business of custom and semicustom chips. The latter involved the use of components called gate arrays, which could be connected in the last stages of manufacturing to suit specific needs. Some leading commodity chip producers ignored this segment, leaving more room for a new batch of start-ups (including LSI Logic, founded by former Fairchild president Wilfred Corrigan).

The industry also kept on innovating. Devices called photodiode arrays, or imager chips, endowed semiconductors with greater "visual" ability and allowed them to conquer one of the last vestiges of vacuum tubes: movie cameras. EPROM (erasable, programmable, read-only memory) chips made "smart" machines much more flexible. Researchers improved the performance of CMOS (complementary metal-oxide semiconductor) chips, which threw off less heat and thus reduced the cooling problems created by very dense concentrations of circuits.

American semiconductor companies also responded to the Japanese challenge through a variety of cooperative measures that sought to gain some of the advantages that Japanese firms have by being part of *keiretsu*—families of companies with great access to resources. These U.S. arrangements included joint development projects, cross-licensing of technology, and cosponsored research. Among the latter was the not-for-profit Microelectronics and Computer Technology Corp. established by a group of electronics companies to do leading-edge research.

The Japanese meanwhile were not sitting still. In the mid-1980s companies such as NEC began challenging U.S. dominance in the microprocessor market. In doing so, NEC got itself into a legal battle with Intel over the issue of whether the instructions embedded in Intel's 8086 and 8088 chips amounted to a program and were thus protected under the copyright laws. A federal court ruled that microcodes are so protected but found that NEC did not infringe on Intel's product.

The ruthless drive for market share by the Japanese in the memory market as well as in EPROMs also brought them legal problems. Following the disastrous year of 1985, during which U.S. producers lost more than $500 million, the Reagan administration finally responded to the complaints of U.S. producers and imposed dumping penalties against Hitachi, Fujitsu, NEC, Toshiba, Mitsubishi, and Oki. At the same time, federal courts began hearing private suits brought by U.S. producers, and the Justice Department and the International Trade Commission were investigating Japanese selling practices in the United States. These actions, along with a rise in demand and a stronger yen, helped put a halt to the steep decline in semiconductor prices.

In the summer of 1986, the United States and Japan reached an agreement allowing American chipmakers easier access to the Japanese market while discouraging Japanese producers from dumping in the United States or in other countries. Yet in the short run it turned out to be of little help to U.S. producers. There were repeated accusations that Japanese chip companies were finding ways to circumvent the anti-dumping provisions, while in Japan there arose a glut that caused prices to plunge. For U.S. companies this eliminated much of the benefit of greater access to that market.

By 1987 the situation began to turn around. In the United States the market for DRAM memory chips was characterized not by glut but by shortages. The decision of the Reagan administration to impose tariffs on a number of Japanese electronic goods in retaliation for dumping caused Japanese companies to cut back chip production and to export less to the United States. American producers, nearly all of whom had abandoned the DRAM business after the Japanese takeover, were not in a position to pick up the slack. The computer companies, enjoying a rise in demand with the introduction of a new generation of PCs based on Intel's powerful 80386 microprocessor, began to run short of the memory chips they needed to put in their systems.

A decline in the growth rate of the microcomputer industry helped to reverse the situation once again, but the memory chip market remained especially volatile, and U.S. producers never recaptured the ground they lost to the Japanese. The industry's response was to step up its cooperative projects in an effort to regain the edge in technology. In 1987 a group of leading chip manufacturers announced the creation of Sematech (short for semiconductor manufacturing technology), a nonprofit consortium that would develop new manufacturing techniques. Patterned after the VLSI Project in Japan, Sematech was supposed to receive one half of its $200 million annual budget from the federal government. Given the panic about the national security implications of a declining American semiconductor industry, Congress went along with the idea. Yet the Bush administration rejected an advisory committee's recommendation that the federal government's support of Sematech be substantially increased.

Another cooperative venture was announced in 1989. In an effort to rebuild America's standing in the memory chip business, IBM and six other companies (Digital Equipment, Hewlett-Packard, Intel, National Semiconductor, Advanced Micro Devices, and LSI Logic) formed an unprecedented manufacturing consortium called U.S. Memories to challenge Japan's 90 percent control of the market for 1-megabit DRAMs. The operation, which was to be funded by computer companies (i.e., chip customers) as well as semiconductor firms, did not receive the support IBM and its partners had expected. The cooperative nature of the project was apparently just too foreign to American business culture. In January 1990 the venture was abandoned and with it American hopes of being free of dependence on foreign memory chip producers. A sign of the leadership of the Japanese producers came in mid-1990, when Hitachi announced the first prototype for a 64-megabit memory chip.

Ironically, many of the same U.S. companies that were wary of cooperating with one another were willing to enter into such arrangements with the Japanese. Advanced Micro Devices entered into a technology-sharing relationship with Sony, and TI formed a joint venture with Kobe Steel to make advanced logic chips. These were in addition to such earlier ventures as those between TI and Hitachi, and between Motorola and Toshiba.

In the microprocessor segment of the business, the U.S. position remains strong, but there is intensifying rivalry between the 32-bit (and more recently, 64-bit) chips and those produced using the reduced instruction set, or RISC, technique. RISC processors, which are faster and cheaper because of their simplified design, were pushed into prominence by their use in Sun Microsystems' powerful workstations and later in similar products from IBM. By 1989 even Intel, which has led the field for the more traditional microprocessors and introduced ever more powerful devices, had decided to employ some RISC circuits in its latest and fastest microchip, the 80486.

While fighting its competitive battles, the industry is also looking ahead to even greater changes in technology. Various companies are exploring a move from silicon to gallium arsenide, which is more expensive but moves electrons faster, uses less power, operates at higher temperatures, and emits light. More daring researchers have begun investigating the possibility of chips made of organic molecules. Such "biochips" could allow much greater levels of integration and create more versatile machines.

LABOR RELATIONS

The fundamental fact about labor relations in the electronics industry is the remarkable success management has had in keeping out unions. A survey by the American Electronics Association in 1982 found that its 1,900 member companies had only 90 union contracts—and those were not at bigger, more prominent firms such as IBM, which has managed to keep its entire U.S. work force unorganized (though several unions and an independent group called IBM Workers United have been trying to change that).

The conventional view is that high-tech companies have created attractive enough conditions—workplace amenities such as hot tubs and tennis courts, generous stock options, and a general esprit de corps—so that unions lose their appeal. It is true that firms such as IBM, Hewlett-Packard, and Wang Laboratories are highly paternalistic, offering extensive benefits and, in some cases, declining to lay off employees even during slumps. On one level, Silicon Valley and other electronics outposts amount to a kind of worker's paradise.

The problem is that there is more than one level. The country-club atmosphere is enjoyed mainly by a narrow stratum of the total electronics work force, consisting of highly skilled engineers, top-level marketing people, and a limited number of other white-collar types. These are the people who, once they gain some experience in a leading firm, have enormous mobility. They hop from job to job, seeking higher pay and perks in exchange for what prospective bosses hope will be specialized knowledge and perhaps the trade secrets of the previous employer. It is a highly unusual sort of labor market.

Yet there is more to the electronics industry than the development, design, and marketing of products. Someone has to mass-produce the chips and computers. It is here that a differ-

The Top 10 Semiconductor Producers Worldwide in 1989 by Chip Sales, Not Including Captive Operations ($ Millions)

Rank	Company	Sales
1.	NEC	$5,015
2.	Toshiba	4,930
3.	Hitachi	3,974
4.	Motorola	3,319
5.	Fujitsu	2,963
6.	Texas Instruments	2,787
7.	Mitsubishi	2,579
8.	Intel	2,430
9.	Matsushita	1,882
10.	Philips	1,716

Source: Dataquest, San Jose, California.

ent story comes to light: Electronics is basically a cheap-labor industry.

As much as the industry has fostered the image of being highly automated, there are still aspects of electronics production that remain very labor-intensive. And given the intense competition of the industry, companies have gone to great lengths to keep the costs of that labor to an absolute minimum.

One strategy has been to move production overseas. The shift to what is called offshore assembly was led by Fairchild when it opened operations in Hong Kong in the early 1960s. Other companies followed suit, and by the late 1960s countries such as Taiwan, South Korea, Singapore, and Malaysia were dotted with semiconductor and other electronics factories owned by U.S. firms. Electronics became a globally integrated system of manufacturing, with low wages more than making up for the transportation costs associated with decentralized production.

These operations mainly employed young women, imposing a military sort of discipline (both in the workplace and in the dormitories in which they were housed) and paying them wages that were barely above the subsistence level. Many of the plants were located in special export-processing zones set up by third-world governments to lure foreign investors with tax breaks, reduced tariffs, and guarantees of labor stability. When labor costs rose slightly in these countries, electronics firms sought out new low-wage havens in countries such as Thailand and the Philippines.

Although the workers were for the most part pushed into submission, there have been notable cases of resistance. In 1982 a group of mainly young, female workers in South Korea held hostage for nine hours two U.S. executives of Control Data Corp. who had come to resolve a labor dispute. Scattered strikes have also occurred in U.S.-owned electronics plants in Mexico and the Philippines. In 1989 a union of several hundred IBM employees in South Korea won recognition and a contract from the company after a bitter struggle that included a sit-in and a hunger strike.

In part because of these labor troubles and in part because of a shift to automation, American electronics firms in the late

1980s began cutting back on offshore assembly and returning production to the United States. It turned out, however, that the labor force employed back home closely resembled the one cultivated abroad. The production workers of Silicon Valley are predominantly low-paid women, and in fact many of them are recent immigrants from the same Asian countries in which offshore facilities have been located.

Whether the workers are foreign-born or not, electronics companies have gone to great lengths to discourage unionization. A *Wall Street Journal* reporter who took a job (incognito) in a Texas Instruments plant found workers so intimidated that they panicked even at the mention of unions. The United Electrical workers, which started organizing in high-tech companies in the early 1970s, joined with other unions in cooperative drives in both California and Massachusetts, but by the mid-1980s the unions had all but abandoned what appeared to be a futile effort.

Labor organizers have insisted that once a major high-tech firm was successfully unionized, the tide would turn. Perhaps the closest a union came to such an achievement was in the case of Atari. In the early 1980s, workers at the home-computer and video-game producer, angered over wage cuts and possible layoffs, contacted the nearest union they could find, which turned out to be the Glaziers. In early 1983, just as the union had signed up enough workers for a representation election, Atari announced that it planned to eliminate 1,700 jobs in Silicon Valley and transfer the work to low-wage operations in Asia. The action, which did a great deal to deflate the job-creating image of high-tech industry—the term *Atari Democrats* was hastily abandoned—also led to the demise of the organizing effort.

Another obstacle faced by organizers is that many of the jobs held by people they are trying to unionize may soon be obsolete. While some aspects of semiconductor assembly are still labor-intensive, automation is coming rapidly. The computer makers have been at the vanguard of this trend. The facilities that Apple Computer built for producing the Macintosh were so automated that direct labor costs amounted to less than 1 percent of the total expenses of producing the machine.

The slump in the electronics industry during much of the mid- to late 1980s also took its toll on employment levels. IBM alone reduced its payroll by tens of thousands of people, usually through early retirement. Yet many others whose jobs were eliminated ended up quitting when faced with the need to uproot their families to take a new job in a distant part of the IBM empire; critics call this "invisible layoffs." The large cutbacks at Big Blue helped to create a more conducive climate for employee activism in the company. Dissident groups such as IBM Workers United found increased (though still limited) support, and the Communications Workers of America inched ahead with its plan to organize IBM. In 1987 representatives of IBM employee organizations from nine countries met in New Orleans as part of an effort to build a network called IBM Workers International Solidarity.

THE HIDDEN HAZARDS OF HIGH TECH

While it was growing in prominence, the electronics industry gained the reputation of being a "clean" business. In place of the belching smokestacks that symbolized old-line heavy industry, the image of electronics was that of white-gowned and masked technicians in the "cleanrooms" of semiconductor facilities. It is true that some aspects of chip production have to be done in a highly purified atmosphere; it is also true that the production of semiconductors and printed circuit boards requires the use of highly toxic substances.

The first signs of health problems in electronics occurred in the 1970s with outbreaks of mysterious ailments among large groups of workers. Eventually it was determined that the symptoms, including fainting and nausea, were linked to poor ventilation in the plants. Occupational health researchers also learned that workers were being exposed to a variety of harmful substances.

These included solvents (such as trichloroethylene, or TCE) used to clean circuit boards, nitric and other acids used in photoetching, arsine gases used in growing silicon crystals, lead oxide fumes from soldering, and radiation from substances such as Krypton-85 used to test for flaws in circuits. Some of these toxic substances were also being used by women performing home labor for electronic subcontractors.

While the high rates of occupational illness caused some concern in the industry, the public did not pay much attention to the issue of high-tech hazards until they spread outside the factory. In December 1981 the local water company in a Silicon Valley neighborhood found that a five-year-old chemical storage drum buried outside a Fairchild plant was leaking a toxic solvent into a public well. After the discovery was made public—some weeks later—local residents argued that the leaks may have been responsible for a cluster of birth defects in the area.

In 1984 the federal Environmental Protection Agency found widespread underground pollution in Silicon Valley and added a number of sites (including facilities of such prominent companies as IBM, Hewlett-Packard, and Intel) to the superfund list of toxic dumps. The following year the California Department of Health Services found a high rate of miscarriages and birth defects in areas where the water was contaminated by toxic leaks from high-tech plants. There have also been incidents involving the emission of toxic gases from electronics plants. While trade groups such as the Semiconductor Industry Association have downplayed the gravity of the health problems in and outside of the workplaces, some companies (including IBM and Fairchild) have spent large sums cleaning up toxic sites.

The issue of the effects of semiconductor production on workers' health arose again in 1986 when Digital Equipment Corp. (DEC) announced that a study of its workers found an abnormally high rate of miscarriages among women on the company's chip assembly lines. Several weeks later AT&T announced that in response to the DEC study it was banning all pregnant women from its semiconductor production lines. The Semiconductor Industry Association, however, issued a white paper stating that the DEC study "falls short of providing a valid basis for drawing meaningful conclusions or taking specific actions." Yet in 1989 the association agreed to fund a $3.5 million study of working conditions in chip factories.

LEADING COMPANIES

Jerry Sanders, cofounder and chief executive of **Advanced Micro Devices (AMD)**, is one of the most flamboyant characters in Silicon Valley. Sanders's showmanship, including some epic Christmas parties costing hundreds of thousands of dollars, goes along with AMD's strong emphasis on marketing. The company, a Fairchild spin-off, has prospered by focusing on three industrial markets: computing, telecommunications, and instruments. In 1987 the company acquired Monolithic Memories in a stock swap, and in 1990 AMD announced plans to sell one of its factories (in Texas) to Sony in exchange for $55 million and help in advanced CMOS technology.

Intel, formed by a group of defectors from Fairchild in 1968, is considered the leading technology innovator in the semiconductor business. Led by Robert Noyce, Gordon Moore, and Andrew Grove, Intel pioneered the microprocessor in 1970 and has remained the preeminent firm in that segment. However, the company, along with numerous other U.S. producers, got out of the memory chip business in 1985 in the face of cutthroat Japanese competition. IBM purchased 20 percent of Intel in the early 1980s (though Big Blue cut its interest to 7.1 percent in 1987). In 1986 the company brought out its powerful 32-bit microprocessor, the 80386, which helped usher in a new generation of personal computers. In the following years Intel sought both to protect its dominant position in conventional microprocessors by introducing ever more powerful chips and to gain a foothold in the move toward RISC processors for workstations. In 1990 Intel began raising its profile as a systems producer with the introduction of several workstations and a supercomputer. While most of the industry has been in a slump, Intel has hummed along and remained a darling of Wall Street.

Motorola began life in the 1930s, producing radios for automobiles (the name is an amalgam of motor and Victrola) The company got a lift during World War II when its portable two-way radios, or walkie-talkies, were adopted by the military. Getting into semiconductors in the early 1950s, the company ended up dominating the production of discrete (as opposed to integrated) devices. Although never a great innovator, Motorola later emerged as the second-ranking producer of microprocessors and the leading U.S. producer of semiconductors overall. After the Japanese took over the DRAM market, the company formed an alliance with Toshiba in which Motorola began to sell DRAMs made with Toshiba technology and Toshiba was given access to Motorola's microprocessor technology. In 1990 Motorola made a move from components to systems with the introduction of its own midrange computer.

The people of **National Semiconductor Corporation (NSC)** are known as the "animals of Silicon Valley." Led by Charlie Sporck, the company is a dogged competitor and has a fanatical obsession with reducing costs. NSC was a small and struggling producer in 1967 when its chairman, venture capitalist Peter Sprague, lured Sporck away from Fairchild to take charge. In the mid-1980s the company began putting more emphasis on its National Advanced Systems division, which distributes mainframes made by Hitachi, and its Datachecker/DTS, which makes retail checkout terminals.

Texas Instruments (TI) started out producing seismic equipment for the oil industry in the 1930s and ended up for many years as the world's largest semiconductor company. In the 1950s TI brought down the price of transistors enough to allow them to be used in radios; and in 1959 Jack Kilby, a TI scientist, invented the first integrated circuit. The company, which has traditionally focused on the commodity end of the business, became notorious in the early 1970s for ruthless price-cutting in the calculator and digital watch businesses. TI suffered heavy losses in home computers—a product it abandoned in 1983—and again in semiconductors in the 1980s. Yet TI was the only major U.S. chipmaker (aside from IBM's captive operations) to remain in the DRAM market in the face of a Japanese onslaught. In 1988 TI formed a joint venture with Hitachi to develop DRAMs, and two years later TI entered into a similar arrangement with Kobe Steel to build a $350 million plant to make advanced logic chips for the Japanese market.

INDUSTRY DATA

Semiconductors	*1989*	*1988*	*1987*
Value of shipments	$28.0 billion	$25.6 billion	$19.6 billion
Total employment	203,000	199,000	183,000
Value of imports	$11.9 billion	$11.0 billion	$7.6 billion

Source: U.S. Department of Commerce.

SOURCE GUIDE

Leading Stock Analysts and Experts

Dataquest, a research firm in San Jose, California.

In-Stat, a research firm in Scottsdale, Arizona.

Integrated Circuit Engineering, a research firm in Scottsdale, Arizona.

Daniel Klesken, analyst at Prudential-Bache.

VLSI Research, a market research firm in San Jose, California.

Trade Associations

American Electronics Association, 5201 Great America Parkway, Santa Clara, CA 95054. Tel.: (408) 987–4200.

Electronic Industries Association, 2001 I Street NW, Washington, DC 20006. Tel.: (202) 457–4900.

Semiconductor Industry Association, 10201 Torre Avenue, Cupertino, CA 95014. Tel.: (408) 973–9973.

Data Sources and Directories

Dun's Electronics Marketing Directory, annual (New York: Dun's Marketing Services).

Electronic Market Data Book, an annual compilation of data on consumer and industrial products (Washington, D.C.: Electronic Industries Association).

Electronic News Financial Fact Book and Directory, an annual volume on the industry from the publisher of *Electronic News* (New York: Fairchild Publications).

SIA Yearbook & Directory, a biennial list of industry firms and compilation of statistics (San Jose, Calif.: Semiconductor Industry Association).

Status (whatever year), an annual report on the integrated circuit industry that also includes a list of firms in different segments of the business (Scottsdale, Ariz.: Integrated Circuit Engineering).

Who's Who in Electronics, annual (Twinsburg, Ohio: Harris Publishing).

Trade Publications

Electronic Business, semimonthly.

Electronic News, weekly.

Electronics, monthly.

Global Electronics, a monthly newsletter from the Pacific Studies Center, Mountain View, California.

Semiconductor International, monthly.

Books and Reports

Borrus, Michael G. *Competing for Control: America's Stake in Microelectronics*. Cambridge, Mass.: Ballinger Publishing, 1988.

Early, Steve, and Rand Wilson. "Organizing High Tech: Unions and Their Future." *Labor Research Review*, no. 8 (1986).

Grunwald, Joseph, and Kenneth Flamm. *The Global Factory: Foreign Assembly in International Trade*. Washington, D.C.: Brookings Institution, 1985.

Hanson, Dirk. *The New Alchemists: Silicon Valley and the Microelectronics Revolution*. Boston: Little, Brown, 1982.

Hayes, Dennis. *Behind the Silicon Curtain*. Boston: South End Press, 1989.

Howell, Thomas R. *The Microelectronics Race: The Impact of Government Policy on International Competition*. Boulder, Colo.: Westview Press, 1987.

Malone, Michael. *The Big Score: The Billion-Dollar Story of Silicon Valley*. Garden City, N.Y.: Doubleday Publishing, 1985.

Massachusetts Institute of Technology. "The U.S. Semiconductor, Computer, and Copier Industries," in *Working Papers of the MIT*

Commission on Industrial Productivity. Cambridge, Mass.: MIT Press, 1989.

National Research Council. *Competitive Status of the U.S. Electronics Industry*. Washington, D.C.: National Academy Press, 1984.

Okimoto, Daniel; Tahue Sugano; and Franklin B. Weinstein. *Competitive Edge: The Semiconductor Industry in the U.S. and Japan*. Stanford, Calif.: Stanford University Press, 1984.

Organisation for Economic Co-operation and Development. *The Semiconductor Industry: Trade Related Issues*. Paris, 1985.

Siegel, Lenny, and John Markoff. *The High Cost of High Tech: The Dark Side of the Chip*. New York: Harper & Row, 1985.

United Nations Centre on Transnational Corporations. *Transnational Corporations in the International Semiconductor Industry*. New York, 1983.

U.S. Congress, Joint Economic Committee. *International Competition in Advanced Industrial Sectors: Trade and Development in the Semiconductor Industry*. Washington, D.C., 1982.

U.S. Congress, Office of Technology Assessment. *International Competitiveness in Electronics*. Washington, D.C., 1983.

PART 4

ENERGY

CHAPTER 16

COAL AND ALTERNATIVE FUELS

The $22 billion industry once known as King Coal is now far from regal. The hope that the oil crisis of the 1970s would restore the faded glory of coal went largely unfulfilled, and the plunge of petroleum prices in the 1980s was another painful blow.

Yet the coal industry has a long history of surviving such setbacks and waiting for the next possible boom. The resilience of the coal business is a reflection of a basic fact: Coal represents America's most abundant and inexpensive source of energy. Estimated reserves in the United States represent about 250 years of output at 1989's level of 973 million tons. A succession of presidents, beginning with Nixon, have looked at this national asset and proclaimed coal the key to U.S. energy independence.

The fundamental reason why these exhortations have not been carried out is that coal is dirty—dirty to mine, dirty to transport, and dirty to burn. The electric utility industry, the biggest consumer of coal, has been reluctant to use more coal, because to do so would exacerbate problems of air pollution and acid rain. Also, the more efficient method of extracting coal, strip-mining, ravages the countryside.

The dirtiness of coal has also contributed to the tumultuous labor relations in the industry. The high risks of coal mining—including black-lung disease, explosions, and cave-ins—give it the highest worker death rate of any industry. In this environment it is no surprise that miners are among the most militant rank-and-file workers in the country.

In the late 1970s there was excitement in the coal industry over the revival of interest in synthetic fuels, a major part of which involved the production of oil and gas out of coal. For a few years it appeared that huge infusions of federal money would propel synfuels, and coal, into a leading role in the energy equation.

The decline of oil prices in the early 1980s put an end to those expectations, and synfuels became a dead issue. A similar fate befell the other main alternative type of energy that came into vogue at the same time: solar power. A slew of big corporations rushed into solar power after the Carter administration began promoting it and rushed out again when lower petroleum costs and Reagan budget cuts eliminated much of the appeal.

At the end of the 1980s coal, synthetic fuel, and solar power all remained in the doldrums, waiting for another energy crunch to be called into center stage again. The Persian Gulf crisis that began in the summer of 1990 made that a distinct possibility.

THE ASCENT OF COAL

Although the first commercial mines were opened in the 1740s, the coal industry developed slowly in America because of the abundance and greater accessibility of wood. Coal's main customers were blacksmiths and ironmakers and, during wartime, the producers of ammunition.

During the second half of the 19th century, coal's prospects improved steadily with the development of industry (especially steel) and the railroads. The coal used to make coke in the steel process and to burn in steam engines was the type known as bituminous. This grade of coal is softer and contains somewhat less carbon than the purer anthracite coal used for heating.

With the switch in coals came changes in both the technology of the industry and its geography. Anthracite deposits are concentrated in northeastern Pennsylvania, while bituminous reserves are scattered throughout Appalachia, the Midwest, and the northern Great Plains. The early form of mining was quarrying, or "trenching," a forerunner of strip-mining. This was replaced by underground tunneling, which was more dangerous but allowed access to greater amounts of coal.

In the early days of underground mining, the coal was recovered from a solid bed with the use of only hand tools and explosives. This labor-intensive production process was also highly skilled. Miners had to learn how to undercut the coal face and insert the blasting powder in just the right way to loosen the most coal without causing a disaster. The coal then had to be loaded into baskets and dragged out, though by the mid-19th century mule-drawn carts on wooden rails were being employed.

Yet it was not until the 1930s that coal extraction began to be mechanized in a serious way. Cutting machines became more common, while mechanical loaders were slower in catching on. In the 1950s larger mining companies began to introduce huge machines called continuous miners. These devices, some 30 feet long, gouged coal out of the mine face and loaded it automatically onto shuttle cars. In the 1960s U.S. producers began to use mechanized longwall systems, which functioned like continuous miners but also saved the time traditionally spent on putting up roofing, by using its own steel canopy held up by hydraulic jacks. Both systems were, in theory, much more efficient than traditional methods, but the equipment was vastly more expensive and was subject to a lot of downtime.

Coal reached its pinnacle in the first decades of the century, when it accounted for some three fourths of the country's energy needs. Yet while coal's importance in electricity generation was rising, it was also being challenged by the expanding use of oil and natural gas. Coal by-products found new applications in drugs, synthetic rubber, nylons, and plastics, but coal was challenged by petroleum on that terrain as well. In 1952 petroleum replaced coal as the largest single contributor to U.S. energy consumption. By the latter part of the decade coal's future was jeopardized even more by what was then thought to be a glorious future for nuclear power. By the early 1960s coal had all but been written off.

While many of the small operators in the traditionally fragmented industry had a hard time surviving the slump, coal developed a new allure for a surprising group of investors: large oil producers and other resource companies. Continental Oil (now part of Du Pont) purchased Consolidation Coal in 1966. Occidental Petroleum acquired Island Creek Coal in 1968, and Standard Oil of Ohio bought Old Ben Coal the same year. Kennecott Copper purchased industry leader Peabody Coal in 1968 but was later forced by the Federal Trade Commission to sell the company, which was bought in 1977 by a consortium led by Newmont Mining.

The major emphasis of the new coal barons was not on the traditional deep mines of Appalachia, with their militant labor force. The focus instead was on expanding the Western open-pit extraction that emerged in the 1950s. Strip-mining involved much less labor and was considerably more productive than tunneling. Much of it was done on land owned by the federal government and leased at low rates.

SEEKING SAFE MINES AND CLEAN AIR

It appeared that these investments would pay off handsomely when the rapid escalation of oil import prices in the early 1970s brought about expectations of a rush to coal as an abundant domestic source. Although coal use did expand somewhat, it fell far short of the 1 billion tons a year targeted by the federal government. The reasons for the disappointing recovery of coal are complicated, but they certainly include the following.

The reliability of coal supplies, though perhaps not as uncertain as OPEC oil, was not seen as entirely satisfactory. One problem was that of productivity, which had been steadily declining since the late 1960s. Coal operators tended to put the blame on wildcat strikes and recent federal safety legislation. In 1969 Congress passed the Coal Mine Health and Safety Act, which established fairly strict rules for an industry that had a poor record (including shockingly high fatality rates) of protecting its workers. Predictably, the coal operators denounced the law as too stringent, and miners criticized the Interior Department for lax enforcement (responsibility was later transferred to the Labor Department). Yet from either point of view it was undeniable that the new safety measures tended to reduce productivity while miners and their employers adjusted to the new ways of operating.

Energy customers, particularly utilities, were also hesitant to switch to coal because of environmental considerations. The burning of coal would make it especially difficult for utilities to meet the emission standards contained in the Clean Air Act of 1970. Subsequent federal requirements on the use of emission-control devices such as scrubbers made the switch to coal a more expensive proposition. In 1981 the utility industry lobbied for and won legislation easing provisions in the 1978 Power Plant and Industrial Fuel Use Act requiring greater use of coal. The problems were compounded by a later discovery that the burning of coal was contributing to the problem of acid rain—airborne traces of sulfuric and nitric acid that were killing aquatic life and damaging cropland.

Although the coal they produced tended to be lower in sulfur and thus less of a pollution hazard, strip miners in both the East and the West also faced environmental challenges. More militant critics pushed for a complete ban on surface mining, while others lobbied for strict laws requiring operators to restore the land to something approximating its previous state. President Ford vetoed a tough strip-mining bill in 1975, but Congress acted again in 1977 with the Surface Mining Control and Reclamation Act.

Coal operators hoped that the arrival of the Reagan administration would put an end to many of their regulatory problems. Mine safety enforcement was relaxed, and the Interior Department did move to reopen federal lands to coal leasing after a 10-year moratorium imposed by Congress. But indications that Interior Secretary James Watt was offering the lands at less than market rates prompted Congress to impose a new ban. Also, complaints from the Canadian government about acid rain caused the administration to restrain its deregulatory fervor regarding coal.

By the mid-1980s the emphasis was on finding cleaner

ways to burn coal. Despite budget cuts in other programs, Congress in 1984 authorized $750 million for research in this field. The funds were not appropriated and came under attack from budget cutters in the Office of Management and Budget. In December 1985 Congress voted a three-year, $400 million clean-coal program, reserving the other $350 million for future use.

The 1988 agreement between the United States and Canada on reducing acid rain prompted Congress to continue funding clean-coal research. Among the technologies being developed are fluidized bed combustion, which uses limestone to turn the sulfur generated by burning coal into a harmless waste product, in situ coal gasification, and advanced emission-control techniques. Clean-coal plants are not expected to be in service until the late 1990s.

With the use of coal in steel production steadily decreasing, the future of coal more than ever depends on the electric utilities. Aside from the environmental issues the biggest question here may be the prospects for nuclear power. Public confidence in nuclear power plummeted after the Soviet Union's Chernobyl accident in 1986, but the nuclear industry has been trying to make a comeback.

Faced with a high degree of uncertainty, the coal industry has focused on consolidating operations and increasing efficiency. Productivity started rising again in the late 1970s and the trend continued through the 1980s. Yet consumption, which had some strong years of growth during the mid-1980s, was flat again by the end of the decade. Oil and steel companies began to dispose of their coal assets, and the number of working mines declined to about 4,000.

The coal equation became more complicated in 1990 when the Senate reached a compromise with the Bush administration on the first amendments to the Clean Air Act in two decades. The plan required more than 100 of the dirtiest power plants in 21 states to cut sulfur dioxide emissions by 5 million tons by 1995. This could be accomplished by burning low-sulfur coal, installing scrubbers, or using other emission-control technology. An additional 5 million tons would have to be cut by those plants and 200 others by the

The 10 Largest U.S. Coal Producers, 1989 (Millions of Tons)

1. Peabody	86.7
2. Consolidation	53.5
3. AMAX	38.4
4. Arco Coal	31.1
5. Texas Utilities	29.9
6. Exxon Coal	28.1
7. Shell Mining	25.5
8. NERCO	24.5
9. Sun Coal	22.8
10. North American Coal	22.5

Source: 1990 *Keystone Coal Industry Manual.*

year 2000, at which time a national ceiling on emissions would take effect. Companies would be allowed to buy and sell pollution rights, but no federal funds would be made available to miners whose jobs would be eliminated as a result of a shift away from high-sulfur coal.

SYNTHETIC FUELS

One of the bases for optimism in the coal industry in the late 1970s was the sudden vogue for synthetic fuels, particularly oil and gas derived from coal and oil extracted from shale. In 1979, amid the second oil shock, President Carter proposed an $88 billion, 10-year program to produce 2.5 million barrels of synthetic oil daily by 1990.

Although at the time there were no commercial plants producing synfuel, as it came to be called, the technologies involved were far from new. Shale rock was used as a source of oil back in the 19th century. Until the 1920s "town gas," a low-grade fuel derived from coal, was used in many parts of the United States in street lamps and home ovens. Germany was a leader in the development of synthetic fuels, which were a crucial source of energy for that country during World War II.

Carter's 1979 proposal sailed through Congress, which appropriated $17.5 billion for research and created the Synthetic

Fuels Corporation to administer the work. Companies such as Mobil, Texaco, and Occidental Petroleum began lining up for huge subsidies for coal gasification, coal liquefaction, and shale oil projects.

The federal government's enthusiasm for synfuels began to wane with the election of Ronald Reagan and the easing of the oil crunch. Several major projects, including a $5 billion shale oil joint venture between Exxon and Tosco Corp., were canceled. The $2 billion Great Plains coal gasification plant was built in North Dakota by a consortium of five energy companies, but its owners ended up writing off the project. Slumping oil prices and federal budget cuts crippled the Synthetic Fuels Corporation itself, and in 1986 the agency was shut down.

SOLAR ENERGY

Whereas coal is viewed by many as a has-been technology, solar power, like synfuels, remains in the yet-to-be stage. The concept of renewable energy—solar energy is often defined to include wind, hydro, and other nonfossil resources—was an esoteric subject until the early 1970s. The oil crisis pushed it to a central place in the debates on the future of energy.

Solar energy advocates found they had an ally in the White House when Jimmy Carter took office. Carter got Congress to create tax credits for solar installations and to fund the Solar Energy Research Institute in Colorado. The administration also supported an event called Sun Day, held on May 3, 1978, to promote public awareness of the potential of solar power. As part of his energy plan President Carter set a goal of having renewable resources account for 20 percent of the country's energy needs by the end of the century.

The heightened interest in solar energy was not limited to the government. As federal funding of solar energy research escalated, big business got into the act. Leading the move were the major oil companies, which had already hedged their bets by investing in coal and uranium. Petroleum giants such as Exxon, Texaco, Mobil, and Atlantic

Richfield joined with other large companies such as General Electric and Grumman in acquiring the tiny firms that had pioneered the industry. By the end of the 1970s about one half of the top 25 solar companies were controlled by billion-dollar corporations. The interest of big business was focused on the photovoltaic (the conversion of sunlight into electricity) market, while solar heating tended to remain in the hands of small entrepreneurs.

Whatever optimism had developed in the solar industry was dashed with the arrival of the Reagan administration. Reagan slashed solar energy research funds, which had reached a peak of $500 million in Carter's last budget, and dismissed most of the employees of the Solar Energy Research Institute. The administration insisted that solar energy research would have to depend on private funds despite the fact that the federal government had spent countless billions of dollars on research for previous energy technologies, especially nuclear power. With the expiration of the tax credit at the end of 1985, the prospects for the solar industry grew even more cloudy.

By the late 1980s many of the large companies were abandoning solar energy, just at the time when it was becoming more economically competitive with conventional power sources. ARCO Solar, the largest make of solar panels, was sold by its parent Atlantic Richfield to Siemens of West Germany.

Yet there continued to be some true believers. Luz International, which is responsible for producing nearly all of the country's solar power, continued generating electricity for Southern California Edison at its fields of solar panels in the Mojave Desert. Chronar Corp., a manufacturer of solar-powered patio lamps, announced in 1988 that it planned to build a 50-megawatt facility north of Los Angeles, also to supply Southern California Edison. Some analysts were even predicting that solar energy could be a leading growth industry by the turn of the century, but that will seem a lot more likely if the nuclear power industry fails in its attempted revival and oil prices remain at the elevated levels they reached after the outbreak of a new crisis in the Middle East.

LABOR RELATIONS

There is little doubt that the coal business has had the most contentious labor relations in American industry. While national union leaders have usually tried to maintain cooperative relations with management, the militancy of rank-and-file miners has made it impossible for those leaders to guarantee a disciplined labor force.

Union organizing among Pennsylvania anthracite miners began in the 1840s. The companies used spies and vigilantes to oppose labor militants, and workers responded with violence. In the 1870s the coal operators depicted militancy among Irish miners as a conspiracy engineered by a group called the Molly Maguires. Although some historians now question whether the conspiracy ever existed, the companies managed to get 19 miners convicted.

Bituminous miners took the lead in creating a national union. After several short-lived organizations, the National Federation of Miners and Mine Laborers was created in 1885. It ended up merging with a division of the Knights of Labor and formed the United Mine Workers of America (UMW) in 1890.

The UMW had difficulty winning recognition from the operators despite a long series of strikes. The anthracite strike of 1902 brought federal intervention and a 10 percent wage increase but still no recognition. In some cases the disputes became bloody, as in the infamous Ludlow massacre of 1914. Gunmen working for the Rockefeller-dominated Colorado Fuel & Iron Co. and National Guardsmen drenched the strikers' tents with oil and ignited them while miners and their families were asleep. When the occupants rushed from the burning tents they were machine-gunned. Twenty of them were killed, including 13 children.

Worker militancy escalated after World War I, but the leader of the more conservative faction in the UMW took over as president in 1920. John L. Lewis went on to become a virtual dictator of the UMW for 40 years and a major figure in the labor movement. In his early years as president, Lewis had to contend with an unprecedented management assault that cut pay and reduced UMW representation of the industry.

In 1933 Lewis took advantage of the National Industrial Recovery Act's affirmation of collective bargaining to launch an intensive organizing drive that resulted in the signing up of more than 90 percent of the coal labor force by the end of the year. The UMW was then firmly entrenched and became a major power in the industry. During World War II, Lewis staged two strikes and won such concessions as portal-to-portal pay.

After the war, Lewis pushed for pathbreaking management-funded retirement and health plans. After a 1946 strike that included a temporary federal seizure of the country's mines, the UMW won the demand. The Welfare and Retirement Fund, which provided comprehensive and free (for the miner) health care, was to be financed by a 10-cent royalty paid by the coal operators on each ton produced.

During the 1950s Lewis developed a close working relationship with George Love, president of Consolidation Coal and head of the Bituminous Coal Operators Association (BCOA), an industry group set up in 1952 to bargain with the UMW on national contracts. Lewis decided that increasing productivity was necessary for the future of the industry, and for that reason he was willing to accept widening mechanization of coal production. Lewis was untroubled by the fact that this process meant declining employment levels; in fact there were reports that Lewis was lending UMW funds to smaller operators to help them mechanize. This kind of cooperation resulted in an absence of national strikes between the early 1950s and the mid-1960s.

In the latter decade the level of discontent among miners began to increase. One target was the national leadership of the UMW. Lewis retired in 1960 and was succeeded briefly by Thomas Kennedy, who resigned because of poor health and turned the union over to W. A. "Tony" Boyle. Boyle had less charisma than Lewis and was even more ruthless in crushing his union opponents. Joseph Yablonski, a reform candidate who opposed Boyle in the 1969 election for president, was later murdered along with his wife and daughter in an attack that Boyle was subsequently convicted of plotting. The Labor Department invalidated the election, and a vote in 1972 brought to power another reform figure, Arnold Miller.

In the meantime rank-and-file activism had reached high levels. Wildcat strikes in West Virginia pressured the legislature in that state to pass a black-lung compensation law in 1969. Similar pressure helped bring about a program of national compensation in the 1969 Mine Safety and Health Act.

Although miners were encouraged by the election of Miller and the triumph of the Miners for Democracy reform movement, the wildcats continued. The rank and file had found that such strikes were a more effective way of dealing with workplace problems than the grievance and arbitration system. The coal operators, naturally, pressed the union for strong contract language to outlaw the walkouts, and this became a major issue in the strike that began in December 1977.

In that 110-day walkout, the rank and file rejected a proposed settlement negotiated by the UMW leadership and defied a Taft-Hartley injunction issued at the request of President Carter. Most of management's retrogressions were dropped, but the operators did win the right to convert benefit coverage from the union's Retirement and Welfare Fund to private carriers.

By this time the rank and file had grown disillusioned with Miller, who among other things was accused of withholding aid that had been donated by other unions during the strike. Support for the leadership improved after Sam Church took over in 1979 following Miller's resignation for health reasons.

Most observers expected the 1981 negotiations to be resolved without a confrontation. But again the rank and file voted down a proposed settlement, this time because of a provision giving companies greater freedom to sublease mines to nonunion operators. The miners stayed out for 73 days to try to prevent a further erosion of the UMW's share of coal production, which had sunk to about 40 percent. After the BCOA made some improvements to its offer, including less-sweeping subcontracting language, the miners accepted it.

Once again the UMW president became the scapegoat for rank-and-file discontent over contract talks. Church fell out of favor and was succeeded by Richard Trumka in 1982. In the face of poor industry conditions and rising nonunion competition, UMW members approved a 1984 contract settlement that provided the smallest wage increases since the Great Depression.

The next important UMW battle concerned the policies of a particular employer rather than the national contract. In 1984 a strike was called against A. T. Massey Coal Co. to oppose the firm's refusal to continue recognizing the UMW in some of its subsidiaries. After a 15-month strike that saw a great deal of violence, Massey agreed to settle National Labor Relations Board charges, and the miners went back to work.

In 1988 the UMW won job security and pension improvements (though modest wage gains) in its new contract with the BCOA, but separate negotiations with Pittston Coal (which left the employers' group in 1987) went much less smoothly. Angered by the company's concessionary demands—including an end to its participation in the industrywide pension and health plans—the 2,000 UMW members at Pittston launched a corporate campaign against the company, though they remained on the job after the contract expired. After more than a year of applying pressure, the UMW decided to call a strike.

The walkout turned out to be unusual in the degree of solidarity the Pittston workers received from local communities, other coal miners (tens of thousands of whom staged wildcat sympathy strikes), and the rest of the labor movement. Thousands of unionists visited the Camp Solidarity encampment that UMW members set up in Virginia, and many of them participated in the campaign of massive civil disobedience used by the Pittston workers to try to thwart company operations being carried out by strikebreakers. In September 1989 Pittston workers swept past guards and occupied a Pittston facility in Carbo, Virginia, for several days—an act believed to be the first labor occupation of a workplace since the 1930s.

Following reported threats by European dock unions to refuse to handle U.S. coal shipments because of the strike, Labor Secretary Elizabeth Dole appointed a special federal mediator for the dispute, and in January 1990 a settlement was finally reached. Pittston dropped most of its concessionary demands and agreed to remain in the industry health and pension plans, while the UMW agreed to work rule changes.

INDUSTRY DATA

Coal	*1989*	*1988*	*1987*
Value of shipments	$22.3 billion	$21.1 billion	$21.3 billion
Total employment	141,500	150,800	161,800
Import penetration	0.5%	0.3%	0.3%

Sources: U.S. Department of Commerce (shipments and imports); U.S. Bureau of Labor Statistics (employment).

LEADING COMPANY

Peabody Coal and nearly all of the other big coal producers are subsidiaries of oil and other natural resources companies. Founded by Francis S. Peabody in Illinois in the late 19th century, Peabody has long been the country's largest coal miner. Starting in the mid-1950s, Peabody moved heavily into strip-mining, and a decade later the company was sold to Kennecott Copper. The Federal Trade Commission found the sale anti-competitive, and after a long battle Kennecott agreed to sell the company to a group of six companies led by Newmont Mining. In 1990 Peabody's ownership appeared to be changing once again, as Britain's Hanson (owner of 49 percent of Newmont) agreed to buy the 45 percent of Peabody owned by Boeing, Bechtel, and Eastern Enterprises.

SOURCE GUIDE

Leading Stock Analysts and Experts

Marc Cohen, coal analyst at Kidder Peabody.

John Kawa, coal analyst at Dean Witter.

Joel Price, coal analyst at Donaldson, Lufkin & Jenrette.

Trade Associations and Unions

National Coal Association, 1130 17th Street NW, Washington, DC 20036. Tel.: (202) 463–2625.

Solar Energy Industries Association, 1730 N. Lynn Street, Arlington, VA 22209. Tel.: (703) 524–6100.

United Mine Workers of America, 900 15th Street NW, Washington, DC 20005. Tel.: (202) 842–7200.

Data Sources and Directories

Coal Data and *Facts About Coal*, annuals (Washington, D.C.: National Coal Association).

Coal Information, an annual international statistical compilation (Paris: Organisation for Economic Co-operation and Development).

Coal Mine Directory and *Keystone Coal Industry Manual*, both annuals (Chicago: MacLean Hunter Publishing).

Monthly Energy Review, International Energy Annual, Weekly Coal Production, Quarterly Coal Report, and the annual *Coal Production* (Washington: D.C.: U.S. Energy Information Administration).

Online Database

DOE ENERGY (Washington, D.C.: U.S. Department of Energy; available via DIALOG).

Trade Publications

Clean-Coal/Synfuels Letter, weekly.

Coal, monthly.

Coal Outlook, weekly.

Coal Week.

International Solar Energy Intelligence Report, weekly.

Keystone News-Bulletin, monthly.

Solar Industry Journal, quarterly.

Books and Reports

Banks, Ferdinand E. *The Political Economy of Coal*. Lexington, Mass.: Lexington Books, 1985.

Braithwaite, John. *To Punish or Persuade: The Enforcement of Coal Mine Safety*. Albany, N.Y.: State University of New York Press, 1985.

Critical Mass Energy Project. *Power Surge.* Washington, D.C., 1989.

Gordon, Richard L. *U.S. Coal and the Electric Power Industry.* Baltimore: Johns Hopkins University Press, 1975.

Investor Responsibility Research Center. *Power Plays: Profiles of America's Leading Renewable Electricity Developers.* Washington, D.C., 1989.

Long, Priscilla. *Where the Sun Never Shines: A History of America's Bloody Coal Industry.* New York: Paragon House, 1989.

Perry, Charles R. *Collective Bargaining and the Decline of the United Mine Workers.* Philadelphia: Wharton Industrial Research Unit, 1984.

Reece, Ray. *The Sun Betrayed: A Report on the Corporate Seizure of Solar Energy Development.* Boston: South End Press, 1979.

Seltzer, Curtis. *Fire in the Hole: Miners and Managers in the American Coal Industry.* Lexington, Ky.: University Press of Kentucky, 1985.

U.S. Congress, Office of Technology Assessment. *Federal Coal Leasing Program.* Washington, D.C., 1984.

______. *New Electric Power Technologies: Problems and Prospects for the 1990s.* Washington, D.C., 1985.

______. *On-Site Solar Energy.* Washington, D.C., 1978.

U.S. Congress, Senate Budget Committee. *Synthetic Fuels.* Washington, D.C.: Government Printing Office, September 1979.

CHAPTER 17

NUCLEAR POWER AND ELECTRIC UTILITIES

By now it is taken for granted, but electric power is one of the major blessings of modern times. The role of electricity in economic development knows no ideological boundaries; Lenin once defined Communism as "electrification plus soviets." Lighting, heating, cooking, and the gamut of commercial and industrial activities rely on the immense network of wires that make up the electric power grid.

This system is largely under the control of the private, or investor-owned, utility industry. In 1989 these companies received revenues of $133 billion for selling some 2 trillion kilowatt hours of power.

This energy is produced by several means, the largest part (about 70 percent of the total) coming from the burning of coal, oil, and natural gas. Nuclear power contributes about 20 percent and hydro about 10 percent. In the early postwar years the hope was that nuclear would provide cheap and abundant power—"too cheap to meter," the forecasts claimed. The federal government spent many billions of dollars to subsidize the effort to attain that dream.

But for the utility industry, nuclear power mainly turned out to be a nightmare. A persistent antinuclear movement challenged the claims that the technology was safe. Accidents such as the one at Three Mile Island in 1979 gave added credibility to these concerns and prompted federal overseers to impose a long list of additional regulations. Construction costs of the nuclear plants went out of control, and the projects fell years behind schedule. More than 100 orders for reactors were canceled, new orders dried up, and by the mid-1980s a number of utilities were even abandoning half-finished plants.

The nuclear quagmire, along with other woes such as a decline in the rate of demand growth, made the 1970s the worst of times for the industry. A decade later the situation had improved somewhat, and electric utilities took the surprising steps of seeking deregulation and branching out into new fields of business.

THE COMING OF ELECTRIC POWER

The electrical power industry had its roots in the breakthrough achieved in 1879 by Thomas Edison and his assistant Francis Jehl in the creation of the first long-lasting incandescent light bulb. The announcement of the device, which consisted of a carbon filament in a vacuum globe, made the stock market go crazy. The shares of gas companies, which had dominated the energy business, plummeted as investors flocked to the Edison Electric Light Company, a start-up firm established by J. P. Morgan and Western Union president Hamilton Twombly.

Edison's vision of electricity transforming commerce and the everyday life of Americans captured the imagination of the country. And Edison was determined to capture the market, both for light bulbs and for the provision of the energy to illuminate them. The wizard of Menlo Park set up the Edison Electric Illuminating Company to build the first central-station generating plant. He shrewdly chose as his first service area a patch of downtown Manhattan that included the financial district.

After the Pearl Street station successfully started operation in 1882, competitors rushed into the new business, both to generate electricity and to produce light bulbs. Edison's poorly written patent application for the bulb was rejected, and the legal monopoly went to a rival. The rights to a refined version of that bulb were scooped up by an aggressive young inventor and entrepreneur named George Westinghouse, who also began producing generating equipment.

Despite this setback Edison's company made money by expanding its service and licensing its equipment designs to others. Yet the mechanical genius was less than brilliant as a manager. He missed a number of important opportunities and insisted on using direct current rather than alternating current. The latter, adopted by Westinghouse, allowed higher voltage power to be transmitted over much longer distances. Edison held to the belief that AC was too dangerous, and as a way of highlighting the point he urged New York State to use a Westinghouse AC generator in building the first electric chair.

The battle between DC and AC was only one of the many differences in standards among the various purveyors of electricity in any given city. The desire to resolve this problem and the quest for economies of scale prompted numerous generating companies to merge with one another. J. P. Morgan, the apostle of corporate consolidation, gained control over Edison Electric and combined it with another firm to form General Electric (GE). Edison had no place in either the name of the new firm or its management. He went back to his laboratory, and GE went on to become an industrial giant. While it and Westinghouse became the dominant figures in the manufacture of electrical equipment, they were forced out of the generating business by federal antitrust pressures in the 1920s.

THE RISE AND FALL OF INSULL'S EMPIRE

The great empire builder in the utility business turned out to be Samuel Insull, a Briton who had come to the United States to serve as Edison's personal secretary. The ambitious Insull made his big move in 1892 when he went to Chicago to take over the management of the Chicago Edison Company.

Insull's approach to the business has been compared to that of John D. Rockefeller in oil: He entered a situation of chaotic competition—there were some 47 generating companies operating in Chicago alone—and ruthlessly proceeded to take over rivals and consolidate them. Yet whereas Rockefeller's creation was eventually undone by the trustbusters, Insull managed to attain official sanction for his empire, called Commonwealth Edison. The way he did it was to embrace the notion of strict government regulation as a quid pro quo for a legal monopoly. Despite some public support for the more radical approach of government takeover, as was occurring in Europe, leading civic reformers accepted regulation, seeing it as preferable to a system of public ownership that would provide inevitable opportunities for corruption. The approach spread rapidly across the country in the early years of the century, and electric generating companies became regulated public utilities.

Insull's innovation was not limited to horizontal integration. He was also a tireless promoter of electric power and insisted that the only efficient way to provide it was through central stations rather than the on-site generators that many commercial customers preferred. He also established the first dual-rate structure: a basic charge for the first few hours and a progressively lower rate for additional demand.

With his success in Chicago, Insull set his sights higher. He assembled more powerful equipment and began expanding his service area to other parts of Illinois and neighboring states. His growing operations were assembled in a holding company called Middle West Utilities. To finance his expansion Insull broke away from the large institutional investors and sold bonds to the public. A pioneer in the use of public relations, Insull made himself into something of a folk hero in the process.

In other parts of the country, utility magnates such as John Barnes Miller of southern California were carrying out similar forms of concentration, gobbling up both private and municipal operations. Consequently, by the late 1920s fewer than a dozen holding companies controlled about three fourths of the country's light and power business.

At the same time, the shares of these companies became some of the most highly prized during the speculative fever of the 1920s. Holding companies changed hands at highly inflated prices. To protect his interests Insull formed an investment trust and went on expanding even after the crash of 1929. It was in 1931 that the fragility of the economy caught up with Insull. The shares of his and other utility companies finally plunged, and before long Insull was forced out of Middle West Utilities. To escape prosecution for fraud he fled the country, later to be hunted down and extradited. While he managed to win an acquittal in his 1934 trial, Insull was a broken man.

With the advent of the New Deal, private (or investor-owned, as they preferred to be called) utilities found themselves out of favor in Washington. With support from the White House, Senator George Norris of Nebraska led a tireless crusade to promote publicly owned generating facilities. That campaign enjoyed a number of successes in the 1930s:

- The Tennessee Valley Authority, a publicly financed yet independent agency, was formed to develop hydroelectric power in the Southeast.
- In 1935 President Roosevelt created the Rural Electrification Administration to help bring electric power to the areas that private utilities had resisted wiring. The REA provided low-cost loans to cooperatives formed to produce and distribute their own power or else buy wholesale from private utilities and resell it at bargain rates.
- The Public Utilities Holding Company Act of 1935 outlawed the kind of pyramiding Insull had done and limited each utility company to owning one integrated operating system (though some exemptions were later allowed).

After World War II both privately and publicly owned utilities enjoyed rapid growth in the demand for electricity. This was due in no small part to the marketing efforts of the utilities themselves. They promoted the increasing use of electric appliances and offered inducements to builders to construct all-electric "Gold Medallion" homes. In this kind of environment, expansion seemed to be a no-lose strategy and one further bolstered by the fact that new plants added to the rate base on which state regulators guaranteed a specific level of return.

THE NUCLEAR GAMBLE

In the 1950s life was secure enough for the utilities that they were willing to go along with the attempts by the federal government to promote an entirely new technology for the generation of electricity. That technology was nuclear power, and several decades later it would nearly be the undoing of the industry.

The possibility of performing nuclear fission (i.e., the splitting of the atom) and harnessing the enormous energy that resulted first emerged in the 1930s in work being done by scientists in Europe. The spread of fascism sent many of these researchers to North America, and one of them, the Hungarian Leo Szilard, became obsessed with the possibility that Germany was working on an atomic bomb. He persuaded Albert Einstein to write to President Roosevelt and urge him to initiate an American effort to do the same.

In 1942 President Roosevelt acted on the recommendation and set up what became known as the Manhattan Project. That same year a group led by Enrico Fermi at the University of Chicago succeeded in creating the first self-sustaining nuclear reaction. Several years of intense work and a great deal of money resulted in the atomic bombs that were dropped on Hiroshima and Nagasaki in August 1945.

In 1946 the Atomic Energy Commission (AEC) was formed, and the federal agency worked hard to promote the idea that the power of the atom was not something to be abandoned now that the war was over. At the same time, a number of scientists who had worked on the Manhattan Project—including some who had regrets about the dropping of the bomb—urged that the nonmilitary uses of atomic energy be developed. The main application was to be the generation of enormous amounts of heat to create steam that in turn was to power electric generators.

The revelation that the Soviet Union had an atomic bomb of its own and the onset of the cold war delayed the commercialization of nuclear power until the early 1950s. In 1953 President Eisenhower made an "Atoms for Peace" speech at the United Nations, in which he pledged the United States to help other countries develop civilian applications for the technology. The American private sector, which had been barred from the nuclear business by the federal government's monopoly, expressed resentment that Washington was willing to share with foreign governments information that it was keeping from domestic corporations.

In 1954 Congress heeded the plea of business and passed legislation permitting the private ownership of reactors under AEC license. The AEC welcomed the development and brought together Westinghouse and the Duquesne Light Company of Pittsburgh for the first private project. Private is perhaps the wrong word for the deal, since the federal government was to pay most of the cost for the reactor that Westinghouse was to build for the utility at Shippingport, Pennsylvania. This plant, which started operation in 1957 and was technically owned by the AEC, was followed by half a dozen experimental reactors built by and for the private sector, with the taxpayers footing most of the bill. The federal subsidies were necessary because business was not yet willing to take a risk on unproven technology. For its part, the AEC considered immediate costs secondary to the goals of demonstrating U.S. nuclear superiority and creating energy abundance: a situation in which, as AEC chairman Lewis Strauss liked to put it, electricity would be "too cheap to meter."

Although utilities were willing to gamble with Uncle Sam's money, many of them were hesitant to go further. Congress created a further inducement with the Price-Anderson Act of 1957. The law limited the damages that could be collected in an atomic accident to $560 million, with the federal government covering $500 million of that. The utilities were still slow to move, because the estimated costs for nuclear plants remained above oil- and coal-fired ones and because no one yet imagined that there could be shortages of fossil fuels.

Commercial nuclear development thus proceeded rather slowly until the early 1960s. The turning point was the announcement in 1963 by Jersey Central Power & Light that it had determined that a large nuclear plant—its Oyster Creek plan called for 650 megawatts—would be cost-competitive with coal. To make the nuclear option more attractive, leading reactor manufacturers Westinghouse and General Electric announced that they would build nuclear plants on a fixed-cost basis. The two electrical equipment giants ended up losing nearly $1 billion on the 18 turnkey plants they built on these terms. Yet they succeeded in establishing their nuclear technology—light water reactors—as the dominant one throughout the United States and most of the world. Combustion Engineering Corp. and Babcock & Wilcox (a subsidiary of McDermott Inc.) also got into the reactor business, with their own versions of the same general technology.

Utilities looked at nuclear plants in a new light and, with the encouragement of Westinghouse and GE, started placing increasing numbers of orders for larger and larger reactors. Thus began what became known as the "great bandwagon years."

The tone was set in 1963, when Consolidated Edison placed the first order for a 1,000-megawatt plant, which it wanted to build right in the middle of New York City. Even the AEC was nervous about locating a reactor amid such a large population center, and Con Ed was persuaded to withdraw the proposal. The 1,000-megawatt figure was soon reached again when the Tennessee Valley Authority (TVA) ordered such a plant for Browns Ferry, Alabama. In 1972 the AEC set a limit of 1,300 megawatts despite industry talk of going as high as 8,000. The momentum continued into the early 1970s, and construction plans became so ambitious that groups of utilities joined forces to carry them out. In 1972, 16 utilities in New England combined to build two 1,150-megawatt reactors at Seabrook, New Hampshire.

THE SAFETY WAR

No sooner had the bandwagon started rolling than the nuclear industry began to be plagued by growing complaints about the safety of reactors. The AEC and the Joint Committee on Atomic Energy, which had exclusive control over atomic legislation in Congress, had long downplayed the safety issue. This was despite the fact that a study commissioned by the joint committee in the mid-1950s concluded that while the chance of a serious accident was remote, if one happened it could cause 3,400 deaths, 43,000 injuries, and $7 billion in property damage. The first serious reactor accident is believed to have occurred in 1955 at an experimental facility in Idaho, where a partial meltdown occurred.

Safety became a public issue in the late 1950s, a period of growing concern about fallout from atomic weapons. In 1956 the United Automobile Workers challenged the AEC's approval of a plan by Detroit Edison to build a nuclear plant on Lake Erie. The Fermi plant was the first U.S. commercial facility involving a liquid-metal fast breeder reactor. This technology, which creates plutonium in the process of using enriched uranium and thus produces more fuel than it consumes, was put forth as the basis of an energy nirvana. However, volatile liquid sodium rather than water is used in the breeders' cooling systems, making them much more dangerous than regular reactors. The Supreme Court ruled against the UAW, but the union's fears were seen to be justified in 1966 when the plant, only months after going into operation, suffered a serious accident that came close to a total meltdown.

The 1960s saw the emergence of an ongoing movement against nuclear power. The first target was the excess heat that plants released into the environment when disposing of nonradioactive cooling water. Critics charged that this "thermal pollution" was harming fish life in the vicinity of the plants.

Nuclear opponents refined their campaign after the passage of the National Environmental Policy Act of 1969. Taking on the Calvert Cliffs plant that Baltimore Gas & Electric was trying to build on Chesapeake Bay, environmentalists got a federal court to agree in 1971 that nuclear plants had to undergo the environmental reviews called for in the act.

Within a few years the debate shifted to the question of the reliability of the emergency core cooling systems (ECCS), which are supposed to serve as fail-safe devices for reactors. The nuclear establishment was heartened by a 1974 report, commissioned by the AEC and conducted under the direction of Professor Norman Rasmussen of MIT, that concluded that the risk of a severe reactor accident was less than the chance of an individual being struck by a meteor.

The opposing position gained more credibility the following year, when a serious fire broke out at the TVA's Browns Ferry plant and operators temporarily lost control of the core coolant, creating a situation that some observers said could have resulted in catastrophe. The incident helped spark the growth of the national antinuclear network Critical Mass and the placement of proposals for curbing nuclear plants on ballots in seven states (most notably Proposition 15 in California) in 1976. Although all of these measures were defeated, many new activists were recruited.

Antinuclear protesters then turned to direct action to try to block the construction of the Seabrook plants in New Hampshire. Starting in 1976 a group called the Clamshell Alliance staged repeated construction site blockades that slowed down work on the facility and focused national attention on the issue.

The election of Jimmy Carter in 1976 did not bring an out-and-out nuclear opponent to the White House, but it did temper federal support for nuclear growth. In 1977 Carter called nuclear energy a "last resort" and reaffirmed a ban begun by his predecessor on the reprocessing of spent nuclear fuel, in order to safeguard against the diversion of material that could be used to produce nuclear weapons.

The theoretical debate over safety became more of a real issue in the early morning hours of March 28, 1979. It was then that a serious accident occurred at one of the two reactors at the Three Mile Island facility operated by Metropolitan Edison (a subsidiary of General Public Utilities) near Harrisburg, Pennsylvania. There was no meltdown in the Babcock & Wilcox reactor, but the combination of mechanical failures, human error, and the lack of clearly defined emergency procedures in the surrounding area cast a shadow over nuclear power. More people than ever began to wonder about the wisdom of what nuclear pioneer Alvin Weinberg once called the "Faustian contract" society had made with atomic energy.

The Three Mile Island incident added another layer of trouble to an industry that was already loaded with woes. After the oil shock of 1973–74, the nuclear industry was set to step in and rescue the nation from the perils of dependence on foreign energy sources. The fly in the ointment here was that in the wake of the oil price increases, the customary postwar growth of electricity demand of 7 to 8 percent a year suddenly halted. This, along with financial problems linked to the higher costs for fossil fuels, caused many utilities to abandon or delay nuclear construction plans. Power companies were also pushed in this direction by the growing delays and rapidly rising costs for the nuclear plants that were already under construction. What was once a six- to eight-year process was stretching to a dozen years or more, and the construction cost per kilowatt climbed from a few hundred dollars to several thousand. Even when nuclear plants were completed, utilities were finding that they were out of service a great deal of the time.

New orders for nuclear plants peaked at 41 in 1973 and dropped to 26 in 1974 and to less than 5 in each of the following few years. Not a single new order for a reactor was placed in the United States after 1978. At the same time, the number of cancellations of reactor orders (seen for the first time in the early 1970s) began climbing. Since 1974 every nuclear project (numbering more than 100) has been scratched.

THE FUEL SQUEEZE

The major reactor builders continued to generate revenues from foreign orders and the servicing of domestic plants, but they found themselves in a bind in their role as providers of fuel. To understand how this came about, it is necessary to review how the nuclear fuel industry has been structured since 1964, when Congress passed legislation allowing private participation in what had been a government monopoly.

The first step is the mining of uranium and the conversion of the ore into uranium oxide, or yellowcake. Next is the conversion of the yellowcake into uranium hexafluoride. These processes have traditionally been done by the private sector, including several oil and chemical companies.

Then the uranium is sent to one of a handful of government-owned plants (operated by private contractors) for enrichment, a process that requires enormous amounts of electricity. The federal government has tried to privatize ownership of these plants, but companies have been reluctant to make the huge capital investment required. (In 1989, a joint venture led by Duke Power announced plans for construction of a $750 million enrichment plant in Louisiana.)

The enriched uranium then goes to private facilities where operators working by remote control solidify the uranium into small pellets and load them into metal fuel rods. The rods are then transported to the generating plant and are ready to be inserted into the reactor.

As part of their sales inducement to utilities in the 1960s, the reactor makers entered into long-term contracts to supply fuel. That was fine as long as uranium prices were stable. But in 1972 the leading international producers formed a secret cartel and conspired to raise prices. This, along with actions by the Nixon administration to raise enriched uranium prices to encourage the private sector companies to take over the government's enrichment business, pushed uranium prices from about $10 a pound to about $35 by the mid-1970s. For a company such as Westinghouse, which was obliged to supply millions of pounds of fuel, the new prices spelled major trouble. To avoid a huge loss Westinghouse reneged on its contracts and later brought an antitrust suit against the uranium companies. The drawn-out case was finally settled in 1981, with Westinghouse receiving a $100 million settlement.

A SEA OF TROUBLES

In the years following the Three Mile Island accident, the plight of the nuclear industry got progressively worse:

• Efforts by the industry to accelerate the licensing process were blocked, and the Nuclear Regulatory Commission issued a blizzard of new regulations. (In 1974 the AEC was abolished, and its regulatory responsibility and development efforts were placed in separate agencies. These were the Nuclear Regulatory Commission [NRC] and the Energy Research and Development Administration, which later became part of the new Department of Energy.)

• The owners of Three Mile Island, facing a $1 billion cleanup job, had to beg for help from the federal and state governments and other reactor operators. General Public Utilities also took the bizarre step of suing the NRC for not regulating the company enough; the case was thrown out of court.

- In 1983 Congress cut off funding for the Clinch River breeder reactor project in Tennessee. The demonstration project, originally authorized in 1970, had been a political football for years. Opposed by President Carter because of the risk that the plutonium produced by the breeder could be diverted for weapons production, the project was finally killed because of its rapidly rising cost.
- The finances of the Washington Public Power Supply System (informally known as Whoops) got progressively weaker and the system defaulted on $2.2 billion of its debt in 1983. The default, the largest in municipal bond history, resulted from the escalating costs of the nuclear plants being constructed by Whoops, a joint venture of 19 publicly owned utilities and four municipalities in the Northwest. The default occurred on bonds issued for the two nuclear plants (out of a total of five planned by Whoops) that ended up being canceled.
- A new NRC safety study found that the odds of a serious accident were much greater than estimated by Rasmussen and that one could be expected every 10 to 15 years.
- The Supreme Court ruled in 1983 that states could ban the construction of new nuclear plants for economic though not for safety reasons.
- There was increasing public controversy over the issue of nuclear waste. After years of debate Congress in 1982 finally passed legislation setting a timetable for the establishment of permanent underground storage sites. However, Congress avoided the issue of whether to permit the reprocessing of spent fuel into plutonium—a procedure that the Carter administration had opposed because of the danger of theft of weapons-grade material but that Reagan supported. In addition the Energy Department faced strong local opposition to any sites it considered for the storage facilities.

By the mid-1980s utilities with nuclear plants under construction found themselves facing a dilemma. Costs on the projects had gotten totally out of hand, and delays were enormous.

Long Island Lighting's Shoreham plant, which was originally supposed to cost $300 million, was up to more than $4 billion and was a decade behind schedule. The cost of the two Seabrook reactors in New Hampshire was estimated at more than $7 billion—eight times the original estimate—and work on one of the reactors was suspended.

The utilities had to decide whether to sink yet more money in these projects, not knowing whether they would be necessary by the time they were done. To make matters worse it became increasingly uncertain whether the utilities would ever be able to recoup their investment.

Faced with this possibility, some utilities began to consider walking away from their huge investments. This was the path taken by Public Service Co. of Indiana, which in 1984 abandoned its half-finished Marble Hill plant, on which it had spent $2.5 billion. A group of Ohio utilities took the less drastic step of converting their troubled Zimmer nuclear project into a coal-fired plant, and in 1990 Consumers Power in Michigan opened a natural-gas-powered plant in a facility that had been built as a nuclear station.

The sorry state of the nuclear industry brought criticism from voices far removed from the antinuclear movement. One of the most dramatic statements came in a 1985 cover story in *Forbes* magazine, which declared: "The failure of the U.S. nuclear power program ranks as the largest managerial disaster in business history."

Yet another blow to nuclear power came in 1986, with the serious accident at the Chernobyl reactor in the Soviet Union. The U.S. nuclear industry hastened to point out that the graphite technology used at Chernobyl was almost unknown in the United States. Yet the incident, which caused 31 deaths in the short run and ultimately thousands of cancer fatalities, represented a serious setback for the proponents of nuclear power.

For the U.S. nuclear industry it was unfortunate that the Chernobyl accident occurred while Congress was considering renewal of the Price-Anderson law on the liability of the industry in the event of an accident. The original 1957 act's $560 million liability limit (with the federal government providing $500 million of that) was to last for 10 years. The law was revised in 1965 and in 1975, with the federal government's share eventually phased out, and the maximum liability was put at the total of the industry's pooled commercial insurance coverage and assessments of $5 million that the owner of each licensed plant would be expected to make. This brought the ceiling to about $700 million by the time the law was up for renewal in 1987. Congress had been expected to raise the limit somewhat, but in the wake of Chernobyl the sentiment was for a much larger increase. In 1988 a 15-year extension of Price-Anderson was enacted with a tenfold increase, to $7.1 billion, in the liability ceiling. Yet if damages exceeded that amount, the president was authorized to request that Congress appropriate additional compensation.

In the late 1980s the major controversy concerning nuclear power was the battle between the federal government and several states on the safety issue. Since states and localities had been given responsibility for developing evacuation plans for nuclear accidents, officials skeptical about reactor safety could create significant obstacles in the licensing process. This is what happened in New England and New York at the Seabrook and Shoreham plants.

President Reagan moved to eliminate this local nuisance in November 1988 with the issuing of an executive order giving the federal government the right to draw up evacuation plans when local authorities fail to do so. The order—withheld until just after the presidential election to prevent presidential candidate Michael Dukakis from using it against George Bush—may not have been of much immediate help to supporters of Seabrook and Shoreham. By the time Reagan acted, the operators of Seabrook were close to getting approval for their evacuation plan. Their main problems were, instead, financial. Public Service Company of New Hampshire, the lead utility in the Seabrook project, had filed for Chapter 11 bankruptcy in January 1988. In March 1990 Seabrook finally received an operating license.

The Nuclear Regulatory Commission also voted to award an operating license to Shoreham in 1989, but by that time beleaguered Long Island Lighting (known as Lilco) had finally reached an agreement with New York State for the closing of the facility. Lilco also came close to a Chapter 11 filing after a federal jury in 1988 found the company guilty of fraud in obtaining rate increases to help pay for Shoreham. The verdict was overturned by the judge, but Lilco nonetheless agreed to a settlement with the plaintiffs under which proposed rate increases would be kept lower for 10 years.

At the heart of the dilemma facing Lilco and other reactor builders was that, even when they overcame the safety obstacles, economics had turned against them. During the 1980s nuclear power, far from being "too cheap to meter," had become more expensive than competing fuels such as coal. When residents of Sacramento, California, voted in 1989 to shut down their municipally owned nuclear plant, Rancho Seco—the first time voters have decided to close a working reactor—the main reason was that it had simply become too expensive to operate.

The nuclear industry began a campaign in the late 1980s to overcome this problem by promoting reactors as environmentally superior to oil and coal plants. Citing global warming, acid rain, and massive oil spills as the consequences of using fossil fuels, the industry once again sought to present nuclear power as the cleaner, safer alternative. By the beginning of the 1990s there were no signs that this campaign was having any great effect. Utilities were not ordering new reactors, even though many operating plants were approaching retirement age. The future of the peaceful use of atomic energy remains very much in question. The Persian Gulf crisis of 1990 did, however, increase the chances of a new focus on nuclear power.

UPHEAVAL AMONG THE UTILITIES

Nuclear problems were only a part of the travails that were plaguing the electric utility industry. In the 1960s the problem was a shortage of capacity, a situation illustrated most dramatically by the huge blackout in the Northeast in November 1965. This shortfall in supply was brought on by rapid population growth and the proliferation of electric devices (air conditioners, dishwashers, etc.) in the home.

The Federal Power Commission was pressing utilities to

improve transmission links between systems in order to make more efficient use of existing capacity, but the companies resisted. Instead many of them focused on increasing their own capacity by building large nuclear plants, with the results discussed above.

The slowdown in the growth of demand in the aftermath of the oil shock stunned both the utilities that were building nuclear plants and those that were relying exclusively on fossil fuels and hydro. The utilities were also hit hard by rising interest rates and the high cost of the pollution control equipment they were obliged to install in the coal-fired generating plants that the federal government promoted during the 1970s. Consumers—acting through groups such as the citizens utility boards organized in a number of states—fought against rate increases; and many state commissions, faced with these protests over "rate shock," rejected utility requests or granted small increases.

More than one third of the states refused to allow the costs of construction work in progress (CWIP) in the rate base, and many state regulatory commissions were becoming resistant to allowing the bloated costs of completed nuclear projects to become permanent additions to the rate base. (The Supreme Court ruled in 1986 that utilities could not recover the cost of plants that were canceled during construction or shut down after completion.)

In the late 1970s and early 1980s the business press began to speculate whether electric utilities were still a viable business, and discussion of government takeovers was increasing among observers not usually given to talk of public ownership of industry. The decline of oil prices and interest rates eased the crisis, and the industry began an ideological counterattack. Less rather than more government intervention was said to be the solution to the problems of utilities; the surprising new topic of debate was the possible deregulation of the industry. This new notion was part of a dramatic transformation of the electric utility industry—involving both the ways in which power was produced and marketed, and the scope of utility business operations—that began in the 1980s. Among the major elements were the following.

Cogeneration

Back in the late 1970s Congress was eager to do anything to encourage energy conservation. The Public Utilities Regulatory Policies Act of 1978 furthered this goal by requiring utilities to purchase power that was produced through cogeneration. This is the process by which large industrial facilities use the heat thrown off in their operations to generate power for internal use as well as extra amounts that can be sold to others.

What started out as an incidental process has now become a big business. Companies such as Combustion Engineering (now part of Zurich-based ABB, Asea Brown Boveri) have put up plants solely to produce power to sell to utilities. By late 1989 nonutility generators accounted for 30 percent of U.S. generating capacity under construction, and by the end of the century they are expected to supply about one tenth of the country's power requirements.

Competition

There has also been a change in the transmission part of the business as large industrial users have begun to purchase power from distant utilities. The power is "wheeled in" over the lines of the local utility, which is paid a fee for that service. Utilities have been doing more wheeling themselves in order to buy or sell excess power from each other, but they don't like it when one of their customers begins to treat them like a "common carrier" rather than an exclusive supplier. To try to hold onto large customers being lured by competing utilities or cogenerators, some utilities began discounting industrial rates while raising residential rates to make up the difference.

Deregulation

Developments such as these gave rise to the argument that market forces are playing a much greater role in the electricity business and thus government regulation (particularly at the federal level) is no longer needed. In 1989 the Federal Energy Regulatory Commission suggested that any power plant be permitted to send electricity anywhere in the country, but the agency set no timetable for implementing this radical change.

Utilities are split on the issue of deregulation. Some are

worried about losing their traditional guaranteed profit margins, while others are worried that competition will drive down prices or that a variety of suppliers could make it difficult to guarantee universal service.

Diversification

There is greater agreement among utilities on the need to diversify into other businesses, in part to make up for the declining profitability of electric power. Lenient state regulators have permitted utility companies, suddenly flush with cash thanks to reduced costs, to take on new activities such as oil and gas exploration, land development, leasing, banking, venture capital, and cable television. Yet many regulators are concerned that the utilities are not paying sufficient attention to their core business.

Some utilities have been attentive to the business of other utilities. Along with diversifying, several power companies have embarked on acquisition binges. One of the most active buyers has been PacifiCorp of Portland, Oregon, which in 1989 purchased Utah Power & Light in the largest utility merger in half a century. An even bigger deal, the $2.6 billion takeover of San Diego Gas & Electric by SCEcorp. (parent of Southern California Edison), as of this writing has not received regulatory approval. Also awaiting the final federal go-ahead is the takeover of Public Service of New Hampshire (driven into Chapter 11 by the financial burdens of Seabrook) by Northeast Utilities.

In all, life is now much brighter for the electric utilities than it was in the 1970s. Lower interest rates and fuel costs and the winding down of many massive construction projects, along with a stronger economy, have helped the bottom line. Yet the consequences of increasing competition and diversification are only beginning to be felt and understood.

LABOR RELATIONS

Initial organizing in the utility business came under the auspices of the International Brotherhood of Electrical Workers and the United Electrical, Radio and Machine Workers of America. A more concerted drive in the industry came in 1938, when the CIO formed the Utility Workers Organizing Committee (UWOC). The UWOC set out to transform into true collective bargaining organizations the company unions that many of the utilities had formed. After accomplishing that objective at New York's Consolidated Edison in 1945, the committee was chartered as the Utility Workers Union of America (UWUA).

The UWUA grew to nearly 75,000 members when the AFL and the CIO merged in 1955, but it was kept relatively weak by the high degree of automation in the industry. Nevertheless, it carried out a number of strikes, the most notable being the walkouts at Con Edison in 1968 and 1983.

Labor activity related to nuclear power plants has been most tumultuous among the construction workers building them. Strikes have occurred since the building of the earliest facilities, though in 1978 construction unions and nuclear engineering companies agreed on a pact restricting strikes and lockouts on nuclear projects. Nonetheless, there have been incidents of labor unrest, including wildcat actions by workers at the Seabrook project in New Hampshire in the mid-1980s. In March 1990 about 3,000 health technicians employed by contractors at several dozen nuclear plants around the country staged a short strike as part of a drive to win union recognition.

There have also been frequent disputes at nuclear testing

The 10 Largest Electric Utility Companies, by 1989 Assets ($ Billions)

	Company	Assets
1.	Pacific Gas & Electric (San Francisco)	$21.4
2.	Southern (Atlanta)	20.1
3.	Commonwealth Edison (Chicago)	17.9
4.	Texas Utilities (Dallas)	17.2
5.	SCEcorp (Rosemead, California)	15.4
6.	American Electric Power (Columbus, Ohio)	14.7
7.	Entergy (New Orleans)	14.7
8.	Public Service Enterprise (Newark, N.J.)	12.9
9.	Philadelphia Electric	12.7
10.	FPL Group (North Palm Beach, Florida)	12.3

Source: *Fortune*, June 4, 1990.

and fuel production facilities, especially with the Oil, Chemical and Atomic Workers (OCAW). Karen Silkwood, a worker and OCAW member at a Kerr-McGee plutonium plant, was trying to expose unsafe conditions at the facility when she was killed in a suspicious car crash in 1974. She later became a heroine of the antinuclear movement. A desire to keep safety problems quiet is common throughout the nuclear industry. In 1989 three utilities admitted to the NRC that settlements they had reached with employees in lawsuits had included provisions preventing the plaintiffs from revealing safety problems.

The nuclear workers that are hardest for unions to organize are those known as "jumpers." These temporary employees are brought in to enter reactors for short periods, perhaps 10 minutes, to make a few adjustments to the equipment before they are "burned out"—that is, they get their maximum dosage of radiation.

LEADING COMPANIES

General Electric (GE), put together by J. P. Morgan in 1892, took Thomas Edison's designs and became the leader of the electrical equipment business—a position that caused it to be a major culprit in the price-fixing case brought against the industry in the 1960s. In the 1950s it also emerged as one of the two leading nuclear reactor producers. GE received its last reactor order in 1974 but continued to earn revenues (albeit a small portion of the giant company's total) from services and fuel for existing reactors. During the 1980s GE was the target of several lawsuits filed by utilities charging that the company's reactor designs were flawed. In 1987 confidential company documents were discovered that revealed the existence of concerns within GE in the mid-1970s about the quality of reactors that were being aggressively marketed. GE settled the most important of the cases—a fraud and racketeering suit brought by the three utilities that sponsored the Zimmer plant near Cincinnati—in 1987 with a payment of $78 million.

PacifiCorp has gone from being an obscure player in the utility business to holding a position at the forefront of the transformation of the industry. While still known as Pacific Power & Light in the 1960s, the Portland, Oregon-based company was a pioneer of diversification, moving from electric power into coal, telecommunications, and financial services. In early 1989 PacifiCorp completed a $1.8 billion acquisition of Utah Power & Light, the largest merger of two utilities in 50 years. Later that year the company offered more than $2 billion for Arizona Public Service (owned by Pinnacle West Capital) and later expanded the bid to include the holding company. The bid was later dropped after Pinnacle West agreed to an arrangement in which PacifiCorp will get low-cost access to power generated by an Arizona Public Service plant.

Westinghouse Electric has been the major rival of General Electric since the turn of the century and has become the nation's leading producer of nuclear reactors. Founded by inventor and entrepreneur George Westinghouse in 1886, the company by the mid-1980s was estimated to be earning as much as one third of its net income from nuclear activities, especially abroad. Its most controversial foreign project was a $2.2 billion reactor project started in the Philippines during the Marcos regime. Westinghouse has been accused of bribing Marcos to get the contract. After taking power, the Aquino government refused to begin operation of the plant because of safety concerns—the reactor was built near a volcano—and evidence of faulty construction.

INDUSTRY DATA

Investor-Owned Electric Utilities	*1989*	*1988*	*1987*
Industry revenues	$133 billion	$135 billion	$129 billion
Total employment	518,584	513,742	523,868
Import penetration	0.4%	1.2%	1.9%

Source: Edison Electric Institute.

SOURCE GUIDE

Leading Stock Analysts and Experts

Charles Benore, utilities analyst at Paine Webber.

Leonard Hyman, utilities analyst at Merrill Lynch.

Ernest Liu, utilities analyst at Goldman Sachs.

National Economic Research Associates, a utility consulting firm in White Plains, New York.

Trade Associations and Unions

American Public Power Association (municipally owned utilities), 2301 M Street NW, Washington, DC 20037. Tel.: (202) 775–8300.

Edison Electric Institute (investor-owned utilities), 1111 19th Street NW, Washington, DC 20036. Tel.: (202) 778–6400.

International Brotherhood of Electrical Workers, 1125 15th Street NW, Washington, DC 20005. Tel.: (202) 833–7000.

Oil, Chemical and Atomic Workers International Union, 255 Union Blvd., Lakewood, CO 80228. Tel.: (303) 987–2229.

U.S. Council for Energy Awareness (nuclear industry lobby), 1776 I Street NW, Washington, DC 20006. Tel.: (202) 293–0770.

Utility Workers Union of America, 815 16th Street NW, Washington, DC 20006. Tel.: (202) 347–8105.

Data Sources and Directories

Electric Power Monthly, Electric Power Annual, Monthly Energy Review, International Energy Annual, and the annual *Commercial Nuclear Power* (Washington, D.C.: U.S. Energy Information Administration).

Electrical World Directory of Electric Utilities, annual (New York: McGraw-Hill).

International Directory of Nuclear Utilities, annual (Lakewood, Colo.: Lotte Ltd.).

Moody's Public Utility Manual, an annual volume of financial data on individual utilities (New York: Moody's Investors Services).

Nuclear Energy Data, annual (Paris: Nuclear Energy Agency/OECD).

P.U.R. Analysis of Investor-Owned Electric and Gas Utilities, an annual directory and data source (Arlington, Va.: Public Utilities Reports).

Statistical Yearbook of the Electric Utility Industry (Washington, D.C.: Edison Electric Institute).

Online Databases

DOE ENERGY (Washington, D.C.: U.S. Department of Energy; available via DIALOG).

ELECTRIC POWER DATABASE (Palo Alto, Calif.: Electric Power Research Institute; available via DIALOG).

ELECTRIC POWER INDUSTRY ABSTRACTS (Washington, D.C.: Edison Electric Institute; available via ORBIT).

Trade Publications

Electric Light & Power, monthly.

Electric Utility Week.

Electrical World, monthly.

Independent Power Report, fortnightly.

Nuclear Fuel, fortnightly.

Nucleonics Week.

Power, monthly.

Public Utilities Fortnightly.

Books and Reports

Bupp, Irvin C., and Jean-Claude Derian. *Light Water: How the Nuclear Dream Dissolved*. New York: Basic Books, 1978.

Critical Mass Energy Project. *On Again, Off Again: The Unreliability of U.S. Nuclear Power Plants*. Washington, D.C., 1989.

Hertsgaard, Mark. *Nuclear Inc.: The Men and Money Behind Nuclear Energy*. New York: Pantheon Books, 1983.

Hirsh, Richard F. *Technology and Transformation in the American Electric Utility Industry*. New York: Cambridge University Press, 1989.

Investor Responsibility Research Center. *Generating Energy Alternatives: Demand-side Management and Renewable Energy at America's Electric Utilities*. Washington, D.C., 1987.

_______. *Mergers and Financial Restructuring in the Electric Power Industry*. Washington, D.C., 1988.

_______. *Plugging into Canada: Prospects for U.S.-Canadian Trade*. Washington, D.C., 1988.

Johnson, John W. *Insuring Against Disaster: The Nuclear Industry on Trial.* Macon, Ga.: Mercer University Press, 1986.

Kemeny Commission. *Report of the President's Commission on the Accident at Three Mile Island.* Washington, D.C., 1979.

Munson, Richard. *The Power Makers: The Inside Story of America's Biggest Business.* Emmaus, Penn.: Rodale Press, 1985.

Novarro, Peter. *The Dimming of America: The Real Costs of Electric Utility Regulatory Failure.* Cambridge, Mass.: Ballinger, 1985.

Stoler, Peter. *Decline and Fall: The Ailing Nuclear Power Industry.* New York: Dodd Mead, 1985.

Taylor, June, and Michael Yokell. *Yellowcake: The International Uranium Cartel.* Elmsford, N.Y.: Pergamon Press, 1980.

U.S. Congress, Office of Technology Assessment. *Electric Power Wheeling and Dealing: Technological Considerations for Increasing Competition.* Washington, D.C., 1989.

______. *Nuclear Power in an Age of Uncertainty.* Washington, D.C., 1984.

U.S. Department of Energy. *The Future of Electric Power in America* (Chiles Report). Washington, D.C., 1983.

U.S. Nuclear Regulatory Commission Special Inquiry Group. *Three Mile Island: A Report to the Commissioners and to the Public* (Rogovin Report). Washington, D.C., 1980.

CHAPTER 18

OIL AND NATURAL GAS

The petroleum industry is one of the main pillars of the American economy. Its output is essential both to the country's energy needs (transportation, heating, power, light, etc.) and as a raw material for a long list of industries, including chemicals, textiles, drugs, and plastics. The value of the crude oil and natural gas produced in the United States in 1989 was some $74 billion, and the products of petroleum refineries another $147 billion. Oil companies account for one third of the 20 largest U.S. industrial corporations, and until 1988 (when it slipped to number three) industry leader Exxon alternated with General Motors for the top spot.

The recent history of the industry has been especially tumultuous. With the rapid increase of oil prices in the early 1970s, the industry became a favorite villain of everyone from consumers to the president of the United States. Yet the fat days of the oil business came to an end with the slump of oil prices in the 1980s. Once-invincible companies found themselves under attack as corporate raiders sought to dismantle some of the giants. The battle prompted companies to arrange friendly mergers that resulted in some of the largest deals in U.S. business history and the disappearance of some of the industry's most familiar names. Other companies adjusted to the new environment and made themselves less vulnerable to takeover by massive restructuring moves. As the 1990s began, the "oil patch" was still trying to recover from the most trying period in its history. Then a new crisis in the Middle East once again made the industry a controversial center of attention.

FROM TITUSVILLE TO SPINDLETOP

The U.S. petroleum industry began in the 1850s with the determination of a man named Edwin Drake to prove that oil, previously seen only in places where it seeped out of the ground, could be obtained directly through the drilling of wells. Drake, working with New York lawyer George Bissell, began his explorations (which were subjected to a great deal of public derision) near Titusville, Pennsylvania. On August 27, 1859, his drill struck oil and gave birth to a new kind of gold rush.

Only five years earlier the kerosene lamp had been invented, and the possibility of a new source of light, to supplant the traditional candle wax and whale oil, was realized. The kerosene in use was derived from coal; Drake's discovery promised a more accessible supply of energy. Within only a few years kerosene produced from oil almost entirely displaced the coal-derived variety.

The large number of undercapitalized entrepreneurs who rushed into the oil business and the irregularity of their output made for a very unstable industry. Prices bounced up and down as supply vacillated. As oil historians like to say, the business was ripe for consolidation.

The man who took on that task as his life's work was a young entrepreneur named John D. Rockefeller. The son of a con artist who abandoned his family and of a deeply religious woman, Rockefeller managed to combine ruthless business practices with a sense of philanthropic responsibility. In 1863 he set up a kerosene refining business with two partners in Cleveland. He soon bought out the co-owners and embarked on a single-minded drive to take over as much of the business as he could—the refining and transportation aspects of the industry, that is, since Rockefeller decided that the exploration end was too risky.

Rockefeller's company went public in 1870 under the name of Standard Oil Company. For the rest of the century Standard employed every device, legal and not so legal, to dominate the industry. It grew large enough to dictate terms to the railroads and thus enjoyed freight charges substantially lower than those paid by its dwindling rivals. Rockefeller allowed competitors to operate in limited areas, but if they grew too large Standard waged unbridled price wars to keep them in place or take them over. Standard was also far and away the leading exporter and the dominant player in the international oil market.

To get around an Ohio law limiting a corporation's ownership of shares of companies in other states, Rockefeller created an arrangement that became known as the Standard Oil Trust, in which Standard's subsidiaries were nominally independent but were controlled by a centralized board of trustees. In 1892 the Ohio Supreme Court struck down the plan, so the holding company for the trust was converted to Standard Oil of New Jersey, a state that had adopted more liberal rules regarding out-of-state ownership.

The first challenge to Standard's domination came with the development of the Baku fields in Russia by the Nobel brothers of Sweden. Working with the Rothschilds of France, the Nobels provided Europe with an alternative source of supply. Then the industry in the United States was transformed by the discovery of oil in Texas. Beginning with the 1901 gusher at Spindletop near Beaumont, the Texas wells began producing at levels far in excess of those in Pennsylvania. The dominance of the Southwest was clinched when additional finds were made in Oklahoma and Louisiana. The leading companies to emerge from the region were Gulf Oil, built with money from the Mellons of Pittsburgh, and the Texas Company, later known as Texaco.

Just as Standard's predominance began to erode a bit, public opposition to the trust reached its height, helped by muckraking books such as Ida Tarbell's unflattering history of Standard. The Roosevelt administration brought antitrust charges against the Rockefeller empire, and in 1909 a federal court ruled that the Standard Oil Trust was illegal under the Sherman Act. The case went all the way to the Supreme Court, which upheld the ruling and ordered the dissolution of Standard into more than 30 independent companies.

The distribution of stock in the new companies was done according to the ownership of Standard's shares, which raised questions as to the degree of autonomy of the firms, but there is no question that the monolithic Standard Oil was no more.

The largest of the spin-offs were Standard Oil of New Jersey (often called Jersey Standard and officially renamed Exxon in 1972), Standard Oil Company of New York (Socony, which went through several name changes until becoming Mobil in 1966), Standard Oil Company of California (Socal, which was renamed Chevron in 1984), and Standard Oil of Indiana (which took the name Amoco in 1985).

OIL PLAYS IN THE MIDDLE EAST

By the second decade of the 20th century oil had become a strategic resource as well as a commodity. The use of motorized ground transportation, airplanes, and oil-fueled ships made petroleum crucial to the war effort. With the return of peace, oil continued its rise to prominence as the fuel of the automobile age.

The importance of oil made the major international powers eager to obtain direct control over supplies of the precious black liquid. Great Britain, no longer able to count on its domestic supplies of coal, focused its efforts in the Middle East. The first arena was Persia, where the British backed William D'Arcy, a speculator who had obtained a 500,000-square-mile concession in 1901. After a major discovery was made in 1908, the Anglo-Persian Oil Company (renamed Anglo-Iranian in 1935 and British Petroleum in 1954) was formed.

The next move was in Mesopotamia (Iraq), which was nominally ruled by the sultan of the Ottoman Empire. A flamboyant Armenian entrepreneur named Calouste Gulbenkian gained the confidence of the sultan and paved the way for the creation of the Turkish Petroleum Company (TPC) in 1912. TPC came to be controlled by the Anglo-Persian Oil Company, Deutsche Bank, and Royal Dutch/Shell (the British-Dutch firm that was established to challenge Standard Oil). For his efforts Gulbenkian got a one-twentieth share and came to be known as "Mr. Five Percent." With the onset of World War I Deutsche Bank's share was expropriated by the British.

By the 1920s the U.S. government grew uneasy over the

British dominance of the vast reserves of the Middle East and the exclusion of American firms. This was a result at least in part of the shortage scare created by the leading producers. In 1920 the director of the U.S. Geological Survey, using data supplied by the companies, declared that American reserves were declining rapidly. The result was a sharp increase in domestic prices and the creation of the Federal Oil Conservation Board, which encouraged higher prices by restricting output, a practice that had been initiated at the state level by the Texas Railroad Commission. Another consequence was a consensus in Washington that greater access to foreign oil was imperative.

Accordingly, the U.S. government began espousing an open-door policy to the British and urged leading American producers to band together to press for a share of the Mideast action. A group of seven companies originally joined the effort, but an increase of supplies in the United States (the shortage turned out to be short-lived) prompted most of them to drop out.

When an agreement for U.S. participation in TPC, renamed Iraq Petroleum, was worked out in 1928, only Jersey Standard and Socony remained. They and their partners, which now included the French state-owned Compagnie Française des Pétroles, agreed not to compete with one another for concessions in a huge area representing the old Ottoman Empire. To supplement what came to be called the Red Line arrangement, the heads of Jersey Standard, Royal Dutch/Shell, and Anglo-Persian met secretly at Achnacarry, a hunting lodge in Scotland, in 1928. Cooking up what became known as the As-Is agreement, the oil barons pooled the world market (aside from the United States and the Soviet Union) and divided it up according to existing shares of the major producers. Any expansion of the business was supposed to preserve those relationships. This was the first international oil cartel.

Although the architects of As-Is continued to dominate the global oil market outside the United States, they were unable to prevent competitors from expanding. Socal got a foothold in Bahrain, and Gulf Oil in partnership with Anglo-Iranian obtained a valuable concession in Kuwait. The most notable defiance came in Saudi Arabia. Socal got a vast concession from King Ibn Saud and in 1938 ended up finding the world's largest reserves. The California company had so much oil that it cut Texaco into the deal. The two firms formed the Caltex joint venture and later turned it into the Arab American Oil Co., or Aramco. In 1945 Jersey Standard and Socony joined the Saudi consortium.

Postwar demand for petroleum products increased smartly with the growth of air transport and the spread of home heating systems using oil and gas. There was also increased use of petroleum as a raw material in chemical production, including plastics and fertilizers, and in the manufacturing of products such as synthetic rubber and pharmaceuticals.

The growing market made the search for supplies a constant preoccupation of the major international producers, known collectively as the Seven Sisters: Jersey Standard, Socony, Socal, Gulf, Texaco, Royal Dutch/Shell, and British Petroleum.

THE ROAD TO OPEC

Yet it became increasingly difficult for the multinationals to exercise over Third-World governments the kind of absolute control they enjoyed early in the century. The challenge to foreign companies witnessed during the Mexican Revolution appeared again in Venezuela in the 1930s and 1940s. After a large oil discovery was made in that country in 1922, the major producers propped up the cooperative despot General Juan Vincente Gomez. When the dictator died in 1935, the government took a much harder line against the foreign oil giants. Taxes were raised, customs duties began to be enforced, and a new protective labor law for oil workers was passed.

The most significant blow to the companies was the government's insistence on a new financial arrangement that gave it a 50 percent share of oil income, a considerably higher figure than the Seven Sisters were used to giving the host country. The Venezuelan deal inspired other oil-producing countries to demand better terms, and before long the 50–50 split was standard.

However, when the Iranian government under Mohammed Mossadegh tried to go farther and nationalize the oil industry, the West struck back: a CIA-aided coup overthrew Mossadegh in 1953. Yet the shah, who was reinstalled in the throne, proved to be difficult to control. He did initially let U.S. companies get a share of Iranian production, but in the late 1950s he asserted greater control over the country's oil operations and turned to the Italian state-owned petroleum company ENI, which offered a deal more favorable to Iran.

The terms achieved by Iran helped to inspire a group of eight oil-producing countries to meet in Baghdad in 1960 and form the Organization of Petroleum Exporting Countries (OPEC), which a dozen years later would turn the world upside down. As *Fortune* put it in 1965, "OPEC wants to do for international oil what the Texas Railroad Commission has done for U.S. oil."

The challenge to the Seven Sisters came not only from their Third-World hosts. The 1950s also saw the rise in the United States of aggressive competitors that became known as the independents. Taking advantage of a tax provision that the majors had won (which allowed U.S. companies to deduct foreign royalties from their American tax liability), companies such as Continental, Marathon, and Getty became aggressive explorers abroad. The accelerating hunt for oil by both U.S. and foreign companies brought about many new sources of supply.

The result was that while demand kept on increasing, the faster growth of supply tended to keep prices lower than the oil producers would have liked. The willingness of the independent producers to undercut the prices of the majors and sell crude to independent refiners at a discount also contributed to the trend. The flood of cheap oil into the United States worried the majors, and they turned to the federal government for help. Persuading Congress and the Eisenhower administration that the country was becoming dangerously dependent on foreign oil, the majors succeeded in getting a provision inserted in a 1955 trade bill that gave the president the right to institute mandatory limits on oil imports. Critics of the program (which remained in effect until 1973) wondered how it improved national security, but there was little doubt that the import quotas boosted prices and restricted the growth of the independents.

THE GROWTH OF GAS

Another element that entered into the changing competitive situation of the energy industry after World War II was the rising importance of natural gas. The history of commercial gas usage in the United States extends back to the early 19th century, when a synthetic version derived from coal was used for lighting in various parts of the country.

Gas use waned with the growth of the oil industry. The natural gas often found along with oil or in deposits by itself tended to be burned off at the well. This was not because the gas was useless; in fact it was and is a very efficient and clean energy source. The problem was the difficulty in transporting the gas over long distances, which contributed to its low price.

In the 1920s the development of acetylene welding made possible the construction of pipelines through which natural gas could be transported over longer distances at high pressure. By the 1950s natural gas was being widely distributed around the country to both residential and industrial users. During the same period techniques were developed for freezing the gas to subzero temperatures, thus converting it into a liquid and permitting it to be transported by ship.

Natural gas was important enough by the late 1930s to prompt Congress to pass legislation regulating its pricing. Yet the wording of the Natural Gas Act of 1938 was somewhat ambiguous, and the gas-producing industry waged a battle against the authority of the Federal Power Commission (FPC) to regulate wellhead prices—that is, what was charged by the producer to the pipeline operator.

In 1954 the Supreme Court upheld the FPC's jurisdiction over wellhead prices, but the producers kept fighting. Congress voted in 1956 to end price regulation. However, the revelation of attempts by an industry lobbyist to make improper payments to members of Congress caused President Eisenhower to veto the bill.

Upon taking office in 1969, President Nixon expressed some sympathy with the complaints of the natural gas industry and appointed a like-minded lawyer, John Nassikas, to head the FPC. The commission did everything possible under the law to ease regulation of the industry and allow prices to rise, but the producers hungered for complete decontrol.

The announcement by the American Gas Association of a sudden plunge in gas reserves amounting to some 5.5 trillion cubic feet was used by the industry to justify higher prices, which were supposed to encourage exploration, while critics charged that the industry was fabricating the shortage to blackmail the country. This dispute became all the more fierce with the actual supply shortages that occurred at times during the 1970s, alternating with dearths of other energy products such as heating oil and gasoline.

The pressures for decontrol persisted, but when Congress in 1978 finally passed such a measure, the Natural Gas Policy Act, it embodied a compromise with the proponents of continued regulation. The law phased in decontrol of newly discovered gas over a seven-year period and in the interim subjected the intrastate sale of gas, which had previously been exempt from federal rules, to the same controls.

UPHEAVAL IN OIL

Meanwhile the oil scene had become even more tumultuous. The late 1960s saw the industry battling on fronts both at home and abroad. In 1968 an upstart company called Atlantic Richfield made a major discovery of oil in the North Slope area of Alaska. Other companies rushed in to participate in the bonanza, but the problem was how to get the oil from the frozen region where it was being drilled to a port from which it could be transported to the rest of the country.

The industry came up with an ambitious plan to construct an 800-mile-long pipeline from Prudhoe Bay down through the entire state to the port of Valdez in the south. The plan, one of the largest engineering efforts of all time, elicited loud protests from the growing environmental movement, which expressed concern over how the 48-inch-in-diameter pipeline (through which oil would travel at temperatures of around 140 degrees) would affect the delicate tundra. The environmentalists, who gained considerable support after the major offshore oil spill near Santa Barbara, California, in 1969, managed to tie up the project for years with court challenges. But in the end congressional intervention allowed the project, redesigned to reduce ecological damage, to go through. Nonetheless, the construction of the pipeline was fraught with engineering setbacks, faulty welding (some of which contractors tried to cover up), and other problems, which ended up pushing the final cost to some $9 billion.

The foreign challenges came from the countries where the bulk of the world's oil was extracted. The OPEC nations had little success in the mid-1960s in raising their prices. But things changed after the radical Muammar Qaddafi took power in Libya in 1969 and successfully pressured foreign companies to part with a higher percentage of their income. Other OPEC members were inspired to demand better terms for themselves. In 1971 the cartel for the first time reached agreement on raising the minimum price for a barrel of oil. The basic price, which had remained steady at $1.80 a barrel throughout the 1960s, thus began a slow ascent that brought it to a bit over $3 by late 1973.

After war broke out in the Middle East in October 1973, the Arab oil producers decided to use their oil as a weapon to punish U.S. support of Israel. OPEC cut back production and declared an embargo on shipments to the United States. The action lasted only five months, but the cartel also began a series of price increases that ended up quadrupling the cost of a barrel of oil.

Although evidence later came out that the United States had actually supported oil price increases to bolster its Mideast allies, the OPEC actions went much further than anticipated. The large run-up in the price of oil created turmoil in the industrialized world and made the "energy crisis" a major concern of government policy for the rest of the decade.

For the oil industry the OPEC price hikes were financially a wonderful development, but they were a public relations disaster. Much of the public believed that the oil majors either had colluded with OPEC or at least were unfairly benefiting from the oil crunch. The energy crisis was often put in military terms, and the oil companies were accused by some of "war profiteering." In 1977 President Carter accused the industry of staging "the biggest rip-off in history."

The industry, of course, denied any improper actions and claimed that its high returns were necessary to pay for the exploration needed to find new energy supplies. To make their case the majors spent millions on advocacy advertising. Mobil was the most aggressive of the bunch, regularly buying space on newspaper op-ed pages to defend the industry.

The companies also noted that the American public was cushioned from the full impact of the oil cost increase by the federal price controls that President Nixon had instituted in 1971 as part of his anti-inflation policies and that Congress insisted on keeping in place. However, the industry was confronted with a series of government investigations of violations of those controls. President Carter announced in 1979 that he would support the ending of price controls but got Congress to agree to subject the industry to a windfall profits tax for the transition period.

Public controversy over the oil companies' actions escalated with the diversification moves that the majors began to make. Mobil completed its purchase of Marcor, owner of retailer Montgomery Ward and Container Corp. of America, in 1976. Atlantic Richfield purchased copper miner Anaconda in 1977, and other companies such as Exxon, Gulf, and Socal made major investments in mineral producers. This was in addition to earlier moves into coal and uranium.

The reputation of the oil companies was further besmirched in the mid-1970s by revelations that a number of firms, most notably Gulf, had made large amounts of improper campaign contributions in the United States and payoffs to government officials abroad.

The industrialized world had largely adapted to the sharp oil price rises of 1973–74 and the slow ascent in the following years, when another shock came in 1979. In the wake of the cutback in oil production during the Iranian revolution, prices on the spot market (oil not under contract) leaped as high as $40, and OPEC hiked up its prices as high as $23. Supply was a problem as well as price: the United States experienced severe gasoline shortages in the spring and summer of 1979. Long lines of angry drivers at filling stations often erupted in violence.

GLUT AND SLUMP

The second oil shock forced individuals and corporations in the United States to make serious changes in the way they used energy. Although many of the conservation measures proposed by President Carter never passed Congress, energy efficiency became the order of the day. This, combined with switching to alternative fuels and the onset of economic recession (induced in part by high energy prices), caused the demand for oil to sink. U.S. consumption dropped from 6.9 billion barrels in 1978 to 5.6 billion in 1982, and imports fell even faster.

A similar pattern through the rest of the industrial world helped put downward pressure on international oil prices. By 1982 spot prices were falling rapidly, and OPEC members and other producing countries initiated a round of price-cutting. In 1983 OPEC officially decreased its base prices for the first time in the cartel's history.

The decline of oil prices spelled trouble for U.S. petroleum companies. The Southwest lost its affluent Sun Belt aura and became one of the most depressed regions of the country. Smaller players went under, and among the larger companies there was a dramatic period of restructuring.

The latter included a series of different processes that changed the face of the oil patch. First, there was a wave of consolidation as giant companies gobbled up one another. In 1981 Du Pont emerged from a complicated takeover battle having bought Continental (Conoco) for $7.2 billion. The following year Occidental Petroleum bought Cities Service for $4 billion, and U.S. Steel (now USX) defeated Mobil in a battle for Marathon Oil, paying $5.9 billion for its prize. In 1984 Texaco bought Getty for $10.1 billion, and Mobil acquired Superior Oil for $5.7 billion. U.S. Steel completed the $3 billion purchase of Texas Oil & Gas in 1986. British Petroleum, which had joined forces with Standard Oil of Ohio in an Alaskan North Slope joint venture in the late 1960s and later acquired 55 percent of

Sohio, completed its takeover of the company in 1987 in an $8 billion deal.

In the case of the Texaco purchase of Getty, the deal turned out to have unexpected and profound consequences. Texaco was sued by Pennzoil, which said it had a prior agreement to buy part of Getty. A Texas court ruled in favor of Pennzoil and awarded it an astounding $10 billion in damages. After failing in its court appeals Texaco filed for Chapter 11 in 1987 and reached a $3 billion settlement with Pennzoil.

The industry was also thrown into turmoil by the actions of a maverick oilman named T. Boone Pickens, chairman of the relatively small Mesa Petroleum. Charging that the managements of numerous large oil firms were not making the best use of their assets, Pickens launched a series of audacious hostile tender offers, with varying results. The assault on Phillips Petroleum led to a 1985 deal in which the company repurchased Mesa's shares at a profit for the Pickens company. But the same year, in the case of Unocal, Pickens was defeated and was excluded when management repurchased more than $4 billion worth of its shares. In the most dramatic battle, Gulf agreed in 1984 to be acquired by Chevron for $13.2 billion to escape the clutches of Pickens.

The industry has also resorted to a variety of financial moves to adjust to the slump and to prevent stock prices from sinking too low. Firms such as Exxon and Amoco announced common-share repurchase plans. In many cases assets have been written down or sold off, exploration efforts have been scaled back drastically, and large numbers of employees have been laid off or pressured to take early retirement. Some smaller companies such as Mesa Petroleum have turned themselves into master limited partnerships, under which their oil properties are packaged as partnerships and sold to the public.

In early 1986 the woes of the industry intensified as the decline in oil prices accelerated. Spot prices dipped below $10 a barrel for the first time in nearly a decade. Oil was becoming so cheap that the industry was warning that the United States was once again becoming dangerously dependent on foreign supplies. There was talk in Congress of instituting an import fee that would discourage use of foreign oil and help prop up domestic prices, but the Reagan administration strongly opposed the idea. There was a change in climate in the summer of 1986 when OPEC members reached agreement on a plan to cut production by about 15 percent in an effort to halt the collapse of prices.

The ups and downs in the oil market have caused similar gyrations in the natural gas business. Following the second oil shock in 1979, many users switched from oil to gas. This and the workings of the Natural Gas Policy Act of 1978 led to a rapid rise in prices, prompting a debate on whether to tighten federal controls or to accelerate the pace of deregulation. The decline in oil prices ended the gas boom and shifted the policy debate in favor of the deregulators, who finally achieved their goal in 1989 when President Bush signed legislation removing all federal price controls by 1993.

By the beginning of the 1990s the pendulum was swinging back for the oil industry. Prices began moving up again, yet U.S. domestic supplies remained low because of cutbacks in drilling and production. Since demand was strong, the result was a surge in imports: 46 percent of the oil consumed in the United States in 1989 came from abroad—the highest level since the gloomy days of the late 1970s. While the petroleum producers were hoping for a return to the $40 barrel of oil, American consumers were not looking forward to a return of energy inflation.

Yet that is exactly what they got after Iraq invaded Kuwait in the summer of 1990 and precipitated a new crisis in the Middle East. Immediately after the invasion, oil prices rose sharply in spot markets, surpassing $30 a barrel in late August. Retail gasoline prices increased dramatically, prompting a new round of allegations that the oil companies were exploiting the crisis.

Once it became clear that an all-out war in the Persian Gulf was not going to happen right away, the energy market stabilized. Yet it remained highly unlikely that, whatever the political outcome of the crisis, oil prices would soon return to the depressed levels of the late 1980s.

The Top 10 U.S. Oil and Gas Producers, by 1988 Total Revenues
($ Billions)

1. Exxon	$96.285
2. Mobil	56.188
3. Texaco	35.656
4. Chevron	32.785
5. Amoco	26.760
6. Shell	21.948
7. Occidental Petroleum	20.068
8. BP America	17.688
9. Atlantic Richfield	16.815
10. Conoco	12.682

Source: *Oil & Gas Journal*, October 8, 1990.

LABOR RELATIONS

Soon after the development of the oil industry in the late 19th century, oil field workers started organizing in Pennsylvania, the main producing area. In 1899 the various small unions were consolidated into the AFL-chartered International Brotherhood of Oil and Gas Well Workers. The brotherhood, facing strong employer resistance and an inability to keep up with the geographical dispersion of the industry, was defunct by 1905.

The birth of the oil industry in Texas brought a new round of organizing, and the unions reached a high point of power during World War I. Yet after the war the industry once again moved to enforce its open-shop policy, and the unions waned. It took the National Industrial Recovery Act of 1933 to revive union activity. A national organization called the Oil Workers International Union (OWIU) achieved a number of successes and went over to the CIO.

During the 1940s and the early 1950s the OWIU suffered from persistent internal political battles and rivalries with other industry unions. Problems continued even after a 1955 merger with the United Gas, Coke and Chemical Workers of America. The combined union—renamed the Oil, Chemical and Atomic Workers (OCAW)—kept a strong foothold in the industry but did not achieve much additional growth.

The OCAW faced obstacles in the increasingly automated

refining sector of the industry and barely managed to keep wages rising and to hold onto its members. The problem got worse with the industry slump of the early 1980s. Management began demanding contract concessions, and in the mid-1980s the unemployment rate among oil workers was well above 10 percent. Yet by 1990 the situation had improved enough so that the OCAW was able to preserve its industrywide contract and win good improvements in wage rates and health insurance.

LEADING COMPANIES

Amoco is the name taken in 1985 by Standard Oil of Indiana, the Standard company that stuck to its knitting in the United States while the other majors were wheeling and dealing around the world. The company did eventually expand overseas, and it is perhaps best known as the owner of the tanker Amoco Cadiz, which ran aground off France in 1978 and created a 70-mile slick along the Brittany coast. A decade later a French court ordered the company to pay $85 million in damages. In 1988 Amoco emerged as the leader in the natural gas business with the $3.8 billion purchase of Canada's Dome Petroleum.

Atlantic Richfield (ARCO) was built over three decades by Robert O. Anderson, a Chicago banker's son who went west to make his fortune. He became a small but prosperous refiner in New Mexico in 1941 and as a wildcatter made a major discovery in the state in 1957. He merged with Atlantic Refining in 1963 and Richfield Oil in 1966. ARCO, as the company is often called, was the first firm to succeed in Alaskan exploration in the late 1960s, and the find propelled the company to a prominent place in the industry. The company, a leading proponent of corporate social responsibility, acquired the Anaconda mining company in 1977. In 1985 ARCO announced a drastic restructuring plan that involved a $4 billion stock repurchase, the sale of a refinery, and the shutting down of all marketing operations east of the Mississippi. This streamlining process, continued by Lodwrick Cook after he took over the CEO spot following Anderson's retirement in 1986, has made ARCO one of the most profitable companies in the industry.

BP America (a subsidiary of British Petroleum) is the company that resulted from BP's completion of its takeover of Standard Oil of Ohio in 1987. Sohio was the original base of the Rockefeller empire. After the breakup of the trust, Sohio remained a minor figure in the industry until it joined forces with BP in an Alaskan North Slope joint venture in the late 1960s. Sohio ended up with an abundance of crude and sold half of itself to BP in 1970 to raise capital for expansion. After a number of years of disappointing results from further exploration and the acquisition of Kennecott Copper in 1981, Sohio found itself in a less friendly relationship with BP, which ousted Sohio's management in 1986 and then acquired the 45 percent of the company it did not already own.

Chevron, known until 1984 as Standard Oil of California, has since the breakup of the Standard Oil Trust in 1911 been one of the world's leading integrated oil producers. The company, which had its roots in the Pacific Coast Oil Co. (founded in 1879), had one of its greatest moments in the 1930s, when it got a concession to explore in Saudi Arabia and found some of the world's largest reserves. In 1984 the company acted as a white knight for Gulf Oil, which was under siege from raider T. Boone Pickens. Gulf, for which Chevron paid $13.2 billion, had its beginnings in the discovery of oil in Texas in the first years of the century. The Mellon family of Pittsburgh took over the pioneering J. M. Guffey Petroleum Co. and turned Gulf into one of the world's largest oil firms. In 1988 Chevron purchased Tenneco's oil and gas reserves in the Gulf of Mexico, and late the following year Chevron found itself the subject of a possible takeover after Pennzoil used much of the $3 billion it won in its legal battle with Texaco to buy a block of Chevron stock.

Exxon, for years the world's largest oil company and now running neck and neck with Europe's Royal Dutch/Shell, was known until 1972 as Standard Oil of New Jersey. Its history goes back to the petroleum empire built by John D. Rockefeller in the late 19th century. The Standard Oil trust was originally based in Cleveland, but Jersey Standard was turned into the holding company in 1892 to get around Ohio laws prohibiting a company from owning shares in an out-of-state corporation. After the Standard Trust was broken up in 1911, Jersey Standard emerged as the biggest of the newly independent pieces. It moved aggressively to set up operations around the world as the leader of the major international firms known as the Seven Sisters. In the 1970s Exxon made an ill-fated attempt to diversify into office products. In 1986, amid the industry's severe slump, the company consolidated many of its operations and eliminated more than one fourth of its work force. That same year the Supreme Court ruled that Exxon had to pay a fine of $2.1 billion for violations of oil price controls in the 1970s. In 1989 Exxon's reputation was further besmirched when one of its tankers ran aground off the Alaskan coast, spilling some 11 million gallons of crude oil into Prince William Sound. The company, widely criticized for not responding to the disaster more quickly, was forced to spend at least $2 billion in clean-up expenses. Exxon also found itself indicted by a federal grand jury on five criminal counts in connection with the spill.

Mobil has been the most ideologically aggressive of the major oil companies. When the industry was under attack in the 1970s Mobil spent large sums on newspaper and magazine advertisements responding to critics. Mobil started life as the Standard Oil Company of New York, or Socony. After the dissolution of the Standard trust in 1911, Socony became one of the leaders among the spun-off producers. The company, which went through several names before becoming Mobil in 1966, made what turned out to be a disappointing diversification move in the mid-1970s with the purchase of Montgomery Ward and Container Corp. of America. Mobil lost out to U.S. Steel in a 1982 contest for Marathon Oil but purchased Superior Oil for $5.7 billion in 1985.

Occidental Petroleum was a virtually defunct company in 1956 when a wealthy entrepreneur named Armand Hammer took it over as a tax shelter. Hammer, who had made a name and a fortune trading with the Soviet Union, struck oil in California and decided to make "Oxy" into a serious business. The company went overseas in the 1960s and ended up with a major interest in Libya. After Muammar Qaddafi took over the country in 1969, Oxy had to hand over a larger share of the income from that operation. Hammer, who turned 90 in 1988 and still resisted retirement, diversified the company with purchases such as Iowa Beef Processors in 1977 (half of which was spun off in 1987). Oxy's Hooker Chemical subsidiary became notorious in the 1970s for its role in dumping toxic wastes into Love Canal near Buffalo, New York, where hundreds of families had to abandon their homes. The company scored a major coup with its discovery of a large oil field in Colombia in 1984. Following the lead of Lee Iacocca, Hammer published an autobiography in the late 1980s that made it onto the best-seller lists.

During the second half of the 1980s **Texaco** was living under the shadow of the largest damage award ever awarded in an American lawsuit. In 1985 a Texas court found that when Texaco moved to buy Getty Oil for $10 billion, it had improperly interfered with an agreement that Pennzoil had made to acquire part of Getty. The damages and interest added up to

INDUSTRY DATA

Crude Oil and Natural Gas	*1989*	*1988*	*1987*
Value of shipments	$74.3 billion	$67.3 billion	$76.8 billion
Total employment	NA	NA	204,000
Import penetration	NA	29.8%	28.9%

Petroleum Refining	*1989*	*1988*	*1987*
Value of shipments	$147.1 billion	$115.0 billion	$118.0 billion
Total employment	NA	NA	74,300
Import penetration	NA	8.5%	8.9%

Source: U.S. Department of Commerce.

$11 billion. After a Texas appeals court in 1987 reduced the damages by only $2 billion, Texaco filed for Chapter 11 bankruptcy. Later that year Texaco settled the dispute with Pennzoil (and dropped its appeal to the Supreme Court) by agreeing to pay $3 billion. But Texaco's troubles were not over. Corporate raider Carl Icahn acquired more than 12 percent of the company, launched a proxy battle (which he nearly won), and kept pressure on Texaco to liquidate assets. Eventually, however, Texaco chief executive James Kinnear prevailed, forcing Icahn to sign a seven-year standstill agreement. (Icahn sold his holdings, which had risen to more than 17 percent, in 1989.) Texaco started life as the Texas Company, one of the most successful producers in the early years of the oil industry in the Southwest. Texaco joined with Socal to exploit the vast reserves of Saudi Arabia in the 1930s and had controversial dealings with Franco and Hitler. After World War II Texaco spread across the country and came to be regarded as one of the Seven Sisters.

SOURCE GUIDE

Leading Stock Analysts and Experts

John S. Herold Inc., an oil consulting firm in Greenwich, Connecticut.

John Lichtblau, president of the Petroleum Industry Research Foundation, New York.

Charles Maxwell, analyst at C. J. Lawrence, New York.

Thomas Petrie, analyst at Petrie, Parkman & Co., Denver.

Bernard Picchi, analyst at Salomon Brothers.

Petroleum Industry Research Associates, a New York consulting firm.

Kurt Wulff, analyst at McDep Associates, New York.

Trade Associations and Unions

American Gas Association, 1515 Wilson Blvd., Arlington, VA 22209. Tel.: (703) 841–8400.

American Independent Refiners Association, 649 S. Olive Street, Los Angeles, CA 90014. Tel.: (213) 624–8407.

American Petroleum Institute, 1220 L Street NW, Washington, DC 20005. Tel.: (202) 682–8000.

Independent Petroleum Association of America, 1101 16th Street NW, Washington, DC 20036. Tel.: (202) 857–4722.

National Petroleum Refiners Association, 1899 L Street NW, Washington, DC 20036. Tel.: (202) 457–0480.

Oil, Chemical and Atomic Workers International Union, 255 Union Blvd., Lakewood, CO 80228. Tel.: (303) 987–2229.

Data Sources and Directories

Annual Outlook for Oil and Gas, Natural Gas Annual, Petroleum Supply Monthly, Petroleum Supply Annual, Monthly Energy Review, and *International Energy Outlook* (Washington, D.C.: U.S. Energy Information Administration).

Basic Petroleum Data Book, three times a year (Washington, D.C.: American Petroleum Institute).

Brown's Directory of North American & International Gas Companies, annual (Cleveland: Edgell Communications).

Gas Facts, annual (Arlington, Va.: American Gas Association).

International Petroleum Encyclopedia, a review of the industry, *U.S.A. Oil Industry Directory*, and *Worldwide Petrochemical Directory*, all annuals (Tulsa, Okla.: PennWell Publishing).

Oil and Gas Information, annual (Paris: International Energy Agency/OECD).

Whole World Oil Directory, annual (Wilmette, Ill.: National Register Publishing).

Online Databases

DOE ENERGY (Washington, D.C.: U.S. Department of Energy; available via DIALOG).

IPABASE (New York: John Wiley & Sons; available via ORBIT).

P/E NEWS (New York: American Petroleum Institute; available via DIALOG and ORBIT).

Trade Publications

Foster Natural Gas Report, weekly.

National Petroleum News, monthly.

Oil & Gas Journal, weekly.

Oil Daily.

Petroleum Intelligence Weekly.

Platt's Oilgram News, daily.

World Oil, monthly.

Books and Reports

Adelman, M. A. *The World Petroleum Market.* Baltimore: Johns Hopkins University Press, 1972.

Anderson, Robert O. *Fundamentals of the Petroleum Industry.* Norman, Okla.: University of Oklahoma Press, 1984.

Blair, John M. *The Control of Oil.* New York: Pantheon Books, 1977.

Liscom, William L., ed. *The Energy Decade: A Statistical and Graphic Chronicle.* Cambridge, Mass.: Ballinger, 1982.

Petzinger, Thomas. *Oil & Honor: The Texaco-Pennzoil Wars.* New York: G.P. Putnam's Sons, 1987.

Sampson, Anthony. *The Seven Sisters.* New York: Viking Press, 1975.

Sherrill, Robert. *The Oil Follies of 1970–1980.* Garden City, N.Y.: Anchor Press, 1983.

Tugendhat, Christopher. *Oil: The Biggest Business.* New York: G. P. Putnam's Sons, 1968.

Tussing, Arlon R., and Connie C. Barlow. *The Natural Gas Industry.* Cambridge, Mass.: Ballinger, 1984.

U.S. Congress, Office of Technology Assessment. *U.S. Natural Gas Availability.* Washington, D.C., 1985.

_______. *U.S. Oil Production: The Effect of Low Oil Prices.* Washington, D.C., 1987.

PART 5

FINANCE

CHAPTER 19

COMMERCIAL BANKS AND THRIFTS

Once the epitome of security and stability, the banking industry has since the 1970s taken on a precarious new identity. Buffeted by roller-coaster interest rates and inflation levels, uneven economic recovery, and other calamities, moneylending has ceased to be a safe business. Bank failures have reached levels unknown since the Great Depression, and the federal government has repeatedly had to intervene to prevent the crisis from getting out of hand.

At the same time, bankers have been challenging state and federal rules governing their freedom to expand into new geographic areas and new lines of business. Congress and federal agencies have vacillated between sympathy for these aims and a sense that continuing problems among the nation's 13,000 commercial banks and 2,500 savings institutions imply the need for more rather than less supervision. The upheaval in banking is far from over.

A CENTRAL BANK OR "WILDCAT" ONES?

Banking in the United States began with the Bank of North America, chartered by the Continental Congress in 1781 to aid the young government in financing the War of Independence. Within a few years institutions such as the Bank of New York and the Massachusetts Bank were established.

Yet the first Treasury secretary Alexander Hamilton felt that a true central bank was necessary to assist in the commercial development of the nation. Congress was persuaded, and in 1791 the First Bank of the United States was established. Yet the agrarian-oriented states' rights opponents to Hamilton's federalism carried on a battle against the bank over four decades.

After the national bank's 20-year charter was not renewed in 1811, state-chartered banks expanded without restraint. The public lost confidence in the bank notes issued by the various state institutions—the only paper currency of the time—and rushed to redeem them for "real" money, gold. Their reserves being depleted, the banks suspended payments in specie (coin) in 1814. The breakdown of the financial system revived support for a central bank; a successor institution, the Second Bank of the United States, was chartered in 1816.

Political controversy over the bank soon resumed, especially during the tenure of Nicholas Biddle as president of the bank. Biddle's aggressive promotion of the bank and expansion of its currency function prompted President Andrew Jackson, an avid opponent of institutionalized finance and tight money, to veto a bill renewing the charter of the bank in 1832.

The following three decades became known as the period of free banking, during which anyone who met minimum state requirements was able to establish a financial institution. Thousands of different kinds of bank notes circulated, most of them of dubious value outside the immediate area of the issuing bank. In fact, many notes were outright counterfeits, and others originated in "wildcat banks," so called because their offices were deliberately located in such remote spots ("out where the wildcats roam") that it was difficult for a holder of the notes to try to redeem them. Even legitimate banks came and went at an alarming rate.

The financial instability in the early years of the Civil War, as well as the government's problems in financing the war, prompted Congress to establish the first national currency in 1862. The Treasury notes were legal tender but not redeemable in specie. The following year Congress went further, creating a system under which banks would be chartered by the federal government and put under the supervision of the newly created Comptroller of the Currency.

The National Bank Act also required every bank with a national charter to redeem at full value the bank notes issued by other national banks. They were also obligated to maintain adequate reserves of gold and to deposit with the comptroller Treasury bonds equal to one third of their capital. The notes circulated by these banks, identical in size and design, were to be the nation's official currency.

To speed the conversion to this new system, Congress imposed a tax (first 2, then 10 percent) on new bank note issues by state banks. The result was not a disappearance of state banks—many still exist today—but there was a steady acceptance of the national currency and a falling-off of counterfeit and fraudulent bank notes. The financial system was more stable than in the era of free banking but not secure enough to prevent crises such as the panics of 1873, 1893, and 1907. In the latter case, which unlike the others was primarily a banking crisis, it took a special effort by leading financier J. P. Morgan to prevent a major collapse.

Events such as these shifted public sentiment once again in favor of creating a new central bank. In 1913 Congress created the Federal Reserve System. All national banks were required and state banks were encouraged to join the system, which consisted of 12 regional reserve banks and a central reserve board. Each member bank had to buy shares in the local reserve bank equal to 6 percent of its capital and surplus. Members had to maintain reserves on deposit and could also borrow (discount) funds from the reserve bank.

The first major test of the new system came in the 1920s, when a depression in agricultural prices seriously weakened banks in rural areas. The Fed was unable to prevent the failure or forced consolidation of thousands of these Main Street banks (as opposed to the larger money-center banks that had emerged in bigger cities to serve corporate clients). After reaching a peak of 31,000 in 1921, the number of banks in the country declined to less than 24,000 by the end of the decade.

THE NEW DEAL FOR BANKING

The stock market crash in 1929 made a bad situation worse. Banks had lent some $8 billion to brokerage houses to finance the margin selling that had fueled the speculative boom. As the effects of the crash spread, banks faced mounting loan losses from both companies and individuals, who had borrowed heavily in the 1920s for houses and automobiles.

In the early 1930s, as in the previous decade, the Fed was unable to halt the crisis. Nervous investors created runs on various banks across the country, prompting governors to declare "bank holidays." The situation deteriorated with reports that Franklin Roosevelt, elected president in 1932, intended to take the dollar off the gold standard. This caused runs on Federal Reserve banks, where people sought to exchange their currency for gold, as well as at commercial banks.

One of the first things Roosevelt did after taking office in March 1933 was to close all the banks for several days and attempt to restore confidence in the banking system. Roosevelt made the first of his "Fireside Chat" radio broadcasts and assured depositors that those banks that were allowed to reopen (thousands weren't) would do so with an official stamp of approval as to their solvency. The panic subsided, and a later action establishing federal insurance for bank deposits further reassured the public. In the meantime Congress passed emergency legislation taking the country off the gold standard and centralizing gold ownership in the Treasury.

The emergency measure was only the first of a series of legislative actions in the mid-1930s that transformed the financial system. The Glass-Steagall Banking Act of 1933 established the Federal Deposit Insurance Corporation (FDIC) to administer the insurance program and to oversee the financial condition of participating banks. It also prohibited the payment of interest on demand deposits (checking accounts), permitted statewide branching for national banks, and mandated the separation of commercial banking and investment banking activities.

The Banking Act of 1935 required state banks with $1 million or more in assets to join the Federal Reserve System. It also broadened the powers of the Fed to regulate bank finances, created an open-market committee in the Fed (which regulates bank reserves through buying and selling government securities), and established the Board of Governors of the Fed, from which the comptroller of the currency and the secretary of the Treasury were excluded.

The periods during and after the war were ones of much greater stability and prosperity for the banking world. If anything, bankers were cautious to a fault. While the economy was booming and personal income was rising to unprecedented levels, commercial banks focused on their traditional commercial customers.

THE RISE OF THRIFTS AND BANK HOLDING COMPANIES

Most of the new retail business went to savings banks and savings and loan associations. These thrift institutions originated in the 19th century. The first savings banks were established in Philadelphia and Boston in 1816 in order to promote thrift among the newly emerging working class. The banks saw themselves as philanthropic institutions helping the poor attain some measure of financial security—if only to have enough saved for a proper burial. Savings banks, which as mutual institutions had no stockholders, spread mainly in the Northeast and reached a peak of 666 in 1875.

Savings and loan associations (S&Ls), which originated in Pennsylvania in the 1830s, were patterned after the building societies of Britain. Their members were initially limited to people who wanted to work together to finance the building of a home for each participant, though later they accepted people who simply wanted to save.

In 1932 S&Ls came under the supervision of the newly created Federal Home Loan Bank Board (FHLBB), and two years later their deposits became insured with the creation of the Federal Savings and Loan Insurance Corporation (FSLIC). The benevolent role of the S&Ls was romanticized in the 1946 Frank Capra film *It's a Wonderful Life.*

By the 1950s the thrift institutions were taking the lead in home mortgage lending, which blossomed after World War II. The S&Ls alone increased in total assets from $17 billion in

1950 to $129 billion in 1965, at which time they were some 6,200 in number.

The thrifts, however, faced a fundamental weakness in that they tended to use short-term funds to finance long-term loans, usually at low fixed rates. This was no problem as long as the spread between the interest rates on the two (that is, the difference between the cost of funds and the rates paid by borrowers) favored the banks. In the 1970s these relative interest rates turned against the thrifts, bringing about a crisis that will be discussed in more detail below.

Meanwhile the commercial banks had awakened from their slumber. One of the first innovations came from First National City Bank of New York (Citibank) with the introduction of negotiable certificates of deposit in 1961. Comptroller of the Currency James Saxon began liberalizing regulations governing national banks, prompting Chase Manhattan of New York to trade in its state charter for a national one. Fearing a mass defection, state regulators began to loosen up as well.

Other changes of the period included the adoption of computer systems by the larger banks and an unprecedented wave of bank mergers. The bigger banks also began expanding their presence abroad, both by entering the emerging Eurodollar market and by following major U.S. corporations to the sites of their foreign investments.

Yet perhaps the most significant event was the decision by Citibank in 1968 to transform itself into a one-bank holding company. This seemingly technical move, the first by a large money-center institution, opened a period of aggressive efforts by banks, led by the newly created Citicorp, to extend the range of their activities.

The creation of the one-bank holding company was a move designed to take advantage of a loophole in the Bank Holding Company Act of 1956. That law restricted the involvement of multibank holding companies in nonbanking businesses in order to prevent them from gaining monopolistic powers. The act excluded holding companies owning only one bank from the rule, in the assumption that they would be small and thus less threatening operations.

Instead giants such as Citicorp used the loophole to enter

a wide range of new activities, such as equipment leasing, data processing services, mortgage banking, travel services, and financial counseling. The banks also began pushing for the right to expand their investment banking business, which since the Glass-Steagall Act had been limited to the underwriting of U.S. government bonds and general-obligation municipal bonds. Amendments to the Bank Holding Company Act passed by Congress in 1970 ended the distinction between one-bank and multibank entities and permitted both varieties to engage in any activity approved by the Federal Reserve.

INCREASING INSTABILITY

The halcyon days for the banks did not last long. By the early 1970s there were signs that the rapid expansion of assets, in both loans and noncredit businesses, was beginning to cause instability. The strain was intensified by the tight money policy adopted by the Fed to rein in the inflation generated by the rise in oil prices.

The most dramatic result was the collapse of the high-rolling Franklin National Bank of New York in 1974. Franklin, among others, had fallen into the dangerous trap of relying on short-term funds to make longer-term loans. This trend (like many others) had been pioneered by Citicorp. But its imitators often lacked the financial expertise to pull it off; when short-term rates started escalating, it was the undoing of Franklin, Security National of New York in 1975, and others.

Federal regulators began to express concern that even giants such as Bank of America (B of A) had taken on large quantities of risky loans in the frenzy to expand assets. In 1974 the Fed rejected proposed acquisitions by B of A, Bankers Trust, and First Chicago.

The next crisis came with the downfall of the real estate investment trusts (REITs). REITs started expanding in 1960, when Congress gave these investment vehicles the same tax advantages as mutual funds. Riding the commercial building boom of the late 1960s, by the early 1970s REITs came to dominate the construction loan business. But REITs, including some established by large banks, also built up a giant pyramid of debt. The collapse of the commercial real estate market left banks with billions of dollars in bad loans.

By the mid-1970s the first stage of the banking revolution—what *Business Week* once called the "wild and woolly growth phase"—was over, brought to an end by inflation, recession, and the excesses of the banks themselves. Whereas five years earlier it was widely charged that the banks were ruining the economy with loose credit, the view now was that the economy was ruining the banks.

Yet the caution that the banks began to exhibit during the recession did not entirely prevail after the economy began to recover, even when another precarious situation emerged. This time it was the problem of Third-World debt.

CRISIS IN THIRD-WORLD DEBT

As part of their expansion in the late 1960s and early 1970s commercial banks took over from first-world governments and international agencies the role of lending to so-called less developed countries (LDCs). When rising oil prices and the international recession (which reduced markets for Third-World exports) exacerbated the LDCs' balance of payments, the volume of bank lending rose sharply. With Citicorp once again in the vanguard, the banks eagerly loaded up countries such as Mexico, Brazil, and Argentina with debt, in part to "recycle" the petrodollar deposits the banks were receiving from OPEC countries.

In 1976, as the foreign loan exposure of U.S. banks mushroomed, various voices in Congress and in the press began questioning whether the LDCs could make good on their massive obligations. The World Bank reported that from the end of 1970 to the end of 1974, LDC debt had more than doubled from $74 billion to $151 billion. The portion owed to private banks nearly quintupled from about $6 billion to $29 billion.

Bankers such as Walter Wriston, head of Citicorp, remained undaunted. They took solace in the assumption that countries, unlike corporations or individuals, could not go bankrupt. They also put their confidence in the austerity measures being promoted around the globe by the International Monetary Fund (IMF), and they insisted that an expansion of LDC export earnings would make the debt entirely manageable. Consequently, the banks kept on lending, and by 1981 total LDC debt soared to more than $400 billion, of which about two thirds was held by Western banks.

Whether the insouciance of the bankers was warranted or not is a matter of interpretation. While it is true that the worst did not come to pass, the world financial system had to survive a series of cliff-hanger situations. In 1982 Mexico announced that it could not pay its debt, forcing banks to scramble to arrange a new repayment schedule—a replay of a drama that had just occurred with Poland. Similar arrangements had to be made for Argentina and Brazil. While the immediate crisis passed, the fragility of the system prompted *The Wall Street Journal* later that year to publish a front-page article offering a scenario for the collapse of the world banking system over 12 days. By this time the banks had started cutting back their Third-World lending.

In 1985 some LDCs began resisting the harsh measures that were necessary to keep up with their debt obligations. Peru and Bolivia restricted their payments, and Fidel Castro was advocating Third-World repudiation of foreign debt. Workers in Argentina demonstrated against repressive economic policies. Unrest over austerity was becoming more and more common.

In response to this climate the Reagan administration proposed a new approach to the debt problem. At the World Bank/IMF meeting in October 1985, Treasury secretary James Baker proposed a three-year lending increase of $29 billion, including $20 billion from commercial banks and $9 billion from the World Bank, which was to assume a greater supervisory role in LDC financial affairs.

The Baker plan shifted emphasis away from the IMF's austerity programs to a scenario based on economic growth, which was supposed to be led by the private sector of the Third World. Critics of the plan charged that it bailed out the banks and allowed them to avoid writing down the value of their LDC loans.

The new approach was applied in mid-1986 when the debt crisis flared up again in Mexico. The agreement put together by Mexico, a victim of declining oil prices, and the IMF included new loans of some $12 billion over two years (half from commercial banks) and measures designed to promote economic expansion, though a reduction in government spending was also part of the equation.

Yet the following year, when Brazil announced it was suspending interest payments on its foreign commercial debt, the atmosphere was quite different. Citicorp took the lead in adopting a get-tough policy toward LDC debtors. Rather than making more concessions to those countries, Citicorp chief executive John Reed proclaimed, banks should simply admit that some loans would never be repaid and adjust their balance sheets to reflect that fact. Citicorp thus took the dramatic step of adding $3 billion to its loan loss reserves, a move that prompted other large banks to make similar provisions.

Reed was not, however, willing to write off all of his bank's $15 billion or so in LDC loans. He also began promoting a process for reducing that exposure that was more profitable to his and other banks. The process was known as debt-equity swaps. Under this arrangement banks began selling their LDC loans to investors (mainly multinational corporations) at a discount of 30 percent or more. The investors then converted the debt to the local currency of the debtor country at a smaller discount and used the money to buy assets in that nation. For example, a company looking to expand its operations in Chile could purchase $100 million of loans for $70 million and swap them for about $92 million in pesos. As a result, the bank rid itself of nonperforming loans, the multinational got investments at bargain prices, and the debtor country freed itself of some of its debt (though in doing so it ceded control over more of its assets to foreign interests).

The Third-World country most enthusiastic about this process was Chile, with countries such as Mexico and the Philippines following along warily; Brazil later joined the trend. U.S. banks that wanted to do the entire swap themselves and get the foreign asset (rather than the cash from an investor) were encouraged by a Federal Reserve ruling allowing them to acquire 100 percent of Third-World companies.

A different kind of debt swap was worked out in late 1987 by J. P. Morgan & Co. and the government of Mexico to make that country's debt load more manageable. The plan called for Mexico to exchange $10 billion in bonds for about $20 billion in loans (which was possible because such loans were selling at a discount of 50 percent). The bonds were to be backed by $10 billion in zero-coupon bonds issued by the U.S. Treasury, which Mexico could obtain for only about $2 billion. (This was possible because zero-coupon bonds, which do not pay interest, sell at a steep discount). In this way Mexico could reduce its debt load by $20 billion with an outlay of only $2 billion. The problem was that not many banks were willing to accept a 50 percent discount on their loans, so Mexico sold only about one fourth as many bonds as it intended.

Financial gimmickry did not resolve the LDC debt crisis. Despite further growth in debt-equity swaps (which, however, began to grow less popular in Latin America), the total indebtedness of the Third World continued to soar, reaching some $1.3 trillion by the end of 1988. After there was bloody rioting in Venezuela in response to austerity policies adopted to please foreign creditors, pressure mounted on the newly installed Bush administration to act.

In March 1989 Treasury secretary Nicholas Brady put forth a plan centered on the goal of reducing LDC debt by 20 percent over three years. To accomplish this the proposal encouraged further debt-equity swaps and looked to the World Bank and the IMF to back securities that would be exchanged at discounted rates for loans held by commercial banks.

The Brady plan also failed to inspire the banks. By late 1989 the banks, led by Morgan, were instead increasing their loan loss reserves once again and thus making it easier for them to avoid making additional loans to Third-World debtors.

The debt problem in the Third World was intensified once again in 1990 when the Persian Gulf crisis brought about a surge in oil prices. The few less developed countries that export oil stood to gain from the situation, but for most of the Third World it meant going further in the hole.

THE INTEREST-RATE SQUEEZE

While the large U.S. financial institutions managed to pull through the LDC crisis, many of their smaller counterparts were not so lucky in dealing with the domestic travails of the banking industry. The major victims were the thrifts, and their major affliction was the galloping interest rates of the late 1970s.

The escalation of rates hit the S&Ls and savings banks in two ways. First, it sharply increased the cost of the funds they obtained in the money market while many of their loans were tied up in long-term, fixed-rate home mortgages at much lower levels. At the same time, their depositors were abandoning savings accounts that paid the legal limit of 5.5 percent and were turning instead to the more lucrative money market mutual funds that had been created.

The latter part of the problem was addressed by Congress in 1980. The Depository Institutions Deregulation and Monetary Control Act of 1980 set in motion a program for the phasing out of Regulation Q interest-rate ceilings over six years. Among its many provisions the act also:

1. Permitted all federally insured banks and thrifts to offer negotiable order of withdrawal (NOW) accounts (i.e., interest-bearing checking accounts).
2. Allowed federal thrifts to invest up to 20 percent of their assets in consumer loans, commercial paper, or corporate debt securities.
3. Preempted existing state usury ceilings on first mortgage loans and allowed states three years to enact legislation overriding the preemption.
4. Raised the limit on federal deposit insurance from $40,000 to $100,000 for each account.

The legislation slowed down the decline of the thrifts, in part by paving the way for adjustable-rate mortgages, which gave the banks greater protection in their long-term lending. But it did not reverse the process. The outflow of deposits continued, and the lifting of interest ceilings made it more expensive for the thrifts to pay for those deposits that remained. The number of federally insured S&Ls driven into merger or liquidation climbed to 24 in 1981 and 48 the next year. By 1982 Congress had to act again. It passed legislation giving federal regulators new powers to help ailing thrifts.

The FDIC and the FSLIC were authorized to exchange capital notes with troubled institutions to bolster their financial condition. The law also allowed federal thrifts as well as commercial banks to offer insured money market accounts, and it permitted S&Ls to offer checking accounts to their loan customers and to begin lending on commercial real estate.

Once again congressional action had limited effect on the beleaguered thrifts. In 1984 the country's largest S&L—American Savings (a subsidiary of Financial Corp. of America)—avoided failure only through a last-minute government rescue (which did not, however, include a takeover). In 1985 there were runs on S&Ls in Ohio and Maryland involving institutions that were insured by private plans. The FHLBB initiated a new program of replacing the management of troubled S&Ls before they failed; 25 institutions were subjected to this process in 1985.

Yet it soon became clear that the problem was much larger. After the deregulatory changes of the early 1980s, countless go-for-broke entrepreneurs swarmed into the S&L business, especially in Texas, Florida, and California. Many of them were real estate developers who committed huge portions of the thrifts' deposits to loans for risky commercial projects that went bad with the collapse of Sunbelt property prices; others were simply crooks who looted the institutions, leaving federal agencies holding the bag.

By the end of 1986 FSLIC was confronted with hundreds of S&Ls that needed to be taken over and restructured, yet the fund's reserves were used up, making it technically bankrupt. To make matters worse, a number of healthier S&Ls began seeking permission to switch their deposit insurance from FSLIC to the more solvent FDIC.

Congress found itself under pressure to rescue FSLIC, which it first attempted to do with 1987 legislation that permitted the fund to issue $10.8 billion in government-backed bonds. That turned out to be woefully inadequate. One third of the country's 3,000 S&Ls suffered losses in 1987, a record total of $6.8 billion in red ink. The following year the losses climbed to more than $12 billion.

There was also increasing criticism of the entire bailout process, which essentially involved the FHLBB paying entrepreneurs such as Texas billionaire Robert Bass to take over failing thrifts. In 1988 it cost the agency $2 billion to arrange the transfer of California's American Savings to a group led by Bass, which put up only $150 million of its own money to gain control of an institution with more than $16 billion in healthy assets.

The incoming Bush administration recognized that dealing with the S&L crisis was one of its most urgent tasks. Within weeks of taking office President Bush announced a rescue plan for the savings industry that involved the sale of $50 billion in government bonds, the interest on which was to be paid by taxpayers and the thrifts, which (along with banks) were to be charged higher premiums for federal deposit insurance. Along with the $40 billion already committed in government-assisted takeovers, the plan was expected to cost taxpayers and financial institutions some $160 billion over 10 years.

The proposal also called for the dissolution of the FHLBB and its replacement with a new agency within the Treasury Department. By putting FSLIC under the control of the FDIC and giving the latter some regulatory power over thrifts, the plan took a large step toward eliminating the difference between S&Ls and banks.

The plan, as passed by Congress in August 1989, created the Office of Thrift Supervision within the Treasury Department to take over much of the FHLBB's regulatory functions. A Savings Association Insurance Fund was created (under control of the FDIC) to insure S&L deposits and to manage the assets of insolvent thrifts after 1992. The Resolution Trust Corporation (RTC) was created to manage the assets and liabilities of S&Ls taken over between 1989 and 1992. (The finances of those taken over earlier were put under the control of the FSLIC Resolution Fund within the FDIC.) The law also increased the capital requirements for thrifts, required S&L investors to put up more of their own money to receive deposit insurance, and allowed commercial banks to acquire healthy thrifts in order to encourage consolidation.

Although the S&L rescue plan, the biggest bailout in U.S. history, was intended to put and end to the thrift mess, it was clear that that was not to be. No sooner was the ink dry on the law than most analysts were saying that it did not provide enough funds and that the complicated new regulatory structure would make things worse. All signs were that the thrift industry, which ended up losing some $19 billion in 1989, would need more rescuing than Congress or the administration had planned.

There was also great embarrassment for Congress when a scandal broke regarding Charles Keating, Jr., and his Lincoln Savings & Loan Association. Keating, the wealthy head of a Phoenix construction company, had waged a campaign against federal regulators in the mid-1980s and won support from a group of senators to whom he had made sizable campaign contributions. In 1989 Lincoln was finally seized by the FHLBB, and a $1 billion federal fraud and racketeering suit was filed against Keating. A House investigation of the Keating affair helped bring about the resignation of M. Danny Wall, the director of the Office of Thrift Supervision (and before that head of the FHLBB) who was faulted for not taking quicker action against Lincoln.

In 1990 there was also a scandal brought to light by a series of articles in the *Houston Post* alleging CIA and organized crime connections to insolvent S&Ls. The mess also touched the family of President Bush. His son Neil was called before a congressional committee in 1990 to explain why as a director of a Denver savings institution he had approved loans for real estate developers with whom he had other business dealings. He was later sued by the FDIC for gross negligence.

The rescue itself was also not going smoothly. The Resolution Trust Corporation, now one of the world's largest financial institutions, had difficulty finding buyers for busted thrifts (many of whom were put off by requirements that 70 percent of their loans be kept in housing). The RTC also found itself stuck with billions of dollars in junk bonds (purchased by various failed thrifts) that were worth considerably less in the wake of the bankruptcy of Drexel Burnham Lambert. In April 1990 the head of the General Accounting Office estimated that the cost of the S&L rescue could end up costing $500 billion. The Bush administration stuck to lower dollar estimates but admitted that the number of S&Ls that would have to be seized would probably exceed 1,000.

The administration was further embarrassed by the revelations that some of the people brought in to rescue failed thrifts had questionable backgrounds. There was an especially loud uproar in 1990 over reports concerning James Fail, a Phoenix businessman who received some $1.85 billion in federal subsidies for 15 Texas thrifts that he purchased for $70 million—of which all but $1,000 was in borrowed funds. In 1976, an Alabama company controlled by Fail pleaded guilty to securities fraud. While Fail was trying to arrange the purchase of the thrifts, he used the lobbying services of a former aide to George Bush.

THE INTERSTATE THRUST

During the travails of the thrifts in the 1980s, the attention of commercial banks was directed to their crusade to break through many of the legal limitations on their activities—both geographic barriers and restrictions on their entry into certain lines of business.

The deregulatory thrust of the banks was directed at a body of law beginning with the McFadden Act of 1927, which limited branching by national banks to their home city (later extended to the rest of that one state). The Douglas Amendment to the Bank Holding Company Act of 1956 barred the purchase of banks across state lines unless the other state permitted it. While banks were free to make loans anywhere in the country, these rules severely limited their potential pool of deposits. As the big holding companies such as Citicorp became major national and international lenders, they hungered for broader

The 15 Largest Savings Institutions, by 1989 Assets ($ Billions)

1.	H. F. Ahmanson (Los Angeles)	$44.7
2.	Great Western Financial Corp. (Beverly Hills)	37.2
3.	Calfed (Los Angeles)	26.2
4.	Glenfed (Glendale, Calif.)	25.6
5.	Golden West Financial Corp. (Oakland, Calif.)	19.5
6.	Homefed Corp. (San Diego)	17.8
7.	Great American Bank (San Diego)	15.9
8.	Crossland Savings (New York)	14.1
9.	Goldome (Buffalo)	13.0
10.	Meritor Savings Bank (Philadelphia)	12.6
11.	Dime Savings Bank of New York (Garden City)	11.7
12.	Firstfed Michigan Corp. (Detroit)	11.5
13.	Franklin Savings Association (Ottawa, Kansas)	11.4
14.	Coast Savings Financial (Los Angeles)	11.2
15.	Imperial Corp. of America (San Diego)	11.0

Source: *Fortune*, June 4, 1990.

sources of deposit funds. The result was a tireless quest for the legalization of interstate banking.

At the same time, commercial banks began to argue once again against the Glass-Steagall Act, which barred them from nearly all forms of underwriting, and against rules that limited their other activities. The banks were concerned about the moves of Merrill Lynch, Sears, and other nonbank companies to create "supermarkets" of financial services. The fact that these competitors were not regulated gave them an unfair advantage, the bankers argued; deregulation would create what industry leaders such as Walter Wriston liked to call "a level playing field."

While deregulation became a drawn-out and inconclusive drama in Congress, the banks began using loopholes in federal law and liberalized state rules to engage in de facto interstate banking and entry into new fields. Bank of America acquired discount broker Charles Schwab & Co. (but later sold it back). Citicorp moved its credit card operations to South Dakota to escape New York's usury laws. Various banks followed the lead of nonfinancial corporations such as Gulf + Western in setting up entities that were given the peculiar label "nonbank banks."

These institutions, which amounted to limited-service banks, took advantage of the fact that federal law prohibiting interstate banking defined banks as operations engaged in both lending and accepting deposits. By limiting their activity to one of the two functions (usually accepting of deposits), the creators of nonbank banks claimed exemption from the law. Federal regulators were divided on the legitimacy and desirability of these institutions, but after a period of confusion the matter was resolved by a 1986 Supreme Court ruling that sanctioned their existence. Yet the following year Congress halted the creation of the nonbank banks.

Faced with faltering profitability, banks also continued their drive to get into lucrative activities previously limited to investment banks. When a number of money center banks began talking about giving up their charters to be free to diversify into these areas, worried regulators started relaxing their rules. In 1986 Bankers Trust received clearance from the Federal Reserve to sell commercial paper through a subsidiary, and the following year the Fed permitted banks to engage in underwriting of commercial paper and asset-backed securities through subsidiaries deriving less than 5 percent of revenues from such activities (the ceiling was later raised to 10 percent). In 1989 the agency approved applications by J. P. Morgan and other banks to underwrite corporate debt securities; in 1990, this right was extended to equities.

The large money-center banks have also taken advantage of a 1982 law that allowed out-of-state banks to purchase failing thrifts. Citicorp was the first to act when it acquired a California S&L in 1982. It subsequently bought thrifts in Illinois and Florida.

Although some commercial banks were in a position to rescue failing institutions—and to serve their own ends in the process—others faced their own crises. Between 1981 and 1983, some 100 banks collapsed. One of the most sensational of these was the Penn Square Bank of Oklahoma, a freewheeling institution that died from an overdose of bad energy loans. Penn Square's demise had repercussions throughout the banking industry, most notably at Chicago's venerable Continental Illinois, which had purchased more than $1 billion in loans from the Oklahoma bank.

Continental Illinois, also saddled with nonperforming real estate and energy loans of its own, experienced a panic among its major depositors in 1984. Federal regulators put together a $7.5 billion rescue package, but the bad publicity caused the run to continue. Unable to find a private buyer for the bank, the federal government in effect took over the institution. After the Continental bailout, only the fourth such government action in U.S. history, FDIC rescues became much more common as the problems of commercial real estate, agriculture, and energy took their toll, especially in the Southwest. First National Bank & Trust Co. of Oklahoma City had to be taken over and reorganized by federal regulators in 1986, followed by the big Texas banks: First City Bancorp in 1987, First RepublicBank in 1988, and MCorp in 1989. The state's other major banks were acquired before failing: Texas Commerce Bancshares by New York's Chemical Bank, and Allied Bancshares by California's First Interstate Bancorp.

These difficulties did not diminish the expansionary drives of the industry, but by the mid-1980s the center of attention shifted from the bold moves of Citicorp to the emergence of so-called regional superbanks. In response to the spread of nonbank banks in their territory, a number of states began to pass laws encouraging bank mergers with institutions in neighboring states. The catalyst for the trend was a regional compact established in New England. A Supreme Court ruling in 1985 affirmed the right of states to restrict interstate banking to specific regions. By the late 1980s it seemed inevitable that aggressive institutions such as NCNB, Fleet/Norstar, PNC Financial, SunTrust, and Banc One would soon be leading forces in the banking world. In 1990 there were more than 20 of these well-capitalized superregionals, accounting for about one fifth of America's banking assets. These banks are strong but not invulnerable: The problem of deteriorating real estate loan quality has spread from Texas to many other parts of the country, affecting many of the superregionals.

The competitive situation was also complicated by the growing presence in the United States of the big Japanese banks. Using extraordinary price-cutting on interest rates, Japanese banks captured 25 percent of the market in California by 1989. Dai-Ichi Kangyo (the world's largest bank) gained a strong American foothold in 1989 when it purchased a controlling interest in Manufacturers Hanover Trust's CIT Financial subsidiary and 5 percent of Manny Hanny itself. The Japanese also became a major player in bank lending for leveraged buyouts. The trend has been even more dramatic on an international basis: From 1983 to 1988, lending by Japanese banks skyrocketed, giving them 40 percent of world market share by the latter year; during the same period the share of U.S. banks sank from 27 percent to 15 percent.

BEYOND LENDING

Behind the headlines about bank failures and federal regulatory policies, a profound change has been taking place in the activities of the commercial banks. The 1980s witnessed an acceleration of a shift away from traditional lending and borrowing. In the search for less expensive financing, companies have turned in large numbers to the market for commercial paper (short-term IOUs issued not by banks but by nonfinancial corporations with excess cash).

The competition from commercial paper has driven down profit rates on bank lending and forced the banks to assume a new role. To an increasing extent banks are serving as middlemen in markets for financing backed by securities. This process of "securitization" turns banks from lenders (i.e., those who originate loans and keep them on their balance sheets as assets) to sellers of someone else's money (the favored term is "distribution"). Traditional corporate lending has not disappeared, but it is the wave of the past, steadily being overshadowed by activities that look more like investment banking than commercial banking.

LABOR RELATIONS

In 1969 *The Wall Street Journal* wrote that in the banking industry "unions have been as welcome as Bonnie and Clyde."

The 15 Largest Bank Holding Companies, by 1989 Assets ($ Billions)

	Company	Assets
1.	Citicorp	$230.6
2.	Chase Manhattan Corp.	107.4
3.	BankAmerica Corp.	98.8
4.	J. P. Morgan & Co.	89.0
5.	Security Pacific Corp.	83.9
6.	Chemical Banking Corp.	71.5
7.	NCNB Corp.	66.2
8.	Manufacturers Hanover Corp.	60.5
9.	First Interstate Bancorp	59.1
10.	Bankers Trust New York Corp.	55.7
11.	Bank of New York Co.	48.9
12.	Wells Fargo & Co.	48.7
13.	First Chicago Corp.	47.9
14.	PNC Financial Corp.	45.7
15.	Bank of Boston Corp.	39.2

Source: *Fortune*, June 4, 1990.

The situation has not changed, and the number of organized bank workers remains miniscule. Today there are labor contracts at fewer than 30 of the nation's banks. Unions such as the United Food & Commercial Workers (UFCW) and District 925 have had little success in the face of strong management resistance. Workers at Seattle First National Bank voted in 1978 for UFCW representation. It was not until 1990 that management agreed to begin negotiating with the union.

The most celebrated struggle of bank workers in recent times took place in Minnesota. In 1977 a group of women at the Citizens National Bank in Willmar charged their employer with sex discrimination, organized an independent union, and sought a contract. Management refused, and eight of the women staged a long but unsuccessful strike for recognition. A 1980 documentary film, *The Willmar 8,* gave the cause national recognition. That struggle inspired workers at another bank in the same town (First American Bank and Trust) to carry out a successful organizing drive and win recognition in 1983. The union, however, faced continued opposition from management, and four years later workers at the bank voted to decertify the union.

A similar course of events occurred in the small town of Mayfield, Kentucky. Ten employees of the Exchange Bank there went on strike in October 1987 for union recognition. After eight months the walkout ended when the union was decertified in a vote that included replacement workers as well as strikers.

LEADING COMPANIES

Bank of America (B of A) grew from a small neighborhood bank in San Francisco at the beginning of the century to become the nation's largest bank by 1945. Led by founder A. P. Giannini, the bank built an extensive retail network throughout California. B of A was overshadowed by the more aggressive Citicorp in the 1970s, but the bank made a bold move in acquiring discount broker Charles Schwab & Co. in 1982 (though five years later it was sold back to its founder). By the mid-1980s B of A was suffering from a large volume of bad loans in the ailing energy, real estate, and agricultural sectors. Samuel Armacost, who took over the holding company BankAmerica in 1981, came in for a great deal of criticism; in 1986 he was replaced by his predecessor, A. W. Clausen. The weakened state of the bank was indicated by the takeover proposal made (and later dropped) by First Interstate Bancorp, an institution less than half the size of B of A. But by the late 1980s the bank was enjoying a strong recovery, and in 1990 it acquired Arizona's second largest savings and loan association.

Bankers Trust, one of the New York giants, caused a stir in the late 1970s when it abandoned its consumer business and moved aggressively into investment banking activities. The bank, founded in 1903, skirted the restrictions of the Glass-Steagall Act and started a trend by acting as an agent for companies in the sale of commercial paper. By the late 1980s Bankers Trust was becoming an important merger-and-acquisition dealmaker and was enjoying substantial profits from bond and currency trading. The company was also beginning to function as a merchant bank by investing some of its own money in the course of assisting in deals such as Alfred Checchi's purchase of Northwest Airlines.

Chase Manhattan, long known as the Rockefellers' bank,

had origins in the Manhattan Co. (which started as the local water utility in New York City in 1799 and branched into financial activities) and in the Chase National Bank, which was established in 1877 and merged with the Rockefeller-controlled Equitable Trust in 1930 and then with the Bank of Manhattan in 1955. Until 1945 Chase was the country's largest bank. The bank suffered sluggish growth under the tenure of David Rockefeller and in the early 1980s suffered losses linked to the failures of Penn Square Bank and Drysdale Government Securities. In 1990, Chase responded to a new period of instability by cutting its dividend in half and eliminating 5,000 jobs.

Citicorp is the largest and most aggressive of U.S. banking companies. Since the late 1960s "Fat City," as the bank came to be called, has been in the vanguard of the efforts by commercial banks to expand their activities across the country and into new fields. Led by Walter Wriston, chairman of Citicorp from 1970 to 1984, the bank branched out across the globe, becoming perhaps the only truly global financial corporation. John Reed, who succeeded Wriston after building the bank's retail business, continued the emphasis on consumer financial services, including the company's dominant position in the credit card business. In 1987 Reed led the commercial banks in a new militancy in dealing with the Third-World loan problem: He opposed further concessions to the debtors and instead added $3 billion to his bank's loan loss reserves (though it later appeared that amount may not have been adequate). By 1990 Citicorp was still aggressively planning for the future but was suffering from immediate difficulties resulting from an increasing volume of problem loans.

Continental Illinois, created by a series of bank mergers in the 1920s and 1930s and one of the powerhouse banks of the Midwest, nearly collapsed in 1984 as the result of bad energy loans and a run by large depositors. Continental was rescued by the federal government, which injected new capital into the bank and in effect became the owner of the institution. By 1986 the bank was recovering and was the subject of controversy over its acquisition of several smaller banks. After former Citicorp executive Thomas Theobald took over in 1987, he moved away from the consumer side of the business and oriented Continental to providing services for corporations and institutional investors.

In the early 1980s **Manufacturers Hanover Trust,** founded in Brooklyn in 1905 and known informally as Manny Hanny, was in shaky enough condition to be lumped together with BankAmerica. The New York-based company took steps to restore investor confidence, including the $1.5 billion purchase of CIT Financial from RCA, but it still suffered from a large portfolio of Third-World loans. CIT also turned out to be a disappointment, and in 1989 Manny Hanny sold controlling interest in the asset-based lending operation to Japan's Dai-Ichi Kangyo Bank, which also took a 5 percent stake in Manny Hanny itself.

Morgan Guaranty Trust, the banking subsidiary of J. P. Morgan & Co., has long been one of the most prestigious and strongest of the New York banks. Some 50 years after it and Morgan's investment bank (which became Morgan Stanley) were separated, Morgan Guaranty was once again aiming at providing investment banking services. There were reports in the mid-1980s that the bank was even considering giving up its charter in order to be able to pursue such services without limitation. That did not happen, but Morgan did charge ahead into the securities business. In 1988 Wall Street was stunned when Morgan was chosen by Hoffmann-La Roche to be its advisor in a hostile bid for Sterling Drug.

NCNB is one of the most aggressive of the upstart financial institutions known as the superregionals. Created in 1968 as a holding company for North Carolina National Bank, NCNB went on an acquisition binge during the 1980s, especially after Hugh McColl, Jr., a brash ex-Marine who has been called "the George Patton of banking," took over as chief executive in 1983. McColl initially focused most of his efforts on Florida, but after the banking debacle in Texas he snapped up various properties in the Lone Star state. The most important of these was a 20 percent interest in First RepublicBank, which had been taken over by federal regulators. By mid-1990 NCNB had 250 branches and $31 billion in assets in Texas alone.

INDUSTRY DATA

Commercial Banks	*1989*	*1988*	*1987*
Assets	$3.2 trillion	$3.0 trillion	$2.8 trillion
Total employment	1.57 million	1.56 million	1.56 million

Savings Institutions	*1989*	*1988*	*1987*
Assets	$1.6 trillion	$1.6 trillion	$1.5 trillion
Total employment	486,000	482,000	481,000

Source: U.S. Department of Commerce.

SOURCE GUIDE

Leading Stock Analysts and Experts

Robert Albertson, bank analyst at Goldman Sachs.

J. Richard Fredericks, bank analyst at Montgomery Securities.

Jonathan Gray, thrift analyst at Sanford C. Bernstein & Co.

Thomas Hanley, bank analyst at Salomon Brothers.

Keefe, Bruyette & Woods, a bank securities firm in New York.

George Salem, bank analyst at Prudential-Bache.

Arthur Soter, bank analyst at Morgan Stanley.

Trade Associations

American Bankers Association, 1120 Connecticut Avenue NW, Washington, DC 20036. Tel.: (202) 663–5000.

National Council of Savings Institutions, 1101 15th Street NW, Washington, DC 20005. Tel.: (202) 857–3100.

United States League of Savings Institutions, 1709 New York Avenue NW, Washington, DC 20006. Tel.: (202) 637–8900.

Data Sources and Directories

Federal Reserve Bulletin, monthly, and *Annual Statistical Digest* (Washington, D.C.: Federal Reserve Board).

Moody's Bank and Finance Manual, an annual collection of data on financial companies (New York: Moody's Investors Services).

Polk's Bank Directory, North American edition published semiannually; international edition annually (Nashville, Tenn.: R. L. Polk).

Rand McNally Bankers Directory, published semiannually (Skokie, Ill.: Rand McNally).

Sourcebook, an annual volume of data (Washington, D.C.: U.S. League of Savings Institutions).

Statistical Information on the Financial Services Industry, annual (Washington, D.C.: American Bankers Association).

Statistics on Banking, annual (Washington, D.C.: Federal Deposit Insurance Corporation).

U.S. Savings Institutions Directory, annual (Skokie, Ill.: Rand McNally).

Online Database

FINIS: FINANCIAL INDUSTRY INFORMATION SERVICE (Chicago: Bank Marketing Association; available via BRS, DIALOG, and NEXIS).

Trade Publications

ABA Banking Journal, monthly.

American Banker, daily.

Bankers Magazine, bimonthly.

Bankers Monthly.

Banking Expansion Reporter, fortnightly.

BNA Banking Report, weekly.

Savings Institutions, monthly.

United States Banker, monthly.

Books and Reports

Adams, James Ring. *The Big Fix: The Inside Story of the S&L Crisis.* New York: John Wiley & Sons, 1990.

Balderston, Frederick E. *Thrifts in Crisis: Structural Transformation of the Savings and Loan Industry.* Cambridge, Mass.: Ballinger, 1985

Brumbaugh, R. Dan. *Thrifts Under Siege.* Cambridge, Mass.: Ballinger, 1988.

Hector, Gary. *Breaking the Bank: The Decline of BankAmerica.* Boston: Little, Brown, 1988.

Johnston, Moira. *Roller Coaster: The Bank of America and the Future of American Banking.* New York: Ticknor & Fields, 1990.

Kane, Edward J. *The S&L Insurance Mess: How Did It Happen?* Washington, D.C.: Urban Institute Press, 1989.

Litan, Robert E. *What Should Banks Do?* Washington, D.C.: Brookings Institution, 1987.

Mayer, Martin. *The Money Bazaars.* New York: E. P. Dutton, 1984.

Moffitt, Michael. *The World's Money.* New York: Simon & Schuster, 1983.

Organisation for Economic Co-Operation and Development. *Competition in Banking.* Paris, 1989.

Ornstein, Franklin H. *Savings Banking: An Industry in Change.* Reston, Va.: Reston Publishing, 1985.

Pilzer, Paul Zane, and Robert Dietz. *Other People's Money: The Inside Story of the S&L Mess.* New York: Simon & Schuster, 1989.

Pizzo, Stephen; Mary Fricker; and Paul Muolo. *Inside Job: The Looting of America's Savings and Loans.* New York: McGraw-Hill, 1989.

Roussakis, Emmanuel N. *Commercial Banking in an Era of Deregulation.* New York: Praeger Publishers, 1984.

Sampson, Anthony. *The Money Lenders.* New York: Viking Press, 1982.

Sprague, Irvine H. *Bailout: An Insider's Account of Bank Failures and Rescues.* New York: Basic Books, 1986.

Trescott, Paul B. *Financing American Enterprise: The Story of Commercial Banking.* New York: Harper & Row, 1963.

CHAPTER 20

STOCK BROKERAGE AND INVESTMENT BANKING

Capitalism needs capital to survive, and one of the primary ways of raising capital is through the issuing of securities. This process has given rise to an industry of intermediaries that help companies plan their financing needs, bring new issues to market, and execute trades of existing securities. There are numerous functions involved in the business; some firms specialize and others do everything. Investment banks "underwrite" new securities by preparing the issue and buying it (along with other firms in what is called a syndicate) in order to resell it at a profit to investors. A total of $307 billion in debt and equity capital was raised this way in 1989. These firms also advise companies in mergers and acquisitions and other matters relating to finance.

Securities firms also engage in the buying and selling of equity (stocks) and debt (bonds) issues for the public (and for their own account). Firms such as Merrill Lynch have vast networks of retail brokerage offices to serve small investors, while other companies focus on serving institutional investors, such as pension funds and insurance companies.

The bull market of the mid-1980s allowed the industry to prosper as never before, but the good times came to an end after the stock market plunge in October 1987. As takeovers waned and the junk bond business withered, many firms were forced to make drastic reductions in overhead, including the elimination of tens of thousands of jobs.

UNDER THE BUTTONWOOD TREE

The securities business in America began during the Revolutionary War as the Continental Congress and the army issued various notes and scrip. The trading of financial instruments gained some regularity in 1792, when a group of 24 brokers gathered under a buttonwood tree at what is now 68 Wall Street and established minimum commission rates and other rules. This clique, which soon moved its operations indoors, evolved into the New York Stock and Exchange Board (renamed the New York Stock Exchange in 1863).

The New York exchange adopted the airs of an exclusive private club, which was in keeping with the genteel character of the brokerage business. Security ownership was limited to a small segment of the population, and they tended to favor stability. Most portfolios concentrated on government and transportation bonds rather than stocks.

In places such as New York there was also a more rough-and-tumble side to the securities business. This consisted of ad hoc exchanges, in which speculation was more common, and "bucket shops," where customers could wager on stock movements without owning shares. These establishments came and went, while the New York Stock Exchange (NYSE) was firmly established as the leading arena for respectable trading. New York brokers who were excluded from the inner circle met on the street for many years—gaining the name "curbstone brokers." This curb market became more formal after World War I and changed its name to the American Stock Exchange in 1953, yet it was still regarded as a poor cousin to the NYSE.

The more rapid economic development after the Civil War stimulated growth in the investment banking side of the securities business. While some firms that could be called investment banks (including Alex. Brown & Sons and Vermilye & Co., precursor of Dillon, Read) were formed in the 1820s and 1830s, underwriting began in a serious way with the financings that Jay Cooke & Co. did for the Lincoln administration during the Civil War.

After Cooke went under in the panic of 1873, the preeminent spot was assumed by J. P. Morgan, whose operation epitomized the WASP-owned private banks that took deposits as well as engaging in underwriting. The other main group in the industry consisted of financiers of German-Jewish origin—most notably Jacob Schiff of Kuhn Loeb—who were excluded from commercial banking but who became important in underwriting and other aspects of corporate finance.

Both groups prospered with the wave of industrial consolidations that arose at the end of the century. The House of Morgan provided the financial wherewithal for many of the emerging industrial giants, most notably U.S. Steel, which was organized in 1901 as the first billion-dollar corporation.

Until World War I the United States was a debtor nation: Much more capital was flowing into the country from Europe than was flowing out. Morgan and the other investment banks often acted as conduits for this investment from abroad. They underwrote U.S. securities and sold them to foreign interests. When war broke out in Europe the relationship changed, and U.S. investment banks found themselves raising funds for beleaguered European powers.

After the war, the securities business expanded rapidly. Investment banks brought out issues for countless new and growing firms. The stock market went wild in the 1920s, drawing thousands of small investors who took advantage of liberal margin requirements. The speculative bubble grew larger and larger until the end of the decade. Some cautious investors saw the warning signs and bailed out. Yet most players were caught off guard in October 1929 when, as the famous *Variety* headline put it, "Wall Street Lays an Egg."

THE DIVORCE OF BANKING

When Franklin Roosevelt took office in 1933, public resentment over the great crash and the ensuing depression had translated into a suspicion of the financial community. The previous year the Senate Banking Committee had launched a probe—called the Pecora Hearings after the panel's chief counsel Ferdinand Pecora—of Wall Street wheeling and dealing. Given a mandate to go after the big financiers, Pecora found a variety of questionable practices relating to stock manipulation, tax evasion, and the like.

The result of congressional deliberations was the Banking Act of 1933 (or, as it is commonly known, the Glass-Steagall Act). The main result of this law was the strict separation of commercial and investment banking. This forced the big banks such as Morgan to spin off or dissolve their investment banking subsidiaries, which led to the formation of firms such as Morgan Stanley and First Boston.

Congress did not stop with Glass-Steagall. Legislation passed in 1933 and 1934 established disclosure rules for companies issuing stock and created the Securities and Exchange Commission (SEC) as a federal agency to oversee the securities business.

Through the rest of the New Deal period and World War II, the securities business was in a state of hibernation. The industry emerged from its sleep and became frisky in the postwar years, especially after federal judge Harold Medina dismissed an antitrust case brought by the Truman administration against 17 leading investment bankers. New York Stock Exchange president G. Keith Funston began promoting wider ownership of stock under the banner of "people's capitalism." Charlie Merrill raised the professional level of brokers (he dubbed them "account executives") and built Merrill Lynch into the leading retail firm.

In 1953 stocks took off, and the longest bull market in U.S. history was under way. Despite a setback in 1962, the rally segued neatly into what became known as the go-go years of the mid-1960s. Along with the general rise of the market there was a frenetic demand for new issues. Underwriters eagerly brought out these stocks, usually with modern-sounding technical names, even though many of them soared briefly and then collapsed. The less scrupulous investment banks paid little mind; as long as they got their profit on the initial offering, they felt the ultimate performance of the stock was the shareholders' problem.

This kind of loose ethical code was most apparent outside of the Big Board, as the NYSE came to be known. A scandal over improper dealings at the American Stock Exchange in the early 1960s prompted President Kennedy to commission the Special Study of Securities Markets. The findings of the study led Congress to enact the Securities Act Amendments of 1964, which established stricter disclosure requirements for over-the-counter securities and more stringent rules for broker-dealers.

The national over-the-counter (OTC) market consisted of thousands of firms that traded stocks outside of organized exchanges. The Maloney Act of 1938 required OTC dealers to form the National Association of Securities Dealers (NASD) to supervise the business. In the 1960s some OTC dealers began defying Wall Street by trading securities listed on exchanges such as the Big Board, giving rise to what was called the Third Market. The large brokerage houses grumbled but did not succeed in thwarting leading Third Marketeers such as Weeden & Co.

In the meantime the NASD, prodded by the SEC, moved ahead with development of an automated trading system. Designed by electronics firm Bunker Ramo, the automated quotation system (called NASDAQ) had its debut in 1971. Thanks to the boom in new issues and the preference of some companies to avoid the strict rules of the NYSE, the NASDAQ system grew rapidly.

While disturbed by these competitive developments, the big brokerages had their hands full trying to deal with all the trades they were executing in the late 1960s. Wall Street was drowning in paperwork as volume on the Big Board jumped to more than 2 billion shares a year. The result was what became known as the back-office crisis: Old-fashioned, labor-intensive methods of processing orders could not keep up with the growth of the business. The immediate response of the leadership of the NYSE was to cut back trading hours in 1967 and 1968, and for a while trading was limited to four days a week so that the back-office people could catch up on Friday. Over the longer term the crunch has forced the brokerage houses to invest large sums in computer equipment.

The market collapse of 1969–70 cooled off Wall Street but

also put the squeeze on a number of the weaker firms. The Big Board leaders turned to Lazard Frères partner Felix Rohatyn—then the leading figure in corporate mergers—to act as a matchmaker for marriages between faltering securities firms and stronger ones. Some firms, which had already changed from partnerships to corporations, took the additional step of going public. Donaldson, Lufkin & Jenrette led the way in 1969, followed by many other leading firms, including Merrill Lynch, E. F. Hutton, and First Boston.

The next major turning point for the brokerage side of the securities business came on May 1, 1975 (now immortalized as Mayday), when the SEC abolished the system of fixed commissions. For the first time Big Board members had to concern themselves with price competition, both among themselves and with the discount brokerage services that were created. The discounters, led by Charles Schwab and Quick & Reilly, gained about 20 percent of the retail brokerage business by 1985.

As it turned out, commission rates did not decline for retail customers who passed up the no-frills services of the discounters and continued using the large brokers. Where the competition emerged was in the rates charged to institutional investors—pension funds, insurance companies, and the like—which trade large numbers of shares and have become the most important customers for many brokerage houses. Commissions for these investors declined from an average of 26 cents a share just before Mayday to about 10 cents at the end of the decade. In the mid-1980s the downward pressure resumed, and nickel-a-share commissions began appearing. Consequently, commission income became a smaller and smaller portion of brokerage house revenues, while trading profits and investment income accounted for the lion's share. Both retail and the institutional trading operations sank even further in the wake of the October 1987 market plunge. Individual investors continued their migration away from stocks, and institutions continued to drive hard bargains with their brokers. Yet as the merger business slowed down, securities firms put more emphasis (and began gaining more profits) from trading for their own accounts.

The 10 Largest Brokerage Firms, by Capital at Year-End 1989 ($ Millions)

Rank	Firm	Capital
1.	Merrill Lynch	$10,048
2.	Shearson Lehman Hutton	6,152
3.	Goldman Sachs	4,018
4.	Salomon Brothers	3,620
5.	Morgan Stanley	2,648
6.	First Boston	1,568
7.	Paine Webber	1,523
8.	Bear Stearns	1,444
9.	Dean Witter	1,429
10.	Prudential-Bache	1,322

Source: Securities Industry Association, New York.

THE RISE OF THE DEALMAKERS

While brokers were hustling to keep up their income level, the investment banking side of the business heated up in more lucrative ways. The genteel practices of the bankers—both the "white shoe" WASP firms such as Morgan Stanley and the German-Jewish ones such as Goldman Sachs—and their unshakable relationships with blue-chip clients started to come unglued in the late 1970s and early 1980s. Encouraged by relaxed antitrust policies and the undervalued state of many stocks, companies became more aggressive in their merger activities. The once-disreputable practice of hostile takeovers gained legitimacy after prominent companies adopted the maneuver.

For investment banks, some of which had never done merger work of any kind, the new wild West environment was unsettling. But the escalation of fees once the deals reached the billion-dollar level dispelled the compunctions of most firms. Some actually embraced the trend as a major new profit area. First Boston plunged into the merger field with a passion, not simply waiting for clients to come to them with merger plans but also concocting likely marriages and then trying to interest the parties. A small group of investment bankers gained the reputation of being essential to any major deal, and their fees reflected this oligopoly. By 1985 it became common for a firm to receive $10 million for working on a single large deal, and in the following years the numbers escalated rapidly. In the $25 billion leveraged buyout of RJR Nabisco, the total fees paid to financial intermediaries amounted to more than $200 million.

Starting in 1987 firms also began profiting from deals by putting up their own money to help clients carry out transactions. Under the rubric of merchant banking, firms such as Shearson Lehman and First Boston provided bridge loans of $1 billion or more to raiders. Once the deal went through, the loans were repaid by selling off assets or issuing junk bonds.

In some cases Wall Street firms became the leaders of buyout groups, such as the 1987 deal in which Borg-Warner was taken private by a group headed by Merrill Lynch. More controversial was Shearson's participation as a partner in a successful hostile bid for Koppers Co. in 1988. Shearson and First Boston were also among the losing bidders in the epic battle for RJR Nabisco.

By the end of the 1980s a number of Wall Street firms were actively involved in initiating leveraged buyouts and holding on to their interests. Morgan Stanley controlled Burlington Industries, Merrill Lynch controlled Supermarkets General, and Prudential-Bache owned 49 percent of Dr Pepper/Seven-Up.

The most daring of the investment banks was, of course, Drexel. A young trader at Drexel named Michael Milken essentially invented junk bonds in the early 1970s, and other partners at Drexel worked directly with the likes of T. Boone Pickens and Saul Steinberg to plan their attacks. Yet Milken was later implicated in the insider trading scandals; in 1990 he pleaded guilty to six felony counts. Drexel itself was also targeted by federal prosecutors. In 1988 the firm agreed to plead guilty to six criminal charges and pay fines of $650 million. In February 1990, amid a collapse of the junk bond market, Drexel declared bankruptcy and ceased operations. (For more on insider trading and mergers see the Appendix to this chapter.)

UNDERWRITING IN TURMOIL

Since 1982 the investment banks have also had to contend with the consequences of the SEC's adoption of Rule 415, which allowed for something called shelf registration of securities. In line with the deregulatory vogue, the SEC decided to permit companies to forgo the customary process of preparing prospectuses each time they wanted to issue securities. Instead companies were given permission to file once for all of the stock they expected to issue over two years and were allowed to keep the stock "on the shelf" until the market looked best for actually selling the issue.

Most of the major investment banks were outraged at this procedure, which they saw as potentially freezing them out of the lucrative business of underwriting. While the worst did not come to pass, Rule 415 did help to diminish the importance of syndication. The breaking up of old relationships and the desire of companies to move quickly when market conditions were best have given rise to a trend of having only one firm bring out a new issue.

By the end of the 1980s a slump in new common stock issues and a decline in the junk bond market contributed to a sharp decline in underwriting fees for Wall Street firms. Merrill Lynch, however, managed to make the most of a weak market in 1989, keeping its place (first attained the year before) as the leading underwriter.

One bright spot for the industry has been the growth of the private placement market: the sale of equity or debt issues directly to an institutional buyer, thus avoiding the procedures associated with a public offering. In 1989 this market amounted to some $170 billion, a tenfold increase in a decade. In April 1990 the SEC gave a further boost to private placements by adopting Rule 144A, which opened the way for institutions to trade such securities freely, making them more attractive to own. Wall Street firms have acted as middlemen in most private placements in the past and hope to continue doing so, but the easing of regulations could allow more institutions to deal directly with one another.

THE BANK CHALLENGE

Yet another problem faced by investment banks has been increased competition from major commercial banks, which have

Leading Underwriters in 1989

	Amount raised ($ millions)	*Number of Issues*
1. Merrill Lynch	$45,689	294
2. Goldman Sachs	42,939	216
3. First Boston	37,985	175
4. Salomon Brothers	32,130	182
5. Morgan Stanley	28,837	169
6. Shearson Lehman Hutton	25,733	165
7. Bear Stearns	17,256	70
8. Drexel Burnham	16,947	93
9. Prudential-Bache	16,465	74
10. Kidder Peabody	8,803	43

Note: Includes all domestic issues, with full credit given to book manager.

Source: Securities Data Company, Newark, New Jersey.

been testing the limits of Glass-Steagall and providing a wider range of financial services. There was a move by banks into discount brokerage after the Federal Reserve approved Bank of America's 1981 purchase of Charles Schwab. Government regulators have allowed banks to engage in underwriting of commercial paper, municipal revenue bonds, and mortgage-backed securities in limited volume; in 1989 the Federal Reserve began to open the door to the underwriting of corporate debt as well. By the end of the decade aggressive institutions such as Bankers Trust and J. P. Morgan were calling themselves merchant banks and seeking to compete with securities firms across the board. Glass-Steagall was cracked yet more in 1990, when the Federal Reserve authorized J. P. Morgan to underwrite corporate stocks as well as bonds.

The challenges to securities firms on both the brokerage and investment banking sides, along with the need for greater access to capital, have brought about a new wave of consolidations and takeovers from outside. In 1981 alone the commodities company Phibro bought Salomon Brothers, Prudential Insurance bought Bache, Sears bought Dean Witter, and American Express (Amexco) bought Shearson Loeb Rhoades. (Amexco later added Lehman Brothers and E. F. Hutton to its financial empire.) General Electric purchased 80 percent of Kidder Peabody in 1986. The following year Smith Barney was acquired by financial services company Primerica. Brokerage houses were regarded as essential elements in the plans of a handful of major companies to make themselves into financial supermarkets.

Many of those firms that survived the merger wave still needed to raise their capitalization to compete, so another batch of them decided to go public. In 1985 and 1986 firms such as Morgan Stanley, Bear Stearns, and Alex. Brown & Sons took that step.

Another tack taken by firms to shore up their capital has been to sell stakes to foreign investors, especially Japanese financial institutions. Shearson sold 13 percent to Nippon Life Insurance, Goldman Sachs sold 12.5 percent to Sumitomo Bank, and Paine Webber sold 20 percent to Yasuda Mutual Life. Newer firms also adopted this approach: Wasserstein, Perella & Co.—set up by two merger stars after they left First Boston—sold 20 percent of its equity to Nomura Securities; and Blackstone Group—a merchant bank established by former Lehman Brothers chairman Peter Peterson—sold an identical amount to Nikko Securities. Nomura, Nikko, and the two other leading Japanese securities firms (Daiwa and Yamaichi) have also been expanding their direct presence in U.S. financial markets.

The Japanese, like their American counterparts, have suffered the effects of the slump in the securities business since the 1987 stock market crash. With takeovers, underwriting, and other activities in decline, firms have made deep cuts in their operating expenses, particularly people. Since peaking in 1987, Wall Street has eliminated tens of thousands of jobs. The young traders and dealmakers earning salaries in the high six-figures and regarding themselves as Masters of the Universe (as Tom Wolfe dubbed them in his novel *Bonfire of the Vanities*) are rapidly becoming extinct.

LEADING FIRMS

First Boston, created in the 1930s out of the investment banking subsidiaries of the First National Bank of Boston and the

Chase National Bank, developed close relationships with a number of blue-chip clients. The firm embraced the takeover mania that started in the late 1970s, and its merger specialists Bruce Wasserstein and Joseph Perella became the hottest practitioners in the field. In precarious condition in 1978, the firm was by 1986 gushing profits, earning $180 million for the year. But the firm was seriously weakened by the after-effects of the 1987 crash. Another blow came early the following year, when Wasserstein and Perella, in disagreement with the strategy of top management, left to form their own merger-and-acquisition boutique. First Boston sought to gain greater stability by merging with its European affiliate Credit Suisse First Boston, creating a new privately held company called CS First Boston (44.5 percent-controlled by Credit Suisse). In 1989 Metropolitan Life Insurance purchased a 10 percent stake in that new company.

During the early 1980s **Goldman Sachs** emerged as an outstanding performer in areas such as block trading and risk arbitrage, as well as underwriting and mergers (though it declined to back raiders). The firm was founded after the Civil War by Marcus Goldman, a German immigrant who was later joined in the commercial paper business by his son-in-law Samuel Sachs. The firm was hit hard by the 1929 crash but was rescued by Sidney Weinberg, who started with the firm as a janitor's assistant and rose to the top. Weinberg and his successor Gustave Levy turned Goldman into one of the most prestigious names on Wall Street. Later the firm, one of the few remaining private partnerships in the industry, prospered under the leadership of Sidney Weinberg's son John and John Whitehead. In 1986 Japan's Sumitomo Bank made a $500 million equity investment in Goldman. Robert Freeman, head of arbitrage at Goldman, was implicated in the insider trading scandals of the late 1980s; in 1989 he pleaded guilty to one count of fraud.

Merrill Lynch is the giant of the securities industry and by far the leader in the retail end of the business. Formed in 1914 by Charles Merrill and Edmund Lynch, the firm got out of the brokerage business after the crash and concentrated on underwriting. After World War II Charlie Merrill expanded his retail business, in part by improving the training of brokers and emphasizing customer relations. In the 1970s under the leadership of Donald Regan (who left the firm in 1981 to become Ronald Reagan's Treasury secretary and later White House chief of staff), the firm diversified into real estate, insurance, and other financial services. Regan also acquired the old-line firm of White Weld in 1978. During the 1980s Merrill built its position in investment banking, becoming a leader in the trend toward providing financing for leveraged buyouts. The firm also rose to the top of the underwriting business but scrambled to cut costs during the slump that overtook the industry.

Morgan Stanley, one of the top names in investment banking, was formed in 1935 by three partners of J. P. Morgan & Co. after Morgan abandoned investment banking in the wake of the Glass-Steagall Act. The firm gained many blue-chip clients and emerged as one of the snobs of the industry, for many years refusing to participate in a stock syndication unless it was lead manager. Robert Baldwin, who ran the firm from the early 1970s to 1984, modernized operations, expanded the merger business, and finally got the firm into trading. But Morgan was slow to enter new areas such as mortgage-backed securities and by the early 1980s had lost its leading position in underwriting. Yet the firm, which went public in 1986, later became heavily involved in leveraged buyouts. Morgan not only acted as an advisor in many of these deals but was also an investor in buyouts at such companies as Burlington Industries and Southern Pacific Railroad.

Salomon Brothers, founded in 1910, was primarily a dealer and trader in government bonds until the 1960s. Billy Salomon, son of one of the three founders, turned the firm into a leading underwriter in the 1960s. John Gutfreund continued the growth after taking over in 1978. Three years later he convinced his fellow partners to sell the firm to the commodities giant Phibro. Tensions between Salomon and its parent soon reached a critical level as the securities business boomed and commodities slumped. By late 1985 Gutfreund engineered a virtual dismantlement of Phibro as Salomon was being hailed as "the king of Wall Street." Over the next few years Gutfreund moved away from his preoccupation with trading and began to push Salomon to become a power in investment banking. One deal that Gutfreund did not want was Ronald Perelman's 1987 bid for Salomon, which was thwarted with the help of investor Warren Buffett, who purchased 12 percent of the firm.

Shearson Lehman Hutton Holdings is the result of the purchase of three leading securities firms by financial giant American Express in the 1980s. The Lehman Brothers firm dated back to a cotton brokerage established by three German brothers in the South in the 1840s. It remained a commodities firm until 1906, when Philip Lehman (son of one of the founders) joined with Henry Goldman (also a founder's son) of Goldman Sachs in a series of joint underwriting ventures. Bobby Lehman, a legendary Wall Street figure, ran the firm in the 1930s, 40s, and 50s. After his death the firm went into a slump, which in 1973 former Commerce secretary Peter Peterson was brought in to remedy. Lehman prospered during the 1970s and in 1977 merged with another old-line firm, Kuhn Loeb. Veteran trader Lewis Glucksman took over in 1983 and, amid feuding among the partners, led the firm into the arms of American Express, which had acquired Shearson Loeb Rhoades (the product of a long string of brokerage house mergers) in 1981. Now led by Peter Cohen, Shearson Lehman continued the consolidation process in 1987 by acquiring troubled E. F. Hutton, the big retail broker that was suffering from the stock market crash and a check-kiting scandal (the firm pleaded guilty to 2,000 counts of fraud in 1985). The combined firm had its own share of woes in the late 1980s, prompting parent company American Express to pump more money into the firm while replacing the brash Cohen with Amexco executive Howard Clark, Jr., in 1990. Later that year Clark split the company into two parts: a brokerage house and an investment banking operation with the revived name Lehman Brothers.

SOURCE GUIDE

Leading Stock Analysts and Experts

Samuel Hayes III, professor of investment banking at Harvard Business School.

IDD Information Services (data on underwriting), New York.

Perrin Long, veteran securities-industry analyst at Lipper Analytical Securities, New York.

Securities Data Co. (statistics on the industry), New York.

Trade Associations

National Association of Securities Dealers, 1735 K Street NW, Washington, DC 20006. Tel.: (202) 728–8000.

Securities Industry Association, 120 Broadway, New York, NY 10271. Tel.: (212) 608–1500.

Data Sources and Directories

Directory of Corporate Financing, a semiannual listing of underwritings (New York: Dealers' Digest).

Fact Book, an annual compilation of statistics on the Big Board (New York: New York Stock Exchange).

Institutional Investor, a leading publication on the industry, produces "M&A Deals of the Year" in its January issue, a review of underwriting, and the closely watched "All-America Research Team" ranking of analysts in its October issue.

Nelson's Directory of Investment Research, an annual volume listing brokerage house analysts by company and industry covered, and *Global Research*, a monthly listing of analyst research reports (Port Chester, N.Y.: Nelson Publications).

Securities Industry Yearbook, a directory of key figures in the industry and data on firms (New York: Securities Industry Association).

Standard & Poor's Security Dealers of North America, an annual directory (New York: McGraw-Hill).

Online Database

FINIS: FINANCIAL INDUSTRY INFORMATION SERVICE (Chicago: Bank Marketing Association; available via BRS, DIALOG, and NEXIS).

Trade Publications

Euromoney (London), monthly.

Institutional Investor, monthly.

Investment Dealers' Digest, weekly.

Securities Week.

Books and Reports

Auletta, Ken. *Greed and Glory on Wall Street: The Fall of the House of Lehman.* New York: Random House, 1986.

Bloch, Ernest. *Inside Investment Banking.* Homewood, Ill.: Dow Jones-Irwin, 1986.

Carosso, Vincent. *Investment Banking in America: A History.* Cambridge, Mass.: Harvard University Press, 1970.

Carpenter, Donna Sammons, and John Feloni. *The Fall of the House of Hutton.* New York: Henry Holt, 1989.

Carrington, Tim. *The Year They Sold Wall Street.* Boston: Houghton Mifflin, 1985.

Chernow, Ron. *The House of Morgan: An American Banking Dynasty and the Rise of Modern Finance.* New York: Atlantic Monthly Press, 1990.

Hoffman, Paul. *The Dealmakers: Inside the World of Investment Banking.* Garden City, N.Y.: Doubleday, 1984.

Lewis, Michael. *Liar's Poker: Rising Through the Wreckage on Wall Street.* New York: W. W. Norton, 1989.

Lowenstein, Louis. *What's Wrong with Wall Street.* Reading, Mass.: Addison-Wesley, 1988.

Seligman, Joel. *The Transformation of Wall Street.* Boston: Houghton Mifflin, 1982.

Sobel, Robert. *Inside Wall Street.* New York: W. W. Norton, 1977. Sobel is also the author of histories of the New York and American Stock Exchanges and other books on the industry.

Stevens, Mark. *Sudden Death: The Rise & Fall of E. F. Hutton.* New York: New American Library, 1989.

APPENDIX: MERGERS AND ACQUISITIONS

During the 1980s, the U.S. business world experienced a frenzy of takeovers and acquisitions that constituted one of the major merger waves of American history. Virtually every issue of *The Wall Street Journal* brought news of another giant tender offer, consolidation, or leveraged buyout. Corporate raiders such as T. Boone Pickens and Carl Icahn struck terror in the hearts of chief executives, who fought back with a variety of antitakeover devices. Yet a number of giant companies—the likes of Gulf Oil, Crown Zellerbach, TWA, and Pillsbury—were either taken over against their will or forced into the embrace of more friendly acquirers known as white knights. Other companies repurchased stock from raiders at big premiums, paying what was called greenmail. Between 1983 and 1989 more than 100 Fortune 500 companies were acquired, merged, or taken private.

The pace and scale of takeovers reached a point at which no corporation seemed immune. In the early 1970s a deal in the $100 million range was considered big news; within a decade that figure had jumped two orders of magnitude.

BIG BUSINESS UP FOR GRABS

The turning point in the road to "megamergers" was the battle for Conoco in 1981. After the Canadian company Dome Petroleum bid for 20 percent of Conoco's shares in an effort to get at its Canadian oil reserves, all of Conoco ended up in play. Seagram made an unwanted offer for a larger portion of the company, whose management turned to Du Pont as a white knight. A bidding war ensued, involving Mobil as well; after the dust settled, Du Pont was the winner with what was at the time an astounding offer of $7.2 billion.

Yet the case that focused public attention—and some degree of outrage—on what was going on in the merger-and-acquisition (M&A) game was the Bendix fiasco of 1982. Early in that year Bendix began quietly buying shares of Martin Marietta and in August announced an offer to buy the aerospace company. Martin Marietta's management, determined to avoid such a takeover, adopted an elaborate defense in which a purchase of the company by Bendix would trigger a process in which Bendix shares in turn would be bought up by Martin Marietta. This "doomsday machine," as it was dubbed, was to be backed up by United Technologies in the role of white knight. When the confusing—and by some accounts ludicrous—process was completed Bendix was taken over completely by Allied Corp., which also ended up owning 39 percent of Martin Marietta, which was otherwise still an independent company.

No sooner had the uproar over Bendix died down than a new wave of takeovers occurred in which the billion-dollar deal rose to double digits. In 1984 Texaco deftly outmaneuvered Pennzoil to acquire Getty Oil for more than $10 billion. (That move boomeranged on Texaco when Pennzoil sued and won more than $10 billion in damages and interest. After a Texas appeals court in 1987 reduced the damages by only $2 billion, Texaco filed for Chapter 11 bankruptcy. Later that year Texaco settled the dispute with Pennzoil for $3 billion.) In the meantime, T. Boone Pickens was pursuing an assault on Gulf Oil. Gulf fought mightily to evade Pickens and ended up agreeing to be purchased by Standard Oil of California (now called Chevron) for a staggering $13.2 billion.

Although the size of the Gulf takeover was not surpassed until 1989, the pace of billion-dollar mergers and acquisitions did not let up. In 1985 the leading arena switched from oil to food, with one well-known company purchasing another in mostly friendly arrangements. In what was dubbed the "brand-name merger wave," Nestlé consumed Carnation, R. J. Reynolds ate Nabisco Brands, and Philip Morris devoured General Foods. Another focus of activity was media companies. In 1985 Capital Cities purchased ABC for $3.5 billion, Ted Turner made an unsuccessful bid for CBS, and General Electric agreed to acquire RCA for $6.3 billion.

A NEW RESPECTABILITY FOR TAKEOVERS

Hostile takeovers, which were previously considered the disreputable domain of a few unscrupulous investors, gained considerably more respectability in the early 1980s. Large corporations no longer hesitated in making unfriendly tender offers or other merger advances, and raiders were regarded in some quarters as champions of small shareholders whose investments were said to be undervalued because of poor company management.

The leading investment banks took advantage of this new climate and in some cases acted as catalysts for major deals. M&A work became a central activity for firms such as First Boston, Drexel Burnham Lambert, Morgan Stanley, and Goldman Sachs. The functions of these bankers include searching for target companies, valuing the target, and structuring the deal. They have advised both acquirers and targets seeking to defend themselves.

The more aggressive investment banks did not wait for clients to come to them. The M&A departments of these firms developed their own list of potential corporate marriages and then made pitches to likely suitors. Superstars such as Bruce Wasserstein of First Boston went even further. When they heard that a deal was in the works, they approached another company about becoming a rival bidder. For example, after Pennzoil announced its plan to buy a chunk of Getty, Wasserstein persuaded Texaco to come in with a better bid—a move that Texaco came to regret.

THE MAGIC OF JUNK BONDS

It was a financing innovation—a device called junk bonds—that made it possible for raiders such as Pickens and Icahn to go after such large prey. Junk bonds were low-grade securities (rated BB or lower by Standard & Poor's or Ba or lower by Moody's) that paid several percentage points more interest than investment-grade bonds. The pioneer of these high-yield securities, to use their polite name, was Drexel Burnham Lambert. A young Drexel trader named Michael Milken began promoting the notion in the 1970s that some investors would be willing to buy high-risk bonds if the interest rates were made attractive enough. Eventually the raiders realized they could raise enormous sums of money through junk bonds, and Drexel became the financier for many of the largest takeover efforts. The firm was riding high until 1988, when the Securities and Exchange Commission charged Drexel and Milken with a variety of securities-law violations, including stock manipulation, false disclosures, and insider trading. By 1990 both Drexel and Milken had pleaded guilty to criminal charges. The firm, also crippled by a slump in the junk bond market, went bankrupt and ceased operations.

GOING PRIVATE

Nontraditional financing was also the basis for a different kind of deal that grew in importance during the 1980s: the leveraged buyout (LBO). This is a process by which the management of a company or other investors takes the firm private by purchasing the public shares with funds that are borrowed using the assets of the company as collateral. The earnings of the private company then serve to pay off the debt. When the company involved is financially strong, the leveraged buyout group is able to raise huge sums of money and invest little cash of its own.

LBOs took off following the case of Gibson Greeting Cards. In 1982 Wesray Corp. (whose chairman was former Treasury secretary William Simon) took Gibson private in an $81 million deal that involved putting up only $1 million in cash. In subsequent years the size of the largest LBOs grew rapidly, reaching nearly $1 billion in the Metromedia buyout of 1984. Even larger deals followed. In 1985 the senior management of the R. H. Macy department store chain proposed taking the company private for $3.6 billion. Then Kohlberg, Kravis, Roberts & Co. (KKR), which emerged as the leading LBO dealmaker, arranged a $6.2 billion buyout of food giant Beatrice, which proceeded to unload billions of dollars worth of assets.

By this time there was a rising chorus of protests against these buyouts. Members of Congress denounced the process as contributing to the decline in the competitiveness of American companies. Economists warned of the consequences of companies taking on such massive quantities of debt. Unions complained about the large layoffs that usually followed a buyout. Other critics noted that these deals were exacerbating the federal budget deficit, since the interest paid on the buyout debt was tax deductible. Even shareholders were outraged at cases in which bought-out companies decimated their operations to pay the debt amassed in the LBO and then went public again, providing fat profits for those who took the firms private. Many of the critics felt vindicated in 1988, when drug store Revco D.S. defaulted on its debt payments and ended up bankrupt.

All of this did not stop KKR, in particular, from forging ahead with its grand plan to remake American industry. By 1988 KKR had become the country's second-largest conglomerate (just behind General Electric) through its control of companies such as Beatrice, Safeway Stores, and Owens-Illinois. Henry Kravis and George Roberts (Jerome Kohlberg, Jr., left in 1987 over differences with his partners) became two of the nation's most powerful financiers since J. P. Morgan. Using a $6 billion buyout fund, they were able through borrowing to command about $40 billion of resources for takeover activities.

That muscle was put to work in late 1988, when KKR made a $20 billion bid for RJR Nabisco, the tobacco and food giant that had just received a buyout offer from chief executive Ross Johnson and Shearson Lehman Hutton. KKR managed to win control over the company even though its final bid of $25 billion was lower than that offered by Johnson, who managed to alienate the board of directors and become a national symbol of greed because of the $100 million he personally stood to make from the deal.

Yet after RJR Nabisco there was a slowdown in the giant buyouts, especially with the softening of the junk bond market. The buyout of United Airlines parent UAL (by management, employees, and British Airways) came apart in late 1989 because of financing problems.

Another blow came when Federated Department Stores (taken over by Campeau Corp. for $6.5 billion in 1988) collapsed under the weight of its debt burden and was put into Chapter 11 in early 1990. The big commercial banks, looking to expand their fee income, have tried to promote an LBO revival. Among other things, this allowed a new buyout plan for UAL to be put forth in 1990.

Aside from KKR, leading LBO dealmakers have included Forstmann Little and Adler & Shaykin. Forstmann made a name for itself during the 1980s by doing buyouts (including those of Dr Pepper and Lear Siegler) without the use of junk bonds, getting its capital instead from pension funds and wealthy individuals. At the end of the decade, amid the collapse of the junk bond market, Ted Forstmann affirmed his position by establishing a buyout fund to be used for deals not involving debt. Despite the change in climate following the bankruptcy of Drexel Burnham, he had difficulty attracting investors.

PAC-MAN AND OTHER DEFENSES

During the takeover wave of the 1980s, corporations facing a hostile bid or fearing that one would occur adopted a variety of defensive measures. The tactic employed by Martin Marietta against Bendix—that of threatening to pursue its pursuer—was dubbed the Pac-Man defense. Calling in a more friendly purchaser was known as seeking a white knight, and paying a premium price to buy back the shares of a raider (but no other stockholders) was labeled greenmail.

Other techniques involved changing the corporation's bylaws to make it more difficult to take control. These included so-called shark repellents, such as staggering the terms of directors so the entire board could be voted out at once or establishing supermajority requirements that up to 95 percent of the shareholders approve a merger. Another preemptive measure was to sell a block of stock, but not all of the company, to a friendly outside party to make it more difficult for a raider to gain control. This use of a "white squire" was employed by CBS when it agreed to let Loews Corp. buy up to 25 percent of its shares after the Ted Turner bid failed but other takeover attempts remained possible.

The most controversial defensive maneuver was known as the "poison pill." First used in Lenox Inc.'s resistance to a bid by Brown-Forman Distillers in 1983, the pill was an adverse financial arrangement that would take effect after a raider had successfully carried out a hostile takeover. For example, stockholders remaining after the takeover might be given the right to purchase additional shares at half the market price, thus substantially diluting the firm's equity. The more extreme forms of the pill would probably have required the liquidation of the company.

Poison pills were meant to discourage raiders in the way that nuclear weapons were supposed to deter hostile action by one of the superpowers against the other. While more and more companies adopted pills in one form or another, no one knew exactly what would happen if a pill were ever triggered. It was also unclear for some time whether the device was indeed effective in preventing takeovers. James Goldsmith managed to evade Crown Zellerbach's pill and still win control of the company. The use of the pill was upheld in a 1985 ruling by the Delaware Supreme Court in a test case involving Household International.

Other court rulings favored the offense. Raiders were strengthened by a decision in the Revlon/Pantry Pride case in which Revlon's arrangement to sell Forstmann Little two of the best parts of the company for a bargain price was deemed illegal. This "lock-up" arrangement to sell Revlon's so-called crown jewels was meant to make the deal more attractive to the LBO people and to discourage Pantry Pride. A similar position was handed down by a federal appeals court in early 1986 invalidating a lock-up arrangement SCM Corp. had been using to thwart Hanson Trust.

Raiders also ended up winning the battle over the "exclusionary self-tender offer," a device used by Unocal to defeat T. Boone Pickens in 1985. The oil company had foiled Pickens by arranging to buy back shares at a hefty premium from all shareholders except him. Although the Delaware Supreme Court sanctioned the technique, it was later banned by the SEC.

Tender offers by raiders became less common as acquirers made use of large-scale open-market purchases of shares to gain control. This technique, used for example by Campeau Corp. in its 1986 takeover of Allied Stores, was facilitated by the willingness of investment banks to supply huge sums of their own money to help finance purchases.

Raiders received yet more encouragement from a change in attitude on the part of institutional investors (pension funds, insurance companies, etc.). Traditionally these investors sided with management. But because they had a fiduciary responsibility to seek the best possible return, they had to take attractive offers from raiders seriously. Institutions such as the College Retirement Equities Fund began to oppose some of the antitakeover tactics being adopted by boards and sought to require companies to get shareholder approval for such measures.

That drive had some effect, but companies found a new means of defending themselves against unwanted suitors. The technique, called recapitalization, involved substituting much of the firm's equity for debt (usually by borrowing heavily to pay a special dividend to shareholders in exchange for a part of their holdings), thus making the company less appealing to a raider. Corporations such as FMC, Holiday, and Harcourt Brace Jovanovich used the method to deter actual or potential takeover bids.

More aggressive defense techniques, a rise in state regulation of takeovers (upheld by the Supreme Court in 1987), and the uncertainty following the stock market plunge in 1987 contributed to a deceleration in takeover activity. But the lull did not last for long. In early 1988 Hoffman-La Roche of Switzerland made a bid for Sterling Drug, the Dart Group went after Stop & Shop, Canadian developer Robert Campeau targeted Federated Department Stores, and Japan's Bridgestone shut out an Italian rival to obtain Firestone Tire & Rubber. One difference from the recent past was that raiders, seeking to get around poison-pill obstacles, were making much greater use of proxy fights to obtain control; Icahn narrowly lost such a battle at Texaco.

By the end of 1988 the megadeals were back with a vengeance, focusing on the food industry. In the course of only a few weeks Britain's Grand Metropolitan made a bid for Pillsbury, Philip Morris announced its intention to acquire Kraft, and the top management of RJR Nabisco launched its effort to take the company private through a leveraged buyout. Pillsbury succumbed to Grand Met in a deal worth $5.8 billion after its poison-pill defense was struck down in court. Philip Morris won Kraft for $12.9 billion. KKR nabbed RJR Nabisco with its $25 billion bid—by far the largest deal in history.

After the poison pill proved ineffective in several cases, companies turned to yet another form of defense: the establishment of an employee stock ownership plan to create a large block of stock likely to be loyal to management. Such a plan (along with other defenses) allowed Polaroid, for instance, to thwart a takeover effort by Diamond Shamrock.

The power of directors to rebuff a takeover bid was also enhanced in the 1989 free-for-all among Time Inc., Warner Communications, and Paramount Communications (the new name taken by Gulf +

Western). Time and Warner had planned a friendly merger when Paramount came along with a hostile offer for Time. The directors of Time rebuffed Paramount and won a court case in which a Delaware judge held that directors have a right to pursue whatever policy they think is best for the company, even if a majority of the shareholders think otherwise.

That ruling gave rise to a series of friendly mergers, including the drug industry marriages of Bristol-Myers and Squibb, and Beecham and SmithKline Beckman.

THE GREAT TAKEOVER DEBATE

Management adoption of extreme defensive measures fueled an already heated debate on the legitimacy of takeovers. Attitudes toward the phenomenon ranged from considering it a dangerous trend that had to be controlled by government action to viewing it as a sign of a healthy, vital economy.

The financial community was split on the matter. While many investment bankers were getting rich off the merger wave, some such as Felix Rohatyn of Lazard Frères and Nicholas Dillon, chairman of Dillon Read, worried that it was getting out of control. Many critics argued that takeovers amounted to a wasteful diversion of resources and that the vast sums being raised by raiders were putting upward pressure on interest rates and making it more difficult for companies to obtain capital for productive investments. They also noted that purchasers often ended up with dangerously high levels of debt.

Managers denounced takeovers as disruptive to companies, and labor leaders noted that takeovers accelerated plant closings and job losses. Robert Reich, a prominent public policy analyst at Harvard University, portrayed the rise of takeovers as part of the "paper entrepreneurialism" that he saw making the U.S. economy less competitive.

The most outspoken defenders of takeovers were laissez-faire economists such as Eugene Fama of the University of Chicago and his disciples at the University of Rochester and elsewhere. One of those disciples, Michael Jensen, published a controversial article in the *Harvard Business Review* in which he argued that allowing the "market for corporate control" to function freely was beneficial both to shareholders and to the economy.

Defenders of takeovers insisted that they served to accomplish a shake-up of American industry that was necessary in the wake of disinflation, deregulation, and the decline of OPEC. While restructuring may have indeed been needed in some cases, it is unclear whether many megamergers contributed to greater efficiency. Many of the large mergers of the past decade have been disasters. Examples include Mobil's purchase of Marcor, Fluor's acquisition of St. Joe Minerals, Exxon's purchase of Reliance Electric, and Sohio's acquisition of Kennecott. But there have also been notable success stories, including the marriages of General Electric and RCA, and Dow Chemical and Merrell.

A WHO'S WHO OF THE TAKEOVER GAME

The takeover world of the 1980s had a large and colorful cast of characters. First, the raiders. There were four leading takeover entrepreneurs:

James Goldsmith. The British-French food magnate and publisher stalked a number of U.S. forest products companies. He acquired Diamond International in 1981 and proceeded to liquidate the company's assets. In 1984 he collected greenmail from St. Regis and made a hefty profit on his holdings in Continental Group even when he lost his takeover bid. In 1985 Goldsmith succeeded in defeating a poison-pill defense by Crown Zellerbach and eventually got himself installed as chief executive of the company. The following year he made a run at Goodyear Tire & Rubber. After a few weeks he dropped his bid and sold back his shares to the company at a hefty profit. In 1989 Goldsmith shifted his focus to the United Kingdom, bidding more than $20 billion for BAT Industries. After BAT announced plans to sell off many prized assets—including the Marshall Field's and Saks Fifth Avenue retail chains in the United States—Goldsmith abandoned his effort.

Carl Icahn. The former stockbroker made plays for a long list of big companies, including Tappan, American Can, Marshall Field's, and Dan River. Although he was often thwarted in his takeover efforts, he usually ended up with hefty profits on his stock investments. In 1985 he made an offer for Phillips Petroleum after T. Boone Pickens dropped his bid, and he also sought Uniroyal. Phillips bought back his stock, and Uniroyal ended up in a leveraged buyout; but Icahn made out well in both cases. He then turned around and initiated a dogfight for TWA. Making a deal with the airline's unions (which preferred Icahn to rival bidder Texas Air, whose chairman Frank Lorenzo was a notorious union-buster), Icahn succeeded in winning control of TWA. In 1986 he made a $7 billion bid for USX but was rebuffed by management. He held on to his 11 percent stake (later increased to 13) and tried to pressure the company to accelerate its restructuring process and leave the steel business. A proposal by Icahn to spin off 80 percent of the steel operations was defeated by USX stockholders in 1990. In 1988 Icahn made a $15 billion bid for Texaco, which was in Chapter 11 as a result of its dispute with Pennzoil. He narrowly lost a proxy battle for control of the oil giant's board, and in 1989 he sold his holdings on the open market at a profit of some $600 million.

Irwin Jacobs. "Irv the liquidator" started off in the closeout business but emerged as a raider of first rank. Based in Minneapolis, Jacobs sought but ended up selling off his holdings in companies such as Kaiser Steel, Walt Disney, Avco, and Castle & Cooke. In 1985 he succeeded in taking over sporting goods maker AMF and started selling off that company piece by piece. The following year he bought stakes in several energy companies, including Pioneer Corp., which found an unusual white knight in T. Boone Pickens. He also made a bid for Borg-Warner but the company ended up going private. In 1989 he made a profitable run at Shaklee Corp. and then accumulated 10 percent of Avon Products and offered $3 billion for the cosmetics company. Avon successfully resisted the bid. By 1990, Jacobs was trying to shake his reputation as a raider by promoting a fund aimed at making friendly investments in troubled companies.

T. Boone Pickens, Jr. The chairman of Mesa Petroleum (later Mesa Limited Partnership) made forays against a number of major oil companies, the most prominent being Gulf, which in 1984 agreed to be acquired by Chevron to escape Pickens. A bid by Pickens for Phillips Petroleum led to a deal in which the company repurchased Mesa's shares at a profit for the Pickens company. But in 1985 Pickens was defeated in a bid for Unocal and was excluded when that company bought back stock from shareholders at a big premium. Pickens later made several unsuccessful runs at Diamond Shamrock as well as bids for Boeing, Singer, Newmont Mining, and Homestake Mining. In 1989 he shook up Japan with his purchase of a large share of Koito Manufacturing and his (unsuccessful) attempt to win representation on the company's board. More recently Pickens has been lobbying against entrenched corporate managements as chairman of an advocacy group called United Shareholders Association.

Other leading raiders of the 1980s included:

The Bass Family. Perry Bass and his three sons made good use of the oil fortune left by Perry's uncle Sid Richardson. The Bass family made a bid for Marathon Oil in 1981, collected greenmail from Blue Bell and Texaco, and made a friendly arrangement with Walt Disney to buy a big block of the company's stock to ward off Saul Steinberg. In the mid-1980s the family ceased pursuing its deals as a group. Robert Bass took the lead in acting on his own. In 1988 the 40-year-old son of Perry Bass was especially active: He bought Westin Hotels from Allegis and sold its Plaza Hotel in New York to Donald Trump; he joined in a leveraged buyout of Bell & Howell; he made a bid for book publisher Macmillian (which ended up being bought by British media tycoon Robert Maxwell); and he led a group that put up only $150 million to gain control of American Savings and Loan (the largest insolvent thrift in the country, with $16 billion in healthy assets). In 1990 he made a bid for the parent company of Florida's *St. Petersburg Times,* which ended up buying back the shares held by Bass.

The Belzberg Brothers. The three Canadian brothers have a reputation as greenmailers (Blue Bell, Masonite, etc.), but in 1985 they purchased old-line manufacturer Scovill for $523 million. They were allied with T. Boone Pickens in the battle for Gulf. In 1986 the Belzbergs again made handsome profits by selling back their holdings in Potlatch Corp., Ashland Oil, and USG. Not so profitable was their investment in H. H. Robertson, which the Belzbergs accumulated over several years and which they watched decline in value as the company suffered a series of misfortunes. The Belzbergs also struck out with their investment in Armstrong World Industries. After losing a proxy battle in 1990, they sold their holdings at an estimated loss of at least $16 million.

Paul Bilzerian. Having made a fortune in Florida real estate in the late 1970s, Bilzerian gained national attention with a 1984 run at Syntex Corp. and 1985 bids for H. H. Robertson and Cluett, Peabody. He next went after Hammermill Paper, which embraced International Paper as a white knight. Bilzerian tried to play the white knight for Allied Stores, which nevertheless ended up in the Campeau retail empire. In 1987 he made a bid for Singer Co. and ended up buying the company (with some financing help from T. Boone Pickens). While Bilzerian was occupied with restructuring that company, he was hit with a federal indictment in 1988 charging him with securities and tax law violations in relation to his previous takeover bids. In 1989 he was convicted on nine counts and sentenced to four years in prison.

Coniston Partners. This firm started out as a money manager but ended up functioning a lot more like a corporate raider, buying stakes in companies and then agitating for change. Run by investment bankers Paul Tierney and Keith Gollust, along with lawyer Augustus Oliver, Coniston made its first splash in 1985 by promoting a liquidation of Storer Communications, which ended up in a leveraged buyout. The following year the firm made a run at NL Industries before Harold Simmons took control and then turned a $49 million profit on shares it purchased in Viacom International shortly before that company was taken private. In 1987 Coniston bought 13 percent of Allegis and called for dismemberment of the company (which did sell off its nonairline businesses and changed its name back to UAL). In 1988 Coniston took a position in Gillette and found itself in fierce struggle with the company's management. Coniston narrowly lost a proxy battle but profited handsomely when Gillette repurchased a portion of outstanding stock. In 1990, amid the decline of debt-financed takeovers, Coniston was disbanded.

Marvin Davis. This Denver oilman bought the Twentieth Century-Fox film studio (with Marc Rich) in the early 1980s, and after selling his half to Rupert Murdoch he embarked on highly publicized but not very successful series of attempted takeovers. He made bids for CBS, NWA (parent of Northwest Airlines), and UAL. The only major deal he completed was the purchase of Spectradyne in 1989.

Asher Edelman. The New York arbitrageur bought into and gained control of a series of computer and other companies, usually in order to liquidate their assets. His largest coup came in 1985 when he won control of Datapoint. In 1986 he made a bid for Fruehauf, which escaped him by arranging a leveraged buyout, and for Lucky Stores, which also successfully resisted him. The following year Edelman joined with Dominion Textile of Canada in bidding for Burlington Industries, which ended up going private in a leveraged buyout. A bid for Telex pushed that company into a merger with Memorex International. While teaching a course at Columbia Business School in 1987, Edelman generated a controversy by offering $100,000 to any student who identified a company he might try to take over. Yet about that time Edelman largely withdrew from the U.S. market and moved to Europe. He profited handsomely from his investment in the British conglomerate Lonrho but was less successful in his run at British retailer Storehouse. At the same time he was the target of a proxy battle by a dissident shareholder in Datapoint.

Carl Lindner. Acting through his American Financial Corporation, this highly secretive, veteran Cincinnati investor over the years bought major stakes in companies such as Gulf + Western, Gannett, United Brands, Penn Central, and Circle K; in the latter three cases he got personally involved in managing the companies. Lindner took a big loss in his investment in Mission Insurance Group, which went into receivership. He acted as a white knight for Taft Broadcasting but then put his three sons on the board of the company and set out to build it into a media empire.

Rupert Murdoch. The international media baron gobbled up newspapers and magazines in the United States and Britain. In 1984 he collected greenmail from Warner Communications and made an unsuccessful bid for Champion International. In 1985 he bought seven TV stations from Metromedia for $2 billion, 12 magazines from Ziff-Davis, and all of Twentieth Century-Fox. To comply with U.S. media ownership rules, he became a naturalized American citizen. In 1987 Murdoch purchased Harper & Row, and the following year he spent $3 billion to buy Triangle Publications, owner of *TV Guide.*

Ronald Perelman. Having built a miniconglomerate (Technicolor, Consolidated Cigar, Pantry Pride, etc.) in his private company, MacAndrews & Forbes Holdings, Perelman caused a stir in 1985 with his drawn-out but successful bid for Revlon. The following year he collected greenmail from CPC International and Gillette. In 1987 he turned the tables on Wall Street by making a bid for Salomon Brothers, but the firm defeated the effort by getting investor Warren Buffett to make a friendly acquisition of 12 percent of the shares. Perelman backed away from raiding in the late 1980s and, aside from purchases such as a group of failed S&Ls, focused more of his attention on managing Revlon.

Victor Posner. The dean of raiders started buying into old-line industrial companies in the 1960s. Operating through Sharon Steel, NVF, and other vehicles, Posner engaged in numerous proxy battles. In 1984 he took Royal Crown private in a leveraged buyout. But in the mid-1980s his empire began to crumble. Sharon Steel went bankrupt in 1987; the same year Posner pleaded no contest to federal tax evasion charges. (He avoided prison by agreeing to spend $3 million for the homeless and to devote 20 hours a week for five years to the same cause.)

Meshulam Riklis. Starting in the late 1950s this former securities analyst began using Rapid-American Corp. as a vehicle for carrying out a long list of highly leveraged deals, including the purchase of McCrory Stores, Schenley Industries, International Playtex, and BVD. Liquidity problems later forced Riklis to sell off many of these properties, though he went on to purchase E–II Holdings, a spin-off of Beatrice. Riklis, who married actress Pia Zadora, outraged E–II bondholders when he tried to take $925 million out of the company in exchange for the Fabergé cosmetics business, which he had acquired in 1984.

Harold Simmons. This Dallas financier made passes at companies such as Pacific Southwest Air, Ozark Air, GAF, Medford (which he purchased), and Sea-Land. He was sued by the Labor Department for using pension fund assets to finance takeover bids. In 1986 he gained control of NL Industries. Two years later he began accumulating shares in Lockheed; in 1990 he was defeated in a proxy fight for control of the aerospace company's board.

Saul Steinberg. Having grown rich from computer leasing, Steinberg first made waves in 1969 with an unsuccessful takeover bid for Chemical Bank. Operating through Reliance Group, Steinberg invested in a number of companies and usually received quite unfriendly responses from management. In 1984 he collected greenmail from Quaker State Oil and Walt Disney. That same year he acquired Days Inn (which he later sold). In 1986 he acquired John Blair & Co. and sold a portion of Reliance to the public. The following year he became chief executive of insurance brokerage Frank B. Hall, which was 30 percent-owned by Reliance. In 1989 Steinberg made a large profit when he sold his stake in UAL.

Donald Trump. The cocky New York real estate developer has attempted to make his mark on the airline and gambling industries as well as the Manhattan skyline. In 1986 he made a run at Holiday Corp., and the following year he collected greenmail from Bally Manufacturing and bought a share in Allegis (now UAL), later selling it at a large profit without having made a formal bid for the company. In 1989 Trump purchased Eastern's Air Shuttle and made a short-lived bid for the parent company of American Airlines. During the same period he became the dominant player in the Atlantic City gambling business. He started one casino in a joint venture with Holiday Corp. (whom he later bought out), acquired another from Hilton Hotels, and ended up with a third (the Taj Mahal) as part of a settlement with Merv Griffin of their battle for Resorts International. In mid-1990 he was scrambling to meet his debt payments.

Oscar Wyatt. The founder and chairman of Coastal Corp. is one of the most controversial figures in the oil and gas world. In 1983 he bid for Texas Gas (which ended up with CSX); in 1984 he engaged in a bitter battle with Houston Natural Gas; and in 1985 he purchased American Natural Resources, which made Coastal one of the largest U.S. pipeline companies. Later that year he collected greenmail from Sonat Inc. In 1989 he made a profit of some $55 million on an investment in Texas Eastern when that pipeline company found a white knight in Panhandle Eastern.

RISK ARBITRAGE AND INSIDER TRADING

The arbitrageurs were called the pilot fish that swam along with sharks such as Pickens and Icahn. Once a tender offer or merger was announced the "arbs" loaded up on the stock of the target company in the expectation that its value would rise. The risk they took was that the deal might fall through and instead of receiving the premium price being offered by the acquirer they would end up with a bundle of stock whose value had plunged below the price they paid for it.

During the early 1980s the most prominent of the arbs was Ivan Boesky, who went to great lengths to argue that he and his counterparts were not mere speculators out for a killing. The service the arbs performed, according to Boesky, was to free small shareholders of the risk and waiting involved in the period between the announcement of a merger and its successful execution. Although arbs made many millions on deals such as those involving Gulf and Getty, they also lost bundles on deals that collapsed, such as the Pickens bid for Phillips Petroleum and Chicago Pacific's leveraged buyout of Textron.

It was customarily assumed that the success of arbs such as Boesky was based on exhaustive research, solid analysis, and good luck. It turned out that the truth was more prosaic and sordid. In November 1986 the Securities and Exchange Commission made a startling announcement. The feds had been investigating Boesky for some time and had uncovered evidence that he illegally obtained insider information on mergers and takeovers before they were made public. Boesky admitted the crime and agreed to plead guilty to a criminal charge and pay a penalty of $100 million. He was also to be barred from the securities business for the rest of his life. At the same time, the SEC indicated that it would aggressively pursue its investigation of takeover activity.

The Boesky case was an offshoot of a wide-ranging investigation by the SEC of insider trading by Wall Street professionals. Earlier in 1986 the agency had brought charges against investment banker Dennis Levine, who cooperated with the authorities and revealed that among his other illegal activities he had arranged to sell Boesky information on deals before they were made public. This allowed Boesky to load up on a stock with the knowledge that as soon as the deal was announced, its value was bound to soar.

Although Boesky paid for his sins (he was later sentenced to three years in prison), he in a sense got the best of the SEC. In the days before his indictment was made public, Boesky unloaded more than $440 million of his holdings in stocks involved in takeovers. Boesky correctly anticipated that these shares would plunge in value after the announcement that the entire takeover fraternity was being investigated. Observers called the move by Boesky to exploit the knowledge of his own legal troubles the ultimate form of insider trading.

Yet federal prosecutors did benefit greatly from Boesky's willingness to cooperate with their investigation; they used information from him as the basis for a wave of subpoenas that were served on leading players in the takeover game. Boesky reportedly also led investigators to an informant who provided the basis for the arrest of three other top arbitrageurs in February 1987: Robert Freeman of Goldman Sachs, Richard Wigton of Kidder Peabody, and Timothy Tabor, who had recently left Merrill Lynch. That informant turned out to be Martin Siegel (formerly of Kidder Peabody), who pleaded guilty to insider trading charges and paid a fine of $9 million. After several months the government was forced to drop the charges against the three arbs because it was not prepared to proceed with the case, though Freeman later pleaded guilty to one count of mail fraud (and was sentenced to four months in prison and paid a fine of $1 million). The investigations of Wigton and Tabor were dropped in 1989.

The next target of the investigation was Boyd Jefferies, chairman of Jefferies Group, a brokerage firm that had worked closely with Ivan Boesky. Jefferies admitted engaging in securities violations including a stock parking scheme with Boesky. This was followed by the announcement in June 1987 that Kidder Peabody had agreed to pay $25 million in fines to settle a sweeping set of insider trading allegations brought by the SEC. At the end of the following year Drexel pleaded guilty to six counts of mail, wire, and securities fraud and paid a fine of $650 million. In 1989 Drexel's Michael Milken was indicted on racketeering charges; the following year he pleaded guilty to six counts and paid a fine of $600 million.

THE LAWYERS

One prominent lawyer once said: "Corporate takeovers are analogous to feudal wars, and the lawyers are the mercenaries." In virtually every one of these wars a particular pair of mercenaries end up playing the key roles on the opposing sides. During the 1980s Joseph Flom and Martin Lipton were the preeminent legal tacticians in the field, and no large company felt comfortable in a merger battle without one of them on its side. Flom, of the firm Skadden Arps Slate Meagher & Flom, was the specialist in offense. His firm was paid large retainers by dozens of companies that wanted to be sure they could call on Skadden's services. Lipton, of the smaller firm Wachtell Lipton Rosen & Katz, was famous for devising defensive measures such as poison pills. In 1988 it was reported that Lipton collected a fee of $20 million for representing Kraft during two weeks of takeover discussions with Philip Morris.

PUBLIC RELATIONS FIRMS

Many hostile tender offers ended up as battles for the hearts and minds of shareholders, with both sides resorting to a barrage of propaganda. The orchestration of these campaigns—which involved such things as blaring full-page newspaper ads and cultivation of reporters—was the province of the public relations specialists. The two names that popped up as often as those of Lipton and Flom were Kekst & Company, led by Gershon Kekst, and Hill & Knowlton, led by Richard Cheney.

The 10 Largest Merger and Acquisition Deals in the United States
(Completed as of January 1990)

Transaction	*Amount ($ billions)*	*Year*
1. RJR Nabisco is taken private	$25.1	1989
2. Chevron buys Gulf	13.2	1984
3. Philip Morris buys Kraft	12.9	1988
4. Bristol-Myers merges with Squibb	12.7	1989
5. Texaco buys Getty Oil	10.1	1984
6. Beecham merges with SmithKline Beckman	8.3	1989
7. British Petroleum buys Standard Oil	8.0	1987
8. Du Pont buys Conoco	7.2	1981
9. Time merges with Warner	7.0	1990
10. Campeau buys Federated Dept. Stores	6.5	1988

Source: "Deals of the Year," *Fortune*, various years.

PROXY SOLICITORS

The job of directly winning over shareholders in proxy battles also belonged to the proxy solicitors. These companies helped to prepare material that was sent to shareholders, contacted individual and institutional investors with their client's pitch, and supervised the distribution of proxy material. The leading proxy solicitors during the 1980s were the Carter Organization, Georgeson & Co., D. F. King & Co., and Morrow & Co. Don Carter, one of the flashiest of the bunch, resigned from the firm bearing his name in 1990 after becoming the subject of a criminal investigation. Carter pleaded guilty to theft and tax evasion charges stemming from what prosecutors said was his practice of billing clients for nonexistent services and inflating expenses for the work he did perform.

SOURCE GUIDE

Data Sources

The Acquisition/Divestiture Weekly Report, a newsletter, and *Merger & Acquisition Sourcebook*, published annually (Santa Barbara, Calif.: Quality Services Company).

"Deals of the Year," an annual list of the 50 largest deals published by *Fortune* magazine in one of its January issues.

"M&A Deals of the Year," an annual feature of *Institutional Investor* magazine, in January.

Mergers & Acquisitions, bimonthly and almanac. This leading trade publication both tracks M&A activity and publishes feature articles.

Mergers and Corporate Policy, a biweekly newsletter that serves as a supplement to the *Yearbook on Corporate Mergers, Joint Ventures and Corporate Policy* (Ipswich, Mass.: Cambridge Corporation).

Mergerstat Review, an annual compilation of M&A data (Schaumburg, Ill.: W. T. Grimm).

Online Databases

IDD M&A TRANSACTIONS (New York: IDD Information Services; available via DIALOG).

INSIDER TRADING MONITOR (North Miami, Fla.: Invest/Net; available via DIALOG).

M&A DATA BASE (Philadelphia: MLR Publishing; available via ADP Data Services).

M&A FILINGS (Washington, D.C.: Charles E. Simon & Co.; available via DIALOG).

Books and Reports

Adams, Walter, and James L. Brock. *Dangerous Pursuits: Mergers and Acquisitions in the Age of Wall Street.* New York: McGraw-Hill, 1988.

Boesky, Ivan. *Merger Mania.* New York: Holt, Rinehart & Winston, 1985.

Brooks, John. *The Takeover Game.* New York: E. P. Dutton, 1987.

Bruck, Connie. *The Predator's Ball: The Junk-Bond Raiders and the Man Who Staked Them.* New York: Simon & Schuster, 1988.

Burrough, Bryan, and John Helyar. *Barbarians at the Gate: The Fall of RJR Nabisco.* New York: Harper & Row, 1990.

Davidson, Kenneth. *Megamergers: Corporate America's Billion-Dollar Takeovers.* Cambridge, Mass.: Ballinger, 1985.

Fleischer, Arthur, Jr.; Geoffrey C. Hazard, Jr.; and Miriam Z. Klipper. *Board Games: The Changing Shape of Corporate Power.* Boston: Little, Brown, 1988.

Frantz, Douglas. *Levine & Co.: Wall Street's Insider Trading Scandal.* New York: Henry Holt, 1987.

Investor Responsibility Research Center. *Corporate Takeover Defenses*. Washington, D.C., 1989.

______. *State Takeover Laws*. Washington, D.C., 1989.

______. *Power by Proxy: More Corporate Conflicts in the 1980s*. Washington, D.C., 1990.

Lampert, Hope. *True Greed: What Really Happened in the Battle for RJR Nabisco*. New York: New American Library, 1990.

Lipton, Martin, and Erica Steinberger. *Takeovers and Freezeouts*. New York: Law Journal Seminars Press, 1979.

Nelson, Ralph. *Merger Movements in American Industry, 1895–1956*. Princeton, N.J.: Princeton University Press, 1959.

Phalon, Richard. *The Takeover Barons of Wall Street*. New York: G. P. Putnam's Sons, 1981.

Segal, Harvey H. *Corporate Makeover: The Reshaping of the American Economy*. New York: Viking Press, 1989.

Taylor, John. *Storming the Magic Kingdom: Wall Street, Raiders, and the Battle for Disney*. New York: Alfred A. Knopf, 1987.

U.S. Congress, Congressional Research Service. *Leveraged Buyouts and the Pot of Gold: Trends, Public Policy, and Case Studies*. Washington, D.C.: Government Printing Office, 1987.

U.S. Congress, House Committee on Energy and Commerce. *Corporate Takeovers: Public Policy Implications for the Economy and Corporate Governance*. Washington, D.C.: Government Printing Office, 1986.

U.S. General Accounting Office. *Hostile Corporate Takeovers: Synopses of 32 Attempts*. Washington, D.C., 1988.

Wansell, Geoffrey. *Tycoon: The Life of James Goldsmith*. New York: Atheneum, 1987.

CHAPTER 21

VENTURE CAPITAL AND INITIAL PUBLIC OFFERINGS

In a March 1985 speech, Ronald Reagan gave presidential endorsement to a notion that had been in the air for some time. He declared: "We have lived through the age of big industry and the age of the giant corporation, but I believe that this is the age of the entrepreneur, the age of the individual. That's where American prosperity is coming from now, and that's where it's going to come from in the future."

Entrepreneurs have indeed become some of the leading heroes of the day. The legends of the electronics industry have gained the most currency: Silicon Valley is hailed as a place where the likes of Steven Jobs, cofounder of Apple Computer, can take an idea and turn it into a fortune almost overnight.

While entrepreneurs ultimately succeed or fail on the strength of their ideas, they are also dependent on financing in order to move from vision to flourishing enterprise. New ventures in emerging technologies are not the kind of risk that the average bank is willing to take; such projects must turn to a different sort of financier—the venture capitalist.

Venture capitalists (VCs) are professional investors who specialize in finding and financing young companies that show promise. The VCs, who had $33 billion of capital under management at the end of 1989, do not do this out of altruism. In exchange for their investment they receive substantial equity in the company, an investment that can yield enormous profits when a successful venture goes public (i.e., begins to sell its shares on the open market). Serious VCs expect an annual return of 50 percent or more for success stories, while other investments—usually the majority of the portfolio—may have to be written off entirely.

IT ALL STARTED WITH COLUMBUS

Venture capital goes back to the origins of America. Christopher Columbus was in effect an entrepreneur who was using venture capital from Queen Isabella to exploit business opportunities in distant lands. Until the middle of the 20th century, venture capital was the province of wealthy individuals who enjoyed bankrolling inventors or entrepreneurs. This is the way that pioneers in fields such as automobiles, electric power, and commercial aviation got their starts.

Beginning in the 1930s some of these patrons began to approach such investments more systematically. Laurance Rockefeller and John Hay Whitney were the leading figures in this regard, and their efforts ended up under the auspices of, respectively, Venrock Associates and J. H. Whitney & Co. Another early promoter of entrepreneurs was Harvard Business School professor Georges Doriot, who ran the American Research and Development Corp., founded in 1946.

Venture capital remained a rather specialized activity until the late 1950s, when Congress moved to encourage less-than-big business. The Small Business Investment Act of 1958 established entities called small business investment companies (SBICs). These were privately owned and operated firms that were allowed to borrow funds from the Small Business Administration and invest them in fledgling enterprises. During the 1960s there was a great surge of SBICs, but in recent years they have declined in importance, in part because of federal budget constraints.

Nearly all the rest of the venture capital industry has grown up in tandem with the development of high technology, especially the burst of advances in electronics since the creation of the microprocessor and the miniaturization of integrated circuits. The venture capitalists made Silicon Valley, and the valley made the VCs. For those who follow the financial side of high-tech, venture capitalists such as Arthur Rock and Thomas Perkins are as celebrated as Steven Jobs and his fellow entrepreneurs.

Venture capital investment took off in the late 1970s, a fact that many analysts attribute to the reduction in capital gains taxes that took effect in 1979. The total funds pouring into venture capital soared from $300 million that year to $1.3 billion in 1981. The influx exceeded $4 billion in 1983.

THE ROLE OF VENTURE CAPITALISTS

Aside from getting rich, venture capitalists have come to play a major role in the development of new industries. By deciding which of the hundreds of business proposals that cross their desks each year are worth backing, VCs are functioning as gatekeepers of technology. They determine which products are going to be developed and marketed and which will become dashed hopes of would-be entrepreneurs.

Venture capitalists are usually organized in the form of limited partnerships. The general partner solicits funds and manages the investments, receiving 2 to 3 percent of the value of the fund for his expenses and 20 percent or so of the profits for his trouble. That trouble can be considerable.

First of all, the general partner or partners and their staff must be expert in evaluating the large number of proposals that come their way. Once the few likely gems are separated out, there is the arcane (some would say arbitrary) process of pricing a deal involving a company that may not yet have any revenues or salable products.

Since many entrepreneurs are inexperienced in business, the VC must often function as a management advisor; some actually usurp the role of chief executive, especially when a company is in trouble and the VC's investment—which usually ranges from several hundred thousand to several million dollars—is in jeopardy.

Although VCs have traditionally invested in projects that have already been incorporated and need capital to grow, in the early 1980s some investors began backing entrepreneurs in first setting up their companies. These so-called seed capitalists (such as Zero Stage Growth Fund of Cambridge, Massachusetts) offered funding in the range of $50,000 to $250,000, whereas most VCs felt that deals that small were not worth the expense of investigating.

The venture capital go-go period of the early 1980s drew new players into the field. Encouraged by liberalization of rules governing fiduciary responsibility, many institutional investors took the plunge. These included public and private pension funds, insurance companies such as Prudential and CIGNA, bank trust departments, and university endowments at schools such as MIT. Banks such as Citicorp and Bank of America joined in, as did corporations such as General Electric. Of these the pension funds turned out to be the most enthusiastic. By the late 1980s roughly one half of all new capital coming into venture funds were from this source.

Most remarkable was the emergence of state governments as venture capitalists. About 20 states set up VC programs in order to promote job creation; some invested directly, and others gave tax breaks to state-chartered VC funds. While most state funds were small (under $10 million), Michigan, Alaska, and Wyoming have each sunk more than $30 million into such investments.

Not everyone is enchanted with the venture capital system. VCs are branded by some as "vulture capitalists" who demand majority stakes and extensive control in exchange for their financing. Critics such as Gordon Moore, former chief executive of Intel, have argued that the presence of abundant venture capital entices key people away from their employers into start-ups, thus disrupting the development of technology. (Moore took this view despite the fact that he and Robert Noyce formed Intel after leaving Fairchild Semiconductor in 1968.) During the VC frenzy of the early 1980s, many observers charged that there was too much money chasing too few worthwhile projects, and as a consequence many marginal enterprises were being funded.

Whether or not the criticism was warranted, the breakneck growth of venture capital investment did pause in 1984. The rest of the 1980s was a roller-coaster ride for the industry. The volume of venture capital commitments declined again in

The 10 Largest Venture Capital Firms, by Capital under Management at the End of 1989 ($ Millions)

	Firm	Capital
1.	Warburg, Pincus Ventures	$1,500
2.	TA Associates	501
3.	Kleiner, Perkins, Caufield & Byers	462
4.	Chemical Venture Partners	450
5.	John Hancock Venture Capital	436
6.	Hambrecht & Quist Venture Partners	424
7.	Summit Partners	391
8.	Prudential Venture Capital	371
9.	Golder, Thoma & Cressey	346
10.	Trust Company of the West	335

Source: Venture Economics, Inc., Needham, Massachusetts.

1985, then increased sharply over the next several years, reaching a record of nearly $5 billion in 1987. It then began sliding again, sinking to about $2.5 billion in 1989.

These figures reflected a series of contradictory trends in the industry. Much of the high-tech sector fell into a slump, yet specific areas such as superconductor applications and AIDS vaccine research remained hot, as did some low-tech areas such as specialty retailing and nursing homes. American VC firms began to turn their sights overseas, while Japanese corporations started offering venture capital to U.S. start-ups. The Japanese tractor company Kubota, for example, invested in a semiconductor firm called MIPS and a manufacturer of supercomputer workstations called Ardent. Increasing numbers of institutional investors were willing to commit funds to venture capital, yet the proliferation of VC funds, which numbered some 650 in the late 1980s, made attractive investments increasingly hard to find.

THE BOOM AND BUST OF IPOs

In order for a venture capitalist to realize a gain on his investment he must sell his equity interest. Sometimes this is done through private placements, but the more profitable and popular method is to take the company public. Along with the boom of venture capital in the early 1980s there was a blossoming of initial public offerings (IPOs). The number of IPOs leaped from 45 in 1978 (with $249 million raised) to 448 in 1981, in which $3.2 billion was obtained.

A handful of smaller investment banks emerged as the leading IPO underwriters in this period. The "four horsemen" was the label given to L. F. Rothschild Unterberg Towbin of New York, Alex. Brown & Sons of Baltimore, and Hambrecht & Quist and Robertson Colman & Stephens of San Francisco. An important role has also been played by D. H. Blair & Co. of New York.

The IPO market declined in 1982 but soared the next year to a remarkable level of 888, in which some $12.6 billion in equity was raised. The IPO frenzy of 1983 brought windfalls to both VCs and entrepreneurs such as Allen Paulson of Gulfstream Aerospace and K. Philip Hwang of TeleVideo Systems, both of whom ended up (on paper at least) as two of the wealthiest men in the country.

The following two years saw a sharp fall-off in IPO activity, but the numbers of new issues and the amounts raised remained higher than at any time before the magic year of 1983. In October 1985 the initial offering of stock in Fireman's Fund brought in $900 million, far surpassing all earlier IPOs. (The previous record was held by Ford Motor Co.'s $658 million IPO in 1956.) But the following year the Fireman's offering was topped by the $1.2 billion IPO of the Henley Group, a collection of businesses spun off from Allied-Signal. This, in turn, was surpassed by the $1.6 billion Conrail offering in 1987.

At this point the general new-issues market was beginning to heat up once again. This time the range of industries was much greater: high tech was no longer dominant, and the popular issues included everything from specialty retailers to yogurt. The stock market crash in October 1987 put a temporary damper on IPOs, yet a record $24 billion was raised in IPOs that year. The new-issues market slipped in 1988 and sank sharply to about $14 billion in 1989 amid the uncertainty about equities. What life there was in IPOs in the late 1980s came from an unusual source: closed-end investment funds. These management investment companies operate like mutual funds but offer shares that trade on stock exchanges or over the counter. In 1987 and 1988 initial offerings from these funds (including the $2 billion one for MFS Intermediate Income Trust in 1988, which exceeeded all other IPOs) accounted for the lion's share of the market, though by 1989 they, too, were in decline.

LEADING PERSONALITIES AND FIRMS

Frederick Adler of Adler & Co. is a New York trial lawyer turned venture capitalist. Known for his aggressive and abrasive personality, Adler is a master at taking charge of troubled companies, such as software developer MicroPro International, and turning them around.

Hambrecht & Quist has played a major role in the high-tech world as both a venture capitalist and an investment bank, underwriting major new issues such as People Express, Apple Computer, and Genentech. Especially hard hit by the VC and new issues slumps, the firm forced general partner William Hambrecht to relinquish many of his responsibilities. In the late 1980s the firm overextended itself and ended up with a large number of poor performers in its portfolio.

Thomas Perkins of Kleiner, Perkins, Caufield & Byers has been one of the most successful VCs. His firm's first fund, established in 1972, grew in value from $7 million to $218 million in five years, aided by major successes such as Tandem Computers and the biotechnology company Genentech.

Arthur Rock first got involved in venture capital in the late 1950s when he was working at the brokerage firm of Hayden Stone. He was contacted by a group of disgruntled engineers who wanted to quit working for William Shockley, the coinventor of the transistor, and strike out on their own. Rock helped them form Fairchild Semiconductor (as a subsidiary of Fairchild Camera & Instrument), which played a key role in the development of electronics and from which numerous people broke away and started other innovative companies with the help of Rock. His firm, Arthur Rock & Co., has backed numerous other successful high-tech ventures.

Sevin Rosen Management, founded by Benjamin Rosen and L. J. Sevin in 1981, is already one of the leaders in the field, boosted by its big successes with Compaq Computer and the software company Lotus Development. Rosen is a former Morgan Stanley analyst who got involved in the early stages of the personal computer industry. Sevin founded the semiconductor company Mostek, which he sold to United Technologies in 1979.

By the mid-1980s **TA Associates**, based in Boston, had become one of the largest venture capital firms in the United States. Founder Peter Brooke was an early backer of An Wang of Wang Laboratories and later helped to build Biogen and Tandon. Brooke later started Advent International, which led the way in the internationalization of the VC business.

Other prominent venture capital firms include the Mayfield Fund and the Sequoia Fund of Menlo Park, California; Sutter Hill Ventures of Palo Alto, California; and Hillman Company of Pittsburgh.

SOURCE GUIDE

Leading Analysts and Experts

Norman Fosback, editor of the newsletter *New Issues* in Fort Lauderdale, Florida.

Stanley Pratt of Venture Economics, the leading VC consulting firm, based in Needham, Massachusetts.

Securities Data Co. (data on IPO underwriting), New York.

Trade Associations

National Association of Small Business Investment Companies, 1156 15th St. NW, Washington, D.C. 20005. Tel.: (202) 833–8230.

National Venture Capital Association, 1655 N. Ft. Myer Drive, Arlington, VA 22209. Tel.: (202) 528–4370.

Data Sources and Directories

Directory of Corporate Financing, a semiannual publication with data on IPO underwriting (New York: Investment Dealers' Digest Inc.).

Directory of Operating Small Business Investment Companies (Washington, D.C.: U.S. Small Business Administration).

Pratt's Guide to Venture Capital Sources and *Venture Capital Yearbook*, both annual (Needham, Mass.: Venture Economics).

Silver, A. David. *Who's Who in Venture Capital*, 2nd ed. (New York: John Wiley & Sons, 1986).

Value Line New Issues Service (New York: Value Line Inc.).

Trade Publications

Going Public: The IPO Reporter, weekly.

New Issues, monthly.

Venture Capital Journal, monthly.

Books and Reports

Organisation for Economic Co-operation and Development. *Venture Capital in Information Technology*. Paris, 1985.

U.S. Congress, Joint Economic Committee. *Venture Capital and Innovation*. Washington, D.C., 1985.

U.S. Congress, Office of Technology Assessment. *Technology, Innovation and Regional Economic Development*. Washington, D.C., 1984.

Wilson, John W. *The New Venturers: Inside the High-Stakes World of Venture Capital*. Reading, Mass.: Addison-Wesley Publishing, 1985.

PART 6

HEAVY INDUSTRY AND TRANSPORTATION

CHAPTER 22

AEROSPACE AND MILITARY CONTRACTING

Back in the 1920s the pioneering builders of airplanes were as dashing and bold as the men who flew them. Over the years the white scarfs have been replaced with pinstripes, but the $112 billion aerospace business remains one of the riskiest around. In the civilian market, companies must invest billions of dollars on new products, never knowing for sure whether by the time they are ready the airlines will still be interested in that kind of plane. This "sporty game," as John Newhouse has called it, represents a unique combination of heavy industry and advanced technology; it is both labor- and capital-intensive.

Until recently, the military side of the business was a bit more predictable, even though companies had to sell to an even more limited universe of buyers: the armed forces, which are subject to the vagaries of politics. Defense contractors benefited from the tendency toward military buildup that, aside from the immediate post-Vietnam malaise, characterized the five decades starting with the onset of World War II. Beginning in the mid-1980s American military spending began to level off, and by the end of the decade changes in the configuration of the world prompted efforts to curb the Pentagon's prodigious appetite.

While the defense industry is famed for producing marvelous new tools of war, it has also gained a reputation for something less than exemplary efficiency and ethics. Cost overruns on weapons systems have been a perennial problem, and numerous contractors have admitted making large amounts of illegal or questionable payments at home or abroad. In the late 1980s there was considerable pressure on the industry to clean up its act. Criminal charges were brought against numerous companies, and the Pentagon seemed to be getting serious about forcing suppliers to compete for lucrative contracts. Yet as their products grow more complicated and expensive and as companies continue to rely on a limited number of potential customers, it is unlikely that the aerospace business will ever function like other industries.

THE INDUSTRY TAKES OFF

The aircraft industry went through a slow ascent in the years following the Wright brothers' first successful flights in 1903. Europe held the lead in aviation until World War I, when the United States, which intended to provide about 2,500 planes for the war effort, was pressured by its allies to supply 10 times that number. Manufacturing companies came out of nowhere, and hundreds of aircraft factories were hastily established. By 1918 the output of aircraft was running at an annual rate of some 21,000 planes. The cooperation of the companies, including a pooling of patents, later led to charges of war profiteering.

The new industrial structure collapsed very quickly after the armistice, and most of the new companies vanished. Those that survived—including Wright Aeronautical (linked to the famous brothers), Curtiss Aeroplane, and timberman Bill Boeing's firm—continued to produce mainly for the U.S. government, given that a significant commercial air transport industry had yet to emerge. Despite the limited market, there were some important newcomers to the business in the 1920s, including Douglas Aircraft, Lockheed Aircraft, and Atlantic Aircraft (an American operation set up by the famed Dutch aeronautical engineer Anthony Fokker). Henry Ford bought into the industry and went on to produce the famous Trimotor, or Tin Goose, the first successful all-metal plane.

The federal government was concerned about the underdeveloped state of the industry, and President Coolidge appointed a study board headed by Dwight Morrow to advise on what public policy should be. The board's 1925 report adopted industry recommendations such as the institution of a longer-term federal procurement policy and the recognition of proprietary designs used on government contracts. Such provisions were embodied in the 1926 Air Commerce Act, and the Pentagon set five-year procurement goals of 1,600 planes for the army and 1,000 for the navy.

During the late 1920s the aircraft industry also benefited from the aviation mania following Charles Lindbergh's famous solo transatlantic flight in 1927 and the growth of the airmail business, which the Kelly Air Mail Act of 1925 put in the hands of private contractors.

The financial wheeling and dealing of the 1920s touched the aviation business. Numerous aircraft producers and airlines were brought together through a series of mergers and put under the auspices of holding companies. The most powerful of these was United Aircraft and Transport Corp., which took over several transport firms and manufacturers such as Boeing, the Pratt & Whitney engine company, and Sikorsky Aviation, which at the time was doing its early work on developing helicopters.

Postmaster Walter Folger Brown encouraged consolidation in the industry in the early 1930s through his power over the granting of the all-important airmail contracts. The convenient arrangement that resulted came under attack after the Roosevelt administration took office. Senator Hugo Black led the charge, leading to the passage of the Air Mail Act of 1934, which instituted both a ban (that turned out to be short-lived) on private transport of airmail and a more permanent requirement that aircraft producers and air transport companies be separated from one another.

The United holding company split into three independent firms: United Air Lines, Boeing Aircraft in the Northwest, and East Coast-based United Aircraft (renamed United Technologies in 1975), which included Pratt & Whitney and Sikorsky. North American Aviation spun off the Eastern and TWA airlines and continued the military aircraft business of what had been Curtiss Aeroplane and Wright Aeronautical.

Despite the Great Depression, the aircraft industry expanded during the 1930s, thanks to the growth of the airlines. Boeing first took the lead with the development of its 247, 60 of which were ordered by United Air Lines. But then Douglas Aircraft responded to a request from TWA and created the DC–1. This, the first of its hugely successful DC (Douglas Commercial) series, turned out to be a prototype, and the production model was the DC–2, which sat 14 passengers and had a cruising speed of 170 miles per hour, compared to 10 passengers and 155 miles per hour for the 247. The enlarged DC–3 (21 passengers) became even better known and more widely used.

The 1930s also saw the development of the famous "flying boats," the huge planes commissioned by Juan Trippe of Pan American to fly across oceans and alight on water where there were no airfields. The planes, dubbed Clippers by Trippe, were originally built by United Aircraft's Sikorsky Division. Beset by heavy losses United abandoned the business in 1938, and a series of other companies such as Glenn L. Martin, Consolidated Aircraft, and Boeing took over production of the flying boats.

By the end of the decade "landplanes" had also been refined considerably. The move to all-metal frames was followed by the development of four-engine planes and the quest to achieve higher altitudes, which required companies to begin work on a system of cabin pressurization.

The growing likelihood of war in Europe brought new stimulus to the military aircraft business, and Lockheed took the lead in selling abroad. The United States soon decided to expand its own fleet—especially after the German blitz of London in 1940 showed what air power could do. In May 1940 President Roosevelt startled the industry and by all accounts his own military establishment by calling for the production of 50,000 planes a year, about five times the existing capacity of the country.

The aircraft makers scrambled to increase production. Automobile companies such as Ford and General Motors were enlisted to help produce engines and later airframes (the bodies of planes) as well. After the attack on Pearl Harbor, output was stepped up even more as Roosevelt demanded 60,000 planes for 1942 and an astounding 125,000 the following year. Huge numbers of workers—including "Rosie the riveter" women joining the industrial labor force for the first time—were pulled into the factories, especially the sprawling facilities of Lockheed, Douglas, and North American in the Los Angeles area. In 1943 aircraft industry employment reached a peak of 1.3 million.

THE JET AGE

Aside from the vast numbers of propeller-driven bombers and fighters built with piston engines in the war years, the industry also developed workable jet engines during the 1940s. In 1941 the federal government formed the Committee on Jet Propulsion, which included representatives of the leading turbine companies. One of those, General Electric, got the contract to produce a jet engine based on a British design. The first American-built jet plane was the XP–59A, which consisted of a Bell Aircraft frame and two of the GE engines; it made its trial flight in October 1942.

After the war there was an inevitable decline in military procurement, but the transition was more orderly than after the previous war, thanks to the provisions of the Contract Settlement Act of 1944. The Pentagon more gradually phased out its orders, beginning with subcontractors, and provided assistance for companies to make the conversion to peacetime production.

The major producers turned back to the civilian market, and Douglas quickly resumed its leadership. But the military business did not remain as limited as it did after the previous world war. As U.S.–Soviet tensions developed into the cold war, the inclination of the American military, reinforced by the recommendations of the Finletter Air Policy Commission, was that air power should be the centerpiece of the U.S. military machine. This commitment led to a sharp increase in aerospace expenditures after the outbreak of the Korean War in 1950.

By the early 1950s jet engine technology was developed enough to be applied to commercial aircraft, but there was some doubt as to whether airlines would want to use the powerful gas turbines, which consumed much more fuel but permitted considerably higher speeds. Boeing, famed for its bombers during the war, decided to take the plunge. The Seattle company was rewarded in 1955, when American Airlines (previously a loyal customer of Douglas) placed a $200 million order for 30 of the 707s. Douglas suddenly realized that its hesitation on jets was mistaken and embarked on the development of a jet-powered DC–8. The company did win a considerable number of orders, but Boeing managed to take over and maintain leadership of the commercial business. The first scheduled flight of a jet plane in the United States took place with an American Airlines 707 in January 1959.

By the mid-1960s the commercial aircraft business—of the world, not only the United States—was dominated by six companies: airframe makers Boeing, Douglas, and Lockheed and engine manufacturers Pratt & Whitney, General Electric, and Britain's Rolls Royce. The early jet planes produced by these companies were noisy and were heavy consumers of fuel. The technology was improved with the placement of a type of fan with 40 or so blades at the front of the engine. These resulting fan-jet engines (the first effective version of which was produced by Rolls Royce in 1960) could handle a larger volume of air and thus develop much greater thrust.

The development of fan-jets, stimulated by the Pentagon's interest in building the huge C–5A cargo planes, made possible substantially larger commercial aircraft as well. The prospect of powerful jets that could carry several times the number of passengers of existing planes was especially tantalizing to a company, such as Pan American, with heavily traveled intercontinental routes. Juan Trippe of Pan Am essentially decided to bet the company on the idea and enlisted Boeing to produce planes with 350 or more seats that would become known as the 747. The purchase agreement for 25 of the jumbo jets was signed in 1966.

That same year American Airlines let it be known that it was also interested in a large jet but one not quite as jumbo as the 747. The domestic carrier was looking for a wide-bodied plane that could carry up to 250 passengers up to 2,100 miles. This sort of plane, of interest to other carriers as well, created an enticing opportunity for Boeing's competitors. Both Lockheed and Douglas (which had gone through a slump and was forced into a merger with military-oriented McDonnell Aircraft in 1967) went after the prize.

The two companies fought hard for what was called the airbus market, and each ended up getting a significant number of orders. The problem was that the airline industry could absorb only so many planes, and there was not enough business around to allow all three producers to thrive.

The weakest link among the three was Lockheed. The company was shaken when its engine partner Rolls Royce was forced into receivership and taken over by the British government. This ordeal scared off both Lockheed's lenders and customers for the L–1011 TriStar. The American company, already weakened by financial problems linked to the C–5A it was producing for the air force, nearly went into bankruptcy itself; it was saved only by a federal loan guarantee program of up to $250 million that squeaked through Congress in 1971.

The aircraft market picked up in the mid-1970s, but the rise in oil prices made airlines eager to have more fuel-efficient planes. The 747s from Boeing and the wide-bodied L–1011s from Lockheed and DC–10s from Douglas had their place in longer, heavily traveled routes, but the carriers were looking to expand their narrow-body fleets and replace aging 707s, 727s, and DC–9s. They also wanted more efficient wide-bodies. Boeing made the biggest commitment to these markets, investing some $3 billion to develop the narrow-body 757 and the wide-body 767.

While the American producers were plunging into this new market they had to look back over their shoulder at the rising threat from abroad. In 1970 a group of French, British, West German, and Spanish aircraft companies formed a consortium called Airbus Industrie to make a foray in the international wide-body business. Their first product, the A300, was a big success, and by the end of the 1970s the consortium had seized one fifth of the international commercial market.

SHAKEOUT AND RECOVERY

In the meantime it became clear that all three of the American manufacturers could not survive. With a pickup in sales of its jumbos and good prospects for the 757 and 767, Boeing became firmly established as the industry leader. So it was a question of whether Lockheed or Douglas would succumb first. For a while observers were betting it would be the latter. A series of accidents involving the DC–10 in the late 1970s undermined the reputation of the plane, and passengers began avoiding flights that used it.

But Douglas managed to recover from the DC–10 debacle and made its way in the market for smaller planes, not by investing billions (like Boeing) in an entirely new product but rather by producing derivatives of the DC–9 and DC–10. Observers were originally skeptical about the willingness of airlines to buy what was essentially old technology, but models such as the twin-engine MD–80 (based on the DC–9) proved to be successes.

Lockheed had no such luck. Sales of the L–1011 remained poor, and by December 1981 the company gave up and announced it would leave the commercial aircraft business and rely on its military contracts.

By the mid-1980s the demand for new planes had improved considerably. The plunge of oil prices bolstered the earnings of the airlines, enabling them to proceed with previously postponed expansion of their fleets. Huge orders began to be placed, such as the $3.1 billion deal announced by United and Boeing in late 1985 and Delta's $2 billion order from Douglas a couple of months later. These were topped by an announcement in August 1986 that British Airways was placing an order with Boeing that could go as high as $4.1 billion.

This favorable new climate for aircraft producers was not without its drawbacks. Having spent years and massive sums of money developing new fuel-efficient technologies, aerospace companies were now finding that the new cheapness of oil was making airlines less concerned about fuel costs. This was a particular blow for Boeing, which (along with engine maker General Electric) was spending several billion dollars developing a new type of engine to be used on Boeing's belated entry into the

150-seat market. The project, which Boeing called the 7J7, involved the use of an unducted fan engine (UDF), a device that made use of external fan blades that looked suspiciously like propellers but which was designed to burn one-third to two-thirds less fuel than existing engines. The Seattle company decided to share the risk and the development cost of the plane with a group of Japanese companies, which were eager to gain access to U.S. aerospace technology. (Those companies have since the late 1970s been major suppliers for Boeing's 767.) Yet the slump in fuel prices and planning problems caused Boeing to delay the project indefinitely.

In the late 1980s the rivalry among McDonnell Douglas, Boeing, and Airbus intensified as the three leaders of the industry fought for the loyalties of airlines that were planning new commitments for their next generation of planes. For customers looking to replace aging DC–10s with a longer-range wide-body, McDonnell Douglas spent heavily to develop the MD–11, which was meant to fit in between Boeing's 747 jumbo jets and its 200- to 250-seat 767. Yet Boeing responded by downsizing the 747 and stretching the 767.

At the same time, Airbus—which in 1986 began to receive serious acceptance from U.S. airlines for its A320 medium-range plane—brought out a long-range A340 to compete directly with the MD–11. Airbus, able to price aggressively because of its government subsidies, began to steal market share from McDonnell Douglas and make Boeing nervous. In early 1988 Boeing strengthened its position by introducing new versions of the 747 and the medium-range 737 that received an enthusiastic response from airlines; the company's 10-year-old midsize 757s also began to catch on. By 1989 Boeing's main challenge was to keep up with the flood of orders. The airline industry's buying spree also fattened (to a lesser extent) the order books of McDonnell Douglas and Airbus.

SPREADING THE RISK

For many years the Big Three engine makers have approached the uncertainty in the demand for their products by spreading their risks through international collaboration. Back in 1974 General Electric created a joint venture with the French company SNECMA. By the mid-1980s such partnerships were the only way new engines were being developed. The biggest combination was International Aero Engines, formed in 1983 by Pratt & Whitney, Rolls Royce, and companies from Japan, Italy, and West Germany.

International Aero stumbled in its development of engines for the Airbus A340, allowing GE–SNECMA (now known as CMF International) to fill the void. GE also shot ahead of Pratt & Whitney in their individual efforts. Starting in the mid-1980s Pratt began falling steadily behind as a result of poor planning and a deteriorating reputation for quality and service. By 1989 Pratt was beginning to regain lost ground, especially with its powerful PW4000 engine, but the company's market share was still far behind the commanding 90 percent it held in the 1970s.

That progress was put into question in early 1990, when GE announced plans for the GE90, which at 80,000 pounds of thrust would be even more powerful than the PW4000. One of GE's partners on the GE90 was supposed to be Daimler-Benz subsidiary MTU. But only a few months after the announcement of the GE90, Pratt, which had worked with the West German company on a limited basis since the early 1970s, formed a closer alliance with MTU, which had to end the relationship with GE.

THE IRON TRIANGLE

Given the many uncertainties of the commercial aircraft business, many companies have traditionally looked to the usually more predictable—and generally more profitable—military side of the business. The industry enjoyed fat years during the heyday of the space program and the 1960s portion of the Vietnam War. Moreover, the decline in defense spending during the period of Vietnamization of the conflict and the aftermath of the war turned out to be short-lived. And by the 1970s the leading aerospace defense contractors (Boeing, General Dynamics, Grumman, Lockheed, Northrop, McDonnell Douglas, Rockwell International, and United Technologies) had developed a secure hold on the lion's share of military spending. Their close relationships with Pentagon officials and members of key congressional committees constituted what analyst Gordon Adams has called the "iron triangle."

The story of defense contracting since the early 1970s has been one of tension between the desire of the military and Congress for the most advanced weaponry and the seeming inability of many contractors to keep the costs of producing these arms under control. Lockheed's massive cost overruns on the C–5A in the late 1960s became emblematic of the situation and contributed to the near-bankruptcy of the company. The problem has been even worse in the complex weapons systems included in the so-called triad (air, land, and sea) of strategic nuclear weapons.

The B–1 bomber, which was supposed to cost $29 million a copy when the contract was given to Rockwell International in 1970, ended up costing $200 million each. (In the interim the project, designed to replace aging B–52s, was canceled by President Carter in 1977 and kept alive by Rockwell until it was revived by the Reagan administration.) Even more checkered has been the history of the Trident nuclear submarine produced by the Electric Boat division of General Dynamics. The management of the project was fraught with problems, and division head P. Takis Veliotis ended up fleeing to his native Greece to avoid indictment on kickback charges.

The reputations of a number of major aerospace companies were further tarnished in the 1970s by revelations that they had been making many millions of dollars in questionable payments to foreign officials to help in getting orders. Lockheed, long a leader in military exports, was implicated in payoff scandals involving the Japanese prime minister, Prince Bernhard of the Netherlands, and a cabinet official in Italy.

There were also controversies regarding the quality of the products being turned out by the industry. Pratt & Whitney, the preeminent military engine producer, was confronted with Pentagon complaints that the company's F100 power plant for the F–15 and F–16 fighters was stalling out and breaking down with alarming frequency.

By the early 1980s the industry was trying to put these unpleasant affairs behind it and take advantage of the trillion-dollar military buildup initiated by the Reagan administration. Aerospace companies and other contractors enjoyed a flood of new orders; observers said that the defense business could hardly have been doing better if the country had been at war. Things were so juicy in fact, with defense contractors enjoying margins about twice the average for corporations in general, that the industry began to come under unfavorable public scrutiny.

Starting in 1983 there was a series of revelations about what appeared to be wildly inflated prices that the military was paying for its supplies and spare parts. The press regularly reported with indignation the $17 bolts and $600 toilet seats the Defense Department was procuring. Contractors decried what they considered a misunderstanding of the complexities of pricing in government purchasing, but the political tide was against them.

Under pressure from Congress, the Pentagon began to get tougher with its suppliers. The Department of Defense started to shift from the traditional cost-plus-fee contracts to fixed-price-incentive arrangements, under which the contractor rather than the government had to shoulder increased costs. The companies also had to absorb much of the initial research and design expenses for their projects.

The new order of the day was competition. The navy and the air force spread their jet fighter engine business between General Electric and Pratt & Whitney to chastise Pratt for problems with the F100. In 1985 the air force announced that it wanted seven contractors—Boeing, General Dynamics, Grumman, Lockheed, McDonnell Douglas, Northrop, and Rockwell—to compete for the contract for an advanced tactical fighter for the 1990s to replace the F–15. In 1986 Northrop and Lockheed were chosen to lead teams to develop competing prototypes for the new fighter. A decision by the navy to encourage McDonnell Douglas to compete with General Dynamics in producing the Tomahawk cruise missile reduced the average cost of the weapon by more than one third. By fiscal year 1987 the army, navy, and air force were each spending more than 50 percent of their procurement budgets through competitive bidding.

Along with the new emphasis on competition, the Pentagon began to seek an end to the sloppy or dishonest billing practices of many contractors. In 1985 and 1986 prominent companies such as General Electric, General Dynamics, and Litton were suspended as authorized government contractors. Skeptics noted that these suspensions were often brief and did little to impede the companies' ongoing relationships with the Pentagon, but they once again put the industry on the defensive. As in the past Lockheed became one of the main culprits. In 1986 the air force accused the company of overcharging hundreds of millions of dollars on the C–5B cargo plane (though the claim was later scaled back). In 1988 Sunstrand agreed to pay a record fine of $115 million to settle charges that it had repeatedly overbilled the military since the beginning of the decade.

In the late 1980s the crackdown on contractor corruption was pursued with great intensity by Henry Hudson, a U.S. Attorney in Virginia. Hudson's Operation Ill Wind started off with a bang in June 1988, when the FBI made surprise searches of the premises of 14 military contractors (including McDonnell Douglas, Northrop, and United Technologies), as well as several offices at the Pentagon.

The investigation focused on charges that various private consultants (including Melvyn Paisley, a former aide to navy secretary John Lehman) had bribed Pentagon procurement officials to obtain confidential documents for their contractor clients, who used the information to gain an unfair advantage in preparing bids. Hundreds of subpoenas were issued in the probe, and the Defense Department briefly suspended payments to all contractors in nine programs in which companies were believed to have won competitive contracts by unlawful means. By the spring of 1990 the investigation had resulted in 32 guilty pleas by defendants including Boeing, Hughes Aircraft, Raytheon, and Teledyne.

Starting in the mid-1980s the defense industry also had to contend with the decision by Congress to put an end to the dizzying growth of the military budget. In 1985 President Reagan reluctantly accepted the decision by the legislature, facing the

The Top 10 Defense Contractors, by Prime Contracts in Fiscal Year 1989 ($ Billions)

1. McDonnell Douglas	$8.6
2. General Dynamics	7.0
3. General Electric	5.8
4. Raytheon	3.8
5. General Motors	3.7
6. Lockheed	3.7
7. United Technologies	3.6
8. Martin Marietta	3.3
9. Boeing	2.9
10. Grumman	2.4

Source: U.S. Department of Defense.

need to get the deficit under control, to limit the increase in defense spending to the rate of inflation.

By the end of the decade, with the disarmament initiatives of the Soviet Union and the collapse of Communism in Eastern Europe, pressure was mounting for substantial cuts in defense spending. While much of the country was debating what to do with the "peace dividend," the arms makers were scrambling to find substitutes for their lucrative Pentagon contracts. Several companies looked to the government's war on drugs as a new market for some of their aerospace products, such as the four radar balloons General Electric sold to the Customs Service for use in detecting smugglers' planes. Yet the more realistic corporate planners were looking to entirely different lines of business outside the military-industrial complex.

The need to search for nonmilitary markets was lessened somewhat by the re-escalation of Pentagon arms spending following the emergence of the Persian Gulf crisis in 1990.

LABOR RELATIONS

The entrepreneurs who pioneered the aircraft industry were none too friendly toward unions. In fact one of the reasons a group of them congregated in the Los Angeles area was to take advantage of the weakness of organized labor in the area. The

Machinists union stepped up its efforts after the passage of the National Industrial Recovery Act, but the industry strongly resisted unionization and set up employee associations to undermine the process.

It took the 1937 Wagner Act to change the balance of power. A sit-down strike at Douglas that year brought recognition, and Lockheed signed with the Machinists after that. Companies such as Grumman continued to resist unionization.

Further organizing in the industry was divided between the Machinists and the United Auto Workers (UAW). The presence of the UAW in the industry created a confrontation when the Ford Motor Co., which was still resisting unionization in its auto plants, became an aircraft subcontractor during the expansion of the industry in the late 1930s. The open-shop policies of leading companies came under repeated attack from the unions, and the firms even defied President Kennedy in a dispute on the subject in 1962.

Labor relations in the industry were frequently turbulent in the following years, and strikes were not uncommon. In 1977 Lockheed became one of the first U.S. companies to seek contract concessions when it sought to erode seniority rights. A 12-week strike by the Machinists ended in a compromise.

The problems of the industry in the early 1980s made the companies tougher at the bargaining table. In 1983 the Machinists signed a contract with Boeing that substituted lump-sum payments for wage increases and instituted a two-tier pay structure. The pact prompted other companies to demand concessions. A UAW strike at McDonnell Douglas to resist similar givebacks collapsed after 17 weeks.

The industry was booming in 1986, but Boeing again got the Machinists to take lump sums instead of increases in base pay. Machinists and UAW members at McDonnell Douglas took a harder line. After rejecting management demands for changes in work rules and the shifting of some medical insurance costs to workers, the unions declined to strike but instead conducted an in-plant campaign to pressure the company. The unions ended up accepting management-imposed conditions that included a small increase in base pay as well as lump-sum payments.

Traditional walkouts were held at the Bell Helicopter Division of Textron in 1987, the Electric Boat Division of General Dynamics in 1988, and at Boeing in 1989. The Boeing strike, which lasted 48 days, ended in a settlement that included both lump-sum payments and moderate increases in base pay.

By the beginning of the 1990s unions in the defense industry were realizing that the future of their members' jobs were in question as a result of declining military budgets. The UAW and the Machinists responded to the situation by intensifying their campaign to get the federal government to plan an orderly transition of military contractors to civilian projects. The unions put their support behind an economic conversion bill sponsored by Representative Ted Weiss of New York, but they faced substantial opposition from the many politicians who fear any policy that smacks of economic planning.

LEADING COMPANIES

Since the mid-1950s **Boeing** has been the leader of the commercial aircraft industry and a major defense contractor as well. One of the largest U.S. industrial exporters, Boeing has manufactured about one half of all the jet planes ever produced outside the Soviet bloc. The company was started as a sideline by timberman William Boeing just before World War I. For a time it was part of the United Aircraft and Transport holding company, and during World War II it became the leading producer of bombers, including the famous B–17 Flying Fortress and the B–29 Super Fortress, one of which dropped the atomic bomb on Hiroshima. In the 1950s Boeing gambled on the introduction of jet planes to the airline market and ended up displacing Douglas as the premier commercial producer. In the late 1960s the company developed the 747 jumbo jet, and in the 1970s it produced a new generation of smaller, more efficient jetliners. Boeing survived a brief challenge in 1987 from raider T. Boone Pickens and resumed work on its high-tech 7J7, a successor to the 727 that uses unusual propeller-driven engines made by General Electric. The 7J7 ran into problems and was delayed indefinitely, but the company was swamped with orders for the latest versions of the 737 and 747 as well as belated demand for its 757. At the beginning of the 1990s it had a backlog of orders worth $85 billion. In 1989 Boeing pleaded guilty and paid a fine of $5 million in connection with charges that the company illegally obtained classified Pentagon planning documents.

General Dynamics, one of the aerospace companies almost exclusively dependent on Pentagon business, has had more than its share of troubles since the 1960s. The company, founded in 1952, experienced heavy cost overruns on the F–111 fighter, major managerial problems in the production of Trident nuclear submarines by its Electric Boat division, and scandals regarding its billing practices. In the mid-1980s its hold over the F–16 fighter business was challenged by a cheaper plane from Northrop, but the air force decided to stick with the General Dynamics product. In 1987 the Justice Department decided not to seek indictments of General Dynamics after a long-running investigation of charges that Electric Boat filed false cost estimates and timetables for delivery of nuclear submarines. That same year a federal judge dismissed criminal fraud charges against General Dynamics and four of its executives in connection with a contract to produce a prototype of the Sgt. York antiaircraft gun. The judge acted after the Justice Department said it was unable to support the allegations.

Grumman has been a leading provider of navy aircraft since the 1930s. Founded by Leroy Grumman at the beginning of that decade, the company in more recent years has been heavily dependent on its expensive F–14 fighter (the featured plane in the film *Top Gun*). The company's E–2C Hawkeye airborne early-warning plane was used to great effect by Israel during 1982 fighting in Lebanon. Grumman lost out on the navy's contract for the Advanced Tactical Aircraft planned as a replacement for the company's A–6 attack plane. By the late 1980s Grumman was putting more emphasis on defense electronics and nonmilitary activities such as data processing.

Lockheed has been one of the most controversial companies in the aerospace business. Founded by Allan and Malcolm Loughhead (who later changed the spelling of their name to Lockheed) in 1916, the company went bankrupt in 1931 and was revived the following year by Robert and Courtlandt Gross. The firm was a major aircraft producer during World War II, but it later had trouble with the performance of both its commercial jet Electra and its Starfighter planes sold to NATO countries. The company returned to the commercial business in the late 1960s by developing the L–1011 TriStar, a wide-body that competed with Douglas's DC–10. Problems with that project and the C–5A transport it was building for the air force nearly put the company under in the early 1970s. It was rescued only by a $250 million loan guarantee from the federal government. Soon afterward the company was embroiled in controversy following reports of some $38 million in questionable payments made to foreign officials to promote orders. In 1981 Lockheed gave up on the commercial aircraft business and focused on military projects. Faced with pressures including the decline in military spending and a possible takeover move by raider Harold Simmons, the company began restructuring itself in 1989. Lockheed chief executive Daniel Tellep made plans for expanding civilian products and arranged for an employee stock ownership plan to purchase 19 percent of the company's shares. Simmons, who amassed an equal stake, was defeated in a 1990 proxy battle for control of Lockheed's board.

McDonnell Douglas was created by the 1967 merger of a leading military aircraft producer and a leading commercial one. James McDonnell (known as Mr. Mac) founded his firm in 1939 and during the war emerged as a major Pentagon supplier. Donald Douglas got started in airplane production in the 1920s and in the 1930s became a leader in the commercial market with his DC (Douglas Commercial) series. Douglas Aircraft was number one in civilian aircraft until Boeing brought out the first jet airliner in the mid-1950s and stole the show. Douglas went into a slump and needed the alliance with McDonnell to keep alive. The combined company jumped into the wide-body race in the late 1960s and was doing reasonably well until its DC–10 ran into a streak of problems in the late 1970s. McDonnell Douglas opted not to follow Boeing in developing a new generation of smaller jets and instead successfully sold derivatives of the DC–9 and DC–10. By the late 1980s the company was enjoying both a surge in demand for its commercial jets and its position as the country's leading military contractor. Yet by 1990 the company was feeling pinched enough to announce plans for eliminating at least 14,000 jobs.

Northrop lived for years on the inexpensive F–5 fighter, which has been marketed to dozens of Third-World countries. Founded by airplane designer John Northrop in 1939 after he left Lockheed, the company has been involved in a number of scandals. Chairman Thomas Jones was found guilty of making $150,000 in illegal contributions to the 1972 campaign of Richard Nixon. In the mid-1970s there were revelations that the company had regularly entertained Pentagon officials and members of Congress at a hunting lodge on the eastern shore of Maryland. In the mid-1980s Northrop, which has traditionally done more foreign than domestic business, waged an unsuccessful campaign to get the air force to adopt its F–20 fighter over General Dynamics' F–16. Northrop also failed to win the huge contract for the navy's Advanced Tactical Aircraft. In the late 1980s the company was the subject of a slew of investigations relating to mismanagement of its production of guidance systems for the MX missile and its role as the prime contractor for the B–2 Stealth bombers (radar-evading planes that are expected to cost more than $500 million each). In 1989 Northrop was indicted on criminal charges of falsifying test results on the air force's air-launched cruise missile and the navy's AV–8B Harrier jet. The following year, just as the trial in the case was about to begin, Northrop pleaded guilty and agreed to pay $17 million in fines. In working out the plea agreement with Northrop, federal prosecutors agreed to close their investigations relating to the MX and the B–2.

Rockwell International has made its name as the largest contractor for NASA and as the producer of the B–1 bomber. Leading aircraft producer North American Aviation (a combination of several early producers) merged with Rockwell-Standard (a diversified manufacturer) in 1967, shortly after three astronauts died in an explosion of an Apollo space capsule produced by North American. The combined company adopted the name Rockwell International in 1973. It took a decade before the company could enjoy the fruits of the B–1 contract it received in 1970. The project, intended to provide a replacement for aging B–52s, was canceled by President Carter in 1977 and revived by President Reagan in 1981 (and redesignated the B–1B). From then until 1988, when the last of the 100-plane program was completed, Rockwell prospered with the $16 billion contract. Although the company managed to find other sources of revenue to replace those from the B–1B, Rockwell suffered from a variety of embarrassing problems in the late 1980s. One of its space shuttles, Challenger, exploded during takeoff in 1986 (though most of the blame ended up being place on Morton Thiokol, the producer of the shuttle's booster rocket, and Rockwell got a $1.3 billion contract to build a replacement shuttle). In 1988 Rockwell was indicted for double-billing the air force on contracts to build a navigational satellite system; the company agreed to plead guilty and was fined $5.5 million. Rockwell has also been the subject of federal investigations of mismanagement and unsafe handling of plutonium waste at the Rocky Flats nuclear weapons plant the company operates for the Energy Department in Colorado.

INDUSTRY DATA

Aerospace	*1989*	*1988*	*1987*
Value of shipments	$112.5 billion	$105.9 billion	$104.4 billion
Total employment	846,000	828,000	816,000
Value of imports	NA	$6.6 billion	$5.8 billion

Source: U.S. Department of Commerce.

SOURCE GUIDE

Leading Stock Analysts and Experts

Gordon Adams, Defense Budget Project, Washington, D.C.

Wolfgang Demisch, analyst at UBS Securities, New York.

Paul Nisbet, analyst at Prudential-Bache.

David Smith, analyst at Raymond, James & Associates, St. Petersburg, Florida.

Trade Associations and Unions

Aerospace Industries Association of America, 1250 I Street NW, Washington, DC 20005. Tel.: (202) 371–8400.

International Association of Machinists and Aerospace Workers, 1300 Connecticut Avenue NW, Washington, DC 20036. Tel.: (202) 857–5200.

United Automobile, Aerospace and Agricultural Implement Workers of America International Union, 8000 E. Jefferson Avenue, Detroit, MI 48214. Tel.: (313) 926–5000.

Data Sources and Directories

Aerospace Facts and Figures, annual (Washington, D.C.: Aerospace Industries Association).

Aviation Week and Space Technology publishes an annual directory issue with a guide to companies in the industry, in December.

Interavia ABC Aerospace Directory, an international guide to manufacturers and airlines published annually (Geneva, Switzerland: Interavia Publishing).

World Aviation Directory, a semiannual volume that includes information on aircraft manufacturers (Washington, D.C.: McGraw-Hill).

Online Databases

AVIATION/AEROSPACE ONLINE (Washington, D.C.: McGraw-Hill).

DMS CONTRACT AWARDS, DMS CONTRACTORS, AND DMS MARKET INTELLIGENCE REPORTS (Alexandria, Va.: Jane's Information Group; available via DIALOG).

PTS AEROSPACE/DEFENSE MARKETS & TECHNOLOGY (Cleveland: Predicasts; available via DIALOG).

Trade Publications

Aerospace Daily.

Aviation Week and Space Technology.

Defense Industry Report, fortnightly.

Defense Week.

Interavia (Geneva, Switzerland), monthly.

Books and Reports

Adams, Gordon. *The Iron Triangle: The Politics of Defense Contracting.* New York: Council on Economic Priorities, 1981.

Bluestone, Barry; Peter Jordan; and Mark Sullivan. *Aircraft Industry Dynamics: An Analysis of Competition, Capital and Labor.* Dover, Mass.: Auburn House, 1981.

Gansler, Jacques S. *The Defense Industry.* Cambridge, Mass.: MIT Press, 1980.

Klare, Michael T. *American Arms Supermarket.* Austin, Texas: University of Texas Press, 1984.

Kotz, Nick. *Wild Blue Yonder: Money, Politics and the B–1 Bomber.* New York: Pantheon Books, 1988.

Massachusetts Institute of Technology. "The U.S. Commercial Aircraft Industry and its Foreign Competitors," in *Working Papers of the MIT Commission on Industrial Productivity.* Cambridge, Mass.: MIT Press, 1989.

Newhouse, John. *The Sporty Game.* New York: Alfred A. Knopf, 1982.

President's Blue Ribbon Commission on Defense Management (Packard Commission). *Quest for Excellence: Final Report to the President.* Washington, D.C., 1986.

Rae, John B. *Climb to Greatness: The American Aircraft Industry, 1920–1960.* Cambridge, Mass.: MIT Press, 1968.

Sampson, Anthony. *The Arms Bazaar.* New York: Viking Press, 1977.

Shaw, Linda, et al. *Stocking the Arsenal: A Guide to the Nation's Top Military Contractors.* Washington, D.C.: Investor Responsibility Research Center, 1985.

Stubbing, Richard A. *The Defense Game.* New York: Harper & Row, 1986.

Tyler, Patrick. *Running Critical: The Silent War, Rickover, and General Dynamics.* New York: Harper & Row, 1986.

CHAPTER 23

AIRLINES

The economic progress of the vast American continent has depended to a great extent on the development of increasingly efficient transportation. The industrial growth of the 19th century was stimulated first by the expansion of inland waterways and then by the spread of railroads. While rail lines and later trucks became the main means of transporting goods, it has been the evolution of air travel that has truly integrated American business on a national level and made possible its wide expansion abroad.

Over the past few decades air travel has changed from a novel and expensive form of transportation indulged in mainly by corporate executives and movie stars into a type of mass transit. The deregulation of the airline industry in 1978 created a free-for-all that resulted in bargains for passengers and challenges for unions. By the late 1980s, however, ticket prices were tending to rise, and as a result of a dizzying series of mergers and takeovers, the $69 billion industry was increasingly dominated by a handful of megacarriers.

FROM MAILMEN TO GLOBETROTTERS

In the years following the pioneering flights of the Wright brothers, commercial aviation was slow in getting established in the United States. The first regularly scheduled passenger line was set up to fly between St. Petersburg and Tampa in Florida in 1914, but the venture was short-lived. While passenger lines were being established across Europe, aviation in America centered on the delivery of mail.

The Kelly Act of 1925 compelled the Post Office Department to open up all but transcontinental routes to private contractors. This encouraged a number of barnstormers to become entrepreneurs and stimulated the growth of commercial aviation. The business became all the more glamorous after Charles Lindbergh's historic solo flight from New York to Paris in 1927; both Main Street and Wall Street became fascinated with flying.

The late 1920s saw the emergence of a slew of companies bidding for the potentially lucrative Post Office contracts. Before long these small firms coalesced into the predecessors of what would become the major carriers, including United Aircraft and Transport, Eastern Air Transport, and American Airways. The mail carriers also began to offer passenger service.

When Postmaster Walter Folger Brown took office in 1929 as part of the Hoover administration, he set about to rationalize and stabilize the airmail industry. He pushed through legislation (the Watres Act) that created a system under which airlines were paid not by the actual weight of the mail they carried but by the amount of space available for mail, thus encouraging the use of larger planes. There were also bonuses for using the most advanced equipment.

Brown also pressured carriers to establish several transcontinental routes and toward that end got Western Air Express, the first successful passenger carrier, to merge with Transcontinental Air Transport, which operated a combination train and plane coast-to-coast service. The resulting company was Transcontinental and Western Air, or TWA (which later changed its named to Trans World Airlines).

What seemed like a brilliant scheme to Postmaster Brown took on the appearance of a grand conspiracy during congressional hearings called by Senator Hugo Black after the Roosevelt administration took office. Brown and the major carriers were accused of carving up the airmail business in an illegitimate manner, and the resulting public outcry prompted Roosevelt to transfer airmail transport to the army air corps.

The army pilots were not experienced in flying at night or in poor weather; after a series of crashes Roosevelt relented and turned airmail delivery back to the more experienced private sector. The major carriers were supposed to be barred from the new system, but the Post Office restored their contracts after they made slight changes in their names and replaced some executives. American, Eastern, TWA, and United were firmly established as the Big Four of the domestic air transport business. The determination of fares and the allocation of routes in that business were placed in the hands of a federal regulatory agency called the Civil Aeronautics Board (CAB).

At the same time, another U.S. company was becoming the dominant player in the international airline field. Juan Trippe, the son of a New York stockbroker, became interested in aviation at an early age, going on to form a flying club at Yale and managing an operation that carried airmail between New York and Boston. Trippe had his eye on Cuba and set up a company with the aim of winning the airmail route between Key West and Havana. He did get the route after merging with two other companies, and the combined operation took the name of Pan American Airways.

Through Trippe's aggressive leadership, Pan Am won a rapid succession of foreign airmail contracts, which were authorized by the Kelly Foreign Air Mail Act—a piece of legislation that Trippe helped to write. By 1930 Pan Am was designated the U.S. government's "chosen instrument" for developing overseas air links, and the carrier had more than 20,000 miles of routes to 20 countries. Trippe turned his attention to transoceanic routes but was dismayed by the European carriers' demands for reciprocal landing rights in the United States.

While that political problem was being worked out, Trippe had airplane manufacturer Igor Sikorsky build four-engine amphibious planes for use in the Pacific. Trippe called these flying boats Clippers in honor of the old clipper ships. After having constructed facilities for stops in Hawaii, Midway, Guam, and the Philippines, Trippe inaugurated the China Clipper's mail and passenger service to Manila with much fanfare in 1935. Transatlantic service began in 1939. Throughout much of the world, Pan Am's planes became the symbol of American expansionism.

After World War II the United States emerged as the dominant force in international aviation, and Trippe sought landing rights in every corner of the globe. Pan Am lost its foreign monopoly, however, as international routes were awarded by the CAB to several other carriers, especially TWA (which was then controlled by millionaire Howard Hughes).

The late 1950s saw the introduction of passenger jets and the reduction of fares to encourage air travel among a wider section of the population. By 1957 more passengers crossed the Atlantic by air than by sea. Trippe saw the potential for mass levels of air travel and in the mid-1960s entered into an agreement with Boeing for the development of a jet capable of carrying 350 passengers. TWA followed Pan Am's lead, and thus began the age of the jumbo jet.

Mass air travel and huge planes, such as the 747s that began flying in 1970, were predicated on the availability of cheap fuel. The age of the jumbo jet had hardly begun when that resource disappeared, and along with expensive fuel came higher interest rates and other elevated costs.

At first the airlines, protected as they were by the CAB, did not have too much to worry about. But by the mid-1970s the rigid pricing structure of the past four decades began to crack as more aggressive carriers pressed for the right to discount fares. At the same time, a deregulatory gospel started to be preached by the likes of Alfred Kahn, chairman of the CAB during the Carter administration. Before long there was serious discussion of abolishing federal oversight of the business aspects of aviation.

THE DEREGULATION FREE-FOR-ALL

This is precisely what happened after Congress passed the Airline Deregulation Act of 1978. That legislation established a schedule for the phasing out of federal regulation of routes and fares along with the abolition by 1985 of the CAB, the industry's stern but paternalistic overseer.

The major carriers lost no time in abandoning their less profitable flights to smaller cities. In the first year of deregulation about 75 localities lost all of their scheduled service. In most of those cities commuter lines stepped into the void, but they used smaller planes and had more erratic schedules.

The major, or trunk, airlines turned their attention to the more popular routes, such as New York to Miami, and the number of those flights soared. Competition in those markets led to vicious price wars, which reduced what is known as fare yield and ate heavily into the carriers' operating income. By 1980 the industry as a whole experienced its first operating loss since 1947.

In order to increase efficiency, the majors (defined as those carriers with $1 billion or more in annual revenues) put more emphasis on hub and spoke systems. Under this arrangement commuter and regional lines brought passengers to the hub airports, from which they could fly around the country on flights of the majors. The desire to build up business in these hubs—which included Chicago and Denver for United, Atlanta for Delta, and Dallas for American—made the price-cutting all the more intense.

The early 1980s brought no relief for the industry. The recession, the curtailment of flights after the air controllers' strike in 1981, increased costs for fuel, interest and landing fees, and the continuing fare wars on the popular routes all prolonged the misery. The larger carriers also saw their business eroding as a result of the emergence of small discount carriers that were able to slash prices by eliminating amenities and using nonunion labor. This approach was pioneered in the 1970s by the likes of Southwest Airlines and Air Florida. Deregulation spawned a new generation of what came to be called upstart carriers. Among them were Midway Airlines, America West, New York Air, and Muse Air.

But the outstanding success story was People Express, which turned into the fastest-growing carrier in aviation history. Built by Donald Burr, former chief operating officer of Texas International Airlines, People challenged nearly all of the major carriers with its no-frills service. The carrier established its hub at the underused airport in Newark, New Jersey, and priced its flights low enough to justify its advertising slogan: "Flying that costs less than driving." Burr, using humanistic management techniques, also turned airline labor relations upside down. His nonunion work force was hired at rates well below industry averages but was imbued with an esprit de corps that put teamwork before work rules and status. Each employee was required to purchase 100 shares of stock (at a heavy discount) and was asked to perform a variety of tasks. Passengers also had to get used to a new ambience, which included the end of free meals, free baggage checking, and other amenities. By late 1985 People was flying to 49 cities and had helped to stimulate a series of price wars. Late that year Burr surprised the industry by acquiring Frontier Airlines for $300 million, winning the support of that company's unions. The Frontier acquisition, along with a subsequent purchase of commuter line Britt Airways, allowed People to expand across the country.

But financial problems plagued the company. Facing a severe financial crisis in 1986, the carrier desperately tried to survive by selling off Frontier. A deal with United fell through because of problems with the pilot's union, and Frontier was put into Chapter 11. People, still vulnerable, succumbed to the advances of Texas Air. Burr agreed to sell People for about $122 million and Frontier for $176 million to Texas Air, which then folded them into Continental.

Frank Lorenzo, the head of Texas Air, was the evil genius of the industry. After establishing tiny Texas International Airlines as his base, Lorenzo stalked many of the leading carriers. He was defeated in his attempts to take over National Airlines (Pan Am won that battle), TWA (twice), and Frontier Airlines. But he did win Continental in 1982 and Eastern in 1986, which along with New York Air (the discounter he established in 1980) catapulted Lorenzo's Texas Air holding company into the number-one spot among airline corporations.

People Express was not the only upstart to suffer in the rough-and-tumble world of deregulation; a number of others went into bankruptcy. While the ranks of interstate carriers jumped after deregulation, from about three dozen to some 125 in 1984, the total then started to decline.

More-established lines continued to reel as a result of increased costs and discounted fares. TWA weakened, Pan Am came close to bankruptcy in 1982, and Braniff and Continental actually went into Chapter 11, although in the latter case it was mainly a ploy to abrogate labor contracts. (For more on the industry's union-management battles of this period, see the Labor Relations section below.) Other leading carriers such as Northwest, Piedmont, and USAir prospered during this period mainly by keeping out of the big brawls and serving smaller cities.

Whether prompted in a particular case by a major or an upstart, the price wars flared on a regular basis. Fare structures became so complicated that even travel agents had difficulty keeping up. The majors amassed thousands of different fares, and they used daily computer analyses to keep track of price shifts by one another. The carriers were locked into this nonstop poker game even when it had disastrous effects on earnings. The common wisdom among the majors was that it was preferable to lose income on account of discounted fares than to give up market share. Intense price competition contributed greatly to the industry's record loss of $733 million in 1982. But an improved cost picture allowed the carriers as a group to move slightly into the black in 1983 and then jump to total operating profits of more than $2 billion in 1984.

Another way in which the majors sought to come out ahead in the competitive jungle was through frequent-flyer programs. These programs originated in 1981 as the carriers sought to solidify loyalty from among those most desirable customers: the ones, usually businesspeople, who fly more than 12,000 miles a year. The airlines began offering free flights to vacation spots when a traveler amassed a certain number of miles flying on business. Corporate travel departments, which were excluded from the game, grumbled about employees who eschewed cheaper flights on certain lines in order to fly with the carrier in whose program they were enrolled. In 1986 several airlines began cracking down on the illicit market that developed to buy and sell frequent-flyer coupons. A few years later the carriers were looking for ways to escape from what had become an enormous and (thanks to triple mileage promotions) rapidly growing liability. Because frequent-flyer programs are such effective marketing gimmicks, the airlines dared not eliminate them, settling instead for imposing additional restrictions on when the free tickets can be used.

Carriers also sought to get a competitive edge through their positions on the computer systems that travel agents use to book the large majority of airline tickets. These systems are provided by some of the carriers themselves, and it is not surprising that the flights that tended to appear on the top of the list when a travel agent keyed in a departure time and destination were those of the supplying carrier. American's SABRE system and United's Apollo, the two leaders in the field, have certainly bolstered the market shares of those carriers. Other lines predictably balked at the treatment their flights received in the systems. (A suit filed in 1984 by a group of carriers against American and United ended in 1989 when a federal jury found that the industry leaders were not guilty of anticompetitive practices.)

In 1984 the CAB required the systems to provide unbiased displays, but a number of carriers still argued for reservation systems that were not owned by single airlines. That did not happen; instead, more carriers got into the game. By the late 1980s the battle for travel agency business was intense among SABRE, Apollo, PARS (TWA and Northwest), Datas II (Delta), and System One (owned by Texas Air, though half of it was later sold to the Electronic Data Systems subsidiary of General Motors).

Also intense was the desire by carriers to gobble up one another. The purchases of People and Frontier were only one element of a dramatic process of consolidation and changing ownership that has characterized the airline industry since the mid-1980s. In 1985 corporate raider Carl Icahn won control of TWA, and United bought Pan Am's Pacific routes. In 1986 Northwest and Republic merged, TWA bought Ozark, Texas Air took over Eastern, Delta acquired Western, and American acquired AirCal. In 1987 Piedmont agreed to be acquired by USAir, but completion of the deal was delayed by regulatory problems. In 1989 a group led by investor Alfred Checchi acquired Northwest. Braniff, which had emerged from bankruptcy in 1984, once again sought refuge in Chapter 11 in 1989 and ceased service. In 1990 control of Eastern (which had been put in Chapter 11 a year earlier after its workers went out on strike) was taken away from Texas Air by the bankruptcy court and given to Martin Shugrue, a veteran industry executive who was named trustee of the beleaguered carrier. During its time in Chapter 11 Eastern sold its Air Shuttle to Donald Trump and its Central and South American routes to American.

As a consequence of all this, the airline business is increasingly dominated by a handful of megacarriers. While the industry as a whole has become an oligopoly, the situation in many individual cities is near monopoly. In places such as St. Louis, Minneapolis, and Pittsburgh, almost all of the traffic is controlled by a single carrier (TWA, Northwest, and USAir, respectively), creating what are known as fortress hubs. Also contributing to the concentration is the fact that many regional carriers have been taken over by the majors. In 1989 the nine majors accounted for 93.4 percent of total U.S. air traffic.

While the quality of service generally deteriorated with the arrival of deregulation, it was not until the late 1980s that customers began to experience an increase in prices as a result of the concentration of ownership. When Texas Air moved away from discounts in late 1988, there was no major carrier left committed to a strategy based on low fares. In December 1989 the Justice Department admitted that it was conducting a price-fixing investigation of the industry.

Some members of Congress were prompted by these trends to consider some restoration of airline regulation, including an increase in the power of the Transportation Department over takeovers. Yet the department itself issued a study in 1990 that concluded there was no cause for alarm in the growing concentration of the industry (though it did acknowledge problems at fortress hubs). Transportation Secretary Samuel Skinner vigorously opposed the calls for re-regulation and instead proposed to increase competition by giving foreign carriers greater access to U.S. cities.

While most U.S. airline executives were skeptical of Skinner's plan, several carriers have formed alliances with foreign airlines. Scandinavian Airlines Systems (SAS) purchased nearly 10 percent of Texas Air and formed a joint marketing

The Largest U.S. Airline Carriers in 1989, by Revenue Passenger Miles (In Billions)

1. American	73.5
2. United	69.6
3. Delta	59.3
4. Northwest	45.7
5. Continental	38.8
6. TWA	35.0
7. USAir	33.7
8. Pan American	28.9
9. Eastern	11.6

Source: Airline Economics Inc., Washington, D.C.

arrangement with its subsidiary Continental. SAS later bought out Frank Lorenzo's share of Texas Air, which had been renamed Continental Airlines Holding. Delta sold 5 percent stakes in itself to Swissair and Singapore Airlines. KLM-Royal Dutch Airlines became a part owner of Northwest by participating in Alfred Checchi's takeover of that carrier. These arrangements are part of a global trend toward the internationalization of the airline industry.

LABOR RELATIONS

Unionization in the airline industry began with the associations formed by Post Office pilots in the 1920s to promote safety practices. The Air Line Pilots Association (ALPA) was established as a national union in 1931 and soon gained a solid foothold in the industry. The organization's first major test came quickly when E. L. Cord, the owner of Century Airlines and the Frank Lorenzo of his day, moved to cut pilots' pay from $350 to $150 a month, prompting a strike. ALPA garnered considerable political support, resulting in a rejection of Cord's bid for a Post Office contract. The pilots did not achieve a complete victory, but ALPA's stature was enhanced.

The first women took to the skies as stewardesses in 1930, but the unionization of flight attendants did not occur until the late 1940s. While the organization of pilots led fairly smoothly to one powerful union, the flight attendants had a more difficult time. Rivalries emerged between independent unions that were formed at several carriers and ALPA, which wanted to control the organization of flight attendants but resisted giving them equal status in the union. It was not until 1973 that the Association of Flight Attendants became a fully autonomous union within ALPA, but that organization ended up representing only about half of the unionized attendants. Those at American, TWA, and Pan Am were in independent unions that broke away from the Transport Workers Union (TWU); Eastern flight attendants remained in the TWU.

For many years relations between airline managements and the unions—which for ground crews included the International Association of Machinists, the TWU, and the Teamsters—were relatively peaceful. The reason is that CAB control of fares allowed the carriers to pass along higher labor costs to passengers without competitive drawbacks.

With the advent of deregulation, this convenient arrangement was disrupted, and in some cases open warfare broke out between managements looking to cut costs and unions seeking to maintain their members' standard of living. By the early 1980s nearly every major carrier was demanding wage and work rule concessions from its employees. The unions came to the conclusion that the crisis of the majors was real, especially after Braniff filed for Chapter 11 in 1982.

The unions were thus willing to go along with concessions, but creative labor advisors got the unions to seek something in exchange: stock ownership for workers. Employee ownership of limited numbers of shares was nothing new, but the deals worked out by the airline unions called for the workers to receive substantial chunks of equity. Pan Am led the way in 1981 with an arrangement that gave employees 10 percent of the carrier and a seat on the company's board. Western Airlines workers got a whopping 32 percent of the carrier in 1983, and later that year Eastern gave 25 percent to its staff as well as four places on the board. Republic Airlines handed over 30 percent of its shares to employees in 1984.

In cases such as Eastern and Western, the ownership of stock initially led to improved labor relations and prompted employees to take a greater interest in efficiency. But when management demanded additional concessions, the era of good feeling ended.

The wage cuts agreed to by the unions were not always adequate to carriers hungry to reduce costs. Led by American in 1983, managements began seeking much larger reductions for future employees by pressuring unions to sign two-tier agreements that in some cases slashed pay for new hires by 50 percent (though in some cases the new hires would eventually reach parity). ALPA, many of whose members were paid more than $100,000 a year, fought hard against these arrangements but ended up agreeing to them in numerous contracts. However, ALPA struck United for a month in 1985 to limit the duration of a two-tier agreement.

The pressure on the airline unions was intensified by the nonunion upstart carriers that arose in the age of deregulation. At People Express, pilots received a fraction of the salaries at the majors, were expected to put in more "stick time" (hours at the controls) per month, and were given ground duties when not flying.

Because labor represents such a high percentage of total costs (one third or more) for major unionized carriers, relations with unions have often been central to the survival of the company. In fact it was the cooperation of TWA's unions that enabled raider Carl Icahn to take over the carrier in 1985. (However, the honeymoon between TWA workers and Carl Icahn came to an end in 1986. Flight attendants went on strike in March after contract talks, in which Icahn sought substantial wage and work rule concessions, broke down. The company quickly shifted reservations clerks, secretaries, and others into the jobs of the strikers and kept on flying. After 10 weeks the flight attendants ended the strike but rejected the concessions.) The unions themselves have at various times attempted to purchase such carriers as Eastern, Northwest, Pan Am, and TWA. None of these have succeeded, though in mid-1990 employees at United were still trying to achieve such a buyout.

Frank Lorenzo of Texas Air has been the most ruthless airline executive with regard to labor costs and unions. He set up nonunion discounter New York Air in 1980, and after taking over Continental in 1983, he demanded major concessions from the staff. When the unions resisted, Lorenzo pushed the company into Chapter 11, mainly to abrogate its labor contracts. While in bankruptcy Continental reduced its payroll by two thirds and chopped wages in half. A strike called by pilots to protest these actions was finally called off in defeat after two years.

As a result of the Continental affair, Lorenzo became the bête noire for airline unions, which worked to undermine his bids for TWA and Frontier Airlines in 1985. But in 1986 Lorenzo got Eastern's board to agree to a takeover after the Machinists refused new wage concessions unless chief executive Frank Borman resigned. Once it became clear that Lorenzo would continue his antiunion policies at Eastern the Machinists and the other unions made a last-ditch and unsuccessful effort to take over the airline themselves.

As soon as Lorenzo was in control of Eastern he found himself in an epic battle with the carrier's unions, which resisted his demands for huge wage cuts and accused him of stripping Eastern of its assets. After a two-year war of nerves the Machinists finally struck Eastern in March 1989; in an unusual show of solidarity the pilots and flight attendants honored the picket line. Within days Lorenzo put Eastern into Chapter 11; and while changes in the law made it more difficult to repeat his actions at Continental, he did use the protection of the bankruptcy laws to pursue his strategy of turning Eastern into a smaller, nonunion carrier.

Eastern's unions tried to arrange a purchase of the carrier by a group led by former baseball commissioner Peter Ueberroth, but the deal collapsed when Lorenzo refused to cede control during the transition to new ownership. Following that, the unions at Eastern put much of their hope in two different tactics. First they tried to organize an industrywide walkout by pilots, but they received little support. Then they put pressure on members of Congress to pass legislation creating a special commission to investigate the issues surrounding the strike. The House and Senate approved such a bill, but it was vetoed by President Bush.

After the veto the pilots and flight attendants called off

their strike, but Lorenzo claimed he no longer had positions for them. The Machinists remained on strike in what seemed a hopeless cause. Yet in April 1990 time ran out for Lorenzo. Eastern's creditors finally decided they wanted him removed, and the bankruptcy court named industry veteran Martin Shugrue as trustee of the carrier. Shugrue indicated a willingness to resolve the differences with the unions, and in June 1990 he began rehiring some of the pilots who had remained on strike through the end of the walkout. But a complete settlement of the dispute remained elusive.

LEADING COMPANIES

American Airlines had its origins in a batch of aviation companies that a group of Wall Street financiers began accumulating in the late 1920s. American prospered on airmail contracts, and by the end of the 1930s it was the leading passenger line. Still led by C. R. Smith, American in 1953 was the first carrier to offer nonstop coast-to-coast service; in 1959 it pioneered the passenger jet age in the United States with the use of Boeing 707s. By that time American had replaced the Pennsylvania Railroad as the country's leading passenger carrier. Smith left the company in 1968 to become Secretary of Commerce but was called back in 1973 after his successor George Spater ran into difficulties, including the revelation of his illegal contributions to the Nixon reelection campaign in 1972. In the era of deregulation the company fared well. Chief executive Robert Crandall used a street fighter's approach to hold on to lucrative markets and resist pressure from the upstarts. Crandall has resisted the industry's merger mania (aside from the relatively small purchase of AirCal, a West Coast carrier) and has instead grown through internal expansion, opening new hubs in Raleigh-Durham and Nashville. He has also expanded American's overseas service by initiating flights to Japan and Europe, and by purchasing Eastern's Central and South American routes. A 1989 takeover bid by Donald Trump for American's parent company AMR was dropped after a short time.

Continental Airlines Holdings is the new name adopted in 1990 for Texas Air, the parent company for the aviation empire put together by Frank Lorenzo. (Texas Air in turn was controlled by Lorenzo's holding company Jet Capital.) Starting with the purchase of Texas International Airlines in 1972, Lorenzo used the new regulatory environment to shake up the industry. After unsuccessful bids to take over National and TWA, he established discount carrier New York Air in 1980 to compete with Eastern's Air Shuttle. Lorenzo then went after Continental and, after a drawn-out battle, succeeded in taking over the company, which had a proud history dating back to the 1930s. When unions balked at hefty layoffs and wage cuts, Lorenzo put Continental into Chapter 11 and nullified the company's labor contracts. Union opposition helped to defeat Lorenzo's bids for TWA and Frontier in 1985, but in 1986 he succeeded in taking over Eastern (see below) and People Express. After a strike at Eastern crippled its operations Lorenzo put the carrier into Chapter 11. Lorenzo kept the creditors at bay (by selling off assets) for more than a year but was finally stripped of control of Eastern in April 1990. In the meantime Lorenzo sought to strengthen Continental (into which People, Frontier, and New York Air had been merged) by cutting costs and forming an alliance with Scandinavian Airlines Systems, which purchased 10 percent of Texas Air. In August 1990, Lorenzo left the industry by selling his stake in Continental to SAS.

Delta Air Lines had its origin in a crop-dusting operation in Louisiana in the 1920s. It came to dominate the air transport business in the Southeast and also expanded to the Midwest, New England (through the purchase of Northeast Airlines in 1972), and a few foreign destinations. In 1987 the company acquired troubled Western Airlines, one of the country's oldest carriers. The uncharacteristically bold move brought new momentum to Delta. To protect itself against a takeover, Delta sold 5 percent stakes to Swissair and Singapore Airlines in 1989.

Eastern Airlines began life as Pitcairn Aviation, which ran the mail between New York and Miami starting in the late 1920s. Under the leadership of World War I ace Eddie Rickenbacker, who was named general manager in 1935, Eastern became one of the Big Four domestic passenger carriers. Eastern gained a reputation for poor service but prospered thanks to its Air Shuttle service between New York, Washington, D.C., and Boston (initiated in 1961) and other lucrative routes. The company ran into financial difficulties in the early 1970s, and former astronaut Frank Borman was installed as president in 1975 to stop the decline. Borman won early wage concessions in 1977 but ran into strong opposition in the early 1980s when he sought further givebacks. Borman threatened to follow Continental into Chapter 11, but Eastern's unions (especially the militant Machinists) only agreed to further cuts after Borman agreed to giving workers 25 percent of the company's stock and four seats on Eastern's board. For a while a cooperative relationship emerged, but Borman's need for more cuts soured that. By early 1986, with Eastern facing possible default on its loans, the company's board consented to a $600 million takeover by Texas Air. The head of that company, Frank Lorenzo, soon found himself in an intense battle with Eastern's unions, which resisted his demands for huge wage cuts and charged him with milking Texas Air and his carriers to the benefit of his holding company, Jet Capital. After a walkout began in March 1989 Lorenzo put Eastern into Chapter 11 and skillfully manipulated the bankruptcy process to keep one step ahead of the creditors and the unions. He also managed to derail a variety of efforts to buy the carrier while succeeding in selling off various of its assets, most notably the Air Shuttle, which was purchased by Donald Trump in 1989. Finally, in April 1990 the creditors lost patience and got the bankruptcy court to appoint Martin Shugrue, a former executive at Pan Am and Continental, as a trustee to take over Eastern. In 1990, Eastern was indicted by a federal grand jury for falsifying maintenance records in the period from 1985 to 1989.

Northwest Airlines, founded in the 1920s, developed a poor reputation for service and was close to bankruptcy in the 1950s. Former CAB chairman Donald Nyrop was brought in to rescue the company in 1955 and stayed for 24 years. Nyrop was famous for his penny-pinching managerial style and his hostility toward the company's unions. Northwest's command over the Asian market was challenged when United acquired Pan Am's Pacific routes in 1985. The carrier's parent company, NWA, purchased Republic Airlines the following year—a merger that took some time to succeed. In 1989 the company was put in play by an offer from investor Marvin Davis, which was followed by bids from Pan American and the Machinists. Yet the $3.6 billion prize went to a group led by investor Alfred Checchi.

Pan American was the pioneer in international air transport and for many years was the American flagship carrier abroad. With the enterprising Juan Trippe at the controls, Pan Am established routes throughout the world, facing competition from other U.S. carriers only in the 1950s. Pan Am started experiencing problems in the 1970s, resulting in part from the costs of adding large numbers of 747s to its fleet. In 1979 the company won a takeover battle for National Airlines and hoped to recover through an expansion into domestic business. But Pan Am had difficulty operating in the deregulated environment, and losses mounted. Chairman William Seawell sold off assets, such as the company's New York headquarters building and the Intercontinental Hotels chain, to keep the carrier alive. In 1981 C. Edward Acker, who had made a name for himself at upstart Air Florida, took over the company and managed to win a wage cut from Pan Am's unions in exchange for 10 percent of the stock and a seat on the board. Relations with the unions remained tense, and the company was hit with a month-long strike in 1985. Later that year Pan Am sold off its historic Pacific routes—inaugurated with the China Clipper in 1935—to United for $750 million. In 1986 the company inaugurated shuttle service in competition with Eastern between New York, Boston, and Washington, D.C. Over the following few years a series of possible purchases of the carrier (many of them initiated by Pan Am's unions) fell through. Among the suitors were financier Kirk Kerkorian and Braniff chairman Jay Pritzker. Pan Am received a boost after unions struck Eastern in 1989, but the competition in the shuttle business resumed and intensified after Donald Trump took over Eastern's Air Shuttle in June 1989. Later that year Pan Am made an unsuccessful bid for Northwest Airlines. Still facing the old financial problems, Pan Am announced in May 1990 that it was putting its shuttle up for sale.

Trans World Airlines (TWA) started life as Transcontinental and Western Air, a 1930 merger of two of the early successful passenger lines. TWA's president Jack Frye ran into opposition from his board while attempting an expensive modernization of the carrier's fleet. Frustrated at this caution, Frye approached millionaire Howard Hughes, a longtime aviation buff, who bought control of the carrier in 1939. Hughes took over the management of the company (Frye was fired in 1947) and made it the technical leader of the industry. Hughes initially subsidized TWA with money from his Hughes Tool operation, but he later turned to outside lenders, who eventually forced Hughes to relinquish control of the firm. TWA became a formidable competitor to Pan Am in the transatlantic business, but it has been one of the weaker performers in the deregulated environment. In 1984 the carrier's holding company, Trans World Corp., which also owned Hilton International, Canteen Corp., and Century 21 Real Estate, spun off the airline. TWA came into play in 1985, and Carl Icahn snatched the company out from under the nose of Frank Lorenzo. Icahn subsequently had difficulty financing the complete acquisition, but labor concessions helped him complete the deal. In 1986 TWA agreed to acquire Ozark Air Lines for $250 million. According to most observers, Icahn's main concern over the next few years was finding a buyer for TWA; his short-lived 1987 offer for USAir was seen as a ploy to get that company to make a bid for TWA in defense. By 1990 Icahn was in a showdown over contract concessions with the carrier's unions, which were instead interested in removing Icahn and taking over TWA through an employee buyout.

United Airlines began as the amalgamation of a large number of early aviation companies, including plane manufacturer Boeing and engine builder Pratt & Whitney, both of which were split off by government edict in 1934. William "Pat" Patterson, a former Wells Fargo banker, built United into one of the leading passenger carriers. It was first in revenues in the mid-1930s but lost that position to American at the end of the decade, only to regain it in 1961. United initially responded to deregulation by dropping routes but then joined the price-cutting wars with a vengeance. Chairman Richard

Ferris, who took over in 1976, maneuvered United into one of the strongest spots among the majors. In 1985, after weathering a month-long pilots' strike, Ferris went on a spending spree to use an accumulation of cash to turn UAL (the name of the parent company) into a travel industry powerhouse. He spent $750 million to buy Pan Am's Pacific routes, paid nearly $600 million to purchase the Hertz rental car business from RCA, and placed $3 billion worth of orders with Boeing for more than 100 new planes. In 1986 UAL agreed to buy the Trans World Corp.'s 88 Hilton hotels abroad for nearly $1 billion. Yet the directors of the company (which had been renamed Allegis) grew dissatisfied with Ferris's strategy and came under increasing pressure (including a takeover bid by United's pilots and the threat of a proxy battle from Coniston Partners, a New York investment firm that acquired 13 percent of the stock) to move in the opposite direction. That is what the board did in 1987 when it forced Ferris out and launched a restructuring plan that involved selling off all but the airline (and changing the name back to UAL). Yet the company remained in play: Marvin Davis made a bid in 1989, and the pilots once again attempted an employee buyout. The directors approved the latter offer (with participation by management, British Airways, and the flight attendants union as well as the pilots), but it collapsed because of financing problems. A revised bid by the two

INDUSTRY DATA

Airlines	*1989*	*1988*	*1987*
Operating revenues	$69.1 billion	$63.7 billion	$56.8 billion
Revenue passenger miles	451 billion	437 billion	418 billion
Employment	586,000	557,000	529,000

Source: U.S. Department of Commerce.

unions (along with the Machinists but not management or British Airways) was accepted by the board in 1990. The action was taken after Coniston Partners once again threatened a proxy fight to replace the board if it opposed the buyout. Yet the unions still had not worked out their financing problems, and the deal was not a certainty.

SOURCE GUIDE

Leading Stock Analysts and Experts

Michael Armellino, analyst at Goldman Sachs.

Lee Howard and George James of the consulting firm Airline Economics Inc., Washington, D.C.

Paul Karos, analyst at First Boston.

Julius Maldutis, analyst at Salomon Brothers.

Trade Associations and Unions

Air Line Pilots Association, 1625 Massachusetts Avenue NW, Washington, DC 20036. Tel.: (703) 689–2270.

Air Transport Association, 1709 New York Avenue NW, Washington, DC 20006. Tel.: (202) 626–4000.

Association of Flight Attendants, 1625 Massachusetts Avenue NW, Washington, DC 20036. Tel.: (202) 328–5400.

International Association of Machinists and Aerospace Workers, 1300 Connecticut Avenue NW, Washington, DC 20036. Tel.: (202) 857–5200.

Transport Workers Union of America, 80 West End Avenue, New York, NY 10023. Tel.: (212) 873–6000.

Data Sources and Directories

Air Transport, an annual brochure of statistics (Washington, D.C.: Air Transport Association of America).

Airline Companies Directory, annual (Omaha, Neb.: American Business Directories).

The Airline Handbook, an annual volume providing descriptions of the services and fleets of 2,000 carriers worldwide (Cranston, R.I.: AeroTravel Research).

The Airline Quarterly, a consulting firm's compendium of data and analysis (Washington, D.C.: Airline Economics).

FAA Statistical Handbook of Aviation, an annual volume of data on U.S. air traffic, carrier fleets, accidents, and other aviation information (Washington, D.C.: Federal Aviation Administration).

Moody's Transportation Manual, an annual compilation of financial data on companies including airlines (New York: Moody's Investors Services).

World Aviation Directory, a semiannual volume containing information on carriers, aviation services, airports, and organizations (Washington, D.C.: McGraw-Hill).

Online Database

AVIATION/AEROSPACE ONLINE (Washington, D.C.: McGraw-Hill).

Trade Publications

Air Transport World, monthly.

Aviation Daily.

Aviation Week and Space Technology.

Interavia (Geneva, Switzerland), monthly

Books and Reports

Allen, Oliver E. *The Airline Builders*. Alexandria, Va.: Time-Life Books, 1981.

Bailey, Elizabeth E.; David R. Graham; and Daniel P. Kaplan. *Deregulating the Airlines*. Cambridge, Mass.: MIT Press, 1985.

Bernstein, Aaron. *Grounded: Frank Lorenzo and the Destruction of Eastern Airlines*. New York: Simon & Schuster, 1990.

Dempsey, Paul Stephen. *Flying Blind: The Failure of Airline Deregulation*. Washington, D.C.: Economic Policy Institute, 1990.

Hopkins, George E. *The Airline Pilots: A Study in Elite Unionization*. Cambridge, Mass.: Harvard University Press, 1971.

James, George W., ed. *Airline Economics*. Lexington, Mass.: Lexington Books, 1981.

McKelvey, Jean, ed. *Cleared for Takeoff: Airline Labor Relations Since Deregulation*. Ithaca, N.Y.: ILR Press, 1988.

Morrison, Steven, and Clifford Winston. *The Economic Effects of Airline Deregulation*. Washington, D.C.: Brookings Institution, 1986.

National Center for Employee Ownership. *Trading Stock for Wages: Employee Ownership in the Airline Industry.* Oakland, Calif., 1987.

Nielsen, Georgia Panter. *From Sky Girl to Flight Attendant: Women and the Making of a Union.* Ithaca, N.Y.: ILR Press, 1982.

Organisation for Economic Co-Operation and Development. *Deregulation and Airline Competition.* Paris, 1988.

Sampson, Anthony. *Empires in the Sky.* New York: Random House, 1984.

Solberg, Carl. *Conquest of the Skies: A History of Commercial Aviation in America.* Boston: Little, Brown, 1979.

"Up against the Gloom and Doom: Aggressive Unionism at Eastern Airlines." *Labor Research Review,* Winter 1984. A special issue; additional articles appeared in the Summer 1984 issue.

U.S. Congressional Budget Office. *Policies for the Deregulated Airline Industry.* Washington, D.C., 1988.

U.S. General Accounting Office. *DOT's Implementation of Airline Regulatory Authority.* Washington, D.C., 1989.

CHAPTER 24

AUTOMOBILES

The manufacture of automobiles is emblematic both of the rise of U.S. industry through most of this century and of the crisis of the 1970s and 1980s. The auto sector pioneered modern mass production and through its relatively high wage rates helped to turn workers into middle-income consumers. The industry has given these and other consumers a wide range of choices in personal transportation but has been less than completely diligent in dealing with the harmful side effects of the motor vehicle age: air pollution and the carnage from highway accidents. For better or for worse, automobiles continue to play a major role in the economy. To purchase, operate, and maintain their motor vehicles Americans spent some $386 billion in 1989, one fourth of which represented new car sales.

THE RISE OF THE HORSELESS CARRIAGE

The quest for a self-propelled vehicle started inching toward fulfillment in the late 18th century as experiments were made with portable steam engines. Significant progress took a century to achieve, and the predominant method of propulsion came to be the internal-combustion engine. Motor vehicles in the modern sense are said to have begun with the machines constructed in Germany in the 1880s by Karl Benz and Gottlieb Daimler. By the 1890s a bona fide automobile industry was in existence in Europe.

The auto business developed more slowly in the United States. The American motorcar age dates from the one-cylinder model produced by Charles and J. Frank Duryea of

Springfield, Massachusetts, in 1893. The Duryea brothers had based their creation on a description of Karl Benz's car published in *Scientific American.*

During the following years scores of other inventors, including Henry Ford and Ransom Olds, jumped into the business with gasoline, steam, and even electric versions of horseless carriages. The entrepreneurs took advantage of the low capital requirements of a business in which they could buy their parts on credit and sell the finished products for cash.

Among the hundreds of entrants, the early leaders included the Pope Manufacturing Co. (the nation's largest bicycle producer) and Olds's operation (Olds Motor Works), which started to establish Detroit as the center of the industry. In 1904 Olds split with his backer Samuel Smith and formed the Reo (for R. E. Olds) Motor Car Co.

A shadow was cast on the young industry around the turn of the century by a patent dispute. An inventor named George Selden had filed back in 1879 for a patent based on a particular kind of gasoline engine he saw at the Philadelphia Centennial Exposition in 1876. Selden engaged in legal maneuvers that resulted in the issuance of the patent being delayed until 1895—that is, until an industry that could exploit the technology had developed. In 1899 the Electric Vehicle Co. bought the rights to the Selden patent and began challenging the right of auto producers to produce gasoline-powered cars without paying a license fee.

Many automakers gave in to the pressure and in fact banded together in the Association of Licensed Automobile Manufacturers to restrict entry into the market. The association sought to undermine independents by publishing ads that warned their potential customers, "Don't buy a lawsuit with your car."

One producer who refused to recognize the claims of the association was Henry Ford, who established the Ford Motor Co. in 1903. Ford led the successful challenge to the patent cartel and also went against the industry's grain by trying to turn autos from luxuries selling at $1,000 or more into products that virtually anyone could afford.

Ford almost became part of an amalgamation of auto producers that William Crapo Durant was trying to put together. Durant had taken over the Buick Motor Car Co. in 1904 and made it into one of the more successful producers. After several deals fell through, Durant succeeded in 1908 in merging Buick, Oldsmobile, Cadillac, Oakland (later Pontiac), and some smaller companies into what he named General Motors (GM).

That same year Ford achieved his dream of an inexpensive "car for the multitude" and introduced the Model T. After first offering the car at $850, Ford worked hard at bringing the price down, eventually getting it as low as $240. The farmers and other people of modest means targeted by Ford made the Model T a historic success. More than 15 million of them were sold over nearly two decades. The "Tin Lizzie," as it came to be called, made auto ownership into a mass phenomenon.

THE AGE OF FORDISM

Ford accomplished this feat by transforming the process of production. Previously, cars were manufactured in small workshops. Ford not only increased the scale of production but also invented a technique, the moving assembly line, that greatly increased the productivity of labor. He also encouraged stability in the work force by introducing a $5-a-day minimum wage rate. This action shocked much of the business world—$5 was about twice the going rate for Detroit factory labor—but it was eventually seen as a shrewd move that enabled Ford workers to become Ford customers as well. Moreover, Ford's wage policy was not part of a liberal approach to management. He ran the company with an iron fist; in 1928 *The New York Times* called him "an industrial fascist—the Mussolini of Detroit."

As Ford took a commanding lead in the industry, General Motors was plagued with financial problems related to its ambitious expansion plans. The company was taken over in 1910 by a banking syndicate, which brought Charles Nash and Walter Chrysler into top management. The ousted Durant then formed an alliance with race-car driver Louis Chevrolet in an effort to produce a low-cost car to compete with the Model T. Durant, an inveterate stock market operator, then began trading Chevrolet Motor Car Co. stock for GM shares, and by 1916 he had regained control of GM and integrated Chevrolet and a group of suppliers, including battery maker Delco, into it. Durant also acquired the Fisher Body Co. and established the General Motors Acceptance Corp. to help customers buy on credit.

By the 1920s the industry was riding high: Annual production reached 2 million at the beginning of the decade, and the number of passenger cars in use climbed from 10.5 million in 1921 to 26.5 million in 1929. At the end of the decade the vast majority of American households owned an automobile.

Many of these customers were being drawn to the more attractive and comfortable models that Ford's rivals were putting on the market in competition with the Model T. Ford resisted the fact that the Model T was passé, and no one in the company was in a position to overrule him. Ford finally accepted the inevitable in 1927 and ceased production even though a replacement model was not ready.

Ford's stubbornness gave an opening to GM, which seized first place in the late 1920s and has never relinquished it. The rise of General Motors was also aided by the managerial talents of Alfred P. Sloan, Jr., who was president of the company from 1923 to 1937 and then chairman until he retired in 1956. Sloan, who took GM from the entrepreneurial era to the age of big business, was brought in by the Du Pont family (the major stockholders in the company) after Durant was pressured to resign amid a personal financial debacle.

While GM and Ford slugged it out at the top, countless other producers fell prey to bankruptcy and consolidation. The number of American automakers dwindled from hundreds to some 44 in 1927. The most successful of these emerged from the efforts of Walter Chrysler after he quit GM in disgust because of Durant and was then called from an early retirement in 1920 to rescue the Maxwell Motor Car Co. Chrysler turned Maxwell around, and after bringing out some successful models called Chryslers in 1924, he ended up taking over the company and renaming it after himself. After acquiring number-five producer Dodge Brothers Manufacturing Co. in 1928, Chrysler joined GM and Ford in what became known as the Big Three.

The 1929 stock market crash and the ensuing depression burst the bubble of the rapidly expanding auto industry. Motor vehicle production peaked at 5.3 million in 1929 and did not reach that level again until 1949. While new-car sales plunged, auto registrations sank much less, indicating that while people could not afford new vehicles, they were continuing to operate the ones they already had rather than abandoning the automobile entirely. The use of the car was made more appealing by the widespread expansion of the highway system that took place during the 1930s, much of it under the auspices of New Deal public works projects.

During the war, passenger car output was eventually suspended, and the automakers turned to the production of jeeps, tanks, aircraft, and other military items. Ford Motor was a bit quicker to aid the war effort than the company had been at the start of World War I, since Henry Ford (an idiosyncratic pacifist) had suffered a severe stroke in 1938 and had passed on control of the company to his son Edsel.

THE RISE AND FALL OF THE TAILFIN

The end of the war brought a tremendous demand for new passenger cars, and Detroit worked furiously to increase output. GM resumed its leading position, while Ford was in serious disarray. After Edsel Ford's untimely death in 1943, the 80-year-old founder returned as a caretaker until his grandson Henry Ford II was ready to step in. Upon assuming the throne in 1945, the 28-year-old Henry II set out to revive an operation that some analysts thought was close to collapse because of poor financial controls.

A total of nine passenger car producers were active in 1946: the Big Three, Studebaker, Packard, Nash, Hudson, Kaiser-Frazer, and Crosley. While the whole industry enjoyed the immediate postwar boom, the Korean War slump that hit the business in the early 1950s threatened the survival of the smaller firms. The result was further consolidation. In 1952 General Tire acquired Crosley and converted it to military work. Kaiser-Frazer merged with Jeepmaker Willys-Overland in 1953 and ended up leaving the auto business. The following year Hudson and Nash combined to form American Motors Corp., and Studebaker and Packard joined forces. By the mid-1960s only the Big Three and American Motors remained.

The mid-1950s was another golden age for the business. Rising income levels and suburbanization made the United States an automobile-based society. And the cars that Detroit produced and consumers embraced became larger, more powerful, and embellished with tailfins and great quantities of chrome. In fact the emphasis on design represented the epitome of the strategy devised by Sloan back in the 1920s: that continual changes in styling and optional features would, despite rising prices, induce consumers to buy new cars more often.

The rise of driving at the expense of other forms of transportation was also promoted by federal policy. In 1956 Congress established the Interstate and Defense Highway System, which used excise taxes on fuel and tires in order to finance the construction of some 41,000 miles of limited access highways throughout the country. (The system was completed by the early 1980s at a total cost of some $80 billion.)

As it turned out, the car-buying public's surrender to complete indulgence was short-lived. The economic downturn of 1957–58 produced the first rush to smaller, more economical models. The problem was that Detroit had few of these to offer. In fact Ford had the misfortune of coming out during this period with its new full-sized car called the Edsel. The reception offered the car was so dismal that the term Edsel has entered the business vocabulary as a synonym for a new-product fiasco.

The one U.S. producer that was sitting pretty during this first small-car trend was tiny American Motors, which had a previously obscure model called the Rambler, originally brought out by Nash. Rambler sales soared in the late 1950s, and AMC president George Romney used the opportunity to denounce the typical offering from Detroit as a gas-guzzling "dinosaur."

The other beneficiaries of the trend were foreign producers. Imports, which had previously accounted for an insignificant portion of the market, jumped to 207,000 in 1957 and reached 610,000 by 1959.

By the early 1960s the bigger producers were finally bringing out their own small-car models, including "sporty" ones such as Ford's popular Mustang. Detroit's move overwhelmed the Rambler and stemmed the rise of imports, though the dirt-cheap Volkswagen Beetle retained a loyal following among the young and hip. This is not to say that the Big Three abandoned their gas-guzzlers. Full-sized cars did end up more streamlined than before, but they tended to become longer and heavier each year. At the same time, small cars became a permanent market segment. In addition to compacts, the industry leaders introduced subcompacts in 1970—the Vega from GM, the Ford Pinto, and AMC's Gremlin.

THE NADER ASSAULT

Issues of automobile size and fuel economy became bound up with the controversy over safety that erupted during the 1960s. Many observers accused the industry of having ignored safety issues for decades. In the late 1950s books such as John Keats' *The Insolent Chariots* brought the issue to the center of public debate, and in 1965 Senator Abraham Ribicoff held influential hearings on the subject. Yet it was publication of a book later that year by a lawyer named Ralph Nader, who had done research for Ribicoff, that galvanized public opinion on the safety issue.

Nader's *Unsafe at Any Speed,* which focused on the problems of the Chevrolet Corvair, opened with the sweeping declaration: "For over half a century, the automobile has brought death, injury, and the most inestimable sorrow and deprivation to millions of Americans." GM responded to Nader's depiction of the rear-engine Corvair as a death trap by trying to discredit the author. GM hired private detectives to spy on Nader, but instead of coming up with dirt on him, the auto giant ended up having to pay Nader $425,000 in damages and publicly apologize to him. The publicity also helped propel Nader into becoming the country's premier consumer advocate.

The uproar generated by Nader helped prompt Congress to pass the National Traffic and Motor Safety Act of 1966. The law authorized the federal government to establish safety standards for new cars, and the result was a steady decline in highway death rates for a number of years. Safety was deemphasized during the industry's economic troubles in the 1970s, and the Reagan administration sought to reverse earlier government rules such as a 1983 deadline for the installation of passive restraints (automatic seat belts or inflatable air bags) in all new cars. The deregulatory crusade ran into legal obstacles, and in 1984 Transportation secretary Elizabeth Dole offered to drop the revised deadline for passive restraints if two thirds of the states passed mandatory seat belt laws. That goal was not met, but in 1987 the Transportation Department extended the deadline for passenger-side restraints to 1993. The prospects for passive restraints became much brighter when Chrysler dropped its longstanding opposition to airbags and announced that it would begin installing the devices as standard equipment on all of its U.S.-made cars. In 1990, GM followed suit and announced that it would install airbags in all its cars built in the United States starting in 1995.

The mid-1960s was also the culmination of years of quiet debate over auto pollution. The link between cars and problems with air quality was first suggested in the analysis of the smog troubles of Los Angeles in the 1940s. The recognition of cars as a culprit escalated in the following decade, and in the early 1960s California established the first emission standards, which forced automakers to install blow-back devices (which controlled crankcase exhaust) on all automobiles sold in the state. Detroit, seeking to avert federal legislation, decided to put the devices on all new cars nationwide in 1963. Yet Congress acted anyway in 1965, passing the Motor Vehicle Air Pollution Act, which authorized the secretary of Health, Education and Welfare to set emission standards and required control devices on all new cars beginning in 1968. Stricter rules were included in the Clean Air Act of 1970.

The energy problems of the 1970s prompted Congress to go even further. Legislation passed in 1975 required the National Highway Traffic Safety Administration to regulate fuel economy by requiring manufacturers to meet certain average levels for their models as a group. Each automaker was supposed to achieve a corporate average fuel economy (CAFE) of 18 miles per gallon by 1978 and 27.5 by 1985. The industry grumbled and lobbied against the rules but succeeded only in winning delays rather than abolition.

SMALL IS UNAVOIDABLE

The auto industry entered the 1970s with visions of continuing prosperity. There was some concern over a rise in imports as well as signs that the auto market was highly saturated. Auto managers were also shaken up by the unrest among blue-collar workers at places such as GM's Lordstown plant. Yet these problems were overshadowed by the expectation that a robust, even if inflation-prone, economy would keep automobile sales healthy.

This optimism was quickly and resoundingly crushed by the 1973 oil embargo. The resulting gasoline shortages panicked auto buyers just after the 1974 models had gone on sale. This, combined with a rapid series of price increases by Detroit, brought about a drop of more than 20 percent in new-car sales in 1974. Detroit was caught with product lines dominated by large, gas-guzzling cars as Americans, much more than in the late 1950s, were demanding smaller, fuel-efficient vehicles.

Surprisingly it turned out that the behemoth General Motors was quickest to adapt to the "small is beautiful" sentiment. GM brought out the tiny Chevette in a record 18 months' time (compared to the usual 36 months for new designs) and redirected billions of dollars of investment toward a new line of small, front-wheel drive compacts. These so-called X-cars, introduced in the late 1970s, were a tremendous success and allowed GM to achieve a substantial boost in market share at the expense of slower-moving Ford and Chrysler. The smaller of the Big Three was also hit much more severely by the rise in Japanese and other imports, from 15 percent of the market in 1970 to 22 percent in 1979.

The U.S. producers resolved to meet both the Japanese challenge and the fuel economy deadlines by investing some $75 billion over a decade to accomplish what amounted to a remaking of the industry: extensive new designs and massive amounts of new plant space and equipment, including a major investment in automation.

The road to revival contained a major pothole—a disastrous dive in car sales that began in mid-1979 and made 1980 into the worst year in the history of the industry. In fact the automakers' aggregate losses of more than $4 billion in net income that year constituted the worst annual performance of any American industry ever.

Chrysler, the perennial weakling of the Big Three, was the hardest hit. The company came close to bankruptcy and was saved only when its new president Lee Iacocca, hired in 1978 soon after he was fired from the same job at Ford in a dispute over strategy with Henry II, turned to the federal government for help.

Iacocca convinced the Carter administration that the collapse of Chrysler would have a disastrous effect on an already weakened economy and thus got Washington to provide the company with up to $1.2 billion in loan guarantees. The deal, which involved substantial concessions from Chrysler's employees as well as its creditors, kept the company afloat, though recovery was slow in coming.

The industry did not show strong signs of revival until some time after the 1981 decision by the Japanese government to observe "voluntary export restraints" (a euphemism for quotas) that restricted the Japanese share of the U.S. market to 1.68 million cars a year, or some 20 percent. By this time total imports had captured more than one fourth of the market.

U.S. automakers used this period of protection to cut their costs and raise their productivity drastically. The quest was to reduce what was said to be a $2,000 differential in favor of the Japanese in the cost of producing a typical subcompact car. This meant repeated efforts to get contract concessions from a sharply reduced labor force, radical changes in manufacturing techniques, and the adoption of Japanese methods such as "just in time" inventory management. The fruits of these policies were seen in things such as the automakers' break-even point; at Chrysler that figure was reduced from 2.4 million units in 1979 to 1.1 million in 1983.

Such cost controls allowed the industry to enjoy a dramatic comeback starting in 1983. While the import challenge had not been licked, U.S. automakers were able to raise their prices and earn a bundle on those cars they did manage to sell. Their combined earnings leaped from a token $82 million in 1982 to an impressive $5.7 billion in 1983 and an astounding $8.9 billion in 1984. Chrysler, the onetime ward of the state, started repaying its government-backed loans seven years ahead of time, and the company's dramatic turnaround made Iacocca into something of a business folk hero.

Despite the recovery of the U.S. producers, the import problem was far from solved. After declining from 21.8 percent in 1981 to 18.3 percent in 1984, the Japanese share of the market climbed to 20.1 percent the following year as the export restraint agreement expired. Total imports in 1985 were up to 25.7 percent.

THE GLOBAL CAR

Moreover, foreign competition was no longer limited to vehicles shipped from abroad. Starting in the early 1980s several Japanese producers established U.S. operations. The projects were in part a response to pressure from the United Automobile Workers and others concerned about the decline of U.S. auto employment.

The first foreign automaker to set up shop in the United States was West Germany's Volkswagen in 1978. Although VW's Pennsylvania operation ended up with a high degree of labor unrest (and was abandoned in 1988), the Japanese followed suit. Honda began assembling Accords in Marysville, Ohio, in 1982. Nissan, which started producing trucks at its Smyrna, Tennessee, plant in 1983, expanded to automobiles two years later. Toyota got involved in both a joint venture with General Motors in California and an operation of its own in Kentucky. Mazda announced plans in 1984 to build an assembly plant in Michigan, and Mitsubishi said it would produce cars together with Chrysler in Illinois. All of this was in addition to French producer Renault's purchase of 46 percent of the common stock of American Motors (AMC) in 1980. (Renault's share and the rest of AMC was purchased by Chrysler in 1987.)

The GM–Toyota and Chrysler–Mitsubishi joint ventures indicate that American producers have used foreign investment as an opportunity to learn the "secrets" of the Japanese success in automaking. GM and Toyota's New United Motor Manufacturing Inc. was established to produce a new subcompact using Japanese designs, methods, and labor policies. GM apparently planned to apply some of what it hoped to learn from Toyota in the wholly owned Saturn subsidiary that the company announced in 1985. Although both Saturn and the Toyota joint venture recognized the UAW, the plan was to completely remake labor relations in a more cooperative mold.

The attitude toward unions of the Japanese companies operating on their own in the United States has been mixed. Mazda, for instance, decided not to resist unionization at its planned Michigan facility, while problems with Honda in Ohio prompted the UAW to abandon its organizing effort at that company. The union was roundly defeated in a representation election at the Nissan plant in Tennessee in 1989.

Foreign investment in the United States and joint ventures are only part of a much larger process of internationalization that has accelerated in the auto industry during the 1980s. The basic trend started some time ago. Ford established a Canadian subsidiary back in 1903 and began assembling knockdown versions of the Model T in Britain in 1911. Ford kept spreading, and by 1920 the company had operations in 20 countries; there was even a licensing arrangement with the Soviet Union.

General Motors followed suit, moving into manufacturing as well as assembly abroad. GM purchased Vauxhall Motors of Britain in 1925 and the German firm Adam Opel four years later. After World War II the two U.S. leaders, along with Chrysler to a lesser extent, became truly global companies.

With the rise to prominence of the Japanese producers in the late 1960s, the U.S. Big Three moved to get a piece of their action. In 1969 Chrysler announced that it would acquire 35 percent of Mitsubishi Motors (though it ended up buying only

15 percent). The following year GM announced a joint venture and technical cooperation with Isuzu as well as a 34 percent investment in that company. Ford revealed that it was negotiating with Toyo Kogyo (now known as Mazda), but it was not until 1979 that Ford's 25 percent investment in the Japanese company was worked out.

Another element of internationalization emerged from the decision by Ford and GM in the late 1970s to go beyond simply producing different cars in many different countries for sale in those same or neighboring nations. The first step was to standardize designs internationally so that what was essentially the same car could be marketed around the world. The leading example of this was Ford's Fiesta, introduced in 1976. The next stage involved producing what came to be called the global car. Plants in a variety of countries were used to produce components that were brought together in several centralized assembly facilities. Ford began assembling its Escort in three countries with components manufactured by Ford factories in nine nations. This technique of "global sourcing" allowed Ford to take advantage of maximum economies of scale in the component plants and also made it less vulnerable to strikes or other disruptions in any one country. GM and Chrysler also moved in this direction by importing parts and components from such countries as Brazil, Australia, Mexico, and Italy for cars that were assembled in the United States.

The inability of the U.S. producers to obtain strong and permanent import restrictions prompted them to make yet another international move: getting into the import business themselves. Traditionally, American automakers produced finished cars for the U.S. market in the United States, and their foreign production operations were aimed at overseas markets. By the mid-1980s they were getting involved in arrangements that once would have been unthinkable. Ford began buying cars from a South Korean producer and selling them under the Ford name in the United States; in addition, the company built a plant in Mexico to produce cars for the U.S. market. General Motors also turned to South Korea, forming a joint venture with Daewoo, and arranged for Japan's Suzuki to produce cars that would be sold under the

Geo name. In both cases the target market was the United States.

Such moves have begun to blur the distinction between imports and domestics and helped undermine the "Buy American" campaigns pushed by the Big Three for many years. (The trend also generated more support for a proposal pushed by the UAW that would have required any car sold in the United States to have a high percentage of American labor and components. "Domestic content" legislation twice passed the House but died in the Senate.) Yet the response from Detroit was that such arrangements were necessary in the face of the increasing competitiveness of the business and the arrival in the United States of new low-end products from countries such as Yugoslavia. The Big Three in effect admitted that they simply could not produce subcompacts profitably and they wanted to make some money selling small cars produced by others. However much this trend toward "sponsored imports" continues, it is clear that the automobile competition will continue to be waged in complicated international arenas.

The competition in the American domestic arena remains complicated as well. By the late 1980s the Big Three U.S. producers had what they so passionately demanded at the beginning of the decade: restraints on Japanese imports, less-costly contracts with the UAW, and a weak dollar to give them the cost advantage Japan had enjoyed when the yen was in that condition. Yet for all of this GM, Ford (to a lesser extent), and Chrysler were still struggling. The reason was that the industry's capacity was out of line with stagnant demand, and Americans continued to crave imports. Part of the problem was of the Big Three's own making: When prices of Japanese imports rose because of the appreciating yen, the U.S. producers did not take advantage of the situation by underselling the imports and winning back market share. Instead, they increased their own prices in order to bolster short-term profits.

Meanwhile the Japanese began penetrating more segments of the U.S. market, breaking out of their traditional emphasis on lower-end models and introducing the type of flashy, expensive cars that had previously been the domain of European producers and a few American models. (This challenge helped prompt several mergers between the Big Three and European luxury producers: Chrysler's 1987 purchase of Italy's Lamborghini and Ford's acquisition of Britain's Jaguar in 1989.)

The Japanese also continued to expand their manufacturing operations in the United States. By early 1990 they had seven so-called transplants (three of them joint ventures with American companies), which were responsible for 22 percent of domestically produced automobiles. In 1989 the Japanese share of the U.S. market rose to 25.6 percent, and the Honda Accord was the best-selling car in the United States—the first time a Big Three model did not attain that honor. It is becoming more likely that the auto industry will still have a Big Three in the year 2000 but that their names will be Toyota, Nissan, and Honda.

LABOR RELATIONS

Collective bargaining and labor relations in the automobile industry were for much of the 20th century the pacesetters for the remainder of American industry. Tentative organizing among autoworkers began as the industry developed around the turn of the century. Such efforts were inhibited by leading companies such as Ford, which initiated the famous $5-a-day minimum wage and established a sociological department to regulate the personal lives of workers. Later the company used a more directly antiunion approach in the creation of an internal security force called the Service Department, led by the notorious Harry Bennett.

It was thus not surprising that the auto sector remained largely unorganized until the 1930s. Following the Roosevelt administration's affirmation of the right to collective bargaining, the AFL began halfheartedly chartering auto unions. Frustrated with oppressive working conditions and seasonal layoffs that kept annual incomes low, autoworkers responded eagerly to organizing drives.

In 1935 the AFL departed from its craft orientation and issued a limited industrial charter to the United Automobile

Workers of America. Industrial union advocates were unhappy with the AFL's restrictions, and in 1936 the UAW joined the newly established CIO.

Given the rapid increase in membership, the UAW moved quickly to win recognition from the Big Three, which had been resisting federal directives on labor policy. GM was chosen as the first target. Short strikes at various sites around the country were followed by a nationwide action against the company in January 1937. The UAW successfully employed the tactic of sit-down strikes and plant occupations, most notably at the Fisher Body plant in Flint, Michigan, where an attempt by police to storm the plant was beaten back by the workers. GM capitulated in February 1937, and Chrysler followed suit later in the year.

Things were more difficult at Ford. The organizing effort was curtailed after an unsuccessful strike at the River Rouge plant, which culminated in the infamous "Battle of the Overpass," in which UAW organizers were attacked by Harry Bennett's private security force. The UAW had more success in 1941, when Ford gave in to strong government pressure and recognized the union.

In the postwar period the moderate faction led by Walter Reuther defeated left-wingers inside the union and went on to lead a number of strikes, including a critical 113-day walkout against GM in 1945–46 in which the union failed in its attempt to win a 30 percent raise to make up for wartime inflation. The union achieved only 18.5 percent, the same amount that had been awarded at other companies without a strike. Other actions against GM culminated in a 1948 agreement that systematized wage increases through annual improvement factors and cost-of-living adjustments.

In the following years the UAW won steady improvements for its members, including pioneering provisions such as supplementary unemployment benefits and company-paid pensions. The union's cooperative relationship with management averted strikes, but it heightened tension between rank-and-file workers and the UAW leadership. The result was periodic insurgencies on the shop floor, especially when a new generation of workers entered the factories in the late 1960s. Militant black workers brought the black-power movement into auto plants with the creation of the League of Revolutionary Black Workers.

This unrest had its most prominent expression in the 1972 strike against oppressive working conditions at GM's Lordstown plant. Lordstown became a symbol of the "blue-collar revolt"—the frustration of young workers with the regimentation of the factory and the demand for a more human work environment.

The ability of the UAW to win steady contract improvements came to an end with the auto industry crisis in the late 1970s. In 1979 the union agreed to $243 million in concessions to ailing Chrysler, and the federal government insisted on another $200 million as one of the terms for the government bailout of the company. At the same time, UAW president Douglas Fraser was given a seat on Chrysler's board of directors.

By the early 1980s, with several hundred thousand autoworkers out of work indefinitely, the UAW felt it had to give in to concessions sought by GM and Ford as well as yet more demands from Chrysler. Some of this lost ground was regained when the industry rebounded beginning in 1983, a process that included a 12-day strike at Chrysler in 1985. Yet there remained a tug-of-war between company claims that the labor-cost differential with Japan had to be narrowed and worker resistance to an erosion in the standard of living.

The leadership of the UAW, taken over by Owen Bieber in 1983, dealt with the problem by promoting a more cooperative relationship with management while seeking to expand job security and worker participation. At the same time, the union sought to slow down the disappearance of auto jobs by lobbying for protectionist policies, as in its unsuccessful campaign for domestic-content legislation. The failure of this effort was highlighted in November 1986, when GM announced plans to eliminate 29,000 jobs by closing 11 plants.

The UAW made it clear in advance of the 1987 negotiations at GM and Ford that increased job security would be a prime goal. The union did win better (though not absolute) job protection in those talks: the two industry leaders essentially pledged not to reduce employment any further except during slumps in sales. The agreements also committed the union to working more closely with management to raise productivity. A similar contract was reached with Chrysler the following year.

The union's productivity commitment—a move toward what has come to be called "jointness"—has been the cause of an escalating internal battle within the UAW. The key figure in this turmoil is Jerry Tucker, a maverick union official who leads a caucus within the UAW called New Directions that regards cooperation with management as a betrayal of the principles of the labor movement. In 1986 Tucker ran for the post of director of UAW's St. Louis-based Region 5. After losing the extremely close election he charged the UAW with voting irregularities and called for a new election. His arguments persuaded a federal judge to order a new vote, which Tucker won. All of this was a great embarrassment to the UAW, which took pride in its reputation as a union free of corruption.

The jointness debate was most intense with regard to the bold experiments in labor relations conducted by GM at its NUMMI joint venture with Toyota in California and its new Saturn subsidiary in Tennessee. In both cases the UAW granted management a greater degree of operating flexibility than had ever been tolerated in a traditional plant. The Japanese-style contract for the Saturn project was criticized by some labor figures, including Victor Reuther (one of the founders of the UAW) because of its use of an incentive pay system, while the productivity-enhancing practices at NUMMI have been condemned as "management by stress."

The UAW's strategy of using cooperation as a way of trying to save jobs has also been applied at the manufacturing operations set up by Japanese companies in the United States. Those plants owned and operated exclusively by foreign firms such as Nissan, Honda, and Toyota managed to remain nonunion. UAW representation was tolerated, however, at the joint ventures established between Japanese automakers and the American Big Three: GM and Toyota's NUMMI operation, the Diamond-Star collaboration between Chrysler and Mitsubishi in Illinois, and the Ford-Mazda plant in Michigan. In all three cases the UAW agreed to extensive workplace innovations, but the contract at the Ford-Mazda facility went particularly far in allowing flexibility, giving management the right to make broad use of temporary workers.

Job security was once again the concern of the UAW in its 1990 negotiations. The union had been stung by the closing of several plants in spite of what the UAW thought was a prohibition against such actions in its contracts. Yet, the union ended up giving GM and Ford greater freedom to downsize, in exchange for increased income security.

LEADING COMPANIES

Chrysler, the traditional weak sister of the Big Three, used a federal bailout starting in 1979 to help it rise from the brink of bankruptcy to reasonable prosperity by the middle of the 1980s. The company was built out of the ailing Maxwell Motor Co. in the 1920s by former GM executive Walter Chrysler. Chrysler jumped to number three with the purchase of Dodge in 1928 and held the position, managing to survive—sometimes just barely—while dozens of other companies fell by the wayside. President Lee Iacocca, who took over in 1978, made himself the personal embodiment of industrial rebirth and as a result got himself touted as a Democratic presidential candidate. In 1987 Chrysler agreed to purchase American Motors, the smallest of the U.S. carmakers, for $1.5 billion. AMC, created by the 1954 merger of Nash and Hudson, had a short-lived moment of glory during the small-car wave of the late 1950s, but the company survived only on the basis of the Jeep business it purchased from Kaiser Industries in 1970. AMC achieved a greater degree of stability when Renault made a major investment in 1980, but the company lost its fourth-place position among U.S.-based manufacturers to Honda of America. Despite the image Iacocca carefully cultivated for Chrysler, the company found itself in a number of embarrassing situations in the late 1980s: It paid $16.4 million to settle fraud charges relating to the practice of disconnecting odometers of thousands of cars that were driven by executives and then sold as new; it was fined a record $1.5 million by the Occupational Safety and Health Administration for workplace violations; and it alienated its workers by announcing the closing of the AMC plant in Kenosha, Wisconsin, and the transfer of its K-car production to Mexico.

Ford Motor Co. was the first great U.S. auto producer. Founder Henry Ford took what was mostly a luxury item and turned it into a new mode of transportation for the masses. He also revolutionized factory production with the moving assembly line and high wages. Ford resisted phasing out his beloved Model T, and the company went into a decline in the 1920s that lasted until the founder's grandson Henry Ford II took over in 1945. The company was modernized with the help of a group of former air force systems analysts (known as the "Whiz Kids") including Robert McNamara, who became president of Ford in the 1950s and later went on to other sorts of fame in the public sector. The company first went public in 1958. During the 1970s Ford was plagued with charges relating to safety problems with its Pinto subcompact and was also slow to respond to the shift to smaller cars following the oil crisis. The company remained very strong abroad, however, and by the mid-1980s Ford was enjoying a recovery due in part to the success of its new Taurus and Mercury Sable cars. Ford continued to ride high through the rest of the decade, thanks to the popularity of the sleek aerodynamic design of it cars (and despite a number of quality problems). In 1989 Ford paid a hefty $2.5 billion for Britain's leading luxury car producer Jaguar.

General Motors (GM) has led the U.S. auto industry since the 1920s. Originally formed as a merger of several early producers, GM was transformed by Alfred P. Sloan, Jr., from an entrepreneurial operation into one of the leading examples of modern corporate organization. During the 1970s GM was quick to respond to the switch in consumer preference to smaller cars, surprising observers with its new creative and aggressive stance. The company went so far as to bring out a subcompact version of its Cadillac luxury car. GM invested heavily in new plant and equipment for the switchover in design, including both a $5 billion commitment to create an entirely new subsidiary, called Saturn, to build subcompacts using advanced technology and a different approach to labor relations. Another bold move was the establishment of a joint venture with Toyota in California. In the mid-1980s the company began diversifying into nonauto businesses. GM spent $2.6 billion to purchase Electronic Data Systems (Ross Perot's computer services firm) and $4.7 billion for Hughes Aircraft. Perot emerged as a persistent critic of chief executive Roger Smith and the rest of GM management, so in late 1986 the company bought out Perot's GM holdings for $700 million and removed him from the board of directors. Yet the problems highlighted by Perot, especially a steady decline in GM's market share, only got worse. The company tried to stage a comeback with its $5 billion GM–10 project—which consisted of redesigns of the midsized Buick Regal, Pontiac Grand Prix, and Oldsmobile Cutlass Supreme—but the cars were not well received. GM did enjoy a sharp rise in overseas profits, but its U.S. market share fell to under 35 percent in 1989 (a drop of nearly 12 points in a decade). Smith's final months as chief executive before his retirement in mid-1990 were further marred by the popularity of a documentary film (*Roger and Me* by Michael Moore) that depicted him as a ruthless destroyer of the communities such as Flint, Michigan, that bore the brunt of GM's cost-cutting campaign. One bright spot for the company was its signing of a $1 billion contract to provide auto parts to the Soviet Union.

INDUSTRY DATA

Automobiles	*1989*	*1988*	*1987*
Value of shipments	NA	$142.1 billion	$133.3 billion
Total employment	355,400	356,800	381,400
Import penetration	28.5%	29.2%	31.1%

Sources: U.S. Department of Commerce (shipments); Motor Vehicles Manufacturers Association (employment and imports).

SOURCE GUIDE

Leading Stock Analysts and Experts

David Cole, director of the Office for the Study of Automotive Transportation, University of Michigan at Ann Arbor.

Ronald Glantz, analyst at Dean Witter in San Francisco.

Maryann Keller, analyst at Furman, Selz, Mager, Dietz & Birney, New York.

Ann Knight, analyst at Paine Webber.

J. D. Power & Associates, auto market researchers, Agoura Hills, California.

Trade Associations and Unions

Motor Vehicle Manufacturers Association, 7430 2nd Avenue, Detroit, MI 48202. Tel.: (313) 872–4311.

United Automobile, Aerospace and Agricultural Implement Workers of America International Union, 8000 E. Jefferson Avenue, Detroit, MI 48214. Tel.: (313) 926–5000.

Data Sources and Directories

Economic Indicators, a quarterly compilation of industry statistics; *Facts and Figures*, an annual data book; and the annual *World Motor Vehicle Data* (Detroit: Motor Vehicle Manufacturers Association).

Ward's Automotive Yearbook, an annual review of industry trends and statistics (Detroit: Ward's Communications).

World Guide to Automobile Manufacturers (New York: Facts on File, 1987).

Trade Publications

Automotive Industries, monthly.

Automotive News, weekly.

Ward's Auto World, monthly.

Ward's Automotive Reports, weekly.

Books and Reports

Altshuler, Alan; Martin Anderson; Daniel Jones; Daniel Roos; and James Womack. *The Future of the Automobile: The Report of MIT's*

International Automobile Program. Cambridge, Mass.: MIT Press, 1984.

Crandall, Robert W.; Howard K. Gruenspecht; Theodore E. Keeler; and Lester B. Lave. *Regulating the Automobile*. Washington, D.C.: Brookings Institution, 1986.

Flink, James J. *The Car Culture*. Cambridge, Mass.: MIT Press, 1975.

Katz, Harry C. *Shifting Gears: Changing Labor Relations in the U.S. Automobile Industry*. Cambridge, Mass.: MIT Press, 1985.

Keller, Maryann. *Rude Awakening: The Rise, Fall, and Struggle for Recovery of General Motors*. New York: William Morrow, 1989.

Lacey, Robert. *Ford: The Men and the Machine*. Boston: Little, Brown, 1986.

Massachusetts Institute of Technology. "The U.S. Automobile Industry in an Era of International Competition," in *Working Papers of the MIT Commission on Industrial Productivity*. Cambridge, Mass.: MIT Press, 1989.

Maxcy, George. *The Multinational Automobile Industry*. New York: St. Martin's Press, 1981.

May, George S., ed. *The Automobile Industry, 1885–1920*. (Encyclopedia of American Business History and Biography series.) New York: Facts on File, 1990.

_______. *The Automobile Industry, 1920–1980*. (Encyclopedia of American Business History and Biography series.) New York: Facts on File, 1989.

Moritz, Michael, and Barrett Seaman. *Going for Broke: The Chrysler Story*. Garden City, N.Y.: Doubleday Publishing, 1981.

National Research Council. *The Competitive Status of the U.S. Automobile Industry*. Washington, D.C.: National Academy Press, 1982.

Organisation for Economic Co-operation and Development. *The Costs of Restricting Imports: the Automobile Industry*. Paris, 1988.

Rae, John. *The American Automobile: A Brief History*. Chicago: University of Chicago Press, 1965.

_______. *The American Automobile Industry*. Boston: Twayne Publishers, 1984.

Rothschild, Emma. *Paradise Lost: The Decline of the Auto-Industrial Age*. New York: Random House, 1973.

Serrin, William. *The Company and the Union*. New York: Alfred A. Knopf, 1973.

Sobel, Robert. *Car Wars.* New York: E. P. Dutton, 1984.

U.S. Commerce Department, Office of Business Analysis. *The U.S. Motor Vehicle and Equipment Industry since 1958.* Washington, D.C., 1985.

U.S. General Accounting Office. *Growing Japanese Presence in the U.S. Auto Industry.* Washington, D.C., 1988.

U.S. International Trade Commission. *The Internationalization of the Automobile Industry and Its Effect on the U.S. Automobile Industry.* Washington, D.C., 1985.

White, Lawrence J. *The Automobile Industry Since 1945.* Cambridge, Mass.: Harvard University Press, 1971.

CHAPTER 25

STEEL

Steel is one of the first examples that comes to mind when one thinks of heavy industry. A country's steel output is considered a primary indicator of its level of economic development. In the United States during the past decade steel has also been a leading symbol of industrial decline. The once-powerful steel sector has been challenged by foreign competitors such as Japan, West Germany, and even Third-World countries such as Brazil and South Korea. By 1986 two leading producers were operating under the protection of the bankruptcy laws. Toward the end of the decade the industry had regained some of its lost vigor as a result of a painful process of restructuring. Yet the future of the $62 billion U.S. steel business remains in question.

STEEL'S GOLDEN AGE

The development of the American steel industry proceeded in tandem with the growth of the entire U.S. economy. Rapid expansion started in the 1860s with the introduction of the Bessemer process and the widening of markets such as oil drilling and the railroads. By the end of the 19th century the United States became the international leader in steel, producing 37 percent of the world's output in 1900. At the same time, what had been a fairly fragmented industry was becoming more and more concentrated. The most significant outcome of this merger wave was the creation of the U.S. Steel Corporation in 1901. Big Steel, as it came to be known, was formed by Judge

Elbert Gary and J. P. Morgan through the merger of the Carnegie Steel Co. and nine other firms, its total capital of $1,400,000,000 making it the first billion-dollar corporation. Many of the other large firms that have survived to the present, including Inland and Armco, were also formed in this period.

Years of consolidation turned steel into a classic case of oligopoly. From 1907 to 1911 the noncompetitive pricing policies of the large steel companies emerged unabashedly out of dinners that Judge Gary hosted for top executives at the Waldorf-Astoria Hotel in New York. Even after congressional antitrust pressure put an end to the Gary dinners, the industry played follow-the-leader, with U.S. Steel setting prices. The inexorable rise of steel prices frequently vexed politicians seeking to contain inflation. In 1962 an exasperated President John Kennedy publicly berated U.S. Steel for an announced 3.5 percent price increase and successfully pressured other companies to break ranks, thus giving rise to the practice known as "jawboning."

The beginning of the end of U.S. predominance in steel came after World War II, as foreign competitors rebuilt their war-ravaged plants using modern technology. The U.S. share of world output reached 56.7 percent in 1947 and began to decline. By 1958 the figure sank to below 30 percent and has remained there ever since. U.S. Steel constructed a new integrated facility (known as a greenfield site) in the early 1950s, but only one other followed in the industry. Meanwhile, foreign rivals, especially Japan, invested heavily in new plants that employed basic oxygen furnaces (which are much faster than open-hearth furnaces in refining molten iron and scrap into steel) and continuous casting (a process that eliminates several steps in turning raw steel into semifinished forms). American steelmakers followed suit but at a much slower rate. Enjoying a cost advantage, foreign producers were able to underprice U.S. companies to such an extent that the share of the American market captured by imports rose from less than 1 percent in the late 1950s to more than 26 percent in 1984.

THE MINIMILL PHENOMENON

The big integrated steelmakers have also faced a domestic challenge. Abandoning the traditional "bigger is better" approach of the industry, a number of companies have prospered by selecting a niche and remaining relatively small. These producers, known as minimills, use electric furnaces and continuous casters (and often nonunion labor) to turn scrap steel into simple products, such as concrete reinforcing bars that are sold in regional markets.

During the 1970s and early 1980s, minimill operators such as Nucor and Florida Steel were hailed as success stories (along with specialty steelmakers such as Allegheny Ludlum) in an industry otherwise beset with endless tribulation. But by the mid-1980s the luster of the minimills was tarnishing a bit as overcapacity and rising costs set in. Still, the 60 or so U.S. minimills, which accounted for some 20 percent of domestic output in the mid-1980s, made it clear they were here to stay.

In the late 1980s, in fact, the minimill companies began to challenge the large integrated producers in their last market strongholds. Nucor became the first of the minimills to begin producing flat-rolled steel, using a new West German technique for thin-slab casting. Birmingham Steel and New Jersey Steel followed Nucor into that market.

The major U.S. producers responded to their increasingly precarious state in several ways. One of the main tacks has been to seek assistance from the government in slowing down the flow of imports. Steel executives (along with steel union officials) have been among the loudest voices calling for a protectionist trade policy, but their efforts have had mixed results.

Starting back in the Nixon administration there were programs to negotiate voluntary import limits with foreign producers. This provided some relief, but the global recession of the mid-1970s prompted steelmakers everywhere to sell more in the world's largest market. The squeeze on U.S. producers brought about major mill closings and layoffs in 1977, and the ensuing political pressure—including the formation of a 200-member Steel Caucus in Congress—prompted the Carter administration to act. Treasury undersecretary Anthony Solomon put together a trigger-price system under which dumping charges would be brought when an importer's price dropped below what was determined to be typical Japanese cost levels.

This trigger-price mechanism did not do a great deal to reduce imports, and some critics argued that it even promoted dumping by exporting countries with higher costs than Japan. The Reagan administration, with its staunch free-trade policy, initially declined to provide any relief to the beleaguered industry. Yet in the midst of the 1984 presidential election the political pressures were enough to get even Reagan to act. His approach was to negotiate a set of "voluntary" restraint agreements with 29 nations aimed at limiting imports of finished steel to about 20 percent of the U.S. market. The industry, in exchange, dropped its dumping suits.

It took some time for the import restrictions to have a significant impact, and in the interim several companies succumbed to their financial woes. Wheeling-Pittsburgh entered Chapter 11 bankruptcy in 1985 and LTV did so the following year. It was not until the late 1980s that the industry began to show signs of a rebound. Along with the import limitations, steelmakers were buoyed by significantly lower costs (the result of the massive layoffs and mill shutdowns) and higher productivity (helped by union contract concessions and an acceleration of the move to continuous casting). By late 1988 the average cost of American steel was below $500 a ton, a drop of 30 percent since 1982. In fact, U.S. steelmakers had become the lowest-cost suppliers for the American market, even though the restrictions on imports were exercising upward pressure on prices.

Despite its relative prosperity (American producers earned a total profit of about $2 billion in 1988) the industry began lobbying for a extension of the import quotas, which were scheduled to expire in September 1989. Steel users argued strongly against further quotas, but the Bush administration was not prepared to return to a free-trade policy for steel. A 30-month extension of the import restrictions was negotiated with 18 countries. The agreement allowed countries to increase their import share if they end subsidies to their steelmakers.

A SLEW OF STRATEGIES

The U.S. steel industry did not limit its response to crisis conditions to calling for import restrictions. The major producers also embarked on one of the most dramatic restructuring processes ever attempted. Big Steel took the lead here as elsewhere. USX (the new name taken by U.S. Steel in 1986) diversified to the extent that steel accounted for only about a quarter of its revenues and even less of its net income. The biggest and most controversial move the company made out of steel was its $6 billion purchase of Marathon Oil in 1982. Three years later it followed that with the announcement that it would purchase Texas Oil & Gas for about $4 billion. Other aspects of restructuring include the following.

Mergers

Steel played a role in the conglomerate wave in the late 1960s as Lykes bought Youngstown Sheet and Tube, LTV bought Jones & Laughlin, and NVF acquired Sharon Steel. Later consolidations included LTV's merger with Lykes in 1978 and LTV's purchase of Republic Steel in 1984, which made LTV the second-largest American producer. U.S. Steel sought to purchase National Steel in 1984 but was rebuffed by the Justice Department.

International Joint Ventures

Although the major producers howl about foreign competition, they have frequently found it convenient to make deals with their overseas rivals. Japanese companies have invested in U.S. firms, as in Nippon Kokan's 50 percent ownership of National Steel (the other half is owned by National Intergroup, though in 1990 the company announced plans to reduce that share to 10 percent) and Nisshin Steel's 10 percent interest in Wheeling-Pittsburgh. Inland Steel formed a joint venture with Nippon Steel for the construction and operation of a cold-rolling mill in Indiana. LTV joined with Sumitomo Metal Industries in an electrogalvanizing operation. In 1989 USX and South Korea's Pohang Iron and Steel began operating a jointly owned mill in California to produce sheet and tin products.

That same year Armco sold a 40 percent stake in its steelmaking division to Japan's Kawasaki Steel.

Worker Buyouts

When National Intergroup decided it wanted to get rid of its huge Weirton operation, it turned to the people with the greatest interest in keeping the mill open: the workers. In 1982 National offered to sell Weirton to the employees through an employee stock ownership plan. The 8,000 workers approved the plan though it involved wage cuts and a six-year no-strike clause. Worker ownership commenced in 1984, and in the following years the company did well enough to pay out more than $100 million in profit-sharing to its employees. Management, arguing the need for additional capital for investment, ended up taking part of the company public in a 1989 offering.

Another major worker buyout occurred at LTV, which in 1989 sold its $800 million steel bar division—the leader in that market—to an employee stock ownership plan. The operation was then renamed Republic Engineered Steels.

The future of the American steel industry is likely to involve more of these strategies along with further retrenchment of older and less productive facilities. Some observers foresee an international two-tier arrangement in which Third-World countries produce the bulk of raw steel while the more developed countries focus on sophisticated specialty steel. Whatever the exact configuration, the steel industry in the United States and abroad is bound to look very different in the years to come.

LABOR RELATIONS

Some observers of the steel industry argue that the root of the crisis of the large producers is the high price of labor. It became commonplace starting in the late 1970s for steel executives, Wall Street analysts, and others to rail against what was alleged to be the $26-an-hour steelworker and to assert that labor costs had risen much faster than steel prices. Union analysts argued that such figures ignored the increased productivity of labor and pointed out that a comparison of the average price of

The 10 Largest Steel Producers, by 1989 Raw Steel Output (In Millions of Tons)

1.	U.S. Steel	14.24
2.	Bethlehem Steel	12.18
3.	LTV Steel	8.44
4.	Inland Steel	5.55
5.	Armco	5.41
6.	National Steel	5.39
7.	Rouge Steel	2.89
8.	Weirton Steel	2.82
9.	North Star Steel	2.59
10.	Nucor	2.51

Source: *American Metal Markets* (New York: Fairchild Publications).

a ton of steel with the wage cost per ton showed the former rising much faster. They also charged the industry with spending too little on capital improvements that would cut costs.

Labor costs and labor relations in steel are the product of a turbulent history. Organizing efforts began in the late 1850s with the creation of the Sons of Vulcan. After nearly two decades of uneven growth, this group merged with other unions to form the Amalgamated Association of Steel and Iron Workers in 1876. Labor agitation increased in the 1880s, and by the end of that decade steel magnate Andrew Carnegie was trying to create a union-free environment in his mills. The conflict culminated in the violent clash of strikers and Pinkerton guards in July 1892 in Homestead, Pennsylvania. The failure of the strike ushered in a period of union decline that lasted until the 1930s.

In the 1930s the newly created Congress of Industrial Organizations established a Steel Workers Organizing Committee (SWOC), which in 1937 succeeded in negotiating a contract with U.S. Steel. Support for unionization spread rapidly among steelworkers, but independent producers (known collectively as Little Steel) refused to deal with the SWOC, prompting a series of bitter strikes. It was not until the early 1940s that Little Steel was unionized, through the intervention of the Roosevelt administration's War Labor Board. The SWOC became the

United Steelworkers of America (USWA) in 1942, with Philip Murray as its president.

After the war the USWA took a leading role in enabling workers to share fully in the postwar prosperity. Industrywide strikes in 1946 and 1949 established a pattern under which the union won regular and substantial pay increases for its members. Because of steel's central role in the economy, the White House took a keen interest in the negotiations and sought to discourage strikes. When contract bargaining was stalled in 1952 during the Korean War and a strike seemed imminent, President Harry Truman took the unprecedented step of seizing the steel mills with the intention of keeping them open. The Supreme Court quickly ruled his action unconstitutional, and the strike resumed until a suitable wage package was agreed upon.

The 116-day strike in 1959 was a turning point for labor relations in steel. Under the leadership of I. W. Abel, who took over the USWA in 1965, the union and the industry pursued what was called a human relations approach, which meant negotiating contracts without the brinksmanship of strike situations. This concept was formalized in 1973 through the Experimental Negotiating Agreement (ENA), under which the USWA gave up the right to strike in exchange for guaranteed minimum-wage increases. As conditions in the industry worsened, the ENA came under increasing attack from both steel companies and rank-and-file workers. The ENA was a central issue in Edward Sadlowski's unsuccessful insurgent campaign for the presidency of the union in 1977.

In 1980 industry negotiators declined to renew the ENA, so the union was free to call a strike when its contract expired in 1983. Because of the crisis condition of steel that year, the talk was not of strikes but of concessions. For the first time in the history of the union the Basic Steel Agreement included givebacks such as a pay cut, loss of cost-of-living adjustments, and reductions in holiday and vacation time. By late 1985 the aggregate value of concessions granted by steelworkers reached $1.4 billion.

A new chapter of militancy began in 1985 at one of the weaker producers. Wheeling-Pittsburgh, after a long time on the brink, succumbed to financial pressures and filed for protection under Chapter 11 of the bankruptcy law. More than 8,000 union workers walked off the job in July to protest the company's successful petition to the bankruptcy judge to allow it to abrogate its USWA contract and demand an 18 percent wage cut. The strike brought about the resignation of Wheeling chairman Dennis Carney, but after three months the workers returned to the job with a new contract, which still included a large pay reduction as well as a less generous pension plan.

At other companies the approach of the USWA under the new leadership of Lynn Williams has been one of accepting the reality of the industry's crisis but seeking something in exchange for concessions. This so-called entrepreneurial strategy has led to agreements with a division of Bethlehem Steel and Kaiser Aluminum in which workers participate in profit-sharing plans and receive shares of stock while giving up some wages and benefits.

In 1986 the USWA, facing the prospect of more demands for concessions, entered separate contract talks with each of the steel producers; industry leaders had indicated the previous year that they wanted to abandon the coordinated bargaining that had been the rule for three decades. The union announced ahead of time that it would agree to givebacks only if a company could show it was in dire economic circumstances. The USWA also decided to let rank-and-file workers vote on contracts for the first time in the union's history.

The first settlement was reached in March with ailing LTV, which even the union admitted was in danger of going bankrupt (as it did several months later). The USWA agreed to cut wages and benefits by $3.15 an hour in exchange for a profit-sharing plan (if profits ever returned to the loss-ridden company). Then the union and National Steel reached agreement on a pact that established Japanese-style job security in exchange for concessions.

The pattern was similar at most other companies, except for U.S. Steel (recently renamed USX). There the USWA—noting the relative health of the company, suggested by its ability to spend billions on acquisitions—resisted management demands for $3.50-an-hour cuts in labor costs and ended up in a labor dispute that the company called a strike and the union a lockout. The work stoppage ended after six months as the union traded wage cuts for improved job security.

The USWA achieved better results in 1989 in negotiations at Bethlehem. The union won an immediate 8 percent wage increase (actually, a restoration of previous cuts) and a total raise of 16 percent over the life of the 50-month contract. The union also restored past wage reductions in settlements with National Steel and Inland Steel. The rank and file stunned the USWA leadership by turning down the National contract, but a second vote on a nearly identical package was approved by the membership.

There was also unrest in the rank and file in late 1989, when two regional officials of the USWA were indicted (and later convicted) along with USX on charges that the company agreed to pay the officials pension benefits they were not entitled to, in exchange for their support of a 1983 concessionary agreement at a mill in Birmingham, Alabama.

COMMUNITY RESPONSES TO PLANT CLOSINGS

Massive job eliminations and plant shutdowns in steel have prompted local union officials and community leaders to adopt unusual tactics in responding to economic dislocation. When Youngstown Sheet and Tube announced in the fall of 1977 that it would close its Campbell works, throwing more than 4,000 employees out of their jobs, people were moved to action. Local religious leaders banded together in the Ecumenical Coalition and initiated a campaign to keep Campbell open under community ownership—which required a $240 million loan from the federal government.

The Carter administration ended up rejecting the plan, but steel communities continued to explore public ownership as a means of saving steel operations that some experts said could be run profitably. A group called Community Steel, headed by a USWA local president, sought to buy two mills in Ohio's Mahoning Valley slated for shutdown by U.S. Steel, which refused to sell. A more radical approach was taken in the Pittsburgh area by religious figures such as Reverend Douglas Roth and local union officials such as Ron Weisen in Homestead who promoted tactics such as disrupting business at branches of Mellon Bank (accused of disinvesting in the domestic steel industry) and picketing the homes of steel executives.

The last major effort was pursued by a group called the Tri-State Conference on Steel, which wanted to use a public authority or worker ownership to purchase the Dorothy Six blast furnace at U.S. Steel's closed works in Duquesne, Pennsylvania. Despite an energetic public campaign, the initiative died after a feasibility study by the investment bank of Lazard Frères concluded that Dorothy could not be operated profitably.

LEADING COMPANIES

Bethlehem Steel was for most of the 20th century the country's second-largest steel producer; it was displaced for a while by LTV in the mid-1980s. The company, established in 1904 by Charles Schwab, was especially strong in the structural steel used in skyscrapers. By the 1980s the firm, along with others in the industry, was suffering heavy losses. Chief executive Donald Trautlein, a former accountant, eliminated a number of less profitable operations—including the huge mill in Lackawanna, New York, which alone caused the loss of 7,000 jobs. Trautlein resigned in 1986 (against his will, according to some reports), and company veteran Walter Williams took over the difficult chore of keeping Bethlehem alive. Williams embarked on what he called Operation Bootstrap: selling off nonsteel assets, getting labor concessions, improving customer service, and reducing the debt load. By the end of the 1980s Bethlehem was a smaller but a more secure company.

LTV (formerly Ling-Temco-Vought) turned itself into one of the country's largest steel producers through a series of acquisitions of old-line mills. LTV was built by James Ling into one of the high-flying conglomerates of the late 1960s. The company bought a majority of Jones & Laughlin Steel in 1968, and despite antitrust problems with the federal government LTV went on to purchase the rest of Jones & Laughlin in 1975, the Lykes Corp. (parent of Youngstown Sheet and Tube) in 1978, and Republic Steel in 1984. Increased size has not enabled LTV to overcome the travails of the steel business. After suffering heavy losses for several years the company went into Chapter 11 in 1986—one of the largest U.S. industrial corporations ever to do so. While in bankruptcy the company tried to get the Pension Benefit Guaranty Corporation to take over responsibility for the company's $2 billion unfunded pension liability, but the federal agency turned the plans back to LTV (though a federal bankruptcy judge later reduced the PBGC's claim against the company). In 1989 LTV sold its steel bar division to an employee stock ownership plan.

In the late 1960s, chief executive F. Kenneth Iverson of **Nucor** decided that his company should begin producing the steel for the roof joists it was marketing. In that way Nucor was in the vanguard of the creation of a new generation of steel operations called minimills that used scrap to produce simple products for regional markets. Using more efficient technology than the big mills and employing paternalism to stay nonunion, Nucor prospered during the late 1970s and early 1980s amid the crises of its larger competitors. By the middle of that latter decade Nucor was much larger than the "mini" designation would imply; it was, in fact, among the Fortune 500. In 1989 the company was the first minimill company to enter the flat-rolled steel market, using sophisticated thin-slab technology.

USX is the deliberately nondescriptive name assumed by U.S. Steel in 1986 to indicate the company's shift away from its traditional business. Although the firm, known as Big Steel, remained the leading producer in the industry, three quarters of the corporation's revenues were coming from other sources. That was the result of the purchase of Marathon Oil in 1982 and Texas Oil & Gas in 1986 for a combined price of $10 billion. Assembled in 1901 as the first billion-dollar corporation, U.S. Steel for many years epitomized heavy industry in America. In 1986 corporate raider Carl Icahn made a $7 billion bid for the company but abandoned the plan several months later after

INDUSTRY DATA

Steel Mill Products	*1989*	*1988*	*1987*
Value of shipments	$62.4 billion	$62.8 billion	$51.5 billion
Total employment	256,000	259,000	251,000
Import penetration	12.3%	14.9%	14.9%

Sources: U.S. Department of Commerce.

management took evasive maneuvers; yet Icahn held on to an 11 percent stake. USX weathered a 24-week work stoppage that same year, and once it was over the company accelerated its restructuring with large-scale asset sales and job eliminations. Icahn, who raised his holding to 13 percent in 1989, kept up the pressure for even more sell-offs, including a complete departure from the steel business. A proposal by Icahn to spin off 80 percent of the steel operations was defeated by USX stockholders in 1990.

SOURCE GUIDE

Leading Stock Analysts and Experts

Charles Bradford, analyst at Merrill Lynch.

Robert Crandall, an economist at the Brookings Institution who has written widely on the steel industry.

Robert Hageman, analyst at Kidder Peabody.

William T. Hogan, Fordham University economist and historian of the industry.

John Jacobson, steel expert at AUS Consultants in Philadelphia.

Peter Marcus, analyst at Paine Webber.

Trade Associations and Unions

American Iron and Steel Institute, 1133 15th Street NW, Washington, DC 20005. Tel.: (202) 452–7100.

United Steelworkers of America, Five Gateway Center, Pittsburgh, PA 15222. Tel.: (412) 562–2400.

Data Sources and Directories

Annual Statistical Report (Washington, D.C.: American Iron and Steel Institute).

Directory of Iron and Steel Plants, annual (Pittsburgh: Association of Iron and Steel Engineers).

The Iron and Steel Industry, annual (Paris: Organisation for Economic Co-Operation and Development).

Metal Statistics, annual (New York: Fairchild Publications).

Trade Publications

American Metal Market, daily.

Iron Age, monthly.

33 Metal Producing, monthly.

Books and Reports

Barnett, Donald F., and Robert W. Crandall. *Up From the Ashes: The Rise of the Steel Minimill in the United States.* Washington, D.C.: Brookings Institution, 1986.

Barnett, Donald F., and Louis Schorsch. *Steel: Upheaval in a Basic Industry.* Cambridge, Mass.: Ballinger, 1983.

Crandall, Robert W. *The U.S. Steel Industry in Recurrent Crisis.* Washington, D.C.: Brookings Institution, 1981.

Hoerr, John. *And the Wolf Finally Came: The Decline of the American Steel Industry.* Pittsburgh: University of Pittsburgh Press, 1988.

Hogan, William T. *Economic History of the Iron and Steel Industry in the United States*, 5 vols. Lexington, Mass.: Lexington Books, 1971.

———. *Steel in the United States: Restructuring to Compete.* Lexington, Mass.: Lexington Books, 1984.

Massachusetts Institute of Technology. "The Future of the U.S. Steel Industry in the International Marketplace," in *Working Papers of the MIT Commission on Industrial Productivity.* Cambridge, Mass.: MIT Press, 1989.

National Research Council. *The Competitive Status of the U.S. Steel Industry.* Washington, D.C.: National Academy Press, 1985.

Paskoff, Paul, ed. *The Iron and Steel Industry in the Nineteenth Cen-*

tury. (Encyclopedia of American Business History and Biography series) New York: Facts on File, 1989.

Reutter, Mark. *Sparrow's Point: Making Steel—The Rise and Ruin of America's Industrial Might*. New York: Summit Books, 1988.

Seely, Bruce E., ed. *Iron and Steel in the 20th Century*. (Encyclopedia of American Business History and Biography series) New York: Facts on File, 1990.

Strohmeyer, John. *Crisis in Bethlehem: Big Steel's Struggle to Survive*. Bethesda, Md.: Adler & Adler, 1986.

U.S. Congress, Congressional Budget Office. *The Effects of Import Quotas on the Steel Industry*. Washington, D.C., 1984.

U.S. Congress, Office of Technology Assessment. *Technology and Steel Industry Competitiveness*. Washington, D.C., 1980.

U.S. General Accounting Office. *The Health of the U.S. Steel Industry*. Washington, D.C., 1989.

INDEX

NOTE: This is primarily an index of individual and family names, companies, unions, and other organizations. The Source Guides and lists of companies are not indexed. Entries in bold refer to Leading Companies sections.

A

B

C

D

E

F

H

K

L

M

N

O

P

S

T

U

X–Z